Loose
on the Landscape

*An Ecologist Looks for Meaning
in the Wildest Places*

Joel Everett Harding

First Edition

Copyright © 2023 by Joel Everett Harding

All rights reserved. No part of this publication may be reproduced or transmitted in any form without permission in writing from the publisher, except by a reviewer who wishes to quote brief passages in connection with a review.

USBN: 979-8-218-25539-8

Published in the United States
Westminster, MD

Willow Oak
Books

An imprint of
Green Peach Publishing

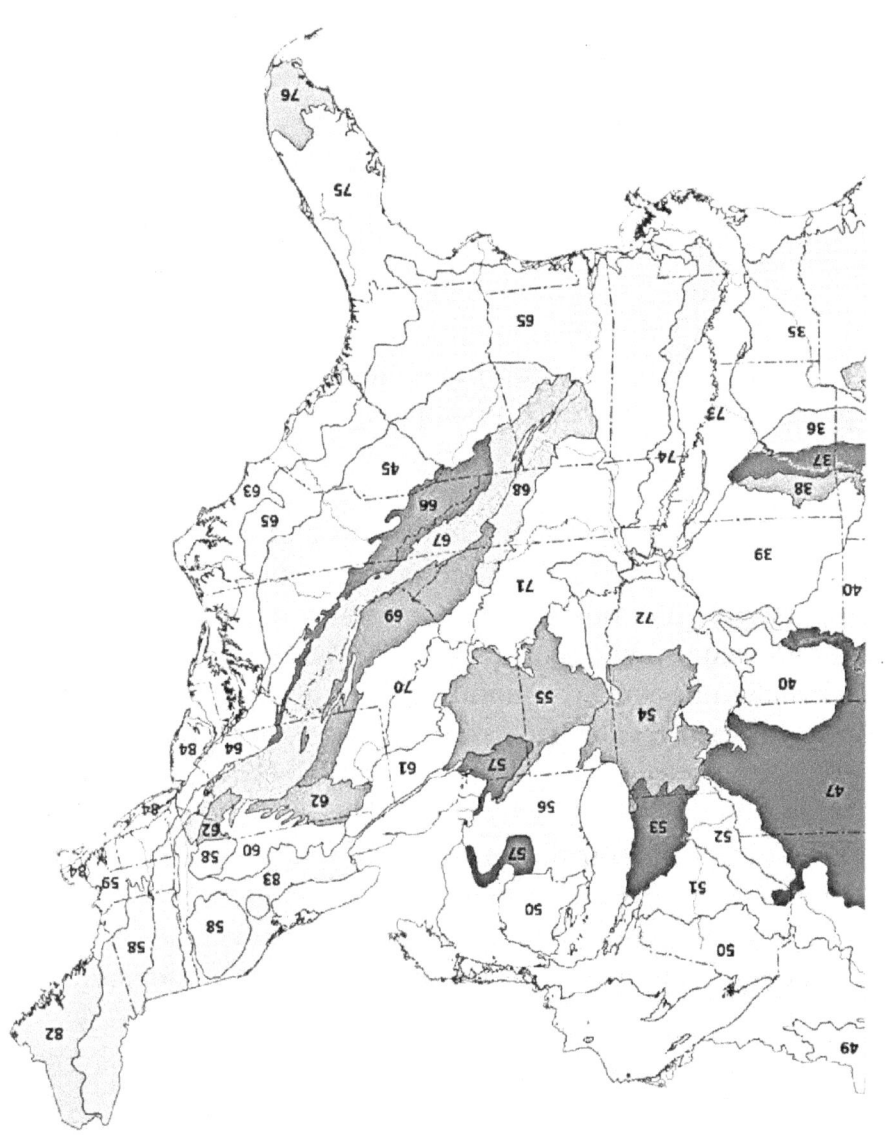

Level III Ecoregions of the Eastern Continental United States

*For my family who shared my landscape adventures
and made them meaningful*

Author's Notes

Names of certain people and places have been changed in this book for security reasons. Events portrayed are true based on the author's recollections, opinions, and known facts. Cover design and all graphics created by the author and are protected in accordance with the above copyright.

The ecoregions used in this work are based on those developed by the U.S. Environmental Protection Agency as revised May 2003 from the National Health and Environmental Effects Research Laboratory, U.S. Environmental Protection Agency. See Appendix for List of ecoregions of the continental United States. The maps used here are not to scale.

Also by Joel Everett Harding
Vagabond Boy

"In every walk with nature one receives
far more than he seeks."
—John Muir

"What is the good of your stars and trees, your sunrise
and the wind, if they do not enter into our daily lives?"
—E.M. Forster

"Nature is the source of all true knowledge."
—Leonardo da Vinci

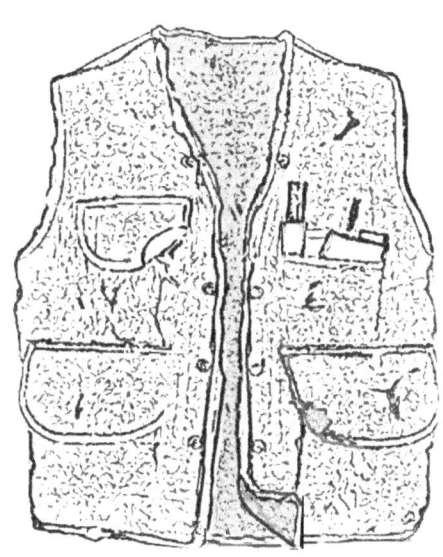

Level III Ecoregions of the Western Continental United States

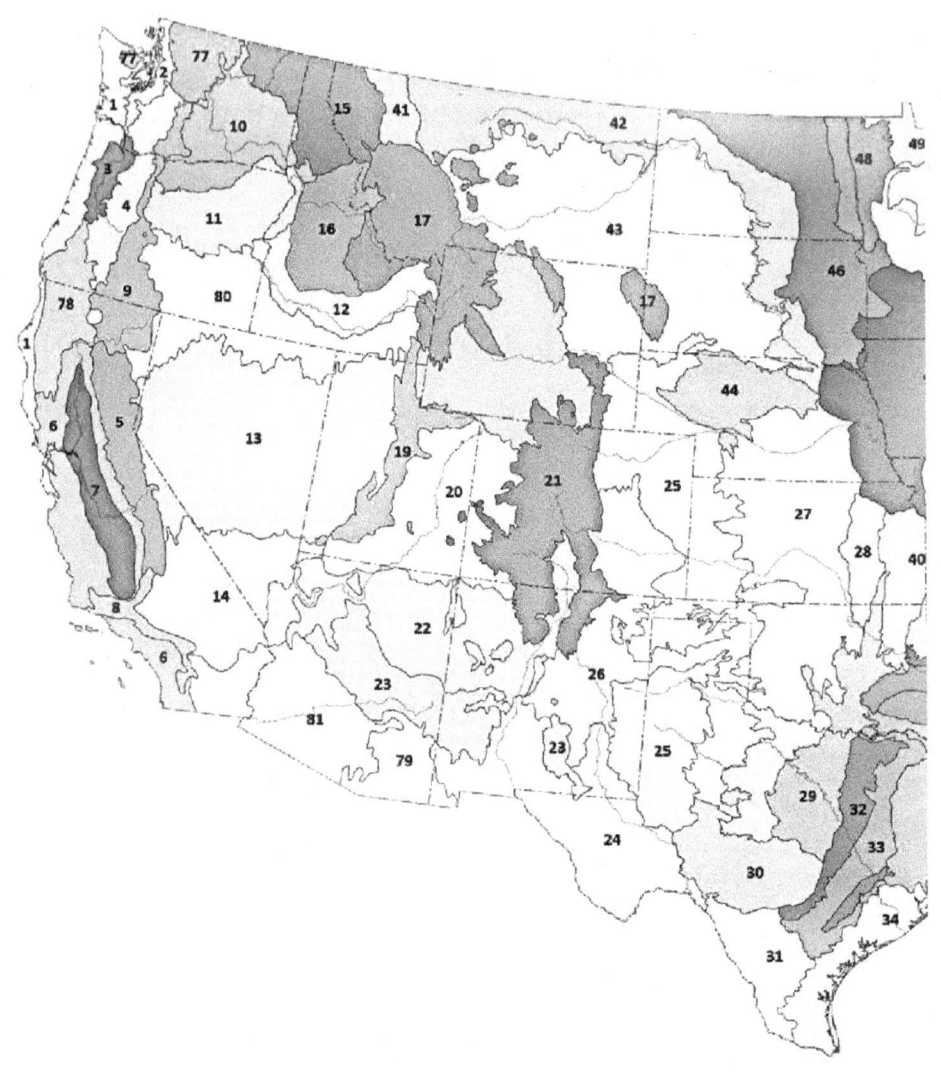

Contents

The Ecosystem Collector	1
Shady Nook	21
There Comes a Season	29
Jeepers Creepers—Peepers	39
Midnight in Maple Marsh	49
Shiawassee Illusions	65
Launching the Duck Patrol	77
Wingmen	91
Rad-Vector Epiphany	107
Umatilla Reconnaissance	125
The Crop Circles of Irrigon	133
Echoes of Falling Water	143
Soda Butte Creek	159
The Lure of Eco-Engineering	177
River Morphing	197
Bootleggers of Cranberry Lake	217
Final Call from Wild-Base One	235
The Batsto Bewitching	251
Riding the Dragon	271
Guardians of the Enchanted Isle	289
Dark Passage in Middle Earth	307
Chara's Wake	325
Lost in Translation	347
Twilight	369
Into the Kootznoowoo	389
A Piedmont Legacy	405
Appendix	427
About the Author	431

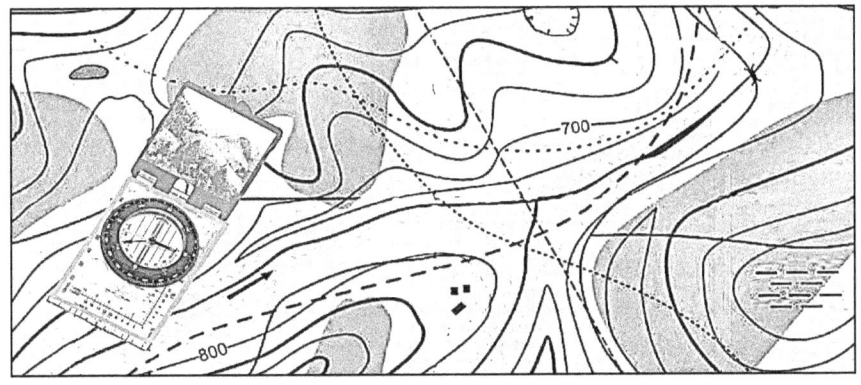

The Ecosystem Collector

If you look closely at a well-worn pair of field boots, they no doubt show a record of the wild places one most often visited. Nicks, gouges, scrapes, and cuts tell tales of the adventures and landscapes encountered. Muddy lugs, seeds in the laces, wear patterns, inform much about the territory you trod, whether flat, rocky, mucky, weedy, or full of thorns.

On a personal level, boots link the wearer with the outdoor settings they traveled through, and allow us to discover intricate and hidden layers of nature. While just sitting in a corner, they can whisper their stories to us through the memories they bring to mind.

As a lad, my curiosity compelled me to explore the nature of landscapes. Over a lifetime of wandering, many of my boots entered retirement with rips and flapping soles, but I usually kept them around a while for nostalgia's sake. A half-dozen worn-out pairs used to sit idle but not forgotten on the basement stairs. They brought warm feelings to mind when I'd grab a working pair, eager to take them afield.

Those retired boots reminded me of my connections with nature and landscapes in the way they gave me access to the wonders I had seen. The experiences awakened insights and truths about myself and the human condition. They allowed me to step into wild places far away and to explore aging puddles just down the lane. Rugged footwear got me there and back, and I never would have collected so many ecosystems through my wanderings without them.

How is it that some of us find a soothing peace when surrounded by natural landscapes, while others cannot see the proverbial forests—except for the trees? Some don't even see the trees, let alone the bark and leaves. Many do not grasp how the forests connect with other realms of nature and the complex rhythms of our planet. And how can some remain unimpressed by the wonders in trunks, stems, buds and twigs?

Then too, I have always felt a soothing calm in the sounds of gurgling streams. There I heard the songs of the river stones, telling tales of ancient flows and events along their banks. They sang of all the wild animals that had come by to drink the cool water, swim in the gentle current and nest among the sedges and rushes. The songs told stories of my childhood exploring small creeks, watching frogs, crayfish, and minnows go about their lives.

Years ago, I had a friend who expressed doubts about the enjoyments obtainable from exploring natural places. He asked me, "Who really needs trees all over the hills and valleys? What would be the problem if most of them did not exist?" He had a college education, a professional position in the financial field, and lived as a productive citizen from dense east coast suburbia.

In response to his question, I began enumerating the ecological values of forests and natural landscapes. But soon I realized it did not matter. Nothing I said lessened his preference for a concrete and steel environment where the incessant blinking of mechanical traffic signals maintained order.

The sentiment prevails for many urban dwellers and rural inhabitants alike. They are content with an occasional visit to the local park. Not everyone, though, considers the smell of mowed grass a satisfying nature experience. In fact, many more people than ever are exploring the great outdoors beyond brick-and-mortar enclaves. Comparisons with the Outdoor Foundation's annual participation reports show that outdoor participation has continued to grow at record levels. Most Americans ages six and above took part in a recent outdoor activity. And the total number of nature recreation participants recently grew to over one-and- a-half million.

The number of enthusiasts fifty-five years and older has increased over fourteen percent within the last few years compared with younger people. Perhaps an old saw provides an answer—with age, wisdom may come. Seniors seem to know that as the pressures of modern living have increased, nature experiences help them defuse and maintain a sense of well-being.

Non-seniors in general would likely spend just as much time with nature if it were not for their more schedule-laden lives. That more individuals of all ages are heading into the countryside shows a deep attraction humans have for the natural world.

Sometimes, though, I wondered if non-nature lovers like my former colleague might have thought I needed an intervention. They probably would recommend I undertake a twelve-step program to cure my dependency on natural phenomena. Perhaps they felt I should seek help through group therapy with similarly obsessed souls—those with bramble scratch-tracks on their arms, who itched with poison ivy for another nature-fix. One where they longed to bask in the euphoria of a natural endorphin-high in some remote woodsy glen.

Though I didn't know of any group program with a name like "Ecological Anonymous," I could imagine myself standing before a crowd, unkempt in muddy hiking boots and tattered field vest. There, at the behest of others, I would search for the magic words of admission that would set me on a fresh path toward a cure from wilderness-addiction. To introduce myself, I might say, "Hello, my name is Joel...and I'm an ecosystem collector."

Like-minded folks in the audience might nod with understanding. They would know what it was like to gouge their skin with needle punctures from the devil's walking stick and locust thorns they stumbled into on their last visit to a nearby forest. Perhaps their responses would sound soothing—"We've been there too, brother, lost amid prickly thickets."

Encouraged, I might confess. "I'm an eco-high freak." "We all feel your mosquito pains," they would mutter.

Such encouragement would allow me to continue my confession. "I realize now, ecosystem collecting is a dirty thing to do, sneaking around in muddy places and poking into the private affairs of innocent floral and faunal inhabitants, and then spying on them with a hand lens, binoculars, and plant identification guides."

Beads of sweat might form on my brow as I admitted to more disturbing behavior. "I've hugged trees without their consent...or any regard to their sexual preferences or pronouns."

The clearing of throats would echo off the stark walls, along with halting whispers.

"I swear, though, it was only to measure their girth and take naked photos for my field investigations— nothing more; I didn't even publish them on social media for revenge. And my personal relationships with trees meant nothing. Believe me...I did it for science."

My voice would falter. "Sometimes I...", then my head bowed— "I...ugh, kidnapped some of nature's residents as a kid, like fireflies and hellgrammites." My inner pain would force me to face myself—"And I would...would...," searching for the right words, hardly able to go on, tears glistening in my eyes. "I held them hostage in glass jars," I might croak, "...until they died. Or I put pins through their bodies and mounted them on cardboard panels. I made them my personal possessions," I would wail, acknowledging my guilt as a serial collector.

By now uncomfortable rustlings might spread among the folding chairs. I'd hear shoes scuffle on the hard wooden floor; someone may bend down as though heaving, and another from the back might call out hoarsely, "Me too."

My head nodded in their direction. "But, as I grew older, I've just never been able to stop myself—or hide my enthusiasm for stalking natural habitats beyond my front door."

I could picture the empathy in their eyes. They knew what it was like to get a big score—connecting with some rare ecosystem experience. The sympathizers in the audience would know what I meant about the rush that could come from immersing yourself in one of nature's unique corners, or somewhere down rabbit holes filled with unexpected awe.

Those peers would recognize that enlightenment as attainable from occasionally enveloping themselves in a natural setting. Like me, many could appreciate the flow of energy that pulsed through an ecosystem while we stood at its edge or waded into its heart.

From where did this craving for eco-highs come? I sometimes wondered. I wasn't sure, but I knew a cure wouldn't come for a long while—I hadn't hit rock bottom yet, nor did I even really want to change myself. In time,

I learned my eco-high experiences came partly from a deeper understanding of the inner workings of ecosystems from my experiences and career in ecological science. Benefits came from bringing basic knowledge with me into the field about nature and habitats. It could produce a deeper, richer experience than a jog, bike ride, or power hike through the woods.

Yet, I preferred to slow-travel the landscapes. Then I could feel more serene from the release of natural hormones and neurotransmitters. These "happy hormones" boost a person's mood, emotions, and even cognitive function. You can produce them through activities like mild exercise, enjoying a meal with loved ones, meditation, social interaction, and laughing until your sides want to split.

How lucky we are that nature experiences alone can do the same. Combining them with other hormone- inducing activities makes for the ultimate in natural highs—it's called healthy living and improving your sense of well-being.

Hundreds of studies have shown this, including those involving thousands of people. It takes only about two hours for an average person to get a large enough dose of nature to express a strong sense of well-being from an outdoor experience.

But wait, there's more. Not only do nature experiences give us positive moods, but they also provide physical benefits. Studies have shown that safely spending time immersed in nature reduces stress, lowers blood pressure, anxiety, and nervous behavior. Wild experiences also enhance immune system function and increase self-esteem. In other studies, researchers in psychiatry found that spending quality time in nature reduced feelings of isolation and social disconnection. I gained all of these at one time or another.

Now we know why so many people find enchantment with nature experiences of all types. Research shows these results are available from many types of green spaces. These include local parks and the countryside, as well as blue spaces like coastlines, lakes, and rivers. And it does not matter that the participants come from different occupations, ethnic groups, income levels, or have chronic illnesses and disabilities.

It is easy to lose yourself mentally in a natural setting, even simpler ones. In my own wanderings, I felt my drooping spirits become elevated when I would go afield. It happened whether I walked along a bubbling stream or sat on a log in a brushy meadow watching birds at dawn. Sometimes nothing was more important than going off into the woods and contemplating the frog chorus of a vernal pool.

This sense of connectedness humans feel with other living things is called "biophilia." It is an instinctual emotional response that developed through natural selection to improve our ability as sentient beings to survive in an indifferent world. Our affiliation with nature is thus a functional adaptation rooted in our DNA. Like many intrinsic traits, though, it is modifiable and can get suppressed in those who spend their lives within cityscapes and indoors.

As our human ancestors spread across the world, they occupied every habitat imaginable. When they discovered enough resources, they called those places home and sought to protect them as territories. Natural selection favored individuals that felt emotionally attached to the environments that provided for their physical needs.

Nature promoted this biophilia connectedness through our sense of contentment when we communed with wild places. People do not need to love their job, their living space or much else. But as humankind evolved, practical living required that we love the natural world in order to survive well within it. Nature always brings humankind back to reality. Millions of edible plants have provided nutrition and medicines for humans since we emerged on the planet's landscapes. What better evidence of our inherent connections with nature do we need than that?

Our attraction to nature and wild places remains just as functional today, because whether we realize it, our kind still depends on the natural world to sustain our individual lives. Humans would not continue to thrive without access to the plants, animals, and ecosystems that occupy the landscapes and waters of the world.

They are the sources of oxygen, drinking water, food, and materials we use in our homes, our tools, and the means to care for those we love. Even concrete, steel, and plastics originate from natural materials. All raw materials come from nature; we cannot escape them.

The mechanisms that promoted biophilia during human evolution remain in our genome. Science tells us human connections with nature preceded those we had with gods and spirits. As our cognitive minds evolved, so did sentience and our need to make existential sense of the world. Our ancestors, like *Homo erectus,* began asking "why" questions about their harsh and fearful lives, but it is believed they had limited means to find satisfying answers.

Nature experiences filled their lives, and as sentience evolved, natural selection favored suites of genes that motivated individuals to seek explanations for phenomena and events. Genes that supported spiritual explanations and contentment made our ancestors' lives easier, more successful. Our "happy hormone" physiology and personality traits evolved along with and supported this genetic association between nature and spirituality.

General spirituality surely is a complex trait influenced by many genes and cultural influences. Organized religious teachings do not necessarily conflict with our inherent need to live in harmony with nature. Many developed from ancient nature worship long before any supreme being may have informed anyone of its omnipotence.

Formalized institutional religions grew as civilization replaced tribal living and individual connections with nature. Spirituality comes in many forms, but they all involve the acceptance of a feeling that something of meaning exists that is greater than oneself, a belief that being human is more than sensory experience.

Such feelings kept bringing me back to wild places where I could never remain just a nature-looker. I needed more than merely standing at the perimeter of inspiring places. I felt compelled to enter them and engage all my senses, listening to their sounds, watching and smelling the processes of life there, touching the soil and rocks, and tasting the air and water. More than that, though, I wanted to know why ecosystems thrived where they did, and what makes them persist.

Like most people, I quick-visited the iconic places too, like the Grand Canyon where crowds ogle for fifteen minutes before heading to the souvenir shop. But when time afforded, I took the slow-travel approach. That meant taking days to explore remote corners of famous and popular places like the national parks of America.

Many people have done as much or more, allowing them to collect such ecosystems and personal memories about their immersive visits. For me, the best were those slower journeys where I melted into the landscape, felt its pulse, and discovered its secrets.

Along the way to such places, I would read the landscape, stopping to examine wild patches away from the tourist routes. My thoughts ran deep where old, covered wagon ruts from pioneers remained in the soils of wide-open prairies. I marveled at ancient bristlecone pine forests in California's White Mountains that still thrived after nearly five thousand years. In Utah, my imagination pondered once-lush Jurassic landscapes while my finger traced ancient dinosaur tracks etched into a remote desert.

Profundity and inspiration came to me in the Joyce Kilmer old growth grove in North Carolina. I once found and touched the bark of the world's tallest tree named Hyperion in a fog-drenched coastal redwood tract. How marvelous, I thought, when I visited General Sherman, the planet's largest organism, as it towered over lesser sequoias. I wandered through smoking calderas, felt the heat of the lowest place in North America, Death Valley. Sometime later, I chartered a light plane in Alaska and flew within feet of America's highest point. There, the peak of "Denali"—Mount McKinley—pierced the clouds.

Other roads took me to the summit of Maine's Cadillac Mountain, where the sun's rays first reach America each day. I've studied sunsets coast to coast and north to south. On Florida's dunes I monitored sea turtle hatchings, where clutches of them pushed above their sandy nests at night and dashed to the surf as though their lives depended on it, which they did.

In the middle of small brushy fields, I have watched woodcocks perform their beautiful mating sky-dance at dusk, spiraling upward nearly out of sight, then fluttering downward with twittering sounds before landing exactly where they launched.

For weeks I tracked bald eagles to their nests to monitor their young and map their ranges. On a wild barrier island, I watched a flock of wild turkeys with hatchlings wander along the beach, dabbling in the surf. I've marveled at networks of winding river channels, remote canyons, tiny flowers in alpine meadows and the diversity of coral reefs.

Odd how my job required me once to travel for days through the mountain hollows of West Virginia to investigate towns flooded by the raging Tug Fork River. Without roads, the only access involved driving a maintenance truck with iron wheels that ran on top of railroad tracks. One day, the route unexpectedly led to a wilderness hilltop where a secluded family brewed sorghum molasses using a mule to grind the stalks. How delicious it tasted later on my breakfast pancakes. It seemed I had stepped into a depression-era landscape where mountain folk survived on old-time skills.

I've taken the scenic route on slow trains through the wilderness, sailed on vintage schooners and river boats, and watched rural landscapes float by in a hot-air balloon. Slow-traveled memories linger longest in my mind. They are the nature experiences I like to add most to my personal eco-collection.

Such marvelous natural wonders made me want to enter landscapes as an explorer rather than a tourist...but I ran both ways as often as possible. In either case, I hungered for a more intense natural high. And I liked to season my outdoor excursions with some practical knowledge to experience the most emotional nourishment from nature.

Add in a smidgin of reflective thought, a dose of curiosity, and a pinch of spicy adventure, and tasty facets of nature usually appeared that I never knew existed. I learned early on that nature is abundant with hidden layers of meaning. But uncovering landscape layers requires a good deal of digging and understanding them comes from keen observation.

Plumb nature's layers and you can find clues to the eternal existential questions of who, what, where, when, why and how. When we make our own footprints toward the truth of things and find it, we earn the epiphanies that follow about the world, and ourselves. If we are not willing to accept the truths about our inner self, how can we expect others to take our thoughts about anything seriously?

Not everyone has easy access to nature. But satisfying experiences do not always require going very far from home or taking extraordinary steps to find a suitable level of eco-immersion. Ecosystems come in all sizes, including puddles, springs, and tiny lazy creeks. Dallying among even simple ones can produce a sense of peace and gratitude for those willing to pause awhile outdoors.

Those who cannot access outdoor ecosystems can still find blissful nature. Thousands around the world gain eco-highs with daily nature documentaries, books, movies, and videos from wild places all over the planet. These days we can watch hours of live safaris on websites in real-time, observing wild animals and habitats in the wild. The internet is full of drone excursions that allow viewers to fly through natural landscapes. Live webcams for virtually every type of landscape and habitat are available for observing nature.

Or, you could watch life unfold within a small terrarium, an aquarium, geraniums in a window pot, pet behavior, or a patch of backyard flowers. Some people insist on keeping their homes spotless as a chemistry lab, purged of all life except theirs and a few mammal pets. But if you are not among them, you can enjoy a bit of nature inside by watching a benign little jumping spider stalk an ant on a window jamb, as I am doing right now.

No need to rush to the phone and call "Pest-Control 911," unless you see an invasion developing. If you feel sweaty about it or have heart palpitations seeing insects, then chances are you are not really a nature lover.

Whether engaging nature in the wild or at home, I prefer to include an encounter in my eco-collection if I have actively gained something meaningful from it. This requires interacting through observations and reflection on how the experience relates to other aspects of life and living.

Meaning might include increased knowledge, new insights, inspiration, gratitude, an uplifted mood providing a sense of wellbeing or adventure. This deeper involvement makes our nature visits worth collecting and turns them into meaningful memories.

With each visit to special places, our subconscious gauges the similarities and differences between them. It finds patterns and makes judgments about the significance of the natural settings investigated. Those of greater significance to us get stored in our long-term memories. We can retrieve them to boost flagging spirits and help us through rough patches in our lives. Additional connections of meaning form with newer nature experiences. If we continue to pay attention, we may find kernels of wisdom about nature, ourselves, and humankind.

More than that, a sense of connection and comprehension may emerge. Epiphanies can clear away confusions the way sunshine evaporates foggy mornings. Such clarity can remind a person how they, too, are an integral part of it all. It can enlighten a troubled mind on how we belong to something much grander, more complex, and wondrous than ourselves, our neighborhood, our worries.

In order to appreciate nature deeply, I found a humble spirit works best, along with a sense of reality as well as compassion. Objectivity can free a mind that is too narrowly focused or emotionally driven. Reason and rational thinking can offer a larger perspective on matters as we search for pathways to wisdom. But when we arrive at a fork in our path to wisdom, both trails need exploring, for wisdom requires a comparison to gain perspective. And perspective can change minds and the world for the better.

Such cognitive expansion regarding nature goes beyond feelings of nature as cute or superficially entertaining. If watching a shooting star does not make you think about your place in the cosmos, then you are not trying hard enough.

Deeper, richer engagements with the outdoors using knowledge and understanding can temper raw passions. Emotionalism without the braking system afforded by a proper dose of reason neglects a million years of advanced human cognition. This ability involves symbolic thinking, language skills, and memory. Keen short-term memory seems to have been the final critical step toward modern cognition in humans. It is only when it fades that we realize its value.

Cognitive thinking allows the brain to retrieve, process, and hold in mind several chunks of information all at one time to complete a task. This sophisticated type of short-term memory involves the ability to hold something in the mind while one is being distracted by something else. It allows us to invent things, develop sequential steps in a process, find the best solutions, see critical patterns, and change our direction.

We now call it multitasking. And it is crucial for problem solving, strategizing, innovating, and planning. This kind of cognition is challenging for many people today because it requires intentional thinking effort. Lazy thinkers miss out on the more intricate splendors of nature. Most humans embrace routines because they are reliable for delivering familiar results quickly.

It is easier to stick to routine tasks, putting the brain on autopilot, like when you drive your car to work, eat the same food, or take the same walk every day. You think little about the mechanics of the task, letting your subconscious take over.

This is frequently a useful strategy for routines, but wringing higher benefits from wild landscapes and immersive nature experiences requires more. It involves a conscious and deliberative approach involving close observation and contemplation. Richer experiences can come when our cognitive minds become part of the experience.

As important as cognition is to find greater meaning in the natural world, it is unnecessary to worship nature as a religion. Appreciating nature and wilderness landscapes can help unlock spiritual portals within ourselves, but nature is not spiritual itself. Landscapes and climates do not care whether you relate to them like a modern pagan or radical environmentalist. Nature is indifferent and does not dispense favors to supplicants—no matter how loud they wail or engage in rituals.

Begging is useless on the seas of life. It cannot make a storm end, the waves subside or rogue whales leave you alone. Nature always has the helm, and we may sometimes avert disaster with our actions. We may alter course to avoid the shoals, and sail faster or slower, but nature allows us the voyage and eventually blows us where we may not wish to go.

Yet, without the seas, no journey is possible, whether it involves oceans or life.

Our advanced cognition, however, allows us to speculate and form beliefs about the role of intelligent design. Nature provides the mechanisms, science helps explain them, and spirituality allows us to tolerate nature's rigors. Beliefs and faith are forms of spirituality that help us deal with such concerns in a brutal world. They are like intuition, insight, and inspiration, in that they do not require cognitive analysis.

Nature can awaken our spirituality so we can find wonder, eureka moments, whimsy, and coincidence on the landscapes we visit. The unexpected is most always our trail-mate. As it turned out, I never joined a support group for nature addicts. I preferred getting hooked on chlorophyll-packed meadows, fresh breezes, mossy slopes, canopied forests, and mysterious watery realms. I never became tired of seeking rocky mountain highs and mind-bending experiences in low-lying meadows.

Excursions into landscapes for adding ecosystems to your cognitive collection need not entail complicated tactical journeys to far-off places. There is much to gain from an average backyard, a flowing ditch or weedy lot downtown. A curious mind can lead to an hour watching gulls bicker over crumbs and chum at the docks, or studying a line of ants carrying dinner leftovers from your countertop. Such fascinations are not just for kids, and anyone can explore the ecosystem in the rock pile by the driveway or the brushy border behind the petunia patch.

And once you gain an understanding of simpler ecosystems, other more complex and layered wild places await to make your list. Challenging opportunities exist out there towards the horizon and beyond the pavement. One just needs to step into their landscapes to find them. Make the most of nature opportunities where you find them.

Sometimes when one goes afield, it is enough just to pay attention to what is going on around you. Concentrate and engage your senses—sniff the air, listen for natural sounds, move your eyes over the scene, stopping to focus on anything interesting.

Even things that do not appear important may hold surprising secrets if you watch and wait. Feel benign textures—bark, stalks of grass, dew on leaves, a handful of stream water. Follow the contours of buds and twigs, which are as unique for every species as fingerprints are for people. Field guides can help with identifying types of plants and where they live—even in winter. Learn to walk, focus, and think about the living realm you are traversing.

For better field experiences, take along a larger perspective about where you go. Before embarking, you can view satellite images of a landscape that show how a place fits within the greater region around it. Interrelationships between landforms and ecosystems become apparent on topographic and vegetation cover maps.

A superb source for these is the *Ecoregion Maps* and their descriptions available from the U.S. EPA's internet site, or many others that help you locate the ones of interest. They depict the general boundaries of every area of the country at four increasing levels of detail.

In my office, I used to keep a wall-sized printed version I would study before going into an unfamiliar landscape. It allowed me to know in advance the kinds of plants, geology, and geographic features to expect before going afield. In the U.S. alone, nearly a thousand different ecoregions fill the most detailed map, and each one is available for collecting—if you can get there and plant your feet in it or wade its waters. Consider basing your list as an eco-collector on these ecoregion categories; it's a great way to organize them by type and landscapes.

Most of the ecoregions described in this book are based on the EPA's Level III and IV categories from 1987. Each classification carries a name and number code in the chapters. Level III categories have a whole number, while Level IV carry the same number plus a letter. Representative Level III ecoregions and codes are listed in the Appendix. However, you may decide that Level II or even Level I is suitable for your ecosystem collecting purposes. Full descriptions and maps are available from the EPA's official website:

https://www.epa.gov/eco-research/ecoregions

Most states and other countries have their own regional descriptions, some based on the EPA classifications. The Counsel for Ecological Cooperation (CEC) has modified those categories and codes. Ecoregions can put the landscapes you visit in an ecological context and should form part of any ecosystem collection toolkit.

With maps and satellite images, you can gain a bird's-eye view of the landscape you wish to visit. Use them to imagine yourself as a hawk soaring high aloft over a complex of marshes, woods, fields, ponds, and streams. Let your eyes roam over the aerial scene. Details will tell what is going on down below. You may not be interested in spotting a field mouse for breakfast like the hawk, but you will see things in context.

With that larger perspective, along with topographic maps, your view of nature will allow you to understand why things exist where they do. When I am searching for ecosystems to add to my collection, I think of all the physical connections, processes, functional layers, diversity, and curious lives that are going about their business. These hint of the food webs and energy pathways that underlie a landscape.

Once you have grasped the context, it is time to set out and begin your wildscapes ramble. Nothing wrong, though, in just slipping into a benign natural place with little preparation and looking at details. But if you first focus on amoebas, flagellates, and ciliates from under a microscope lens, you aren't likely to know whether they came from a pond, wetland, stream eddy, or your neighbor's own gut. From a medical perspective, you may not care. But ecologists and nature lovers want to know because the species involved can tell them about the health of an entire ecosystem. That is why an initial bird's eye view is important.

Perhaps you find it difficult to think like a hawk, and if so, then virtually hop into the basket of a hot-air balloon that rises above a city. Close your eyes and picture yourself a few hundred feet high in your wicker perch, drifting through a Piedmont landscape on a sunny afternoon. As you float along with the breeze, country landscapes replace city structures. The air becomes clearer and smells fresher, fewer noises from below reach your basket. More diversity in landforms and terrain appears, and water in ponds and lakes sparkle, streams and rivers dissect the topography, and a myriad of different colors cover ridges and valleys.

You get a similar view from an aircraft, but faster and less satisfying. The balloon lets you slow-travel the landscape. Sweep your eyes over the mosaic of living communities and observe how they connect to each other. Look where their edges meet, and you will see transition zones called ecotones. These are hybrid ecosystems, vigorous with mixtures of adjacent habitats. Streams thread between woods and fields, and lead to soggy habitats containing marsh and swamp communities. Your balloon follows gentle slopes and rolling hills that lead to enticing valleys where meadows, pastures and farm fields carpet the landscape in natural hues.

The view from your balloon is like what the hawk sees soaring nearby. Fundamentally, the difference is the meaning the scene offers. The hawk does not recognize beauty, and the meaning it gains stems from its hunting and navigational motivations. As a sentient human, however, floating through the sky does not satisfy any instinctual motivation because nature never designed us for flying or hanging about in high places. So, when we go aloft, many of us feel disoriented and even fearful at first. Soon, though, your mind adapts and becomes free to soar into higher planes of appreciation and cerebral thoughts.

Whether in a balloon basket, aircraft, or high atop a panoramic vista, my heartbeat would quicken. I would feel a sense of wonder and curiosity about the landscapes below. In the balloon. I wanted to be lowered down from the basket and explore the details and niches of the places that caught my attention.

While high among the breezes, I would think of the incalculable number of creatures and plants carrying out their lives on the ground and in the waters below. Everywhere, from the tiniest microbes and plankton to the largest trees and beasts—energy, nutrients, and water undergo processing and transformation.

Earth abounds with life. It is in the biosphere, on the landscapes and in the bucket of muddy water you left by the backdoor for a week. Worlds to explore lie in the humblest of places. How marvelous it is to behold their essence—the inherent beauty, perseverance, and ingenuity nature exudes in finding endless ways to manifest.

While looking down from your floating balloon, marvel that far below, wherever there is a suitable niche, some form of life likely has made a home there. And if we appreciate such qualities in nature, we gain new insights. Eco-explorers may find their own place in those grand cycles and the important roles we all play as integrated inhabitants of the ecoregion where we dwell.

Millions of vibrant, unexplored ecosystems remain in the world, and new habitats pop-up each season. Many of those might exist near your home. Inevitably, they will change, so before they do, why not spend a little time getting to know them better? When you insert yourself into a wild place, even for a short time, and you gain something meaningful from the experience, then your collection of ecosystems will grow. You may become an even more enlightened person by intentionally slow-traveling landscapes, and you are likely to feel good about more things in your life.

Ecosystem collecting can be habit-forming. Once I started tripping through natural landscapes, nature continued to supply me with regular eco-highs. It was exhilarating to stand ankle-deep before a crowd of spring peepers in a wet meadow on a warm April night. Perhaps someday you will find yourself in some place similar, and you may feel sufficiently confident to make your confession. Address it to the audience of frogs, toads, and salamanders attentively listening from the water's edge. You might start off with, "Hello, I'm [*your name*], and I'm an ecosystem collector."

Shady Nook

A lovely and secluded spot once existed on the banks of a great river, where towering trees provided shade and framed the view across the wide channel. Beneath the trees, a carpet of lawn surrounded a vintage single-wide trailer. Small but tidy, a local family used it for decades as their summer residence, though they lived just a few miles down the road. Reached by back roads, the quiet setting provided a perfect place to relax and enjoy the peaceful river on a sunny day.

Steeply sloped banks twenty feet high bordered the channel for up to a mile along this reach of the river. As a result, access to the water occurred only where the few modest summer homes peeked through the trees. The rural town of Selinsgrove and a small university named after the river bustled only a few minutes away. But most locals were not aware of the tiny hamlet on the riverbank. Old-timers and current residents called it "Shady Nook." When mentioned, locals nodded sagely and knew exactly where the soft breezes blew and nature seemed to spend her leisure time.

Though built in the 1950s, the owners had taken good care of the seventy-foot trailer. But by now, the once bright yellow siding, white trim, and skirt had faded gracefully. The owner's children had grown up and the family rarely used the property anymore. They had abandoned the shade in the yard offered by the mature trees. Perhaps they no longer cared about the flowing Susquehanna River and the forested land across the channel. Tranquility lived there still, but no one noticed.

Shady Nook lay within the *Ridge & Valley Ecoregion (67)* and *Northern Shale Valleys (67b)*, which extend from northeastern Pennsylvania to near the James River in Virginia. It is characterized by rolling valleys and low hills and underlain mostly by shale, siltstone, and fine-grained sandstone.

One blistering day in August, my wife Laura and I moved into the trailer, intending to rent it for the next year while I completed my final year of college studies in biology. During 1970 and over the next year, the trailer served as a delightful first home for us—and our new son a few months later. The little tow-headed boy arrived the following winter, and we named him Trey.

The Susquehanna River began wooing me on my first drive along it. That occurred three years earlier when I started college. In nice weather, the river presented beautiful scenes—a silvery ribbon winding mile after mile. Its passage stitched together the unfolding landscapes of changing fields, forests, mountains, and scattered Pennsylvania towns.

The great river had carved its way into seemingly endless valleys and deep passes of the Appalachian Mountains—among the oldest in the world. Its wide channel had been carrying its relentless flow for more than a billion years by the time my little 1957 VW "beetle" chugged along its banks.

The Bug served us well for driving locally, and for exploring our surroundings on lazy weekends. It didn't take us long to discover how vast an area the Susquehanna River drained—its channel wound nearly 450 miles through large parts of New York, Pennsylvania, and Maryland, before emptying into the Chesapeake Bay. Not only is it the largest contributor of freshwater to the bay, but it is also the longest river on the East Coast of the United States.

At Shady Nook, we parked the little Bug next to the trailer beside the riverbank. Sometimes we stepped down to the water's edge and cast a line out into the flow where we hooked bass for dinner. How soul- satisfying it was to gather such fresh food from our backyard. We lived in paradise, it seemed, where idyllic nature filled our young lives with a sense of well-being. We knew it could not last, because once I finished college the following June, we would need to move on. Time was like that, pushing us forward into new moments and fresh beginnings. Shady Nook was the perfect place for me to contemplate the concept of time.

During warm weather, I would bring my textbooks to a rustic picnic table in the yard under the trees. I used to study there on the high bank, enjoying the solitude. When my mind became fuzzy with science facts, I would look up and watch the mass of water slowly moving passed—the relentless flow fascinated me and would stir my thoughts. I pondered the river's secrets, and how it shaped the lives of others far upstream and downstream from me. I wondered how many of them watched the flow just like I did. Perhaps they engaged in similar existential musings at that very moment.

I thought how curious the flow that might stimulate their thoughts occurred in their present time, as it did with me. But the mass of water witnessed by upstream gazers would pass me in my future hours or days ahead. The reverse applied for those people living downstream of me. But they did not know that the brushy log I watched drift in the current would come into their view and minds later—long after I abandoned my reverie at the picnic table.

But before I did, other questions about time would swirl in my mind. I sometimes recalled Thoreau's thoughts in his book Walden, where he spoke of making the most of our moments, of using time to our advantage—"In any weather, at any hour of the day or night, I have been anxious to improve the nick of time, and notch it on my stick too; to stand on the meeting of two eternities, the past and future, which is precisely the present moment; to toe that line."

The present moment often demands all our attention but living just "in-the-moment" misses two- thirds of what time offers us—our pasts and potential futures. We get the best from our present experiences on landscapes when we place them in context with their pasts and possible futures.

The past provides clarity for much of what we do in the present and where to go in the future. Those who neglect the past keep repeating the same mistakes because they do not learn from similar historical events. This lack of perspective often shrouds the way forward with uncertainty and leads to unsuitable outcomes. Using time effectively requires more than just watching it pass moment-to moment. Time is an ally for the wise.

The present is but a fleeting moment, an infinitesimally narrow point on the timeline which is being encroached upon by the past and the future. Unlike other creatures, we can use all the facets of time to great advantage, like dealing with change. Change comes from the past, and when our present differs from the past, then change has taken place. Change only occurs in the future. Thus, the past, present, and future are linked, and show cause and effect are at work in the universe. Existence and events move in an irreversible succession from the past, through the present, and into the future.

Still, the fundamental nature of time puzzled me as a young man. Some scientists believe time may not even exist. But experience tells us that something happens between events, which we recognize as the passage of time. We know this intuitively because things change, passing from state to state. Nothing we can do alters this sequence of events. In the relentless flow of time, we get transported along as circumstances change.

While studying on the banks of the Susquehanna, time seemed like a river that connected events and carried me in its current that took me somewhere different. For most of us, we never know in advance exactly where we will end up, or which connecting channel or course we will slip into next.

Yet we cannot say what exactly happens when time passes. We can see its tracks, however, in the changes that occur in matter, events, and nature. We can detect how the state of something differs between observations. If we could not consciously compare changes that have occurred, daily life would seem timeless to us—no reference points, no sentience. We would not know we existed any more than a barnacle would, clinging to a slippery rock filtering seawater.

Time becomes evident through motion—sunrise sunsets, night and day, the changing seasons, the movement of the celestial bodies. All of these indicate continuous change. The aging process is a reminder that molecular motion and interactions are also at work and are a part of time.

Time also changes the meaning we attach to a memory. The experience gets tumbled around with older and newer events in our subconscious the way shirts get tossed in a hot clothes dryer. Both our memories and shirts can come out shrunken or stretched, damaged, or fit to wear, but changed by the events they experienced.

Each ecosystem collector gains cognitive meaning about their experiences from the memories they keep. Without connected memories, time means little to humans beyond the effects it leaves in the changes it manifests. Memories allow learning and useful decision-making beyond mere survival in-the-moment.

Our capacity to perceive and long-remember the passage of time may be our greatest attribute as a species. It allows us to dwell successfully in many habitats through adaptive inventions. Time allows us to learn from our past mistakes, create new solutions, and realize our dreams. Without it, we would have no long- term plans or memories, no reason to visit old friends, and no pleasure from watching our children grow.

In Walden, Thoreau offered more than a caution about using time wisely. He emphasized how we can individually gain knowledge about ourselves and nature through keen observation and reflection. Such knowledge transcends, provides insights beyond what we can perceive through our senses or feelings. In that way, nature inspires and enlightens. In some ways, it seemed our Shady Nook was akin to Thoreau's Walden Pond; a place in a landscape where my feelings about nature took root.

Like Thoreau at Walden, I became a fact-finder of natural phenomena that helped me render deeper meaning from my experiences. Thoreau surmised that complicated and high-intensity living often masked humanity's innate connection with nature, which remains linked to our pasts, present, and destinies. He found soul-satisfying value in natural landscapes, self- reliance, and wilderness experiences.

The great Susquehanna River never faltered during our stay on its banks, always providing sustenance for the creatures and people who depended on it. We gained new perspectives in its changing patterns, seasons, currents, and the volumes of flow it carried. The river seemed in harmony with its landscape and the communities within its valley.

Good fortune, however, is fleeting. New realities would occur on the Susquehanna's banks where we had dwelled in peace. The currents of change were coming. They would bring something unexpected and unimaginable to Shady Nook.

There Comes a Season

When we first arrived in Shady Nook near the end of summer, the heat of August baked the landscape. The growing season moved along in full swing, though the local plants and animals had started to wind down production for the year. Weeds in the vacant fields along the lane worked diligently to produce mature seed heads. Grape vines burst with ripened fruit while moths and butterflies slurped nectar in every patch of flowers. The air lay hot and thick; lonely cicadas buzzed in the distance hoping for a last chance at love.

Already, squirrels scouted where the best acorns and hickory nuts might drop for later retrieval. Songbirds, done with the weary tasks of parenting, were making plans for extended trips to their favorite vacation spots down south. Bunchgrasses had already switched over from putting out impressive top growth and focused now on bulking up their roots.

Fall lay a month away, though creeping inevitably down from more northern latitudes with cooler temperatures. When we had time for our strolls down the lane next to the trailer, we gradually noticed fresh changes in our surroundings. Besides color shifts on large swaths of the rural landscape, evidence of typical summer ravaging was everywhere. Leaf tips and edges had turned brown after weeks of blistering afternoons and windburn. Ragged leaves attested to relentless munching by insects and herbivores. The bright greens of spring and early summer settled into more olive hues.

As autumn moved along, brighter and more intense colors saturated the landscape again. But this time, the dull greens of summer woods and shrub borders were sporting more flashy colors. Chlorophyll supplies had ebbed, slowing photosynthesis and biomass production in the plant communities. The leafy greens on shade trees along the river had paled, cloaked now in a palette of reds, yellows, and oranges—a visual feast for humans like us who contemplated the splendors of nature.

The herbaceous fields displayed a more subdued mantle, mostly light browns and tans, punctuated by tiny flowers of pink, blue, and white asters, yellow goldenrods, milkweeds, and lanky dogbane. Hundreds of grass varieties occupied the open spaces, knitting the broad-leaved forbs together to form living mats as tall as our waists. An ocean of seedheads bobbed in the breezes, all pregnant with their respective germplasm to produce the next generation in the spring season to come.

Last summer's blooms had faded from the landscape into a memory, their mission accomplished of pranking insects to stop by for a bit of pollen to take home. The Queen Anne's Lace stood tall, their once flat, white flowerheads folded up into little green baskets to hold the developing seeds. Roots of many plants had become starchy, storing carbohydrates to kickstart the next spring season. Rhizomes and tubers nuzzled each other underground, secure in their bunkers against the coming winter.

Pleasant weather prevailed through September and mid-October, even as the planet moved further away from the sun. While the earth zipped along its elliptical orbit at nineteen miles per second, changes appeared in the landscape. Puddles froze overnight and wild geese began flying downstream along the river. Acorns dropped from trees near the riverbank, and silky milkweed seeds floated across the nearby field.

Freezing temperatures took hold of the valley in November. Cold air regularly sneaked down from the surrounding mountains, settling into low areas, and warning every living thing about how harsh conditions would soon become once again. We knew fall had peaked when we saw orange frost-covered pumpkins poking through their withered vines in local farm fields. They sat unharvested, unwanted, and rejected. They would decay where they sat, welcomed by herbivores and decomposers.

Living plants focused mostly on their roots, and abandoned their tender above-ground parts, ceasing to pump nutrients up stems and stalks. Metabolisms had slowed to a crawl by late autumn. At the end of October, we put a seed feeder out for those hardy songbirds that would stick around through winter.

The earth marched to its own ancient rhythms, unbeholden to either man or beasts. Every living species in the region could endure the hard times ahead because the pattern of passing seasons was predictable and reliable. Year-round resident species had adapted to the cycle eons ago, evolving suitable strategies built into their genetic structures. The seasonal fluctuations in weather and shortened daylight hours triggered physiological and behavioral responses in resident lifeforms.

By late November, annual plants had finished shedding their seeds to the breezes and the palates of birds and wildlife, which later dropped them in their scat. Others had packaged their seeds in burrs and spiky capsules, which they surrendered to the serendipity of passing animal travelers, who brushed against them and carried them further afield in their pelts. Insects stayed snug in cocoons, cases, and chambers. Reptiles and amphibians had gone dormant in nice hidey-holes among the litter or underground.

Winter banged on our trailer one night with blustery winds, rattling the aluminum storm door, warning us of hard times ahead. Soon, the season of frozen pipes and coaxing heaters for warmth was upon us. Frozen water was soon on everyone's agenda, plants and animals alike. Those whose habit was to hang around the valley for the next few months would usually do fine when sleet, frozen ground and snow gripped the countryside. Daily we heard flocks of Canada geese honking their way down the river corridor they used as a flyway for navigating southward.

During a week in January, we watched the water surface buckle into a rugged jumble of boulder-sized chunks of ice. The ice thickened, but below it the waters continued to flow unimpeded toward the distant Chesapeake Bay.

Frozen landscapes made life harsh for most wild species. Dormancy was a strategy many of them used to survive. Now physiological processes only crept along—just enough to sustain life. All the bright- colored tree and shrub leaves nature had showcased for us last fall lay discarded—left to themselves in the bitter winds of winter. It was nature's triage approach, redirecting energy reserves where each organism's survival had the best chances.

But not all living things became inactive. Resident songbirds around Shady Nook remained busy, scavenging for what food they could find. Squirrels slept in dense leaf nests high among sturdy branches in our trees. On milder days, they scampered down trunks and made dashes to grab nuts from their buried caches. Their memory maps seemed impressive, though inevitably they would forget where they buried some nuts. Those would sprout next spring to start a new grove and fill gaps where old trees had fallen along the river.

Many of the songbirds had discarded bright costumes in favor of drab wardrobes, though some preferred to wear the same flashy outfits all year long. Cardinals, for example, were easy to spot in their lavish scarlet cloaks and fancy crests. Blue Jays harassed others with bright blue and white uniforms sporting basic-black collars. They swooped into the feeders clamoring at the gang gathered there like a swarm of SWAT police.

Male house finches, though, preferred more subdued colors and behavior, pecking seeds in brown capes with red patches—not nearly as flamboyant as cardinals. Goldfinches knew never to wear yellow after Labor Day and had slowly replaced their golden summer coats for winter olive tones.

Nuthatches kept their contrarian ways, hanging upside down on our tree trunks. They came to the feeder looking debonair in black, white, and blue trim, then clung topsy-turvy on the suet block. There they tossed out comments with Ank, Ank calls. Chickadees landed near the feeder and demanded a place at the table with a Chickadee-dee-dee. Then they would dart to an open space ready to dine in their black caps and bibs.

By this time, other wild animals in the Susquehanna Valley had abandoned breeding. Mammals such as deer, bear, and squirrels had become pregnant in late fall to deliver babies when spring arrived again. Expecting mother squirrels gestated during the cold months when food became scarce, compensating by hibernating between winter warm spells when they could forage briefly.

With the cold weather limiting outdoor exploring activities, I became interested in learning to identify the wild plants that inhabited the landscapes in our surroundings, including their winter and summer variations. In the university library, I found several field guides and took them with me when I wandered outdoors between cold snaps and bad weather. It was how I learned to identify winter forms of local plants.

By early-March we looked for signs of spring. The Canada geese flew back up the frozen river. They rarely landed because their mission involved heading to their breeding grounds in the far north. As mid-March approached, more geese came through in waves, along with a variety of ducks. They all moved up the valley with a sense of urgency and purpose, intent on reaching Canadian prairies to find nesting spots.

By the end of March, the ground softened around Shady Nook, and mud replaced the last remnants of snow. In mid-April, the river ice broke up. We heard great cracking sounds during the nights and watched chunks of ice jostle in the slushy current during the day. Within two weeks, all the ice had washed out of the channel. The flow resumed without restraint as it had last done nearly three months before.

Spring arrived when nature replaced the gray-tawny shades in the landscape with lime greens and lemon yellows of fresh growth. Birds with new color patterns began appearing at our feeder near the end of April, as though they had gotten fresh makeovers while they were away for the winter.

May moved into high gear with warmer temperatures. Plant life erupted down the lane and throughout the Susquehanna Valley. Fields turned green again, leaves appeared on trees, and songbirds sang frenetically and darted around the yard taking care of business. In early June, my classes had ended, and so was college for me. Eager fresh growth emerged everywhere; the Susquehanna Valley had transformed from a seemingly lifeless gray landscape the previous winter into a vital natural garden suffused in chlorophyll green.

New crops of baby squirrels hopped about near our brushy borders. Nesting birds called from the trees along the river and tended their hatchlings. Many insects had gotten active, having waited to go a- buzzing until the last of the freezing weather ended.

We came to appreciate how plants and animals in the region developed in-tune with Earth's changing rhythms. These changes triggered new metabolic and behavior patterns according to each species' adaptive strategies. Yet, invariably, there comes a season or event when conditions fall outside the norms. Sometimes they even exceed survival capabilities.

Such aberrations in weather patterns, sunspots, geological processes, and other phenomena occur within great cycles so complex and subtle we barely understand them. Nature is filled with rhythms...lots of rhythms, which sustain local landscapes and the biosphere.

Rivers change like everything else—usually more so because they are highly dynamic, subject to constant turbulence, changing water levels, and random meandering across valleys. Rivers are among natures' most relentless energy processors, turning potential energy into kinetic energy by its ledge-drops and waterfalls, and back again in quiet pools and eddies.

In comparison with many other river systems, the Susquehanna River Basin is one of America's most flood prone. Since the seventeenth century, the main stem has flooded an average of once every twenty years. But even when it doesn't flood, water levels rise with every storm in its valley. Fish and other aquatic organisms must struggle with higher currents, more debris, and heightened stresses in finding food and protective cover.

In Shady Nook, the water level needed to rise twenty feet from normal flow to overtop the bank where our trailer sat. At twenty-two feet, water would begin sloshing onto the floor inside the trailer.

That would be a nuisance. But consider a flow that reached, say, three feet higher than that. It might be something worth fleeing to the hills to escape. And such an event happened in mid-June 1972 when Agnes came to town...Hurricane Agnes.

That tropical storm dumped so much rain on the Susquehanna Valley over four days that the cumulative runoff from the landscape and tributaries produced over twenty-eight trillion gallons of water that roared past our trailer. The resulting flood was the nation's most destructive and costly disaster of the time. Agnes took seventy-two human lives within the Susquehanna River basin alone.

Fortunately, we had moved out of the area less than two years before. We were living on high ground then, sixty miles away. But that did not mean we experienced no effects from the Agnes storm.

Several weeks later, when the floodwaters receded, and the flow returned to normal, Laura and I had an occasion to pass through Selinsgrove again. We were eager to see the old trailer and how it fared during those high-water conditions.

When we turned onto the lane at Shady Nook, we expected to see at least some damage. But the pad where the trailer had stood was empty. We decided the owners had received plenty of warning before the storm, and had moved it out of harms' way. A large rectangular patch of dirt remained on the spot where we had lived just months before.

We parked the car in the driveway and got out to look things over. All the trees remained along the riverbank; the lawn appeared intact. Except for the missing trailer and picnic table, little had changed.

The day remained sunny; a pleasant warmth encouraged us to take a walk down the lane in Shady Nook one last nostalgic time. We wandered past perhaps a half-dozen homes and noticed some had sustained damage. In the overgrown field between the lane and the railroad tracks lay someone's green and white trailer, in good shape though a bit banged up. It appeared as though floodwaters had lifted and carried it hundreds of feet.

We walked further down the road and encountered a haphazard pile of debris in the field. Someone with a dozer might have pushed together rubble from houses along the riverbank. Pieces of wood framing, drywall, broken boards, and aluminum siding lay jumbled and broken a dozen feet high.

While we stood next to the heap, I noticed part of a different mobile home that lay in the jumble, with its end missing. This one had dark lines, also unfamiliar to us. Then I realized two trailers lay in the pile, wrapped around each other, frozen in a mechanical death hug.

This second trailer was our old home. With that realization, our spirits slumped steeper than the sunken roof that now filled our previous living room. Crushed and mangled—the trailer's insides lay exposed, ribs of rafters arched out, dangling pieces of pink insulation like raw meat drained of blood. The remains lay rotting in the sun; the furnace appeared smashed and gashed like a wounded heart. It would never pump soothing warmth again to sustain a young couple and their son in their first home…along a peaceful riverbank in Shady Nook.

Loose on the Landscape

Jeepers Creepers—Peepers

Hundreds of them sat in the darkness of a moonless night. Each one tried its best to out-screech all the others. It wasn't me they clamored for, since they all but ignored my presence as I stepped into the soggy depression of an old field. Right away, I could sense lust filled their hearts and possibly rape, though they wouldn't have thought of it that way.

Earlier, the weather radio predicted conditions perfect for a mass gathering after sunset in the wet fields and swales of central Michigan. The area lies within the *Southern Michigan/Northern Indiana Drift Plains (56)* and *Lansing Loamy Plain Ecoregion (56g)*. It consists mostly of gently rolling ground moraines—a blanket of till deposited by a glacier. The terrain comprises hills with well-drained soils alternating with poorly drained depressions.

As I drove into the countryside later, I began hearing the crowd noises a quarter mile away—a cricket-like, soothing backdrop to the otherwise quiet evening. But the intensity and volume increased the closer I drove. A few miles from East

Lansing, the landscape seemed filled with alarm clocks going off at once. No longer soothing, the crowd ranted at a high pitch, urgent with its demands.

When I stepped into the shallow patch of water, my ears begged for silence. I stood directly over a bunch of the celebrants in the chill water, my knees bent in the ready position with my unholstered flashlight clasped in both hands, ready for action.

One perp suddenly screamed from below, and I flicked my flashlight on and fired the beam at my left boot. There he sat, half submerged in the shallow water...a tiny frog. His throat was all bulgy and pulsating, pushing out his signature chant in a strong falsetto. The brown throat with dark wrinkles announced him as a male.

Females had white throats without wrinkles and remained silent. The gals just swished their way past a gauntlet of males—window shopping for love. Males tossed out froggy seduction calls, but for the gals, only the most virtuoso tenor among them would do.

The male at my boot sat perfectly still as he belted out his message with an intensity that seemed impossible for his size, since he was no bigger than the upper half of my thumb.

I reached down, picked him up and examined him. His singing had immediately stopped when I touched him, and he now looked poker-faced at me. His body appeared as though he hadn't worked out in a gym or taken a hike his whole life...kind of flabby in the middle with undeveloped abs.

"So, what's going on here?" I addressed him. "What gives you the right to show up in this swale naked in a Woodstock-like mass gathering? Fess up, are you here intending to perpetrate random sexual activities in public?"

The little fellow just blinked at me, no doubt searching his amphibian mind for a suitable answer. I noticed an inhuman grin smeared across his tight snout and knew he didn't feel like talking. What happens in wet springtime depressions stays in springtime depressions...until the new tadpoles grow up and head out onto the surrounding landscape a few weeks later.

The big black "X" tattooed on his back confirmed him as an eastern chorus frog, *Pseudacris crucifer*. Most everyone who has heard these tiny frogs call on warm April nights knows them as "spring peepers."

I had heard about these characters before but had never been this close to a whole gang of them. For years, every spring, I heard distant puddles full of them singing, their seemingly happy peeping bringing me nostalgic memories of growing up in the countryside. But when amid a clamoring gang of them, curiosity rather than nostalgia held my interest.

This night, a mass of adult males and females, each one spaced a few feet apart, communicated in a language I only partially understood. They had chosen a vernal pool for the party, where males seemed to badger females verbally with incessant come-hither trills for attention.

Gatherings like this commonly occurred across the eastern United States in early spring when the temperatures stayed mild, the wind blew gently and an inch of water lay in small wetlands, pond edges and gravel borrow pits along roadways. Such signals prompted me to grab my field gear and head out into the darkness to surveil the situation.

Once I arrived on the scene, I saw that this gathering involved more than group sex for mere fun but took place for intentional breeding...perfectly legal by the laws of nature. Sometimes I noticed a male bumping another male, pushing a competitor out of his square- foot territory, like a sumo wrestler.

This way a peeper-gal could see his big and beautiful body and judge his strength, the way men flexed their muscles and sucked their bellies in. He had an amazing voice and owned real estate, at least for the next week. He hoped a few fertile females might decide "What a catch." Even better if they sidled over signaling, "I can't wait to have your babies...along with that guy's over there, his by the piece of bark, and the other one next to the skunk cabbage." These gals, you see, were very particular about whom they selected for group sex, accepting only the alpha males.

Some other males called a few feet away from me, but their trills sounded tepid and tentative. I set the frog in my hand where I found him and stepped over to investigate the others. Not a single flirty female flashed her slim legs at those squeaky low-testosterone dudes.

It seemed almost pitiful to see a gorgeous one-inch lady peeper with silky-smooth skin ignore an off-key crooner. With a bold leg kick, the gals sailed right past these limp-wristed, wet-behind-the ears, weak-voiced, puddle-plopping males.

The breeding females instinctively knew that these wannabe poppa-peepers just did not have the moxie to fertilize more than a few dozen fertilized eggs—hardly qualifying as a legit peeper family. She had plenty of other prospects nearby that could service over three- thousand of the eggs she carried. You go, girl.

"Sorry, guys," I said to the crooners-without- partners. "Maybe next year. Eat more beetles, ants, flies, and spiders, and stay off the vegetarian diet—it's not for you." I smiled, feeling at home dispensing advice to sex-crazed hoppers at this froggy concert who didn't care a whit that I stood among them.

Though I felt more at peace standing among the frogs, they clamored and screamed out of compulsion. My senses approached overload from the cacophony, the wetness, damp earthy smells, tiny throbbing throats, hordes of little black Xs slipping about the still water, males begging for a hook-up with any female that sauntered by. I felt their urgency; biological imperatives were at stake...no less than the survival of their species.

In a few weeks, the wet patch would dry up, most likely after the tadpoles' metamorphosis into proper froggies and left the swale. New generations depended on the few weeks of the year when spring rains created similar temporary wet spots on the landscape. Adults had been making hundred-foot journeys to such sex- party venues for millions of years.

I swerved my flashlight around and could see that the vernal pool comprised a half-acre. A field of tall, dry grasses and weeds surrounded it and stretched over a mile in any direction. Bunch grasses and sedges poked up as markers that helped the male frogs stake out their crooning turf. They would guard them for breeding well into June all over the natural landscapes of eastern America. Though they go dry by summer, until then such pools offer habitat for many forms of life after they accumulate water from spring rains and a high water table.

I had often come across pond edges in the past where female peepers had lain their fertilized eggs. These floated in masses of gelatinous clumps, each surrounding hundreds of dark specks— amphibian eggs basting in the warm waters. Each egg had its own jelly-like wall for added protection within the larger wobbly glob. This told me frogs rather than salamanders had deposited them.

In similar locations, I had seen salamanders deposit eggs without individual gelatinous walls, encasing them all within a common jelly clump. Toads, unlike frogs or salamanders, laid their eggs in long lumpy ropes, translucent and reminiscent of piles of strange intestines lying in the shallows.

All amphibians need a wet environment for breeding. But terrestrial male salamanders and toads usually spend little time in water after mating—they flee the scene as soon as the females lose interest in them. Typical.

Then the females lay their eggs and adult salamanders lope off individually to a local hideout or crack-house—usually the crack is under a rock, root, pile of leaf litter or a muddy bank where they bushwhack prey. Toads are nomads—roaming the landscape with hunting on their minds, mostly for unsuspecting bug and grub victims just out for a pleasant wiggle.

Male spring peepers hang around the wet spots until the gals ignore them and the testosterone juice runs out. Once the big mating party is over for the season, the males typically stagger off to their favorite heap of leaf litter in the uplands. There they sit around sucking bug juice all day and snacking on crispy crickets.

Life isn't always easy for peepers, though. Many predators stalk the pools, looking to land a dinner of frog tartare. Another major hazard, drought, could leave vernal pools baking and drying in the sun.

After the male peepers hop away to commune with nature and sunbathe during their off-season, the females stay around the breeding ponds for up to two weeks. They keep an eye on things, inspecting the nurseries, then laying their jelly-filled packages all over the bed of the shallow pool.

Then, their mission completed, lady-frogs leave the water too, retreating to woods and grasslands for the summer. There they fatten up at their favorite spa retreats near groundwater springs and pond edges.

The gelatinous globs that hold the peeper eggs act like individual trojan horses. When tadpoles hatch, they don't move very much at all for the first two weeks after emerging, spending their time absorbing the remaining yolk from their egg for nutrients. Then they burst out to exploit their puddle's food resources. All the adults had slipped out of town, leaving their squiggly progeny to survive completely on their own in a harsh place. It is the natural way for them—let the little ones raise themselves, like many human parents do these days.

Once the tadpoles chew through their jellied cloaks, they swarm by the hundreds of thousands throughout the pond, gobbling up algae at a furious rate. Gradually they switch to raw meat, munching on tiny crustaceans, protozoa, and other zooplankton.

By July, the tadpoles grow into genuine cartilage- carrying adult peepers and get a hankering to leave their confined pools to seek their fortunes in the greater outdoors like their parents. Puddles soon evaporate, exposing great numbers of late-maturing tadpoles to the harsh sunlight, dehydrating them into crusty lumps of frog jerky.

When the cold days and rains of fall blow in, the vernal pools fill with water again. But the frog's clocks have ticked, and no well-adjusted peeper will venture there with breeding in mind. Energy reserves now need conserving to survive the coming winter.

Unlike birds and mammals, amphibians cannot regulate their internal temperatures, but rely on basking in the sun to gain enough body heat to drive their metabolism. The peepers grow torpid when the weather turns colder than sunny days can recharge the frogs' daily temperatures. Barely able to move anymore, the frogs cannot even eat as their metabolism ebbs.

Instinctively, they find a safe place to enter a dormant state and pass the cold season. Most peepers and other frogs sit patiently for months under logs, rocks and in loose bark and holes in trees. They cannot dig a burrow, so depend on the hospitality of nature's crevices and hidden places for protection.

Freezing conditions often reach into these cracks and crannies and produce freezing within the bodies of the peepers inside. The skin, muscles, and tissues become stiff with ice crystals, but the frogs rarely die in normal winters—their species has adapted...and therefore will persist.

This is because nature's remedy is to store high concentrations of glucose in the frog's vital organs. When a peeper freezes solid, it will stop breathing, memory cells get erased, and its heart stops beating. It becomes functionally dead, like a Star Wars character frozen in a block of "Carbonite." There, the little frogs spend the long winters, oblivious to the howling winds and frozen landscape above them.

And yet it returns to life when the vernal pools fill again with the arrival of spring. Each April is like a separate lifetime that gets recycled—new scenes, fresh memories, prepping for the next mating convention.

I have often imagined what it is like for a frog when the snow and ice melt away, the weather first warms enough, and its internal clock goes off. Might it sense one day a new drowsy warmth in its chest, where its heart begins to beat, very slowly at first, then stronger with a new rhythm. Blood flows to its lungs again, allowing the peeper to breathe freely once more after months of holding its breath.

The eyes focus, though at first it sees only a dimly lit blur. Soon, a spark of consciousness descends as the sun's warmth seeps through the skin and penetrates its other organs. Leg muscles twitch slightly, then more urgently as the ice-crystals inside melt.

Finally, dormancy breaks, another spring has arrived, and the great emergence begins. If this is its third or fourth year, it will be the last opportunity for the peeper to breed. The peeper kicks its way out of the winter cleft and begins the trek to the local puddle.

When a male gets there, he searches for a log, stone, or clump of soil to gain height. It will climb on top and sit, winking in the sunlight. He has fully warmed up and can feel the energy flow through his miniature body. Hormones surge, and an urgency builds in his mind, which soon becomes nearly overpowering.

He looks to the left, then the right. Finally, he shifts to face the open water. The urgency is overwhelming now, and he instinctively knows one thing. He knows that now is the time. He takes a great breath, the biggest he ever has for nearly a year. His throat bulges to a third the size of his body. Then suddenly he lets go.

All the waiting, all the suffering through a long frigid winter, and the previous spring when he pushed other tadpoles aside to grab his share of algae and bugs, dodging water birds, wandering turtles and later, a man with a flashlight in the dark. He doesn't care anymore about any of it.

All he feels now is to let loose. He just wants to sing. He must sing, his mind tells him. His song bursts forth then, and he holds it for half a minute. He swallows, then takes another mighty inhale— and sings again his beautiful song.

He directs it to the group of females sitting nearby. Every ounce of energy he has is focused on his song. He sings with a glorious sense of release. Ahh, he sings. And performs for hours because he must. He is a spring peeper, and he was born to sing.

Midnight in Maple Marsh

I slid silently through the dark water, alone under the cloak of darkness. Tall reeds and rushes parted before me, drifting past the rowboat. A kerosine lantern sputtered on the bow seat, casting a weak glow ahead. I slowly moved deeper into the blackness.

Somewhere far ahead, the dense vegetation should give way to open water. The only map I had was a state highway rendition of the road networks in the region—unsuitable really for field navigation. It was only good for getting me to where the road ended near the marsh and pointing me in the direction to go from there. I had earlier marked a red dot on a location in a blank space, and using my compass, oriented the boat toward the dot once onsite.

The flat-bottomed craft was full of gear and soon left the shallow bank and disappeared into the black void. Eleven-thirty, and I expected to find the target area just before midnight. Ripples splashed softly when I dipped and pushed the oars. They sometimes bumped against the gunwale with a low thud. The only other sound that breached the night was my breathing. The jon boat crept forward with each stroke I made from the rear seat. With my back braced against the metal stern, I focused on the bow just above the lantern.

This position made rowing awkward, swinging the oars toward the bow, dipping and pulling the boat forward. Unconventional compared with powering it through the water from the middle seat while facing the stern. My rhythm, inefficient, was the only way to navigate the boat safely in the murky surroundings.

Beyond the glare of the kerosene lantern, I could see only more black space ahead. Enough to make my mind wander a moment in abstract musing. What if nothing existed beyond the bow cleat, only a dark matrix, an amorphous nebula of gas and dust of interstellar space? It was 1972, and I had watched "2001: A Space Odyssey" for the second time a few nights earlier, so that may have been part of the reason for my flight of fancy while rowing in the featureless gloom.

Maybe a black hole containing a million suns awaited me a moment ahead, where nothing escapes and time bends. I speculated about crossing its edge, the event horizon, leaving the marsh behind. It would age seven-hundred earth-years while the boat and I navigated the black hole for just one minute...just like the Dave Bowman character in the film.

Weird for sure, but without reference points that our minds can associate with previous knowledge and familiarity, one cannot know where they are—again like Bowman. He inexplicably found himself in a large room decorated in French Provincial furnishings. The aliens had provided them as familiar reference points from his own memories, so things would not seem surreal to him. In keeping him calm, he felt no anxiety during his new mission as an emissary to Earth.

Cosmic musing seemed to work for me, because my mind soon returned to concentrating on navigating through the inky labyrinth of the marsh. Without landmarks for reference, the rough map beside me was all but useless. The boat made slow progress, often rolling up on a tussock, backing off, shifting angles, probing again like a bumper-car in traffic. These disturbances released bubbles of air that rose to the surface from the base of the tussocks.

At least the boat's low draft allowed it to move through the shallows the way a muskrat might. In fact, I picked my way along their open travel lanes, barely wide enough for the boat. I nudged against a few of their "push-up mounds" now and then. Most of them likely hid a few of the rodents deep inside, where they no doubt slumbered away the night.

The mounds stood knee-high—piles of cattails, reeds, brush, and mud with underwater entrances. There, the sleek furbearers raised their young and hid from predators in the treeless marsh, oblivious to black holes and galactic plasma.

Muskrats did not concern me much, for they posed no problem. Other things did, though, like paying attention to avoid banging hard into an old mound with shrubs on top, where a startled water snake could fall into my lap. Fortunately, in Maple Marsh none of them were poisonous…they just sank their teeth only through the first few layers of skin. I found out once, years later, after sticking my hand under a log to get something I dropped. Several of the snakes had hidden there unseen until a pair lashed out and chomped my hand. They slithered into the water while I wiped off drops of blood.

Now and then I heard a dull splash erupt somewhere in the dark. I imagined a snapping turtle had dragged a bullfrog under the surface. Or perhaps a black-crowned night-heron had speared a shiner that rose for a gulp of air.

Without landmarks, I had to use my wristwatch to estimate how far I had rowed—about a quarter mile. I figured it from multiplying the boat's estimated speed by the elapsed time.

Field navigation remained a primitive endeavor based on old-school techniques— no GPS or cell phones then.

Before launching, I set my analog field compass with a bearing to follow. After adjusting from true north to magnetic north, I moved by dead reckoning. It told me I had gone only half-way to the marsh's center, where the actual work would begin.

The marsh sat in the broad floodplain of the Maple River, fifty miles north of Lansing and still within the *Southern Michigan/Northern Indiana Drift Plains Ecoregion (56)* and *Lansing Loamy Plain (56g)*. My purpose at that late hour was to collect evidence. The kind a science graduate student at MSU needed to complete an advanced degree. I had selected five different wetlands besides the one whose dark waters I now explored. They lay scattered in different locations throughout the state. At various times during the day and night over the next year, I planned to visit each one multiple times.

I wanted to know how water-based ecosystems like wetlands, ponds, and lakes thrived during periods when sunlight is weak or absent—cloudy days and dark of night. Most of us know that multicellular life in all ecosystems depends on the availability of sunlight. Green plants and plankton in algae mats use the sunlight to produce biomass and oxygen from sunlight in their leaves and stems. These microscopic creatures form the base of marsh food webs and energy pathways.

Theories floated about in the scientific literature involving how the marsh could remain productive without sunlight for half the day. I had come to Maple Marsh to take a closer look for myself—go where theory ended and facts dwelled.

Plants extract carbon dioxide and oxygen molecules from the air to support themselves. Organic carbon gets produced and used for plant tissues, and the oxygen dissolves in the water as a byproduct. All consumer organisms require the carbon and oxygen for building anatomical structures and providing a source of energy. The living biomass and inorganic elements in marshes present many opportunities for organisms to exploit resources. Every species has its special means for mining these resources, which comprise its particular modus operandi known as its ecological niche.

Similar niches of different species form the hierarchical trophic structures of the ecosystem. Plant producers called autotrophs provide food for herbivores. Carnivores that eat herbivores form the next level, then predators that feed on first-level carnivores form the top of the food chain. Decomposers get the scraps and the last laugh, for they consume the dead parts of everything, and send them for recycling. Then they die and decompose too.

Without sunlight, carbon fixation and dissolved oxygen, the Earth would remain as lifeless as its moon. But oxygen metabolism by some aquatic microorganisms can also breakdown many pollutants through chemical reactions. This became my second mission that night—to learn if the marshes I investigated suffered from the busy roadways nearby. Chemical pollutants like oil and gas byproducts, asbestos, deicing chemicals, often became deposited into adjacent still-water habitats from the unending flow of vehicles.

A state highway crossed over Maple Marsh a half-mile from my target spot. The other five marshes also bordered roadways. I surmised these constructions might affect the marshes' functional capacity to remain sustainable. But I needed facts based on objective data; speculation wouldn't do. For this, I needed to get my hands dirty with squishy things that lived in the mud. I knew wisdom lies in the dirtiest places.

There, life slugs it out every moment to physically survive. I pictured the whole earth as a battleground where relentless forces tug and push, shape, reorganize and transform matter into energy and vice versa each moment. Armies of creatures and plants use every manner of adaptive strategy in constant struggles to persist in the harsh trenches of life.

The intricacies and connections involved fascinated me, but many of their inner workings still remained unstudied back then. Perhaps some answers, I thought, lay somewhere in Maple Marsh at midnight. Maybe the muskrat trail I followed would lead to some cognitive treasure—even a wee epiphany would suffice. Enough of those, and I may find enlightenment and awareness involving nature and myself.

The bow of the boat brushed past another stand of reeds. Once again, I lifted the oars and swung them forward for another stroke. A loud rushing sound erupted out of the still darkness mixed with a staccato whistling. It was so unexpected I jerked an oar too much while in mid-stroke. The tip hit the lantern and knocked it off the seat into the open boat, extinguishing it immediately. The globe shattered, sending pieces of glass flying like shrapnel.

My heart rate shot the line, and a jolt of adrenaline caused me to slam the oars against the hard hull. I shipped them and sat unmoving in complete darkness to let the thumping in my chest dwindle. The boat had likely invaded the sleeping spot for a pair of ducks— most likely mallards based on the high-pitched beating of flapping wings. They had flushed at the last second instead of quietly swimming away. Their choice had caused a chain reaction of events that instantly made me blind in an already dark place.

My original backup plan was to employ a flashlight in case of such an event. When I reached for it beside me, I saw it floating in a puddle near the dead lantern. I grabbed it and pushed the switch. No beam. *Flick, flick*...dead, shorted out.

I took the unit apart by feel, fiddled with the batteries, bulb, and switch. Useless. A spare flashlight sat in the truck, which I had somehow overlooked when loading my equipment into the boat. That one was waterproof. I felt my lips pucker; "...for want of a nail, the shoe was lost..." Somber reeds seemed to nod agreement in the gloom, yet in their soft rustling I sensed their mirth. I sighed; get a grip.

My options seemed limited. I needed to get to open water this night during the new moon, when complete darkness reigned. Otherwise, the data I needed might disappear with the dawn.

I turned the boat around and eased back through the narrow channels toward the truck. If I kept the compass heading on the reverse course, I couldn't help but hit the shore eventually, though not necessarily near the truck.

The boat slid onto the muddy bank near the truck a half-hour later. Gravel crunched softly when my foot stepped onto the dry land. I walked over and retrieved the flashlight. When I turned it on, the beam shot out in the sudden brightness only a fresh battery could provide. A single large square one powered it, and I also snagged the extra battery next to it. All set, I returned to the boat and pushed off again. In seconds, cattails closed their ranks behind me.

To conserve power, I switched the light on and off occasionally. Forty minutes later, the vegetation vanished, and open water surrounded me. My night vision had peaked—pupils dilated to the margins. I could make out more features now, including the shape of a distant forested shoreline. It lay silhouetted against a slightly lighter shade of dark purple on the horizon.

A few days earlier, I had scrutinized maps and aerial photographs in my student office. I selected and marked eight locations within this marsh to collect my data. My "office" was a peeling desk in a former broom closet at the university that I shared with five other graduate students.

The room was as spacious as an elevator with furniture—two desks and chairs, stools, and a pair of drafting tables. Whoever got there first had their choice, but they had to squeeze through the half-blocked door. We all had different schedules and projects, and we used the closet as our base while on campus. It was supposed to be a place for us to study, but that was usually impossible. Much of the time, we jabbered between classes and research projects.

Space wasn't a problem, however, while deep in Maple Marsh. I used the dim wooded shoreline as a reference, and with the map and flashlight, estimated my general location for collecting the first samples. Soon I shipped the oars again and flipped open the latches of a cooler-sized container next to me. The inside resembled a portable chemical lab with water-testing devices, equipment, and chemical reagents, all neatly packed.

I pulled out the sounding gauge with the attached lead weight and measuring line. After a quick inspection, I dropped the weight over the side like a sinker until I felt the tension on the tape slacken. Just over three feet deep. I winched up the tape, set it aside and recorded the reading in my field notebook.

Five more soundings followed from various positions in the boat. As I worked, Thoreau's narrative came to mind—plumbing the depths of Walden Pond in a quest for objective reality and spiritual growth. He too went out on the water alone, seeking facts and the cognitive edge of man.

He used the same type of sounding gear I did and eventually mapped the entire pond's bottom. When I read his works as a freshman, he had traveled quite far along the road to wisdom. He spent two years out there on his pond…I hoped to be back in my usual bed before dawn.

I replaced the equipment and lifted out a hand-held digital oxygen meter the size of my hand. A thin cable connected to a sensing probe at the end. It detected dissolved oxygen in the water but needed calibrating before I dropped it over the gunwale just below the water surface.

More measurements from different depths found their way into my notebook. To confirm the meter data and test for dissolved oxygen and pollutants, I collected water samples in glass bottles at the same depths to analyze back in the university's lab.

For the next ten minutes, I bombed the depths with more samplers to measure turbidity, pH, and temperature. An amazing amount of biological and chemical action happened in wetland substrates, and to investigate, I sent a fifteen-pound steel contraption hurtling to the bottom. It was a bulky grab sampler—an industrial version of the carnival crane-claw, except the two steel jaws snapped closed like a bear trap when it hit the muck. I felt the cable tension drop, then hauled the gear up and scooped the dripping mud into jars and labeled them.

Soon after, I finished the testing, collecting, and documenting, stowed the instruments, then rowed to the remaining seven sample sites. Out came the instruments again, and testing resumed using the same procedures and tests. When completed, my watch said four-thirty in the morning. My arms ached from all the rowing and hauling dredge and bottle samples to the surface.

I packed everything up, then sat awhile in the dark and soaked in the utter peacefulness of the moment. The water remained calm; a soft breeze rustled the reeds. A handful of stars peered through dark clouds against an even darker sky.

I closed my eyes and felt my muscles relax. Tension ebbed. My thoughts drifted large—it seemed I was the only creature in the world, waiting in the gloom for...what? I didn't know. Perhaps this was what it was like near the beginning when life first emerged—but with mists; there are always mists when someone describes origin of life scenes.

The first atomic particles that became life are not only still with us today, but they also form parts of the matter that became us, our offspring, other creatures. The cosmos is a most efficient recycler and distributor of matter.

I opened my eyes to the dark sky, the void surrounding me, the still waters, the silence. I pictured this marsh scene of ten thousand years ago. Maybe I was a proto amphibian then who had just climbed onto a lily pad, throat pulsing, waiting for a mayfly to flutter by. The next second I might be slipping down the gullet of an egret, floundering in confusion. It would be dark inside the egret—even blacker than Maple Marsh at midnight. My shoulder twitched, then I turned the boat toward my rusty truck and focused on the next muskrat mound ahead.

The surrounding solitude belied the factory-level energy transforming activities that were taking place in the water, soils, air, and sediments. Hidden plants and animals were busy as machines processing dissolved oxygen into energy and biomass, competing with their own kind and their neighbors for the precious molecules.

Fierce competition for space and resources occurred within every square foot, but it wasn't just here. Many wetland ecosystems peppered the continents as transition zones between terrestrial and deep-water environments. And every one of them provided both a harsh and homey place for something.

Landscapes are theaters of war where indifferent tactics, ambushes, and battles are constantly underway. Wherever water and surfaces abound, plant and animal life soon come knocking. If suitable, a spot on the landscape becomes a habitat. Families move in, then neighbors, and right after that, it's war.

Every crevice, crack, and crease are both a life and death zone. Whether of sea, air, or dry ground, landscapes are where every life tries, and every life dies. They are the interfaces where existence is possible for living things.

At that very moment, untold populations of organisms were stalking, snatching, grabbing, piercing, chewing, munching, crunching, dissolving, absorbing, swallowing, excreting. Yet, I could detect none of it—my human senses were far too coarse. Besides, stealth and camouflage were the keys to survival in the marsh food web.

As a kid, I used to watch similar battles through a microscope— copepods tearing apart Daphnia, paramecia absorbing algae cells. Rotifers propelled through the water like tiny helicopters, sweeping in bits of detritus and plankton. Hydras injected a potent neurotoxin from their tentacles to stun, entangle, and kill their prey before eating it. But despite the violence, I heard no screams or war slogans among the miniscule marsh consumers.

The producers were also vulnerable to consumption and decay both night and day. While I floated on the marsh, green plants, and phytoplankton waited in huddled masses for the dawn and life sustaining sunshine to arrive once again. Then they would go back to work extracting carbon from the air and manufacturing new carbohydrates to grow and maintain their structures. These chemical reactions produced oxygen as a by-product, where the molecules dissolved in the water.

Tiny silent herbivores feasted on the green banquet as I rowed, and predators fed upon the grazers. It was a feature of the planet's grand energy processing system—the global exploitation of resources, all driven by a rather ordinary sun in a backwater galaxy.

One way or another, all living beings, from one- celled algae to swaddled babies and old codgers, depend on sunlight and carbon. This means every organism collects and sequesters carbon—the living, the dead, the fossilized. There is no such life form on earth that is not composed of carbon.

Yet, without a constant stream of photons, photosynthesis would not occur, and carbon would not get extracted from carbon dioxide by the plant tissues in the atmosphere or natural waters. Plants would disappear and life up the trophic line would cease.

And so would life down the line. Many life forms are decomposers that spend their time deconstructing dead animals and plants back into basic elements. These bacteria, fungi, and molds then offer the bits and nutrient scraps to the energy flow market. Decomposers need carbon and oxygen too, except for anaerobic bacteria. Undoubtedly, there were scads of them in the muck below the rowboat. I may have scooped some up in my claw grab-sampler, but the oxygen depletion zone might be deeper. There, the pores between the soil particles would be too tight to hold much water for dissolving oxygen.

As both living and dead matter became ingested and processed in the surrounding marsh, new growth would emerge over subsequent days, new beings, new generations. Ecosystems like the marsh change every moment as species numbers rise, expand, shrink, or become extinguished. They wax and wane as the physical environment, weather, and climates change. On the whole, however, sustainable ecosystems remain functionally balanced within their general ranges of tolerance.

Physics tells us that whether subtle or catastrophic, every change at the atomic level occurs within the structures and rules imposed by universal forces. Whatever happens in the world is controlled by gravity, electromagnetism, strong interactions between atomic particles, and weak ones. Events around me might seem random, I thought—dripping oars, gliding through the water, pushing through the reeds, flapping wings, darkness—but I knew a marvelous orderliness and sequencing applied to all of it.

A fugue of cause and effect occurred around me every second— under the boat, above the surface, within the mud, and on stems and leaves of the vegetation. Life and non-life were transforming their elements back and forth, cycling and recycling in response to entropy's rhythms.

In studying Michigan's geology earlier, I knew Maple Marsh had existed since the glaciers retreated. Thick ice had gouged out low spots in the landscape that held the melting ice waters.

At first, the open water evaporated and became replenished periodically by precipitation. Later, life moved in. Water vapor rose from the surface and mixed with the atmosphere, continuing the next phase of the global water cycle. As the gases dispersed, they interconnected the living marsh with other landscapes of the region—and beyond. Maple Marsh's streams and creeks brought nutrients and new living pioneers to downstream habitats.

Some of those human pioneers settled around the marsh's fringes, where they tapped its resources—its waters, fish, waterfowl, mammals, edible plants. As their numbers grew, the humans became the top exploiters of the marsh. Generations later, many moved on to larger productive habitats and regions. Yet the marsh persisted, and Atlas shrugged.

I rowed back to the truck through the dense cattails without incident. After loading the equipment and muscling the aluminum boat onboard, my arms burned with fatigue, feeling stretched like hot boardwalk taffy. The truck engine sparked to life, all perky and ready to prowl.

I backed around the small space, then eased the rig down the dirt lane. Metal rattled on metal, but at least a trail to follow existed. Soon I came to a country road and not long after, my headlights pierced the darkness on an open highway.

A sliver of pale sky seeped over the horizon when the truck eased into my driveway. I stowed everything, then entered the house and dropped into bed. Three hours until my first class of the day.

Over the following months, I continued to visit the five wetlands and collect data. Eventually, I had enough to analyze and draw factual conclusions. The still waters of Maple Marsh had revealed some of their secrets to me about how the resident plants and animals deal with lower oxygen levels when sunlight is scarce.

During the day, plants released plenty of oxygen into the water through photosynthesis. When the sun disappeared, plants and animals continued to respire and drew what little oxygen remained from the water. Plants needed oxygen too for metabolic functions, but without photosynthesis to replenish what they produced, oxygen levels plummeted.

These levels swung wildly from day to night, creating hypoxia in dead zones of the marsh. The low oxygen in the shallow water can kill plants and animals alike. But wetlands are also resilient, and the communities have backup systems. For one, a reserve of dissolved oxygen can remain in the bottom muck.

Plants absorb oxygen from the water through their roots. They transport what they need to other plant tissues, then store the rest in the submerged roots. At night, the roots release the stored oxygen waste and continue supplying other tissues. In this way, the ecosystem breathes with little interruption all day and night.

Natural catastrophes and excess pollutants from human activities, however, can permanently degrade and destabilize an ecosystem. But despite the busy roadways, pollutants did not seem to interfere with the marshes production activities where I visited. Much of it lay buried in the mud next to the roads, suggesting the quantities remained largely unavailable. Also, the marshes were large relative to the roadways, with sufficient capacity to tolerate the cast-offs of modern transportation.

While floating upon Maple Marsh's dark waters at night, a sense of clarity had descended over me. I had plumbed its depths, checked its vital signs, watched it breathe in the air bubbles released by plant roots that rose to the waters' surface, and heard the marsh move in the cattail rustlings.

Beneath a deep purple night sky, I had found my way to its heart. I had pulled back some of its layers one by one and peeked inside.

In doing so, I gleaned a hint of the marsh's complexity and marveled at its connections to other intricate layers of the universe. While alone upon the waters of that wild place, I sensed how everything there, including myself, all formed part of a massive whole. Something so dense with layers of actions and reactions, stimulus, and response, cause-and-effect, teeming with lifeforms struggling for persistence.

After completing my work in Michigan's marshes, I felt ready to investigate new natural mysteries in other landscapes. I would keep nibbling the cognitive fruits that might inhabit other wild places. I was eager to examine the whole and all its parts of living landscapes in order to find the meaning of it all.

Perhaps more layers of knowledge awaited me to find. If I encountered grit out there, then all the better. But if any unicorns grazed the landscapes, I intended to find them as well. Perhaps they preferred some other marsh, where instead of midnight darkness, sunlight beamed down upon the waters and gave the muskrats a reason to sigh.

Shiawassee Illusions

The dried corn stalks rattled loudly as I pushed past them through the flooded field. Water sloshed over my feet, but they remained dry from the rubber hip boots I wore. The thin crust of ice crunched loudly with each step. In the pre-dawn light of mid-November, visibility extended only a few rows ahead.

Soon, I stood only six feet from the deeper water at the opposite edge of the planted corn strip. Bulging unharvested cobs hung in their husks, and many had burst open and dropped yellow kernels that reminded me of small golden nuggets. Good omen? I hoped so.

The stalks would serve as camouflage, and I was careful to keep them standing intact. Next to me stood a knee-high tussock of thick grass, where I set my gear down to keep it out of the ankle-deep water. My breath froze in the chilled air as I glanced to my left and saw my companion, Chuck, twenty feet away. Dave, on my right, rummaged in his duffel bag. I knew what he was looking for— supplies for the ruse we had planned.

In the pre-dawn light, I could see across the open water in front of me to another corn strip a hundred yards away. My stomach growled; still a half-hour before go-time, so I ate a granola bar. "How about some hot coffee Chuck, plenty of time for it?" I called.

"You bet; got my thermos right here. Don't even need to stir the cream with a spoon—this icicle on my nose should work fine." I chuckled politely while pouring some of the steaming brew from my own thermos into the lid and then sipped it. The hot liquid slid along my throat with a soothing slug of warmth all the way down. It felt good, but did nothing for my cold toes. I checked right again. "Hey Dave, does this spot look as good as it did on the map at headquarters?" But with his back toward me, he didn't answer.

Then I heard corn stalks clatter and frozen vapor disperse upward from below his waist. He was jettisoning the remains of his own earlier coffee-break onto a corn stalk.

A metallic zip reached my ears—the universal announcement of male voiding achievement. "Yeah, it's got everything a greenhead would want; we just have to lure them in."

Our cornfield sat in the Shiawassee River State Game Area, within an hour's drive of Lansing. One of Michigan's best waterfowl preserves, it occupied ten- thousand acres of lowland hardwoods, overgrown hay fields and marshes interspersed with corn and grain plots. A system of low-dikes, canals, and water control structures flooded mature crop fields seasonally, and turned them into temporary wetlands. We had come here to hunt ducks.

The area provided a paradise for waterfowl, with an irresistible mixture of habitats, food, and protective cover. No weary flock could resist landing there—any more than a fleet of eighteen-wheelers approaching a neon-flashing truck-stop filled with breasty waitresses. No one worried about hordes of hungry ducks pouring in to gobble up acres of crops—federal wildlife agencies intentionally planted the blocks of corn and grain just for them. They managed Shiawassee as a refuge and hunting reserve for nearly fifty-thousand ducks and geese during the fall migrations, and more in other seasons. Most of these included mallards and Canada geese. Hunters commonly called male mallards drakes and, in the fall, "greenheads" because of the solid metallic green color above their necks. They displayed maroon chests, and the body plumage contained light gray. Females, or hens, stayed mostly brown with a black streak behind their eyes. When flying, both sexes displayed a bright blue patch on their rear wing feathers closest to their bodies.

The Shiawassee area is part of the H*uron/Erie Lake Plains Ecoregion (57), Saginaw Lake Plain (57e)*. It is mostly flat and underlain by clayey lake deposits from Lake Michigan, with some beach ridges and low dunes. Some sand occurs associated with beach formations, but the soils are mostly poorly drained.

Lotteries and fees from participants made hunting a highly regulated activity. The revenues went back into the management budget each year. Thus, hunters became a primary means of financial support for this and many other refuges. Only selected areas opened for hunting, rotating to keep the flocks healthy and at sustainable levels.

I had come there to hunt with my two companions who had been to Shiawassee once before. They were also fellow grad students of mine enrolled in MSUs' fish and wildlife management program. For this trip, they offered to pick me up at my house at three in the morning. We needed permits to hunt on the refuge, available only through the lottery held at five in the morning at the onsite refuge headquarters.

After driving an hour from Lansing, a long gravel road snaked through the darkness off the main highway. It ended at an isolated barn-like building within the vast refuge. Pickup trucks, trailered boats, and men in full camouflage dress packed the parking lot. Engine noises and vehicle lights pierced the gloom that carried guarded voices heading inside the building. It seemed as busy as a swat team staging-area preparing to deploy.

We followed a troop of outdoorsmen into the building. While I stayed at the counter as a place-holder, Chuck and Dave went over to scrutinize a wall-sized colored board containing a map of the available hunting locations. They picked a promising one with an unclaimed tag, pulled the card off the peg and joined me at the counter.

With our chosen hunting spot, we could register for the lottery with a hundred others. Everyone hoped to win a plot before the total allotment was filled. Registering involved presenting proof of the other permits we had paid for days earlier—driver's license, Small Game Hunting License, Waterfowl Hunting License, Federal Migratory Bird Hunting Stamp, and Harvest Information Endorsement. In those days, it was more difficult to enter a government-controlled marsh than board a commercial airliner— just ask D.B. Cooper.

By five-thirty, everyone had registered, and the staff put the cards with plot numbers into a barrel-shaped bin with a crank handle. One of the staff spun the drum, and another reached in when it stopped and withdrew a slip.

An announcement informed each group of lucky winners, who immediately went outside, gathered their guns and gear and headed into the vast wetlands to find their hunting spots. Most comprised small groups of three or four hunters who backed their camouflaged outboard power boats down the ramp outside the lottery building and into the canal. They motored the waterways lined with low, grassy dikes for several miles to their plots, pulling or winching their boats up and over the berms to the next canal.

We had no boat, apparently the only group of poor grad students like us. Our only choice—set out on foot in the frosty

November air, carrying our gear along a narrow dike. My companions toted quite expensive guns, but mine was a more basic model.

Boat wakes surged alongside us, outboard engines whined, men's voices rose above the noise, bow lights blazed, combatants scrambled aboard as though launching a river offensive. The entire landscape seemed to pulse under the coming invasion, and we all carried weapons—armed and dangerous and out for blood. No attack helicopters or napalm showed up, but this water assault still looked like "Apocalypse Now" in the marshes of Shiawassee. The slaughter would soon begin.

Dozens of twelve-gauge shells hung from elastic loops on my vest, one band across my chest and another on each side. I had enough firepower to take down an entire corn patch—with or without ducks. Each of us carried our own shotgun, a bag with decoys, ammo, binoculars, hand warmers, flashlight, sandwiches, thermos, and canteen. Multiple layers of clothing, heavy parkas, and gloves, plus bulky chest waders, hindered our progress.

We trudged several miles along the tops of narrow connecting levees, and the further away we hauled ourselves from headquarters, the fewer boats and other hunters we saw. Dawn awaited, still two-hours away. The temperature settled at more than brisk—bone- chilling. I exhaled frozen breath, and ice crystals on the ground crunched with each step. Most of the time, that sound and our collective breathing were all I heard. An odd stillness permeated the air and the sounds we made seemed extra crisp and clear.

As the first rosy hints of dawn showed on the horizon, we turned onto another connecting berm. It ran through a long, flooded field. On both sides, strips of brown corn stalks extended seventy feet wide. They alternated with strips of open water, forming a linear pattern across the landscape like the stripes on an American flag.

We followed the berm until we spied a post with our plot number on it. Our permit allowed us to hunt anywhere along that strip, and we chose a spot halfway down its length. I hauled my gear down the berm slope and into the shallow water at the bottom. The other two did the same, slipping and sliding on the icy ground. We spread ourselves ten feet apart, and in unison we took a step forward, and disappeared into the corn.

After Dave relieved himself in the corn patch, I returned the thermos to my duffle and pulled out a half-dozen decoys. I dragged them through the last few corn rows to the water's edge and deployed them a dozen feet away in the open water. Each had a cord attached to a lead fishing weight to keep it from drifting away.

We chose our cornfield because we knew the prevailing wind came from in back of us. Ducks and geese approach their landing areas by flying into the wind. They cup their wings to create drag, and then touch down feet first. The ducks would come to the decoys facing our guns.

I stepped back among the stalks where I snapped off and husked a few ears of corn. I tossed the kernels among the decoys so any incoming ducks would think a contented feeding party was whooping it up there. Mallards (Anas platyrhynchos) were "puddle ducks" or "dabblers" because they inhabited shallow waters and tip their bodies vertically. It is their habit to snatch food off the bottom— seeds, tubers, and pondweeds, as well as insects, worms, snails, and crustaceans.

Refuge rules allowed hunting to start when dawn officially arrived, which fast approached. I uncased my twelve-gage shotgun and inserted five duck loads. We had seen no birds moving in the skies around us yet, though my pulse had changed from a shuffle to a trot. On that day, I intended to engage nature on the battlefield as a volunteer combatant rather than a scientist. This outing promised plenty of natural grit— noise, gunpowder, blood, death. It might even cause any lingering unicorns on the landscape to disappear. I wasn't at all sure if ducks or unicorns would survive my presence on the landscape that day. I felt loose with pre-battle anticipation, but I wasn't worried—I carried a gun.

The idea was to shoot the ducks in the air just as they set their wings to land near the decoys. While perfectly legal, shooting a "sitting duck" in the water is unsportsmanlike. No duck hunter with any conscience would shoot a duck sitting on the water, unless it is crippled or they are trying to retrieve or to avoid starvation.

When my watch showed seven, hunting could start. I flipped off the safety switch. My right finger tightened against the trigger guard, while my left gripped the wooden slide tightly. I was prepared to pump lead into some hapless living creature. Immediately, I heard explosions in the distance. Then I heard many more. I was about to become a wanton killer, one who did it for fun rather than survival—just another beast...a rogue predator.

"Someone got lucky early," Chuck said.

"Or maybe not," I said. "Might have missed." "Right," Dave nodded, "Most of them get away."

We kept our eyes on the sky in front of us, ready to shoulder guns should a flock descend. So far, though, we had seen nothing flying except some starlings.

"So, what's the likelihood of bagging some ducks?" I asked Dave. "Well, in a typical season, only about ten percent get harvested, but those get replaced by the following spring breeding season."

More shots echoed far across the fields. I scanned the sky again for wings. "Seems like they keep the hunting parties far apart."

Chuck responded. "Yeah, at least a hundred yards, and usually more. Otherwise, the birds would stay out of an area—too much disruption."

"And it's also far beyond shotgun range of other hunters," said Dave.

We stood in silence then, urging the heavens to deliver a small band of dabblers we could unload upon. But none came toward us. Every few minutes we saw flocks moving in the distance across our view—too high and out of range.

Soon I started shifting from one foot to the other. My toes felt numb from standing in the freezing water. In another half hour, my feet lost feeling. The numbness in my toes subsided in favor of a persistent ache. Shortly, everything up to my knees hurt. My waders contained no insulation, and I only wore two pairs of wool socks. My mind couldn't shake the thought that my feet had been soaking in a bucket of ice-water for hours, and I was getting desperate to pull them out.

The gray stillness that started the day remained. Neither the water nor the surrounding air had seemed to warm a single degree. As time passed, and despite my parka and knit cap, I felt my body core chill like an oyster kept on ice at a raw bar. Only my hands kept a hint of warmth because I had thrust them deep in my coat pockets. Each grasped a small metal flask that held a glowing wick soaked in lighter fluid. The three-hour fuel supply, however, approached empty.

My mind wondered why I was standing in a flooded cornfield getting more hypothermic by the minute, just to annihilate a couple of hungry ducks. My companions seemed to have no qualms. They and most of the other graduate students in the MSU Fish and Wildlife Department were training for research careers or operation management positions on wildlife refuges and hunting lands. I didn't know what I would do after graduating, but felt certain it had to involve landscapes; something practical, hands-on.

Managing critical habitats through hunting and wildlife preserves made sense. Keeping populations from exceeding the carrying capacity of a landscape prevented mass starvations and ecological catastrophes. Historical incidents had shown this all over the planet, including the Kaibab Plateau on the north side of the Grand Canyon. After mule deer hunting became banned, the animals overgrazed and destroyed the landscape and mass starvation ensued.

Other cases involve kangaroos that are eliminating endangered plants and reptiles, monkeys in India breaking into homes and biting people, wild dogs and rabies in China, beavers in Argentina destroying forests, Canadian feral cats decimating local wildlife, English badgers rapidly causing the spread of bovine tuberculosis.

I didn't have hostile feelings about hunting to put food on the table. Like everyone else, I had descended from a long line of ancient omnivores who acquired most of their protein needs from other animals over the last several hundred thousand years.

Even sport hunting wasn't all about bloodlust and dysfunctional male egos seeking control over nature. I suspected hunting was popular for its many positive benefits—connecting with nature, historic cultural roots, survival, the thrill of the hunt, bonding time between fathers, sons, daughters, mothers and extended families and friends.

The day before our Shiawassee trip, I stocked up on ammunition. After exiting the gun store parking lot, I passed a Chinese restaurant. My head nodded as I sniffed the air. "Ahh, roast duck." Soon I would be stir- frying my own mallard Lo-Mein.

Waterfowl had been winging south in fall and back in spring since the Pleistocene—nearly 150,000 years. But centuries of land development had destroyed substantial portions of their flyways and choice feeding and resting areas. These aerial travelers desperately needed areas like Shiawassee. Without them, waterfowl populations would plummet.

Flocks of weary ducks and geese swarmed into Michigan refuges from as far south as the Gulf Coast, migrating along the wide Mississippi Flyway. They stopped for a layover on their way to their breeding grounds on the northern Manitoba prairies.

Convoys of thirty or more ducks form before the birds undertake their journey, equipped with a variety of navigation mechanisms to stay on course. They can use the axes of polarized light to determine their position relative to the sun, and are able to perform compass orientation in their brains.

They learn key landmarks from veteran travelers in the flock. Sun and topographic features, however, are not useful for flying at night. For that, many waterfowl species use star orientation for navigation, like ancient mariners.

Before coming to MSU, I spent two years at Penn State studying animal and human behavior and observing ducks and geese in the wild. The way ducks approached a promising site from the air was familiar to me. Incoming flocks would eyeball the landscape below, looking for signs that a spot fits their criteria for food, cover, and water. If things appeared a little off, they keep moving.

But if ducks like what they see below, they usually circle the area to better inspect it before landing. Previous unwelcome encounters with hunters at other sites elevate their natural wariness. If other ducks are already below in their chosen spot, they will listen to the nuances of their quacks and check for visual cues before committing themselves.

Once convinced an area is safe, the birds set their wings like elevator flaps on a plane, and splash down in the shallows. A waterfowl hunter's success often depends on how well he can deceive his targets—create the illusion that all is safe below using decoys in the water.

When all the distant shooting started after daybreak at Shiawassee, I scanned the horizon for a wedge of flapping wings but saw no birds. More shooting, more empty sky. Time passed slowly, and still no ducks came. Distant bangs periodically broke the silence. A few times our hopes rose when a mallard group occasionally appeared over us, then circled out of range and banked away. Dave tried to woo them in with his duck caller, but they did not seem impressed. Another failed illusion attempt.

The thermos had gone empty hours ago and bobbed in the water at my feet. I had eaten the nearly frozen ham sandwich that once sat in my vest pocket, and drank most of my canteen water. After vigorously wiggling my toes in my boots, they began aching again. Our stake-out is useless, I concluded. We didn't deceive any ducks at all. They weren't stupid—they had us made from the beginning. We were the ones fooled every time the ducks feigned to land. What a bunch of jokers freezing our testosterone-engines off on a perfectly frigid day in their own backyard.

My watch said ten-fifteen. "What do you think, guys?" I finally mumbled, stiffening my jaw to mask my teeth from chattering. "We've got to check-out at headquarters by eleven; think we should start heading back?

The others agreed, and we packed the gear. The return trek along the dikes and canals to the reporting station was more miserable than the outbound one. By the time we arrived at the station, my feet were barking silently in pain.

Boats returned to the docks. Men and dogs disembarked. Laughter, broad grins, and thumbs-up signals flashed from the victorious hunters. Most of them carried fistfuls of duck feet upside down at their waists, with green heads dangling and flopping while they walked.

Each hunting party had to turn in a report of numbers and species killed, crippled and knocked- down—hit, but status unknown. When we submitted our plot card, all of our boxes were full of zeros. It had been quite a successful day...for the ducks that hovered high above our frigid corn patch.

The hour's drive home with the car heater turned to atomic blast was just enough to turn my howling feet to a whimper.

No one had much to say, and as the miles clicked by, I became consumed by an overwhelming urge to doze.

But every time I nodded off, my mind would fill with the day's images of flocks of ducks flying toward me. They came closer. I saw the pupils in their eyes, heard them quack to the decoys. Their wings cocked in unison, and they circled. Then, one after another, they broke away on a glide path toward the decoys. Almost within shooting range. But then one of them would utter a warning quack, and the others did the same. Immediately they veered off—flapping up, up, and away.

That raucous calling, I suspected, was their way of laughing—guffawing really—that our ruse had not worked. The real illusion that day was mine...that I was an avid hunter. I heard their hysterical chatter echo in the wind as they slowly disappeared into a deeply clouded sky. I was certain I heard devil-laughter in the distance, but it might have been just an illusion as well.

Launching the Duck Patrol

Soon after my failed Shiawassee hunt, and while I remained busy with my marsh research and heavy course load, another research project demanded more of my time. The university offered me a graduate assistantship grant that paid me for conducting additional research. It provided half our income, and we desperately needed it. In exchange, I was required to collect a boatful of data on Lake Erie that involved an environmental warming trend taking place in its waters. Once again, I would face the elements to hunt ducks, but not to kill them—just count them.

The western basin of the lake is thirty miles wide between the Detroit River, south to Toledo. Historically, it served as a migration stop-over for hundreds of thousands of waterfowl, especially during the fall seasons. Here ducks congregated in giant rafts of individuals—some extended over eight miles long. Diving ducks rested and fed on fish far below the surface before the lake surface froze.

Dabbling ducks and geese also formed rafts on the lake and flew to inland fields to feed on insect larvae and corn before flying south for the winter. Once the lake surface froze, waterfowl vacated the area for the winter the way they had done for over four-thousand years.

Then suddenly, things took a different turn. A mini climate-change arrived that warmed habitat conditions dramatically around the small city of Monroe, Michigan. The altered environment there affected a ten-mile section along the western lake coast. A guy named Enrico and the giant megawatt machine named after him were responsible.

Known as the "Enrico Fermi II Nuclear Power Plant," it was still under construction next to the lake when I first arrived there. Pumps pulled water from Lake Erie to cool the radioactive rods. Temperatures reached nearly six-hundred degrees Fahrenheit, and valves routed the resulting steam to a pair of massive cooling towers. Only one had started partial operations at the time, the other remained only half-way completed.

Visible from miles away, the cooling towers stood like the world's largest pair of beige, flat-topped traffic cones two-and-a-half times the height of the Statue of Liberty. As the steam rose inside the towers, it swirled upward, gradually cooling before exiting the gaping hole at the top of each one.

Clouds formed above the volcano-like opening from the condensed steam, but during this phase of construction, most of the heated water returned to the lake. Though the power plant remained offline for commercial operations, it still needed to produce power daily for construction activities and regular testing of the intake and discharge systems.

The landscape surrounding the Fermi plant is associated with the *Huron/Erie Lake Plains Ecoregion (57)* and *Maumee Lake Plain (57a)*. It extends along the western shores of Lake Erie, and is covered by fine- grained glacial till and lake sediments, with some coarser deposits originating as terminal moraines and beach ridges.

The underlying bedrock consists of limestone and dolomite, which is occasionally exposed at the surface. This region has soils that are highly fertile, but poorly drained.

Before construction began, regulatory agencies had raised concerns about whether heated water might affect ecological conditions and waterfowl usage in the lake around the power plant. A swarm of aquatic biologists regularly came onsite to study changes in the lake's limnological conditions.

My mission, however, was to monitor waterfowl use during the upcoming winter, when heated discharge water from the power plant kept the western part of the lake ice-free. In past years, this area froze solid by December, causing waterfowl to move out and head south by then.

The key question my research intended to answer involved whether the heated power plant discharges caused ducks and geese to remain in those previously frozen areas during the winter months. The arrival of heated effluent water acted as a rapid miniclimate change for the western basin of Lake Erie. If so, that meant it was anthropogenic—caused by humans, but regional rather than global, since it only involved ten miles along the shoreline and a mile or two wide. Even so, it served as a controlled landscape experiment on the effects of regional man-caused climate warming long before today's climate change hysteria became a new religion.

On the perimeter of the power plant property, the project team used a construction trailer as field headquarters. Various lake scientists from the university set up a lab and sleeping quarters and worked in teams on the lake for a couple days at a time each week. I also traveled two hours weekly, but alone from Lansing to Monroe to conduct waterfowl surveys.

Though crews of other specialists came and went at different hours during each week, I rarely encountered them since my survey schedule differed. They collected samples of phytoplankton, zooplankton, fish, various other aquatic species, and physical measurements. Sometimes they worked through the night and slept in the trailer the next day. The crews collected samples out in the lake from a boat kept at a dock off the power plant property. My surveys started at the same place, just a mile from the construction trailer.

In the years before I arrived there, the facility had not discharged any effluent, but similar data collecting had occurred, including for waterfowl. That set of data served as the baseline for comparing the data I would collect when the discharges began. While heated water flowed into the lake, my role required driving to Monroe on Thursday evenings and sleeping in the same construction trailer.

By the time the sun rose the next morning, I would drive off the power plant site to conduct the surveys. I expected to return home by early evening. Weekly data collecting would occupy my Fridays between October to April for the next two years. That would tell us if the heated effluent in winter had any effect on duck and geese populations and migration patterns.

On the initial trip I made to Monroe, my graduate program adviser came along, Dr. Benjamin Underhill, "Bud" to his students. We went to Monroe together in mid-October so he could instruct me on the data collection procedures for the project.

When we pulled up to the small rural dock on that first day, only two boats bobbed on their lines. One sparkled in the morning sunlight—a gleaming inboard mid-sized cabin cruiser tugging at its spring lines, its classy captain's chairs waiting. It looked ready to take off at full gallop through the water, snorting white spray and streaming colors, its hull pounding the surface in a thunderous roar of horsepower.

Bud glanced at me. "Pretty nice, huh?"

Launching the Duck Patrol

"Oh, yeah...for sure." I smiled, thinking how much fun this project would offer, skimming across endless water under a balmy sky.

While I could hardly wait to come aboard, Bud stepped into the other boat next to it. It was not a cabin cruiser and had no cabin at all—nor any seating, not even a hard bench. It reminded me of Captain Ahab's open whale boat while hunting Moby Dick, or an oversized bathtub. I recognized it as a Boston Whaler with a small, wood-framed steering pedestal in the center. It looked like a waist-high stepstool set in the center of the boat. A single outboard motor hung over the stern.

When I tossed my gear bag inside next to Bud's, it fell as hard as my disappointment. Other than two six- gallon portable gas tanks, the boat had little else—no windscreen, canopy, radio, or safety railings.

"The limnology crew uses that one, but you'll be taking this out," Bud said.

I vaguely heard him droning instructions. "...first, check the gas cans. The water quality sampling crew also uses this boat, and will fill them earlier in the week before they leave. But check them just in case."

"And if they don't fill them?"

"You'll have to take them to a gas station in Monroe first. Usually one tank is enough, but sometimes you may need the other one to finish the last leg and get back here."

"What are my options if I get stranded out there?" "Other than swearing, not much. Ten miles out is a long way to paddle...or flag down a passing boat." "You're kidding, right?" But I knew he wasn't—since he expected me to take this little open boat out in winter swells without a survival suit, or even a life preserver.

After I slipped the tether lines off the pilings, Bud eased the Whaler away from the dock while standing at the center wheel housing. With nowhere to sit, I stood next to him, clutching a piece of the pedestal in my left hand, wondering if it would stop me from catapulting overboard with the first wave.

We puttered out of the little boat basin and into the Huron River. From there, we headed eastward into the rising sun. Bud throttled up to cruising speed in the channel. Several minutes later, the Huron River joined Lake Erie, and the horizon suddenly expanded as though we'd just come through a tunnel and into a wide stadium.

A quarter mile from shore Bud pulled back the throttle, and the boat slowed to an idle. "Here's where you start the survey. Confirm your landmarks, then run south along the coast, keeping this quarter-mile distance offshore. You'll need to maintain a fast, steady speed until you see any ducks or geese, then stop and map the approximate location."

He started scanning the water between us and the shoreline, shading his eyes with his palm. "As you cruise, you'll have to look for flocks of ducks and geese rafting on the water or flying overhead."

"I can manage that," I nodded, swaying unsteadily in the rocking boat. Truth was, I didn't have the foggiest idea how to do that while hanging onto a bucking whale-catcher bounding through rough water at top speed. I pictured myself out on the water alone, fighting against hypothermia again.

"Make sure you identify each species in the flocks— and count the number of individuals you see. Mark them on the map and write notes on whether they are resting, flying, landing, or launching." Bud pulled out a sketch of the shoreline from his jacket pocket and handed it to me.

"Of course," I squeaked, as though this was all routine for me—done it a million times...piece-of-cake. My collar suddenly felt hot and clammy in the cold air, and I pulled my jacket zipper a few inches lower so I could breathe easier.

Bud throttled-up and maintained a southward heading, keeping the shoreline on our starboard side. I had never been on any lake as large as this one before, and never on any of the

Great Lakes. Everything was big—water and sky and shorelines that stretched forever.

The boat zipped along at a steady clip of twenty knots—galloping speed, full throttle. This was about as fast as the hull design could handle. Above the engine roar, Bud shouted something, but the wind carried it away before the words reached me.

The boat skipped across the calm surface of the lake like a flat stone, the hull just gently slapping the surface. A light wind caused ripples on the water. I held onto the pedestal-mount, and my concerns about getting bucked overboard dwindled. Maybe this would be a piece-of-cake after all.

Both of us kept a lookout for any waterfowl on the water or in the air, but so far, we had found none. I scouted the shoreline for any special landmarks I could use when I went out there on my own.

It seemed we moved through a live impressionist painting where green smudges suggested trees and marshes set against the cyan sky of a new day. Distant banks of ochre merged with the cobalt blue water that sparkled like sapphires.

After a few minutes of steady cruising, the shoreline seemed to disappear, but it had merely rounded a peninsula. Bud gestured and yelled over the engine noise that it was Stony Point, as he throttled back to idle. We rocked in place with the lake's rhythm.

Bud motioned for the map and tapped his finger on our approximate position. "When you see the point from this perspective, you've completed the first leg of four miles. Now we'll turn and head the boat straight out further into the lake for one mile." His finger slid across the map and stopped. "From here, you'll turn north by swinging left for the second four-mile leg, staying a mile out. Then turn left again and head to shore and dock."

I nodded while his finger traced the rectangular route, ending at a quarter mile off-shore. He tapped the sketch. "Here's where you start and end."

I nodded. "So, it's a ten-mile rectangle a quarter-mile from shore and a mile wide. Plus, I've got two miles each way between the dock and the lake and back."

"That will add another half-hour." He powered up again and swung the boat to go further into the lake.

Once we reached a mile out based on shore landmarks, Bud stopped the boat again. I glanced down at the sketch. It remained unmarked so far. I looked up at the empty expanse of water and the immense space above the horizon. Small gray clouds now peppered the once-clear sky. The shoreline appeared less distinct, and rolling swells had replaced the sapphire sparkles. It looked like a storm might be brewing.

My grasp on the steering pedestal tightened— weather, another hazard to worry about. I wondered how many people drowned here from lake storms during winter before ice covered it. No worries, I thought, since graduate students came and went, among the few crazy enough to be out then— expendable fodder for the glory of research.

I hoped the final project report would announce that "No harm to any research assistants occurred during the production of this experiment." Though nature designed waterfowl to handle rough waters, humans were made to inhabit the land. I imagined if I went overboard in Lake Erie, my organs would shut down in twenty minutes from the forty-degree water temperature—Shiawassee on steroids. I felt a lump in my throat.

Bud shouted, "Let's see if we can find some birds." He pushed the throttle all the way, and I stumbled backward. We were off again, shooting spray behind our stern in cascades of white turbulence.

I brought the binoculars to my eyes to scan, but the motion of the boat made it impossible to see anything. The rushing wind forced my eyes into a squint, reducing my view to a bouncing glare of blue and white. Bud leaned my way and hollered. "Keep checking your speed and direction to stay on course." He nodded at the compass housing.

So many questions to ask. "So, how do I deal with sex at this speed?" I yelled.

Bud swiveled his head my way. "I don't advise it out here—you need to keep your hands on the wheel...better to wait until you get back to the dock." He winked a smile. "Seriously though, females of many species look similar, mostly dull brown, but the males have bright and unique colors. That makes it easier to first tell males apart by their markings, then do the best you can with the females.

I nodded with a lopsided grin. Minutes passed, then the boat slowed to a putter. Bud pointed off the bow. "You see over there? That's a flock of goldeneyes; you can tell the males by that little white circle near their bills."

I looked where he was pointing and saw a darkened blob on the surface in the distance. A duck raft, but it resembled a large oil slick. I searched for orange bills and little white dots, but suddenly the entire dark patch suddenly erupted upward into a blanket of flapping wings and whistling sounds.

"They've taken off...count them quickly before they're gone."

I stared at the undulating mass in the sky, mesmerized by the synchronized shifting and twisting of so many bodies, their wings flashing dark, then white, dark, then white. I hoped a number would magically appear in my head, a tally that my subconscious had counted. But none did. The flock began moving further away. I counted furiously in my mind until only a smudge remained on the horizon— fading fast, gone, out of sight...over the rainbow.

Bud side-eyed me. "How many did you count?"

"I'd say four-hundred before they disappeared; give or take a couple, here and there." I had no idea.

Bud looked at me directly, doubtfully, as though rethinking his choice of graduate assistant. "Actually, fifteen-hundred were in that flock—give or take a couple, here and there."

I winced.

After jotting down the data, Bud revved the engine. For the next thirty minutes, we flushed flock after flock of ducks on either side of the boat. Some flotillas held only a few hundred individuals, but we also found large rafts composed of thousands. Bud kept up a rapid-fire lecture until we burbled into the lagoon and docked the boat where we started.

We had mapped fourteen flocks and six species of ducks. Bud estimated the total number of birds was forty-two thousand. It had taken nearly two hours, mostly due to all the extra stopping to give me instructions. That was twice the time Bud had allotted for doing the survey myself—beginning next week.

When I stepped off the boat and onto firm ground, my legs wobbled, struggling for a few seconds to hold my balance. Weak-kneed, I helped Bud secure the boat while my legs sensed a phantom boat bouncing under my feet.

The feeling disappeared by the time I slipped into the vehicle's passenger seat. My eyes soon drooped from all the fresh air, frenetic activity, and mental overload. I wanted to doze, but that couldn't happen— not yet, not when we still had a second survey to complete. The car did not head home, but to the local airport outside Monroe.

Two different surveys needed conducting the same morning each week, and it seemed daunting. I planned on going to bed early that night once we returned to Lansing. But I knew that wouldn't happen for many hours. The morning had just begun.

We completed the other surveys, and Bud dropped me off at home in the late afternoon. Laura commented I looked weary, and my head barely nodded. We ate supper, then I took a shower and went to bed, enveloped in a warm cloud of homey heat.

Between classes during the following week, the university library became my second home. There I stalked the aisles of books on waterfowl identification. Most catered to hunters who held dead ducks they had just blown out of the sky. It wasn't hard then to handle them and check the carcass for wing and pattern markings.

But hundreds of live ducks at a distance while bobbing on a lake or in flight, were very different cases. Out on the lake, I had only seconds to identify the species and count the individuals. Worse, the birds usually took flight before one could approach anywhere near them. What I needed was a means for quickly decoding the birds' markings while they swam or flew.

In the library stacks, I found several field guides, but most were reference materials and not loanable. I pulled them off the shelves and secluded myself at a remote table behind banks of musty racks. There I spent hours studying the intricacies of seasonal plumage patterns and silhouettes, burning them into my mind.

Bud had said twenty-six species of waterfowl used Lake Erie. I needed to memorize the subtleties of wing and body shapes and markings for each one—and quickly...next Friday was coming up fast.

It wasn't just identifying flying birds that needed my attention. I couldn't afford to miss any of the steps in the entire survey process. These included time milestones and data recording mandates. To keep things straight, I developed a guide and checklist of the steps involved.

The following Thursday night, I left Lansing by myself to find the trailer on the power plant site. I awoke in darkness, dressed, and gobbled down two hard-boiled eggs I had brought. Mission Day had arrived. Time to go solo, get mobilized to execute.

Once at the boat dock in the pre-dawn light, an overcast sky greeted me. I checked the Whaler and found the gas tanks full. Thank you, limnology team. I held my breath and flipped the ignition key on the steering pedestal. The outboard chugged to life. I tossed the fore-and-aft lines into the boat and eased the throttle forward, inching away from the pilings.

The throttle stayed at half-speed on the way out to the lake, allowing time for me to adjust to handling the boat by myself. As I approached the estimated starting point a quarter mile out, I glanced at my watch. The second hand ticked past the bezel mark I had set for official sunrise. Beefy clouds produced a grayish cast to the scene; less sunlight meant duller colors for identifying birds—not what I hoped for.

I mentally calculated the distance from shore using the constant speed of the boat and the elapsed minutes. A few seconds later, I throttled back. The boat swayed with the waves, idling while I double-checked our position with the shoreline features. They matched my memory from the week before. The binoculars around my neck swung up to my eyes just as a swell lifted the bow. Immediately, my legs danced for balance, and I had to brace my knees against the pedestal.

No ducks. I let the glasses drop and inched the throttle lever forward until it couldn't go any further. The boat leaped through the waves with spray exploding all around the hull. A minute later, I spotted something dark floating off the port side. I swerved toward it, yanked the stick back to idle and squinted through the binoculars. There it floated, a few hundred feet off—a dark shape. I expected it to fly away, but it didn't. After focusing furiously, I determined it was a raft without ducks, just a large wooden pallet. I throttled up once again looking for further bounty.

Shortly, my eyes caught sight of a prize worthy of the quest. There it was, a floating treasure trove of duck data, ripe for the taking. A huge flotilla drifted with the current. I stopped the boat and swept the glasses over the feathered fleet, looking for colors to stand out from the floating silhouettes.

I smiled. You beautiful birds; caught you flat-footed on the water. But in the next instant, the entire flock went vertical. White spray obscured their bodies, then the sky billowed into a fluttering cloud as thousands of wings beat the air at once.

They quickly executed a flanking move above me, intending, no doubt, to make a run for it to some secluded cove. I spun the helm leeward, desperately darting my eyes, looking for some pattern on the birds' bodies that would identify them. Ah, there—dark heads and chests, lots of white bellies. Uh...mallards, yep that's it. Or maybe gadwalls. Wait! Don't female gadwalls look the same from below as male mallards? What about redheads? Mergansers, anyone?

In a flash, the flock had moved too far away to see anything but a vague patch of gray. I watched it disappear, then grabbed my clipboard and wrote some notes and marked the raft on the map plot. I wrote "Gadwall" then erased it, scribbled "Redheads," erased that and re-entered "gadwalls." Somehow, it just felt right.

But I had forgotten to count and sex the birds. My eyes closed, picturing the flock. I mentally compared it with images of flocks we saw the previous week. The number five thousand came to mind for this raft, but hunches could not substitute for real data. I needed to get much better at this, and quickly.

The clipboard went back in my pack and the sketches and notes I'd made in the library came out. It was better to spend a few minutes there in the boat reviewing duck identification cues than continuing onward, uncertain about them.

For the next twenty minutes, I sat on the floor bobbing with the swells while reviewing waterfowl indicators and markings again. My attention focused on the dozen or so species most common in this western region of Lake Erie. It seemed better to blow the schedule a bit than to continue without feeling confident in my identification abilities.

My review paid off, and I finished the survey more self-assured, and headed back to the dock with seven additional flock sightings logged. I felt sure about the identity of the birds in four of the seven flocks, and added question marks for the rest, all solid hunches. The idea that I could do this task made me smile as I left the Whaler gently tugging its spring-lines. I'll be back, I thought—now that I'm a duly qualified commander of "The Duck Patrol."

Wingmen

When Bud first came along with me in mid-October to conduct the waterfowl survey, the surface of Lake Erie remained free of ice. This made it feasible to cruise for ducks in the Whaler. My surveys proceeded each week until ice formed on the lake. When it did, the boat stayed at the dock and I had to follow the back-up plan. That involved hiking each Friday to a half-dozen land observation sites along the wild shoreline. Bud had chosen them for their views of where the heated power plant discharge kept the water from freezing.

Those land surveys took two-hours and sometimes more to complete, but did not begin until January. Trudging across frozen landscapes through snow-drifts and biting winds made for brisk mornings. By the time I reached the car after returning from the last ground observation site, I usually needed a nap.

But that couldn't happen because I had to scoot to the local airstrip on the other side of Monroe, where Bud had taken us on my first day after finishing the Whaler survey. The project schedule required an aerial patrol each week, in addition to either the Whaler or hiking surveys, depending on the weather. Not only did I need to master how to identify and count ducks from a fast-moving, bouncing boat, I also had to do it from hundreds of feet up, flying a hundred miles an hour.

After docking the Whaler on that first day out with Bud, we drove a half-hour west over rural roads. Soon the car turned onto a narrow access road. It led past hay fields to a long, single-story building alone in a wide- open country landscape. Bud eased the vehicle across the gravel lot and parked the front wheels at the curb blocks in front of double glass doors and a large plate- glass window. Bold yellow letters arched across the glass and spelled "Custer Airport." The place looked deserted, perhaps closed.

The *thunk* of our car doors closing broke the silence, and I wondered how this rural airport in central Michigan got its name. I didn't recall any bloody battle between Indians and cavalry around that region.

Inside, dark navy carpeting covered the spacious floor and supported several tables and shelves. They neatly displayed advertising literature, aviation magazines, and airplane models. The natural lighting produced a subdued and quiet atmosphere. Along the opposite wall, a glass counter extended the full length of the room. It displayed various gizmos pilots needed. Leaning against the front side of the counter stood a well-dressed man in his fifties, his hair nicely trimmed, graying a bit at the temples. It complemented his neatly pressed khaki slacks and long-sleeved collared business shirt. Only the three of us stood inside. Bud and I approached him in our dingy field clothes, and the man greeted Bud as though they were well- acquainted. Then Bud introduced me to him—Jack Deets, the municipal airport manager.

Jack was expecting my arrival since Bud informed him the week before. We discussed the flight arrangements and my taking over the surveys at this time each Friday. Then Jack led us out to a line of small planes parked on the grass near the only runway. He stopped next to a single-prop Cessna, white with blue markings. Bud got in the front passenger seat, and I squeezed in the one behind him.

It was the first time I sat in an aircraft of any sort. It seemed far too small and flimsy to launch into the air and stay up there. I looked at the window frame next to my arm—only a thin sheet of aluminum stood between me and a horrible death. My jaw clenched, recalling how I ate lunch out of tuna cans with thicker walls.

Bud and Jack chatted amiably in the front while I wondered where they kept the parachutes. Jack instructed me to put on the headphones lying on my seat, and my voice crackled with a crispness I wasn't used to hearing.

Jack taxied across the grass to the runway takeoff point. The wings wobbled like the balance pole of a high-wire walker, and the engine put-putted the way an old farm tractor did along a country road. But in another few moments, the engine revved to a loud whine when Jack accelerated down the runway.

Through the windscreen, I watched the distant tree line barreling toward us as the engine whine increased to a roar. I could feel a vibration through my seat and my eyes closed, but that quickly the vibration ceased, and the nose of the plane tilted up. I looked down and saw the runway and fields retreat rapidly—we had lift- off.

Soon, only blue sky surrounded us as Jack banked the plane, then leveled off. In ten minutes, I noticed the power plant several thousand feet below our wheels. At that altitude, heavy equipment and construction trailers appeared the size of pebbles. But the massive cooling towers loomed under us like the open maws of giant hatchlings, eagerly waiting for the tiny plane to drop into their hungry gullets.

We avoided the downdrafts created by the towers' evaporative cooling process and continued until we reached the same offshore starting point of the boat survey. From that altitude I could identify the entire ten-mile length of the shoreline, with distant Stony Point jutting out in a hazy smear.

Wavelets rolled across the lake surface, boats carved white trails with their wakes, smoke rose from chimneys, and cars dutifully followed one another along roadways. Purpose and function played out in the moving patterns below. Subtle changes occurred moment to moment down there, where lighting shifted with each angle and attitude of the plane.

All the parts of the landscape seemed knitted together—lake, meadows, woodlots, fields, housing clusters, streets, rivers. They linked to form something larger and cohesive—a living landscape. A textured carpet unfolded, full of vibrant habitats that supported life in every wrinkle. I wanted to swoop down like a hummingbird and examine each one, poking in and out of interesting places.

We descended to five-hundred feet to conduct the survey along the same route we ran in the Whaler. I noticed a dark patch of water, but quickly realized the large raft I thought contained ducks was only a cloud shadow on the water's surface. Bud soon saw something else, then pointed out the streamlined bodies and heads of a flock of flying mergansers. He explained their silhouettes and compared them to shallow water ducks like mallards, and color patterns with other types of deep-water diving ducks, including redheads and canvasbacks.

It seemed easier to count blocks of birds from the plane than from the bouncing boat, because we soared above them and gained a larger field of view. But the plane flew four times faster than the Whaler and could circle around rafts and confirm sighting details before the birds flushed. Once we completed the survey, our log sheets showed twice as many ducks counted as for the boat survey an hour earlier.

Still, during the drive back to Lansing, worry dabbled at the edges of my mind. Would I ever get the hang of running an accurate and efficient duck patrol? So many complexities involved—miss one step or fail to get the data and the whole project nose-dives. How could I identify and count waterfowl accurately while flying a hundred miles an hour in a tuna can?

But with each later boat and aerial survey, my mind became better at recognizing reoccurring patterns in the flocks that became distinctive to the different species. My confidence grew, yet without Bud along, I had no way of knowing the accuracy of my sightings.

At least I stopped thinking about the thin metal aircraft shell, the flimsy stick of a propeller, and the roaring lawn mower engine laboring to hold us up in the blue yonder. Now I soared with the snow geese and ducks, making their acquaintance among the clouds as my feathered wingmen.

After two months on my own logging ducks, Bud came along once to confirm that I conducted the surveys properly, and could effectively identify and count those I encountered. Afterward, he nodded and congratulated me with a warm smile and pat on the shoulder.

Over the next six months, Jack and I got on like a pair of old pilots up there, chatting between sightings, him helping me locate flocks. I looked forward to finishing a boat or land survey, then driving over to the airport where Jack waited for me, ready to soar.

But the flights weren't always routine. It was at such times I remembered that humans who flew the skies were just playing craps with gravity—every flight a risk of disaster. Gravity was death for an aircraft, but otherwise I always had a warm feeling about that force of nature. Most of the time I thought it was fortunate it exists, especially whenever I sat on a toilet.

Sometimes it felt as though the pilots Jack substituted when he wasn't available didn't respect gravity enough. They seemed to gamble with it, where losing meant crashing us into the lake. Not Jack, of course. He was far too lucid for such shenanigans. Jack was a professional, which was why I liked him.

One morning when I walked through the double-glass doors at the airport, Jack wasn't there. Instead, leaning against the counter stood a much younger man. He appeared just a few years older than me, well-dressed, with a white-collared shirt open to the third button, dark slacks, and shiny black hair slicked-back like a mafia enforcer from old movies I'd seen.

He wore a thick swirl of gold-plated chains and a heavy medallion around his neck—the suave fixer look. The medallion gleamed on a dark hairy chest like a fake Olympic trophy sitting in a bird's nest.

"Is Jack around?" I asked, focusing on the shiny bauble protruding through the hairy nest on his chest. For a second, I wondered if a family of mice lived in there all wearing similar gold chains, about to pop their heads out, singing a squeaky version of "Mack the Knife."

"No, he can't make it today; I'll be your pilot." Smooth, suave-like, ultra-confident grin.

"You spoke with him personally?" Surprised by the replacement; he didn't fit the image of a business pilot in the mold of Jack, or any of the hero flyboys I'd seen in movies. Nor did I have any evidence this dandy was even a qualified pilot.

He nodded. "Wheels up in five." He handed me a pen to sign the flight authorization form. Then he crossed the expanse of carpet and headed out the door. I watched him saunter off; he had the swagger of a trust- fund playboy…nothing to worry about, ever.

A few minutes later, we reached the accustomed starting point for the aerial survey over the lake. As I reached into the back seat for the clipboard and map, the plane banked into a turn and leveled out on the accustomed southward course. When I looked up from my lap, ready to spot ducks, the scene was not the one I expected. I did not see any shoreline, shadows or defining landscape features—no perspective, no context, just a gauzy solid-gray mass against the window glass.

Then a dark, tennis ball-sized spot erupted from the gray mass, producing a cascade of white confetti. It was an American coot running on top of the water surface, desperately seeking lift-off.

My head jerked back from the window glass, and I knew instantly that something was wrong. My eyes flicked to the altimeter gauge, but it seemed broken—the needle twitched against the zero mark. The coot appeared too large, filling the window frame. That could mean just one thing—the plane was about to collide with the bird and the lake surface.

During the banking turn, while I fiddled with my survey tools, the pilot had plummeted to a much lower altitude. I never noticed it. Yikes, my mind screamed. If I opened the door, that coot would run right into my lap.

I tapped the altimeter gauge. "How high are we?"

He glanced at the dial. "About ten feet—maybe a little less." He showed no hint of concern, almost as though he wanted to prove something to the college kid.

My mouth went dry as I shifted my head back to the passenger window. I couldn't take my eyes off the scene. The moving lake surface seemed mesmerizing, but I snapped out of it and braced for the crash I knew was coming.

"Look, I need more elevation—take it up to four- hundred." I cocked my head once and back so he'd know it wasn't a question.

The pilot shrugged with a smirk, but he yanked on the yoke and the nose lurched upward with a deafening whine. The plane angled away from the water.

Pressure on my sphincter muscles relaxed and relief poured over me like a warm shower. Still, I wanted to take my clipboard and smack this suicidal maniac on the head with it—where did Jack get this Dapper-Dan with a death wish? Instead, I squeezed my pen tighter against my palm until the red spot it left there seemed to smolder.

Even a non-pilot like me knew you didn't fly that low—ducks could become caught in the propeller when they flushed. I had heard about planes flying through flocks of flamingos that fouled propellers and crashed planes. I also knew the plane's wing could hit a boat mast or antennae. Nor did I need to examine the ducks' nostrils to identify and count them.

When the plane reached a saner altitude, I could again see the horizon ahead of me, and began scanning for rafts of ducks, focusing on the mission instead of Dapper-Dan the Medallion Man. Though the hot-shot that flew me that day was a maverick, he wasn't the only pilot who showed up to fly me on the duck patrol. For several months, another one substituted for Jack. His name was Harold, but he preferred Hal.

I met him at the same airport counter as the others. On a bleak Friday morning, I walked in after the boat survey became a bust—Whaler engine iced up and both gas containers empty. Darn limnologists.

The man I would know as Hal looked about fifty-something, well-groomed, with a crop of thinning gray hair and a white mustache that drooped around his chin. He stood with his arms crossed and legs spread as though watching a new fleet of aircraft take off.

His black slacks and dress shoes contrasted with his long-sleeved turquoise shirt with white and black patterns. The aquamarine shirt color matched his eyes, and they both exuded a sense of pleasant calm— someone's granddad, I imagined. He smiled. "You must be here for the duck patrol."

"Yep; looking for Jack." I smiled back.

"Sorry, he's out today. Just you and me this time."

"Did Jack explain how we do the survey?" I wanted to avoid any random nosedives this time.

He patted his shirt pocket. "I've got the coordinates right here. Jack and I go way back—flew fighter planes together during World War II."

I pictured old newsreel clips of dogfights in the skies, screaming engines, rat-a-tat-tat gunfire, wings on fire, parachutes ejected, balls of flame exploding, victory- rolls. My head nodded. "I'm ready to go."

Hal grabbed a worn brown leather flight jacket from a nearby chair, slipped it on, and ushered me to the door. Flying with Hal became as enjoyable as it was with Jack. He always seemed to have some story to share along the way or a bit of obscure knowledge I found interesting.

He mentioned that most days he drove a long-haul truck, cannonballing across the country in his own rig. On later occasions, I often found him between trips hanging out and jawing with Jack when I walked into the airport. In the air, Hal would expound on things like the proper ways to tie down different loads on his flatbed trailer. Other times, he explained how every truck was custom made to match the specific cargos it hauled when fully loaded. Thanks to Hal, I could tell by the trailers' fittings, shapes, sizes, and the number of wheels and bolt patterns they rolled with.

I had learned some time ago that new knowledge and nuggets of information often brought new perspectives to seemingly unrelated events and phenomena. Eureka moments emerged when those info-nuggets waited patiently in their memory cells until my subconscious saw a connection between them and another issue.

Then recognition would dawn in the cognitive mind as new understandings and meanings emerged. it was my budding intuition asserting itself, and I gradually came to appreciate its value. It was only useful, however, when the info-knowledge was based on reality. Imaginative thinking was useful and enjoyable, but on the landscape, I wanted to find where the fanciful ended and reality began.

Hal seemed a gentleman of solid judgment and competence to me, whether gear-jamming tractor- trailers or practicing dogfight maneuvers high in the sky. Had things been different, I would have gladly signed up as his wingman. I felt the same way about Jack.

As winter progressed, usually one or the other flew the plane. On the way to and from the lake, I frequently asked about the various controls in the little cockpit. Neither of the two hesitated to answer my questions and seemed pleased to do so.

On one flight during the second year of surveys, Jack made me an offer I could not refuse. He mentioned he could teach me to fly on the way over to the starting point of the surveys, as well as on the returns.

The thought had never entered my mind before, and it took me a moment to digest it while a flock of Canada geese flew under our wing. It was a tantalizing idea, but I knew my student income barely afforded me leftover meatloaf sandwiches for lunch, let alone weekly flying lessons.

"That would be great." I imagined myself commanding the aircraft in a spiffy leather jacket like Hal's, dodging rafts of duck squadrons. Now that Dubious-Dan seemed long gone, the aircraft felt less like a tuna-tin and more like a marvel of finely tuned engineering. And now, Jack had offered me a chance to join the legion of mysterious sky pilots—for free. I wanted to execute a barrel roll, but I didn't know how yet.

Each front seat had its own gauges, steering, and control system, along with a separate pair of pedals. On both sides, the pedal's narrower top portions braked the aircraft while taxiing on the ground. Before flying back to the airport that day, Jack told me to put my hands on the passenger seat yoke. He was referring to the control column that protruded from the instrument panel like the bottom half of a car steering wheel.

Jack told me to push the yoke gently inward. I nudged the wheel forward, and it slid toward the instrument panel. At the same time, the plane's nose pitched down into a dive. The response caused me to jerk both hands away, and Jack calmly suggested I pull the yoke toward me, more slowly. I did, and the plane returned to level flight.

Then Jack had me rotate the wheel to the right, which extended the back edge of the right wing rearward, called ailerons. This created drag and made the plane roll sideways to the right in a banking maneuver. When I pressed the left aileron, the plane banked that way.

Banking by using just the yoke to extend the wing ailerons put great stress on the aircraft, Jack explained. To reduce that, he had me press me press the wider lower portion of the left or right pedal toward the direction I wanted to go while turning the yoke on the same side to extend that side's ailerons. The lower pedals moved the rudder on the tail back and forth, changing the aircraft's yaw— side-to-side turning, like an automobile does when it changes direction. Using both yoke and pedals made turning easier, smoother.

Jack took over and landed the plane, and explained how to taxi by pressing on the upper rudder pedal section alone to go left or right. The steering yoke didn't function while taxiing to stop the plane, Jack pressed the upper part of both pedals at the same time, which controlled the wheel brakes, and we stopped.

When we returned to headquarters, Jack had me fill out some papers, then he handed me a small black book—my pilot logbook. He told me how to fill it in for my first flight, and I always brought it with me after that.

Gradually, I became comfortable reading the gauges and operating the throttle, ailerons, flaps, elevators, rudder, trim tabs, and brakes. I began flying the aircraft each week. Soon I had full control from the passenger seat, while identifying and counting the rafts of ducks below, and having Jack take the notes.

One day, Jack showed me how to conduct the required pre-flight check of the aircraft, running down a long checklist of mechanical, electrical, and electronic mechanisms. Then he motioned me into the pilot's seat, where he gave me instructions on taking off. I had never done that before, but didn't flinch because I trusted Jack to know if I could do it safely.

I checked the air-sock halfway down the runway to determine wind direction and speed while I taxied to the run-up spot at the launch apron on the runway. It was a space near the edge used for final systems checks. There I ran the engine hot and fast at high RPMs while pressing hard against both brake pedals to keep the plane from shooting down the runway. I worked the controls for smoothness...check, and studied the instrument panel...check, all systems go.

My eyes scanned the sky above the runway for incoming aircraft. Nothing; I glanced over at Jack in the passenger seat. He nodded. I did the same, then fixed my eyes on the runway that filled my windshield. Nothing else mattered except the white line before me that extended forever. Everything depended on what I would do in the next thirty seconds—like seeing my family again, having a career, eating tacos, belly-laughing. I released the brakes.

The engine roared and rushed us along the asphalt toward a wall of trees, then I drew the yoke back and the nose lifted upward. I felt the wheels leave the ground, then nearly skimmed the treetops. We climbed toward the clouds, slipping into the wind-stream at full velocity, watching the runway and fields fall away, growing smaller by the second. My pulse raced until I leveled off at our cruising altitude of 2,500 feet.

Once over the mission target, I rolled the plane right and headed south as usual. I ran the circuit while calling out rafts of ducks and geese to Jack, who recorded the data on species, numbers, and sex. Sometimes I had to maneuver around an airborne flock for a closer look. So, this is what it feels like to fly among the ducks, I thought, sharing airspace and seeing the world below as they do. My spirits soared with the aircraft while I dove toward a flock of redheads as though the Red Baron hid in there for cover.

When we crossed the starting point again, I set the compass heading for the airport, and Jack suggested I land the plane. Though I expected this, hearing it made my pulse quicken with an image of the runway whooshing toward my face like headlights on a deer in the road. I would only have seconds to execute the move properly or die on the tarmac.

To put myself on the correct alignment, I set the plane on a southeast heading from the lake and maintained five-hundred feet of elevation. Four miles from the airport, I spotted the cluster of trees in the distance that Jack said to use as a landmark. Then I descended to four hundred feet.

Since the small airport had no tower for radioing traffic conditions and clearance, I needed to conduct a visual check from the air. That meant flying a rectangular pattern around the runway at a designated altitude and distance, starting about a mile-and-a-half out from the runway edge—where I had first started my take-off.

To gauge that distance, I waited for the tree cluster to appear in the middle of the copilot window. Jack said it was the right distance from the runway edge. At that point, I banked the plane right and headed toward the cluster, parallel to the runway. When about a mile and a half beyond, I turned left toward the airstrip. There I turned left again, and as I ran the third leg of the rectangle, I set the nose pitch attitude so the airplane stayed level and maintained it by keeping the horizon gauge a couple degrees above the level-line.

I checked the manifold pressure gauge—thirteen inches; good. The airspeed indicator read shy of ninety-knots, so I adjusted the throttle a bit until it did. This put the engine RPMs at 2,100.

When the plane reached a mile and a half beyond the runway landing edge, I verified the absence of other nearby planes in the sky. No planes, so I was "cleared for the option," meaning it was okay to land. I turned ninety-degrees left and began closing the gap to the runway.

Setting the glide path came next, and I began the descent from the 400 foot elevation by nudging the yoke forward. Then I reduced power and trim, which involved turning a crank handle on the ceiling above me. In a few seconds, I throttled back to 1,500 RPMs and lowered the flaps one-third in order to create air friction that slowed the plane. But lowering them caused the front of the plane to elevate, so to compensate I eased the yoke down to keep the level attitude.

After a last instrument and alignment check, I applied full flaps. By this time, the plane flew only twelve feet off the deck heading into the wind. Jack preferred "power-off landings," which meant I needed to ease the throttle knob inward as the plane passed over the runway edge. The engine noise immediately dropped, changing to a clattering idle seemingly about to stall the hot engine— *choppity...choppity...choppity...chop...*

But even without throttle, the plane continued to hurtle toward the tarmac at seventy mph. In effect, the aircraft had become a meteor at the mercy of gravity and I was diving a perfectly good plane into the rapidly looming ground. Only a handful of seconds remained for me to remember how to execute the next moves accurately…or the duck patrol would end in a splat.

The plane lined up perfectly with the prop pointed down the runway straight ahead. I saw the airstrip within the center-third of the windshield frame, and another third in grass on each side. But then the runway edges slowly expanded toward both windscreen frames as the grass spaces shortened.

Suddenly, the runway edges rapidly accelerated to fill the entire lower edge of windscreen frame. That was when I knew the plane soared only a few feet off the ground—it would all be over in eight seconds one way or another. One second, two seconds, three…flare the nose, my mind screamed—no time left.

I immediately pulled back on the yoke while my heart pounded, hoping my timing was right. The nose elevated a few degrees and changed the plane's flying attitude. We glided then, five feet above the beautiful runway's welcoming alabaster centerline—gently coasting closer…closer, until the wings had no more lift and the soft tires and their shadows kissed on the ground. Touchdown.

Loose on the Landscape

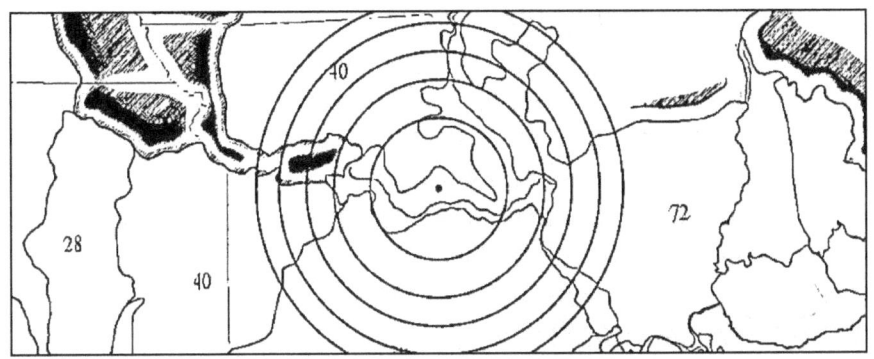

Rad-Vector Epiphany

Something made me bolt upright in bed. The pillow and sheets felt damp with sweat, my pulse rapid, breathing shallow, thoughts all a jumble. Disoriented, I sat staring at the wall beyond the foot of the bed, and then I remembered I lay in a dark motel room a thousand miles from home. An image flickered on the otherwise bare wall as though an old black and white film was playing in a frame.

My eyes tried to focus on the shifting light patterns in the frame, and for a few moments, I let my mind transition from dreaming to reality. Then I noticed the right side of the image on the wall merged with a subtle shaft of light, and I let my eyes follow it to a window on the adjacent wall. The same image appeared there...but it seemed slightly different somehow.

As my mind tried to make sense of things, my breathing rate subsided. Subdued lighting from a lamppost outside filtered weakly through the window, and I realized it caused the shadows on the wall in front of me. A light breeze outside in the trees made the shadows move in patterns of light and dark on the dim wall across from the foot of the bed.

My agitation subsided as I studied the reflection. I understood then what was different about the window and wall images...they were mirror images—reversed.

As I watched, the shadow patterns remained intact but their edges became more defined, sharper. The branch and twig reflections morphed into line sketches of everyday objects. First an animal face appeared, then when I altered my gaze to a different part of the projected image, a portrait of a strange person appeared.

I looked away for a moment, then switched back to both areas in the wall frame, and the same line images still appeared. My subconscious mind seemed to fill-in parts of the outlines with more line details, and retained them as retrievable short-term memories.

This wasn't the first time I'd had such an experience; it had happened now and then since childhood when conditions seemed right. I wasn't sure exactly what those conditions involved, but usually I was in a fairly quiet room with textured walls, floors, or other surfaces, and my mind was in an active state.

A few times as a kid, images appeared on the walls of canvas tents while camping. I woke up at dawn one morning before my tent mates and lay in my sleeping bag, enjoying the sunlight filter through the light- colored fabric. All sorts of sepia-toned images began to fade-in—a cowboy, ship, animals. It was like watching a slide show with emerging and dissolving images.

As I observed the sketches on the motel room wall, a sense of calm defused my agitated state like a deep- breath. My mind took the cue, and I began breathing normally again.

Some time ago, I learned this process of quickly seeing patterns without prompting is called "pareidolia." It's a genetic trait that appears unprompted for many people, whereby the subconscious can quickly make judgments about ambiguous scenes. Natural selection favored such manifestations in many humans as a rapid way to assess the mental and emotional state of others regarding their threat potential. This evolved early-warning system relates to intuition, insight, and imagination. Each of these can provide an individual the opportunity to flee or attack before a perceived threat gets nasty.

For some people, pareidolia might occur under particular circumstances, such as after an encounter with a creepy person or event. Unprompted images of the event might appear on a surface like an omen. But it's just a byproduct of an agitated subconscious mind trying to work things out. Some folks see famous people and landmarks in their mashed potatoes, or disaster ahead in the swirls of their takeout lattes.

That kind of thing never happened to me, for I perceived the phenomenon more rationally—an artifact of our natural early—assessment system. Just because random images appeared occasionally didn't mean any cause-effect was involved. But if one's intuition and factual evidence also fit the perceived message of an image, then perhaps one should examine things more closely.

Pareidolia is the gut-feeling one gets about scenes and images subconsciously before the brain routes them to other cognitive parts for more detailed processing. It can speed up judgment and decision- making when a quick reaction needs expression.

The pareidolia episode that night in the motel room became a tipping point for me—the final climactic stage after days under stress, feeling I was on the verge of failure.

After two winters of collecting waterfowl data on Lake Erie, things had gone well. The project results confirmed the idea that warmwater discharges from the Fermi power plant were a magnet for migrating ducks and geese. Rather than continue southward along the flyway, birds stayed around the open waters of the western basin for longer periods, some for the entire winter season. This new knowledge became valuable for state and federal wildlife managers responsible for conserving duck and geese populations.

Though the nuclear power plant activities had caused a permanent mini-climate change within the western basin of Lake Erie, it had almost nothing to do with fossil fuels. Humans were responsible for the increase in water temperatures of 50°F. But the changes produced far-reaching benefits for winter resident and migratory waterfowl and the lake's ecology. It allowed hundreds of thousands of birds to rest and feed in an area that once froze over every winter.

With my research completed at MSU, I graduated and went looking for a job. A promising position opened for an environmental scientist with a state transportation department back east. I would investigate landscape impacts from human activities such as highways, bridges, rest stops, river crossings. We moved to a rural area of the Piedmont region where the commute took only a half-hour to Baltimore.

The work interested me at first. Within three years, however, I came to realize that working for the government did not suit me—too much bureaucracy often stifled corrective actions I might recommend for reducing environmental impacts from the agency's projects. My enthusiasm began suffocating; I had a need to actually accomplish something meaningful on the landscape, and bureaucratic torpor made that very difficult.

I wanted to work where I could direct efforts myself to improve landscapes. Those opportunities seemed to lie with the consulting industry. Soon I quit my agency job and detoured into the private sector.

I landed a position as the lead terrestrial biologist for a large environmental consulting company headquartered in Washington, D.C. This well-regarded international firm occupied the eighth floor of a downtown office building, complete with elevators, lobbies and crowds of people always milling about. My commute lengthened to more than an hour each way, because neither my family nor I wanted to move.

Fortunately, the job offered a good deal of travel to project sites around the country, investigating environmental problems and conducting research in distant landscapes.

About a week into the new position, I still waited for a project assignment and remained unfamiliar with all the company's operations. But soon the firm sent me halfway across the country to Missouri...to another nuclear power plant. But this one wouldn't involve bouncing Whalers or piloting a plane. I did not realize, though, it would produce a bunch more worries than those missions.

My involvement began when I received a call from one of my company's satellite offices in Chicago. The project engineer needed my help in dealing with regulatory compliance issues for the power plant. This facility needed a special field study performed before it could gain approval from the federal Nuclear Regulatory Commission, NRC, to begin operating.

My objective involved mapping radiation vectors—locations surrounding the facility where humans produced food plants and animals, such as farms, gardens, greenhouses, barnyards, plant nurseries. Using this data, the government could assess how radiation fallout from a nuclear accident might spread through the human population from ingesting home- grown radioactive food.

That kind of survey did not sound difficult—until the engineer mentioned the company needed me to map all these individual radiation vectors within a fifty-mile radius of the nuclear facility in rural Missouri.

"Double-check that, will you?" I said. "Fifty miles sounds absurdly complicated and time-consuming to me."

"Sure; I'll get back to you if it's different, otherwise proceed as mentioned."

"Okay, but get back to me soon...time is short."

When I asked what exactly the company wanted me to do, the engineer wasn't sure because the regulation was new. He said, "We decided you're the expert, and you'll figure it out."

I felt my forehead ripple into a frown. "Expert" was not a term I applied to myself and had always wondered when anyone actually qualified for the generic label; learning never stops. In the public's view, all "experts" seemed equivalent, which made me wonder how to distinguish lousy or adequate experts compared with the best and the super experts.

I much preferred variations on the word "competent" followed by one's job title. At least one's record could show competency, but the "expert" label required nothing to prove it applied to a specific situation. And I had found a world of difference between armchair and scholastic "experts" and those in the applied disciplines, whether field scientists, farmers, construction engineers, plumbers, carpenters, commercial fishermen, miners. I had known quads of campus academics that rarely spent time beyond ivy- covered walls, where they issued pompous universal pronouncements based on their cogitations and opinions.

"Take a couple of weeks to finish if you need it," the engineer said. My frown deepened like the ridge pattern of a corrugated roof panel. I pictured myself stuck in a Jefferson City motel room over the upcoming Thanksgiving holiday. A few days before, I had celebrated both my and our spunky daughter, Jordon's, birthdays.

The thought of eating turkey at an all-night diner rattled my corrugated frown like a nasty wind had banged against it; but maybe it was just giving me a headache. I put the phone receiver back in its cradle— just a tad harder than intended.

I will find a way, I said to myself. Then I felt my scowl soften as I accepted reality—new company, different expectations, fresh adaptations. I had left academia for the landscape, and here I stood in charge...just as I'd wanted. Deal with it.

By late afternoon the next day, I found myself at the Jefferson City airport renting a car. I soon checked into a motel room in town along the highway. I tossed my suitcase on the bed as my eyes swept the room—assessing, judging, nodding approval—not pretentious yet inviting and cozy. The building looked like a large log cabin structure that reminded me of a safari hunting lodge, with its own restaurant, bar, and comfortable fireplace in the lobby.

Since the remote project site lay twenty-five miles away, the lodge had a strategic location. I could come and go quickly without fighting elevators or parking spaces. After emptying my suitcase into drawers, I returned to the lobby to relax.

I noticed airline pilots and flight attendants in uniforms going in and out with luggage. If fellow pilots stayed here, I thought, it's good enough for me. Dinner was still an hour away, but I felt weary from traveling and my mind remained unsettled about the mission ahead.

Several soft armchairs sat empty next to the fireplace. I stepped over and sank down in one near the flames. I let my thoughts drift while I watched well- coiffed flight attendants tote their bouncy little briefcases behind them. Shapely legs milled about the check-in counter, sauntering, turning, shifting tight hips.

All I needed now was a drink. My mouth tasted like old beef jerky, so I rose from the chair and found the bar, where I ordered an ice tea with lemon. The tart flavor and tannins burned out the gamy taste. My armchair in the lobby remained empty, so I reclaimed it and sipped my drink. More little tight briefcases came and went, but my attention had shifted internally to the project.

Questions still needed resolving. Among them, how was it possible to count every milk cow, steer, hog, chicken, garden, orchard, goat, sheep, rabbit chute or anything else people raised to eat...within fifty miles of the nuclear plant? Were these idiots aware that it actually included an area about the size of New Jersey?

Well, I thought they'll probably be cattle, though I'm sure I won't find any elephants within that radius. But figuratively, I will need to eat one...and I'll have to do it one bite at a time. I got up from the cozy chair feeling refreshed and ambled back to my room, where I changed into casual clothes for dinner. Steak, I was thinking—a nice juicy porterhouse...with au poivre sauce, a baked potato with butter and a tossed salad. Maybe that would make one less steer I'd have to find out there on the landscape.

The next morning, after a lumberjack breakfast—pancake stack, fried eggs over easy, bacon on the side, and black coffee—I was eager to start working. One thing stood in my way...instructions on how to proceed. I only had an empty notebook and a roadmap that I picked up at a gas station the day before. My company hadn't supplied any other resources. The highway map would help me navigate, but the scale made it useless as a base for mapping rad-vectors.

Back in the room, I changed into field clothes and tossed my binoculars and camera in my daypack. With my belly full of flapjacks, I was no longer hungry, but the motif came to mind again about how to eat an elephant. I wrote "One Bite at a Time" at the top of my empty notebook, tucked it in the pack, then saddled up the rental vehicle and left the motel parking lot.

Traffic moved heavily with morning commuters, but I merged with the flow and headed toward the nuclear plant to get a sense of the landscape. I was just another stranger alone in a strange land. All the other vehicles out there were also looking for something, but I suspected it had nothing to do with the elephant I was tracking.

I picked up its spoor outside of Jefferson City, where the land lies hard against the Missouri River about a hundred miles due west of St. Louis. I drove along the north side of the river where the road curved away through a vast level floodplain. For the next twenty miles, barren autumn croplands filled the floodplain and lent a monotonous look to the landscape. Raw tawny soils and crop stubble lay exposed in the early sunlight.

Uplands with gentle low slopes and flat valleys sat next to the level floodplain on my left. They contained a mosaic of oak woodlands, sugar maple, pastureland, and farmed crops. Grains and hay for livestock occupied many of the fields. A network of small streams with wooded banks dissected the land.

This land constituted the *River Hills Ecoregion (39)*, a hilly region surrounding the floodplains of mostly the Mississippi, Illinois, and Missouri rivers. It's underlain by limestone and sandstone, and layered in thick loess deposits. This region was not glaciated in the most recent glacial period. Some areas of karst topography exist, with underwater streams, sinkholes, and caves cut out of the soluble limestone.

I drove through a rural countryside with scattered houses and farms along a web of back roads. After a half-hour, I turned off the main road and drove north for another few miles without seeing another vehicle. As the car rounded a curve, I noticed a large white plume in the distance—one of the power plant's cooling towers.

I pulled over into a wide spot on the country road shoulder and turned off the engine. The power plant stood tall above the flat terrain of mixed fields and woodlots. The notebook lay next to me; I grabbed it and jotted some observations.

The map showed the power plant's location, and I marked it as ground-zero for this project. No need to go onto the plant property, since my job entailed investigating the landscape around, not within, its perimeter.

I retrieved a measuring scale I kept in my field vest. I used it to determine how far out fifty miles went. A grunt escaped my lips— twice the distance I had just traveled from Jefferson

City. Did the government actually expect me to inspect each house, yard, and farm for rad-vectors within nearly 8,000 square miles?

Nuts, that should take me until Thanksgiving...not the one upcoming, but the one next year. Eating an elephant one bite at a time was one thing, but I was sure I wouldn't enjoy eating pachyderm chops for that long. Actually, I hadn't yet had much of a bite of the thing. But after chewing it over the past hour, I wasn't liking the taste of this one—something smelled funny about it—like a putrid mammoth carcass unearthed in some tundra ice cave.

The car idled while I contemplated the cooling tower. The chill in the air suddenly seemed to settle in my stomach like a lump of glacier ice. When I started the car and pulled back onto the road, I realized my grip on the steering wheel had turned my knuckles white. I swerved the car into a U-turn and headed back toward Jefferson City, taking a completely different route. At least I would see the region from a different angle.

The return route had the same dull gray look as the outbound route—a seemingly dejected land with bleak prospects...Ozark-fringe, perfect for hiding rad- vectors of all kinds.

I decided to draw the line at mapping crop fields— too many, too complicated, too little time. The project engineer had not mentioned estimating sizes of corn, vegetable, and grain fields. That was more easily done back in an office using remote sensing—aerial photographs supplied by state agencies. Without more specific instructions, I would do the job my way— practically. Someone had to insert reason into this survey project, and I seemed the only one to think so.

With the balance of the day ahead of me, I wandered further afield on other roads. Near every promising farmhouse and country residence, I pulled over and raised my binoculars. They allowed me to peer into yards from the

Rad-Vector Epiphany

roadside looking for elusive vectors, recording their numbers, types, health conditions.

At times, I expected someone to burst through their front door and confront me, or worse, call the cops that they had a peeping ecologist lurking in their bushes. Fortunately, I didn't see any flashing lights in my rear- view mirror all day. I soon realized that the state roadmap was far too small in scale to map anything accurately; I'd need to come back with a better map.

Sunset reds and yellows brushed the November horizon as I parked the car and walked into the motel lobby. After a shower, I changed into casual clothes, grabbed an ice-tea at the bar and settled into my easy chair again by the fireplace in the lobby. A new gaggle of flight attendants walked in, all curvy and chatty. The pleasant ambience eased my thoughts away from radiation plumes and vectors, and I soaked-in the fire's warmth.

I sipped my drink and closed my eyes, wishing I had passed on this project, ready to return home. What I wouldn't have given for a seat on one of these attendant's next flight. Imagining myself reclining the back a bit, I would smile serenely as I took a Bloody Mary from her flawless hands, and absently stirred it with a fresh stalk of celery. I'd be on my way home where I would arrive and swoop up the kids in my arms and lose myself in Laura's deep brown eyes and gentle smile. I'd be home for Thanksgiving.

Over the next few days, I resumed my road canvasing in widening concentric circles around the nuclear plant. I had sketched twenty such rings on the highway map to minimize running over the same routes more than once. Despite a dreary forecast, the woods weren't snowy yet, as I peered into adjacent pastures along so many back roads. I had a schedule to keep—and miles to go before I'd sleep. Robert Frost's poem repeated in my head much of the afternoon...miles to go... How many? I didn't know.

Each evening back in the motel room, I spread out the highway map to check my progress. After the fourth day, I had completed only two circles of the twenty. That made my pulse jump an octave and my jaw clench. I found my way to the lobby again to clear my mind.

This time, two men occupied the comfy chairs, and wet firewood spit sparks at my legs. I went to the bar, where I ordered two bottles of beer that I took back to my room and drank. At dinner, I wasn't in the mood for a steak, and ordered a stir-fry instead. Small pieces of chicken and vegetables lay tossed in a heap, drowning in a sauce like vinegar that soaked my enthusiasm as I ate.

Later in bed, I found myself sweating, tossing, turning. In the morning, the face that looked at me from the mirror appeared bedraggled, with shadows darkening my eye sockets from lack of sleep. So, this is corporate industry, I thought. What the hell have I gotten myself into? I knew if I didn't get things together soon, my days as a consulting scientist would come to an end faster than a rad-vector slipping down someone's gullet.

This time when I went to breakfast, it wasn't flapjacks that stared back at me, but a plate of runny eggs over too easy, fatty bacon, and cold, brittle toast—bland grits on the side. In the background, an old love ballad by the Everly Brothers played mournfully.

My mind began offering its own lyrics to the familiar tune as I wiped a glop of yolk from my chin—

Bye bye job,
Bye bye happiness.
Hello incompetence;
I feel like I know why.

Bye bye job,
Bye bye office space.

*Hello saving face,
I think my time is nigh;
Bye bye my job goodbye.*

*There goes employment to someone new,
They'll sure look happy, I'll sure be blue.
This was my baby 'till fate stepped in;
Goodbye to projects that might've been.*

*I'm through with stalking another rad,
I'm through with missing what I had.
And here's the reason that I'm so free,
My private comp'ny is through with me.*

Back on rural roads again, I'd find myself humming the tune, playing with the lyrics. When something suspicious appeared, I put the binoculars to my eyes— hunting for turnip patches and runaway pigs, goats, and the odd chicken that wanted to cross the road.

A farmer and a lady in curlers hanging wash chased me off when they thought I was spying on them for the IRS. A back tire went flat, and I had to change it along a country road next to a pasture. Two horses watched me from the wire fence several yards away, heads nodding, tails swishing. I had to think a moment if horses were on the vector list—many countries ate them regularly, but I wasn't sure how the NRC felt about it. Forget 'em, I decided; the horses seemed to agree.

It was the least productive day so far out on the Missouri landscape—the elephant was growing rancid. That night I managed an hour of restless sleep, when suddenly I awoke and had my pareidolia episode.

As the line drawings in the wall reflection became crisper, more detailed, my mental turbulence subsided into a quiet pool of calm. Respiration slowed, pulse steadied, sweats halted. I sensed clarity rising from the lucid stillness of a soulful mood.

A way out of my dilemma began taking form in my thoughts. My subconscious may have worked it out while I slept, weighing my options against project objectives and practicalities. A different approach had crystallized in my subconscious while I slept...and now was pushing its way into my cognitive mind. It was so strong that it had jolted me awake. I was having what I can only consider an epiphany.

The sudden rush of understanding and revelation occurred because all the important pieces of my problem had suddenly come together. My subconscious did the heavy work. It was like throwing a box of puzzle shapes onto a table and seeing them all come to rest, fitting perfectly into the pattern of the final picture all on their own.

As with most people, epiphanies had not occurred often with me. But when they did, a sudden cognitive jolt would flash into my mind. It was the moment all the critical pieces linked-up properly—when the dots connected to form a recognizable picture in its entirety. Answers would shoot into my consciousness in a fugue of awe and understanding. A grand release of tension would quickly follow, along with a heightened sense of mental and emotional well-being. Useful epiphanies are always messengers of truth, reality—personal wisdom. They can tell a person that now they are knowledgeable about something relevant that they never realized before.

Intellectual and emotional freedom lie in such knowledge, but to make these last requires confirmation by experience and testing. Enlightenment, epiphanies, eureka moments, and insights are among the most sublime and satisfying perceptions that a mind can offer a human being. They get stored in our memory cells along with similar events and become manifested later as intuition and insight.

Epiphanies seem like punctuation dots marking major perception events, and intuition and insight are the lines that connect them and forecast trends. My guess is that the frequency of epiphanies tends to fade with age and the learning of life lessons—because intuition accuracy grows more effective. Epiphanies then become lessons that our conscious mind stores and retrieves under similar conditions, freeing the subconscious to focus on other matters. Then the mind says, "You don't need an epiphany on this event because you already had it previously."

In the Jefferson City motel room, my epiphany involved the realization that I actually had the power to control the impossible situation I found myself in—if I chose to do so. My cognitive mind was telling me I could handle this—move ahead despite any adverse consequences that might result. It was time to decide for myself how I should proceed, make my own decisions here in the field, act accordingly...take charge.

All I could do was my best, consistent with my experience, knowledge, industry standards, and ethics. I would deliver a defensible product, and if rejected, then the company I just joined wasn't for me anyway. Then it would be me singing *Bye bye my job goodbye*—happily.

The project manager had left it all up to me to solve the company's rad-vector problem with no guidance, resources, or assistance. I had felt the project beast consuming me, but now I was ready to put my big-boy bib back on and dig in myself. It looked like elephant was back on the menu and I was hungry again.

I slept soundly that night. In the morning at breakfast, I felt in the mood for a Belgian waffle, omelet, and a side order of pachyderm bacon...no, hold the bacon, make it pork sausage instead to thin the herd. After breakfast, I drove out into the countryside again, but this time away from the power plant. I needed to investigate the surrounding landscape more efficiently.

Over the next two days, I gathered resources and information. Without computers or cell phones, the best I could do was look through the telephone yellow pages for the local offices of the USDA and Soil Conservation Service. I needed an accurate topographic map of the county at a useful scale to map all the radiation vectors. Since I knew these agencies worked directly with farmers, homesteaders, and agricultural enterprises, it seemed logical they knew where those might be located.

I also made calls to every organization that might have useful information. These included garden clubs, 4H centers, the local University of Missouri's agricultural extension services and their master gardeners list. Other places included large-animal veterinarians that knew of livestock farms and facilities.

In addition, I contacted local butcher shops and produce companies that produced goods that would become unsafe for people if contaminated by radiation. At the public library, I pored over the previous Sunday editions of local newspapers for ads of places that dealt with vector-likely commodities. I stopped by a convenience store and picked up several local classified-add newspapers that sold homestead equipment.

For days I drove every single road, lane, and byway. I stopped at farms, peered into backyards, and noted every potential vector I could find, and plotted them on the topographic maps acquired. All the research I'd done the previous days helped me locate potential locations that I then confirmed on the ground.

After nearly three weeks since arriving, I decided my job was done. I had mapped every rad-vector I could find and driven for miles and miles. Along the way, I got scowled at and asked by curious landowners in the "show-me state" to show them what I was doing snooping around. I'd had enough, and Thanksgiving was two days away. Yet, I had covered less than the whole fifty-mile radius—not even close. The best I could do was half that.

I called the Chicago office, informed the project manager I had completed what was practical within the time and budget allotted; if he needed more, then additional resources and time were required.

He agreed—after all, I was the "expert."

When I mentioned I'd completed only a twenty-five- mile radius, I heard a pause on the line, and I waited for the objection.

But he said, "Fifty miles? You know, I realized soon after we spoke before that you only needed to go out five miles, but I forgot to call and tell you."

My hand clenched the receiver, and I wanted to tip him off about what a useless numbskull he was. Instead, a few seconds of dead air passed before I told him I was heading home, regardless.

"So, when can I get my maps?" He sounded urgent now that the fieldwork was done.

"Check with me in a few weeks. They need some cleaning up— smudges, scribbles, dirt—you know."

"Few weeks? No, I need them the day after tomorrow—two at the max."

Usually I avoided passive-aggressive responses, but I couldn't resist. "I'll try to double-check and get back to you soon if I'm not too busy otherwise. They'll arrive in a cardboard tube...you'll know what to do with it. Take care."
"Wait a min..." *Click.*

Let him stew awhile. I didn't care anymore because whatever fallout developed, I'd handle it. Minutes later, I checked out of the motel and drove to the airport. During the ride, I crooned the Everly Brothers tune, substituting more upbeat lyrics. Why not? I got paid well for the work I did chasing rad-vectors and learned something valuable along the way about myself.

An hour later, I reclined in an aisle seat with my legs stretched, stirring a spicy tomato juice with a crisp celery stalk. Another one of these, I thought, and I won't be able to eat lunch—wonder what they'll serve. Hope it's not elephant since I just ate a whole one. Still, I kind of felt I may have developed a taste for the darn things.

Umatilla Reconnaissance

For a second, I thought my foot had kicked up a stone and sent it clattering across the hard basalt surface. My eyes glanced downward and darted over the broken rocks, not seeing any skidding stone. I stopped moving, but the clatter continued.

The sound seemed louder now, and immediately I knew what it was. I still didn't see it, but my mind insisted it was there somewhere, lost amid the textures and stark shadows of the low rocky outcrop. Then I noticed soft edges against the rock—a small mound where I expected solid rock. My body stiffened. There, a few steps off to my right, a rattlesnake coiled to strike.

Its elevated head and neck formed a zig-zag formation while the tongue flicked toward me, rapidly sampling the air for my scent. The tail vibrated louder, hurling the rattling noise toward me in warning. I studied the animal while carefully stepping away and recognized it as a western rattlesnake (*Crotalus oreganus*).

After a few more steps, it slowly uncoiled and slithered off its basking rock toward the opposite direction. I watched it slide effortlessly over the rocky terrain, its ribs rippling in perfect synchrony. Brown and tan patches on its skin matched the substrate almost perfectly—desert camouflage. Here moved a creature perfectly designed for the landscape where it lived.

The snake slithered away to find a more private place to sunbathe. Unable to control its body temperature, it had lain exposed on the rocks. It needed the morning sun to warm itself enough before it could hunt for a field mouse breakfast. It had no interest in harming me, but rattled to let me know I entered its front yard and to back off or it would show me its cranky side.

I yielded by stepping back and continuing my investigation. It had not occurred to me when I awoke that morning that I'd be dodging rattlesnakes, but finding one didn't surprise me.

The terrain baked in the parched landscape at nine o'clock on a sunny September morning. Nearly a year had passed since my epiphany regarding the Missouri rad-vector project, and now I moved on foot, traversing rocky ground in the state of western Washington.

The night before, I had flown to Portland, Oregon. Then I arose before dawn and drove a rental car east for three hours along the Lewis & Clark Highway, hugging the Columbia River. I arrived by nine at this sparse, desiccated spot in the rain-shadow of the Cascade Mountains.

My environmental engineering company had sent me there near the town of Umatilla to investigate the state of ecological conditions. A major gas pipeline company wanted to cross the Columbia right there with an underground pipe. Prevailing laws required a reconnaissance-level ecological investigation to issue construction permits.

My effort focused on uncovering indicators about the site's terrestrial ecology, vitality, and stability. Such indicators might reveal the potential for significant ecological impacts, and so I would also evaluate the Umatilla site's likely responses to the proposed construction. A more detailed investigation could take place at a later time. The pipeline company had contracted with my firm to conduct the work, and so here I poked around, facing off rattlesnakes in the desert.

Over the past year, I often had to pack my bags quickly and scoot around the country where needed for a few days or weeks. Sometimes these trips involved environmental investigations for large civil projects— hydroelectric dams, power plants, cross-country transmission lines, bridges, factories, and complex land developments. Some involved reconnaissance investigations, while others required complex studies and a team of scientists collecting and analyzing data over months.

Before going to a project site, I usually had a couple of days in the office to conduct as much pre-field research as I could. My efforts centered on aerial photo features of the eco-region, the ecology, critical environmental factors, public concerns, pertinent regulations, maps, published materials on flora, fauna, geology, soils, topography, hydrology. I would search for reports and historical references. In a time without personal computers, this proved a difficult task, and sometimes I landed in a landscape with little to go on, as in Missouri.

Most of the drive from Portland passed through sagebrush plains grilled well-done, seared on top and piping hot. After nearly two-hundred dusty miles, I turned off the primary road and took an unmarked dirt track that headed toward the Columbia River. The track dead-ended at a lonely spot beside the channel. A few miles west lay the small desert community of Umatilla. The dirt road ended fifty feet from the river. When I opened the car door, a blast of heat made me want to stay in the air-conditioned interior. A moment later, though, I climbed out and let my eyes scan the scene. The river flowed twenty feet below the sloping bank. On my left, a cluster of white barrel-sized pipes with wheeled shutoff valves emerged out of the ground. Putty-colored soil and clumps of dried yellow grasses dominated the ground surface.

The far bank, a half-mile away, sported a smear of green vegetation contrasting with low dirty hills that rose in the far distance. No buildings anywhere, nor humans, nor a bird, insect, or anything on four legs; just some dried stalks and me on two legs sizzling in the heat.

I ducked back inside the car and grabbed my hat and field vest off the passenger seat, along with my binoculars, a topographic map, and a large aerial photo of the area. Heatwaves shimmered off the hood like a hotplate left on high, but no other usable surface allowed for spreading out the materials. Even the paper surfaces burned my elbows when I leaned on them, and the maps seemed about to start smoking at any moment.

Matching the few landscape features on the ground with the maps and aerial confirmed this as the right location. The sun glare reflected off the putty-colored soils, making squinting mandatory.

Nothing moved except the water flowing below the banks; a quietness saturated the air—solitude. However, like all ecosystems, this one presented a deceptive view; much more occurred around me than its appearance suggested. To find out what, all I had to do was read the landscape. The first step meant recording my impressions and basic observations in my notebook...

Ecoregion: *Columbia Plateau (10); Subdivision: Umatilla Plateau (10c),* Vegetation Community: arid sagebrush steppe & grassland. Sagebrush species and bitterbrush dominant, interspersed patches of short- stemmed bluegrasses, cheats, wheatgrasses within an undeveloped riparian corridor.

My ecoregion comment recognized landforms based on geological and ecological categories. Few field ecologists had yet to adopt the system and seemed unaware it existed. For me, however, its usefulness lay in providing a universal classification of landscapes. The system labeled, described, and coded each ecoregion so ecologists could recognize and immediately understand the kinds of physical and ecological features to expect on a site before going there.

I closed the notebook, rolled the maps and aerial into a tube, then set out to explore the area on foot. The yellowed stalks rustled in the dry heat as I passed, their seeds mostly dispersed by now in the early fall. The area seemed intact, free from erosion and disturbance.

But something bothered me; an anomaly I had not expected. The engineer had described the pipeline crossing as a proposed project waiting for permits. But the curved three-foot diameter steel pipe valves with wheeled shut-offs should not be here, I thought. My analytical antennae twitched, realizing that these structures represented one of those unseen things below the surface. By the paint scuffs on their surface, someone installed them in the past— quite some time ago.

The valve caps connected to pipes that disappeared underground. Most likely, another matching set existed across the river. Odd, if so, unless an old pipeline already lay under the river. Perhaps our client just wants to repair it or add a second one next to it. Either way, it would not alter my reconnaissance activities, only the severity of impacts. I would confirm my suspicions once back in the office.

The heat seared the back of my neck while I roamed the area, looking for clues about how the disturbances from the project on the river, banks, and surroundings might affect the region's ecosystems. In my field vest, I carried several magnifying glasses to examine plant parts, insects, soil particles, rocks, and small critters I could pick up. Other items included an optical rangefinder to determine distances, a clinometer for measuring topographic slopes, six-inch measuring rulers and a few other instruments.

The vest trapped the heat and chaffed my neck, and I wished I'd brought a lighter version while slipping down the riverbank to the water's edge. A buffer of rushes and sedges formed a band of vigorous plants, still green and robust. From the topographic map, the depth of the river reached twelve feet in the middle—I would need to cross the bridge in Umatilla to reach the other side.

Here the river extended just over a half-mile wide and flowed at a leisurely pace. I did not intend to investigate the aquatic resources, since my friend and colleague Bill Levi, a fishery biologist, would do a separate study a few days later. Once back in the office, we would work together to evaluate our results and produce a formal report. The permitting agencies would review it and decide about any further permitting actions needed.

After completing the reconnoiter, I returned to the car, tossed in the gear, and drove back to the main road. From there, I headed a few miles east to Umatilla.

Named after the early native tribe that inhabited the region, the town of a few thousand served as a significant trading and staging area during the gold rush in the 1800s. Typically a dry place, it averaged less than ten inches of rainfall a year. Now, in September, the area would see barely a half-inch of rain.

After crossing the steel bridge, I turned west toward Portland. A small side road soon appeared near a patch of shade trees directly across the river from where I had first parked. I eased the car along it, but shortly after the pavement ended, a sign cautioned about going further. Our pipeline company client owned a utility right-of- way easement encompassing the dirt path that led toward the river and stopped short of it.

A heavy lock held the gates closed. I stopped the car and walked around the barrier until I reached the river. Clumps of sagebrush dotted the parched ground with their nodding tips in shades of vermillion, gray and silvery-green. I passed another set of genuflecting pipe valves.

 Further along, the terrain changed abruptly when I stepped off a rocky slope onto lower ground, still some distance from the river's edge.

I had reached a lush, vibrant wetland community nourished by the river water—a functional ecosystem where lack of moisture was not a problem. No stresses, discolorations, or evidence of contamination visible.

All the signs told me that things were operating as expected. Life and natural processes chugged along, extracting nutrients, transforming energy into a myriad of pathways, sustaining food webs between the aquatic lotic system and the adjacent arid plateau.

My reading of the landscape suggested conditions had not changed anytime in the recent past. The evidence lay in how stable the channel appeared, the features of its floodplain, and how deep the river had cut through its valley. Most of what I observed had been the same for millions of years. Geological reports I had found earlier showed evidence lava flows covered the region in ancient times up to two miles deep. These had hardened into basalt rock outcroppings. But as eons elapsed, these had all eroded down to the level of my boot soles.

Flooding had not occurred recently, judging by the lack of indicators on either side of the river—no debris piles, rack-lines, sediment deposits, flattened vegetation, relict channels. But in ancient times, cataclysmic floods and wind widely deposited silt and sand. Over time, winds scoured the floodplain and laid down more of these materials across the landscape. The region presently consisted entirely of lowlands, with an arid climate, cool winters, and hot summers.

Yet I knew unseen activities continued all around and under me…beyond the macro-scale of casual human observation. It would take more than a quick field recon to discover those complexities, and the meanings they portended about life and death for the inhabitants of this landscape.

Though my recon proved rather easy to conduct, it provided additional opportunities to hone my observation skills, figuring things out on the fly. And I had found evidence on the site about the landscape's prospects for responding to the proposed pipeline project. I could confidently report that little would change at the site or in the ecoregion…assuming the construction activities proceeded properly. Perhaps once it started, I would have the chance to return and monitor the operations to confirm my assessment, as often happened.

The Crop Circles of Irrigon

With my recon done at the Umatilla crossing, I hiked back to the car. Soon after I reached the main road again, a cool breeze blasted out of the air conditioner vents. I swung the steering wheel right, deciding to return west toward Portland by driving along the south side of the Columbia River. Several hours lay ahead of me for thinking about the report I needed to produce.

It would include my observations, plus my colleague's fishery and aquatic findings. Then I would review the construction blueprints, procedures, and materials proposed. In this way, I would assess the environmental effects expected and provide guidance for minimizing any potential adverse environmental consequences.

But something interrupted my thoughts a few miles down the road near the small settlement of Irrigon. The landscape had changed dramatically from sagebrush desert to vibrant green oases that seemed completely out of place in the otherwise bleak setting.

Giant disks lay upon the land, each one a half-mile in diameter like some kind of alien message system based on crop circles. Indeed, that is what they were...crop circles, but they came from somewhere other than the cosmos.

These curiosities began erupting around me until they appeared everywhere. Clearly, though, hoaxers did not make them to prank the public. Those jokesters typically made their geometric circles with a short flat plank tied at each end with a rope like a hunting bow and string. They hold the rope and press stalks to the ground as they walk to create intricate patterns within extensive grain fields. Such tricks crush the living plants to death for no useful purpose—unless you consider this form of landscape "art" meaningful.

Many do, especially "croppies," as they are known in some circles. These cultish devotees consider the hoaxers a nuisance and believe the seasonal geometric patterns are messages, signs and prophecies from aliens or entities from some other dimension.

At least, the crop circles along the Columbia River had a reasonable explanation and purpose—using advanced technology to grow human food in the dry climate. This did not destroy crops like the hoaxed versions but produced life from the ground-up through cultivation—bravo earthlings.

The view from the road did not reveal the full extent and scale of the circular patterns, so I pulled the car over and parked on the shoulder. The satellite photo for Umatilla lay on the seat next to me and included a portion of the Irrigon area. It displayed a larger perspective of a landscape peppered with multi- colored splotches, as though someone had set hundreds of wet coffee cups down, then removed them. These round shapes not only looked like water rings—water, in fact, created them. It spewed out through holes along a thousand-foot-long overhead irrigation pipe stretched across each circular diameter.

Tall scaffolds attached to wheels supported the pipe every hundred feet or so. At the center of each circle a motor and wellhead connected to a pump that fed groundwater into the horizontal pipe. Power from the motor acted as the geared minute-hand on a clock, revolving the rig's outer end around the circle's perimeter using the wheels on the pipe-structure. The arm rotated at a walking pace around the hub, spraying fresh water over the crops with automatic timers.

For a moment, these large irrigation systems evoked fanciful thoughts in my head of an alien invasion involving galactic dragonfly creatures crawling around inside the circles, eating the fresh vegetation. Hmm, herbivorous aliens—who knew?

The irrigation arm traveled the entire way around each circle over the course of a full day and night, spraying water, nutrients, and pesticides over rows upon rows of vegetable crops. Thanks to wells, pumps and circular irrigation, the dry plains of Irrigon had blossomed with agriculture.

Yet, questions arose in my mind as I drove west about the ecological future of such areas. I wondered about the heavy use of groundwater pumped up from the depths by hundred-foot wells that constantly fed the eternally thirsty land.

How long would the underlying aquifer survive this relentless sucking of the earth's life-fluid up their steel proboscises? Water-slurpers infested the landscape, a stealth invasion of which the public was hardly aware. Those who passed through miles of vibrant corn, beans, tomatoes, and strawberries saw expanses of nurtured crops that fed growing populations of hungry humans. Humankind had rescued nature from a monotonous landscape and turned it into a green plain that supported food, agricultural jobs, steel manufacturing, pipe production, and a well-digger economy.

The center-pivot irrigation system became established in the 1950s. Tens of thousands of wells pierced the depths throughout the Great Plains. Each gulped water while yearly droughts on the surface plagued the already dry plains.

Since irrigation arrived, the water table had dropped by more than one-hundred feet in many areas. But it stayed out-of-sight and mostly out-of-mind because it happened deep underground. Many of those who knew seemed unconcerned, perhaps because billions of gallons remained...and they had fresh basil and tomatoes on their tables.

And yet, those billions of gallons occupied a thin underground layer less than four-hundred feet thick— the massive Ogallala Aquifer. Even today, it remains spread over a vast territory involving eight states. In many places, the aquifer level is less than a hundred feet thick...reduced to perilous levels that threaten natural and human communities. The problem is the sheer number of wells siphoning more ground water at a faster rate than nature can replenish through the planet's hydrological cycle.

Water is the most valuable resource on planet Earth...the great diversity of life here would not have arisen without it. When the water goes, so do ecosystems, species, and everything else that depends on it. And the deeper the groundwater lies, the less it becomes available to support life and humans in particular.

But where did all the planet's water come from in the first place, and why is there so much of it? Scientists have long thought most of it came from outer space— asteroids and comets.

Well now, it seems aliens caused the crop circles of Irrigon after all. Over eons, the water from such space debris fell to Earth and soaked deeply into the ground through porous soils until it reached the bedrock—the aquifer zone.

For a long time, I harbored suspicions about this otherworldly explanation; it seemed inadequate to explain the vast volume of water that exists all over our planet. Other explanations have recently arisen, suggesting a vast cloud of magma coalesced to form the earth nine billion years after the Big Bang occurred.

According to this idea, the primordial earth started as a glowing orb with oceans of steaming hot magma. It slowly cooled, releasing large quantities of the water molecules within the magma into the earth's atmosphere as steam. With the water set free, it cooled and condensed enough to remain on the earth's surface in liquid form.

Volcanic activity continued over billions of years, and brought new water to the atmosphere, as it does to this day. The prototype for the hydrological cycle had formed, creating and maintaining the surface and groundwater quantities of the Earth.

Also known as the "Water Cycle," it is one of the great rhythms of our planet that controls the continuous movement of water on, above, and below the surface. Water is always changing states between liquid, vapor and ice through intricate land and ecosystem pathways. Some of these transformations can happen quickly, the way cubes of water freeze to ice in the refrigerator, or steam erupts from a geyser and turns to water as it falls. Other processes take thousands of years to complete—the accumulation and melting of glaciers, volcanic eruptions, continental drifting.

If not for our sun, the water cycle could not exist— nor could any life it sustains. This is because most of Earth's water still exists in its oceans, where the sun heats the water and evaporates some of it into the air as vapor. Plants, including phytoplankton, also produce water vapor through transpiration from their stems, stalks, and leaves. These vapors rise and pull the water molecules up into the atmosphere where cooler temperatures cause them to condense into clouds.

Once water vapor returns to the atmosphere as clouds, air currents tug and pull them over the landscapes that lie below, growing and dwindling, shifting their shapes and densities. Clouds collide, water molecules coalesce, and fall out of the sky by gravity as precipitation.

Some of it drops as snow or sleet and accumulates in ice caps, glaciers, and land surfaces. As the weather warms, snowpacks thaw and meltwaters flow overland in streams and rivers that bring it back to the oceans. Along the way, runoff and groundwater seepage accumulate in freshwater lakes, ponds and wetlands.

Water soaks into the ground through the bottom of lakes and rivers, where it encounters no impermeable layer of rock or soil—or asphalt. Gravity pulls it even deeper, towards the Earth's core...until the pressures and heat from molten magma set it aboil. Eventually, these pressures thrust the magma up through lava tubes and into the air as geysers and volcanoes, adding more precious molecules to the water cycle. All these events allow the global water cycle to continue indefinitely.

Around the planet, water resources keep moving, changing state, transforming landscapes, nurturing ecological communities, slaking our thirsts, and improving our lives. Water allows our food to grow, metabolisms to function, and decay to remove our wastes. Without it, mummified animal carcasses would litter the world for decades— until they eroded away by sunlight and wind-driven grit, or buried by dust and landslides.

We drink it, bathe in it, and use it to make our childhoods happier with the likes of backyard swimming pools, soft drinks and sodas. Water is so precious to us we cannot be away from it for more than a few days...or we die. Villages and communities thrive where it is abundant, especially when it is easily accessible. If we are lucky, we can turn on a tap and watch it pour fresh into our hands. Best of all, it naturally restores itself, if given the chance. All because of Earth's magnificent water cycle.

And is there any other more interesting and useful substance that can appear on the landscape within a few minutes out of thin air, change form, then disappear a short while later? Puddles can do that. And if a few pollywogs and toads find their way there? Well then, the possibilities expand for discovering even more enchanting lives out there...and just down the lane—and beyond. Water connects every living thing to nature and to other living things, every minute of every day. Even in deserts.

Without water, no habitats could survive, no ecosystems thrive. Though Earth itself is not a living thing, it is a global vessel that contains the habitats where the living can dwell. Wherever an accessible body of potable water becomes available, people, plants, and animals will gather...even boiling hot springs provide habitat for a variety of bacteria.

Sometimes, even now, a sense of awe and gratitude comes over me when I look at a glass of water in my hand with floating ice cubes. The water atoms inside remind me how they found their way into my glass after over four-billion years. During that time since the Earth formed, the oxygen and hydrogen atoms in my glass had changed partners as conditions broke them apart and recombined them into other states of solids, liquids and vapor. The water cycle processes sent them to untold corners of the world and atmosphere until they landed in my mouth. Eventually, all of them would return to the cycle and become part of something else when I breathe, perspire, pee and die.

Who knows what configurations these oxygen and hydrogen atoms had previously seen, what landscapes or steaming pile of lava, what creatures they once belonged to...what stars they had whizzed past once upon a time within a comet. And most likely, not even once did any oxygen atom combine with the same two hydrogen atoms in those four billion years.

It made me feel gratitude for water's marvelous ability involving its solid form that can float in its own liquid. Think of that a moment; how many things can you name whose solid and liquid forms can co-exist within the same enveloping space? Ice will float in the liquid that melts from it.

Only a few substances on Earth can do this— perhaps less than a handful—and water is by far the most prevalent. Known substances that are also lighter as solids than their liquid form include plutonium, bismuth, germanium, gallium and silicon. Try drinking eight glasses of these every day and see what happens...on second thought—don't.

You can see this reverse-density behavior in an icy pond and ocean icebergs...or a glass of water containing ice cubes. Ice is quite amazing that way. And besides liquid, solid, and gaseous states, water can stay in transitional forms under the right conditions—think slush, fog, mist, bubbles and the foam in an ice-cream float.

Water is very plentiful in frozen landscapes such as glaciers and in the permanent snowpacks of mountains. The problem for life in such places is that water remains unavailable because of its solid state. Lifeforms require water in liquid or vaporized states to exist. But no global water shortage problem exists, nor will it...as long as the water cycle remains intact.

During droughts, local and regional stresses occur in susceptible ecosystems. Water-dependent landscapes shrink, re-shape, come and go—just as they have done when climates changed in other geological epochs. New water-based ecosystems pop up on landscapes all the time; our planet is not even close to becoming a desiccated wasteland.

Wherever water appears on the surface for a time, life will come to it. But when it lies deep underground, it behooves us to manage it properly so that we can sustain ourselves and those around us. Irrigation is one way. Using wells has brought better lives to untold numbers of humans and desolate landscapes. But excessive drawdowns of groundwater aquifer supplies adversely affect entire above-ground ecosystems in adjacent regions. That has already happened or is underway in many dry environments.

Part of the solution is to replenish aquifers. This is usually impossible where extensive landscapes become urbanized and paved over with increased hard surfaces. Roads, rooftops, parking lots, commercial, and industrial developments prevent rain from soaking back into the ground, interrupting the water cycle.

This is not a significant problem in places like Irrigon and Umatilla, with low-density populations. But it doesn't always take a lot of urban infrastructure to draw down an aquifer—just lots and lots of wells. Too many wells will over-pump groundwater resources before natural recharge can keep pace. In cities and high- demand crop circle agriculture, ground-water levels keep dropping and can stay dangerously low for long periods during droughts.

Aquifers can, however, recharge by artificial means. The most common methods for direct artificial recharge use excavated ponds and injection wells. Recharge ponds are shallow holding basins constructed so drainage runoff enters them, and the water can take its time to infiltrate. These basins may hold permanent water or not, depending on the design and climate.

Injection wells are a more energy-intensive method that uses high pressure pumps to force water down into aquifers. In order for injection pumps to work, a reliable non-aquifer source of water is necessary. Often, surface water gets diverted from rivers and streams during high spring flows, when crops need less water.

But because pumping wells lower the water table, less groundwater feeds nearby rivers and streams to sustain normal flows. Much of their baseflow comes naturally from sufficient groundwater seeping into channels under banks and up through the beds. Lower baseflows from over-pumping can dry up streams and adjacent wetlands, ponds, and lakes. This can bring catastrophe to landscapes as ecosystems collapse.

New technologies in pump equipment efficiencies, drought-tolerant crop varieties, and other advances may help counterbalance the accelerating rate of groundwater depletion. They might prolong the availability of aquifer resources for another hundred years.

If we do not manage things prudently though, then someday the taps will no longer flow. Then the pumps will cease, and the plains of Irrigon will become barren again when crop circles vanish. Local tomatoes and basil will no longer be available, and well-diggers will have moved on.

No one will be there any longer to wonder if the crop circles once came from chatty aliens sending messages in grain fields, or space rocks bearing gifts of water molecules. Either way, the water came from some galaxy far, far away.

Echoes of Falling Water

The crop circles that covered the Columbia River flood plain suddenly evaporated from view a half dozen miles west of Irrigon. Gray soils, sagebrush, and dust again reclaimed the landscape. The topography had warped into more rugged and highly dissected slopes, where erosion made them unsuitable for farming.

Seventy-five miles later, the land rose abruptly, uplifted to over a thousand feet as dry rounded hills. These arid slopes contained few trees except along drainageways.

I turned the car onto a short side road at a copse of tall trees and parked near the river. It was right here, I thought, gazing across the wide Columbia. On the far bank, I could see a small village; it was Wishram, Washington, where only a few hundred people dwelled. I studied the flowing water and tried to see any evidence of what had happened on this spot. But the only things out there—a handful of colorful wind surfers—skimmed the flat water. Interesting, but mundane—a scene available in benign waters the world over...a wide flat river, two banks, trees beyond, big sky above.

It wasn't always like that here, I thought. The magic was gone now...snuffed out. One day everything operated normally, spectacularly. Then the next—one of the world's great wonders had disappeared right in front of where I stood.

I walked to the bank and tried to imagine what it must have been like for those who were here when it happened. It both started and ended on March 10, 1957. By day's end, silence descended here for the first time in thousands of years—when the hydrological big- sleep occurred; and still it slumbers...under the windsurfers' boards.

My route had taken me to a different landscape, the *Pleistocene Lake Basins Ecoregion (10e)*, though still part of the *Columbia Plateau (10)*. It is a nearly level to undulating lake plain that once contained vast temporary lakes that were created by flood waters from glacial lakes named Missoula and Columbia.

While standing on the riverbank, I thought of when the river was geologically young, how it began carving itself down through the earth's crust. The land elevation sat higher then, but frictional forces persisted for millions of years. Water flowing over the channel bedrock scoured away the river bottom and lowered the elevation along its course.

The Columbia's flow originates high in the Rockies and drains to the Pacific Ocean. A hundred million years ago, sea levels began dropping because of global cooling—glaciers formed by locking up much of the water in ice. Ocean levels dropped faster than the Columbia's channel bed could erode deeper. This created a waterfall far downstream where the river met the ocean.

Constant flowing water erodes the edges of waterfalls the way the front edge of a block of ice melts when the back edge is tilted up slightly. A crease soon forms downslope, channeling water that cuts a notch at the front edge of the block. The water is warmer than the ice, so the bed incises faster there, cutting its way back "upstream" toward the higher side of the ice-block. As the ice continues to melt and migrate upstream, the notch becomes a waterfall.

The same process occurred in the Columbia until the flow encountered exceptionally resistant rock. The forces of friction and resistance used to clash in spectacular fashion exactly where I stood that day. Resistance held strong then, with hard basalt arresting the river's march upstream.

From the ocean to the city of Dalles, the flow had created a smoothly graded channel. But basalt cataracts developed upstream of there. They continued for a dozen miles to Wishram. Here the flow tried to wear down the more resistant rock. But unyielding surfaces and the kinetic forces of hydraulics dueled for dominance.

The rocks held firm, stronger than the channel bed material just downstream. Resistant rocks forced the channel to narrow, causing the flow to rush faster. The softer downstream bed kept abrading away, lowering the bed elevation more quickly than at the hard basalt surfaces upstream.

And that could only result in one outcome...a great waterfall formed where the bed change occurred—right where I stood. Back then, the river flow dropped into a turbulence of thundering water.

Natives called this natural wonder "Celilo Falls." Downstream from there, rapids, cataracts and smaller falls extended to The Dalles. The flow surged through the smaller channel at the falls and roared over a twenty-foot-high wall of immense hydraulic power. So immense that the volume of flow over the falls became the sixth greatest in the world—ten times more than that over Niagara Falls today.

The crashing and extreme turbulence of water at Celilo Falls presented an environmental wonder for those who witnessed it. And, for those who lived nearby, it meant survival. For thousands of years Native Americans lived in large villages along the banks there, netting salmon and steelhead for food and trade. Chinookan people, who lived at the mouth of the Columbia and along the coast, came to fish and trade with the inland Sahaptin-speaking people of the Columbia Plateau.

A half-dozen regional tribes built permanent villages between the falls and The Dalles. The tribal peoples that lived and fished at Celilo Falls had long called the site Wyam—"Echo of Falling Water." These people, the Wyampum, left a record of their lives in the ashes of campfires and burial sites of their dead. Tools and weapons, items of adornment, and samples of their art have remained. During fish migration seasons, thousands of tribal folks gathered to fish and trade at the Wyam area.

Celilo Falls became a significant trade depot, where the goods exchanged included seashells, obsidian, buffalo meat and hides, pipestone, wapato, and slaves. Native Americans trafficked in slavery long before the river's Italian namesake opened that door. The general trade network stretched north into present-day Alaska, south to California, and east of the Rocky Mountains.

These people fished for steelhead (*Oncorhynchus mykiss*), anadromous rainbow trout, meaning they migrate back to the sea for breeding—unlike salmon. Salmon migrate from the sea to the freshwater tributaries where they first spawned. Once they finish breeding in late summer, the adult steelhead die. Juveniles return to the sea after reproducing and can breed in multiple years.

Natives also harvested three other main species of salmon that migrated in the Columbia. Chinook, also called King Salmon (*O. tshawytscha*) were the most plentiful. The other important species included the coho (*O. kisutch*) and sockeye (*O. nerka*).

Fish migrating upstream had to leap their way up Celilo falls, so the deep pools below the falls became a natural bottleneck where large concentrations of fish gathered ready for the taking. The Indians built extensive wooden platforms that hung from massive rocks and crags...ending just feet from the crashing waters.

The falls thundered so loud fishermen talked by sign language. From the high platforms, men pulled nets through the water on twenty-foot poles, trying to grab their catch. Slippery rocks made for dangerous, back- breaking work. Untethered fishermen who fell into the roiling waters had little chance of survival and became swept away in a blur.

Those who caught fish among the lower rocks lifted the nets up to the platforms, where others clubbed them to death with heavy sticks. Villagers dried the catch for winter food or traded the fish for goods with other villages. The fish caught there could feed whole families through the winters.

The chinook salmon run began in early spring. By early summer, immense specimens of chinook migrated through, known as "June Hogs." These fish often weighed up to eighty pounds—longer than the height of the fishermen who caught them. June hogs became extinct with the construction of the Grand Coulee dam far upstream. It and other modern dams blocked their migration route to their spawning grounds in the deep Canadian wilderness.

The blueback salmon run followed the chinook's, which peaked in early July. Even predatory sea lions and seals chased salmon up the Columbia River as far as Celilo Falls. Imagine that...sea lions two hundred miles from the ocean—in a freshwater river—through a desert...next to a roaring, churning waterfall.

Lewis and Clark and their company camped in this area for three days in 1806. During this time, they observed life in the native villages and portaged their canoes around Celilo Falls and miles of downstream cataracts. Clark referred to the falls as the "Great Falls of the Columbia" in his journal.

The falls sustained early American cultures for generations. But our modern civilization changed that. It was all due to the opening of the downstream Dalles Dam, which still operates today. Upon its completion, workers shut the floodgates permanently on a March day in 1957 to raise the water level behind the dam wall to drive the turbines. This caused the river to begin slowly backing upstream of the dam toward Celilo Falls. Hundreds of people gathered to say goodbye to the great falls that day.

At the time, more than five thousand people still relied on fishing at Celilo for their livelihoods. Never before had they watched the river waters run upstream as the entire flow of the river continued to back up behind the dam. They saw the water level slowly rise at the falls—the lowest rocks disappeared early. Soon, wooden fishing platforms wobbled; some crashed into the deepening water. When the scaffold timbers and ladders vanished, the water soon flooded the nearby native village on the bank.

It only took four hours for rising waters to submerge the fishing platforms, silence the falls, consume the native village, destroy river habitat, and create a lake environment. When the last rock went under, the water level reached the previous top of the falls—and moments later the river grew still. And nothing flowed but the tears of those who watched it all. The roar of water disappeared that had existed long before humans came to North America. The echo of falling water was no more. A way of life for people and animals that depended on the falls had ended.

During Lewis and Clark's time, up to sixteen million salmon and steelhead jumped through the falls and migrated upstream annually. At the time the Dalles Dam became operational, only one-and-a half-million fish traveled the river. Today, the numbers are down to a million.

The dam's planners and operators had one significant objective—to provide jobs and power for thousands of modern homes. Was it worth the cost of eliminating an awe-inspiring scene, loss of salmon habitat, extinction of the June Hog ecotype, and a native fishing industry? The answer depends on the collective choices we make regarding our society's crucial priorities, because we humans have the ability to choose solutions.

Humans have the power, and therefore the objective freedom, to change habitats and landscapes. But despite our highly developed brains, we still lack enough knowledge, tools, and foresight for accurately predicting the consequences and magnitudes on a landscape. Good solutions come from objectively bringing many scientific, technical and humanity fields into the evaluations, rather than just lofty socio- political goals and whims.

But scientists cannot determine with certainty what the unintended consequences might arise for higher trophic levels of an entire ecoregion or landscape. Mathematical models of complex environmental systems cannot provide that degree of predictive accuracy—too many variables, random events, unknown linkages between ecosystem components. This applies whether the impacts come from dams or climate change. Despite modern-day hoopla, no person or mathematical model can predict how long- term weather patterns affect global habitats, ecosystems, and landscapes.

And those who try to implement climate engineering like blocking the sun to control Earth's surface temperatures, should experience a few months in a cave or some gloomy dungeon, for they are dangerous fools to the world at large.

When it comes to big ideas, enthusiasm should be tempered by erudition. Impounding the Columbia River at The Dalles brought major changes to its ecology and adjacent ecosystems. As did all the fourteen other dams on the Columbia's main channel...and the four-hundred-fifty dams within the Columbia's thirteen-hundred miles of tributaries.

On one hand, electricity, flood control and increased water storage within the new impoundment provided human benefits. Those benefits, however, came with costs to native cultures that had thrived there, as well as to natural habitats that depended on the rivers' flow.

The once active floodplain became inactive. It had sustained marshes and ponds along the river's edge, but rarely ever flooded anymore. Once-productive wetlands along the Columbia became drowned and eliminated by the higher artificial lake levels.

Now, only the most severe storms produce floods, and those often cause great damage to properties built in the floodplain. The Columbia's fish evolved adaptations for moving through water, where they depend on currents to bring food to them. Since a still- water lake replaced the natural flow, fish must struggle in the placid waters.

Without a current to assist them, migrating fish must spend more energy in the lake waters to find food that had always arrived with the currents. This reduces their stamina and competes with the energy needed to continue migration. It is not natural for the native species, and their numbers continue to decline.

The native fish species that once lived in the Columbia's waters, and those that still do, evolved as the river naturally changed over thousands of years. The Columbia River developed when the last ice age ended, and the glacier that carved the valley melted. At first, massive dams of ice up to two-thousand feet high bordered a huge glacial lake further east in Montana, called Lake Missoula.

As the climate warmed and volcanism and earthquakes altered the regional landscape, the ice dams periodically melted and gave way to cataclysmic floods. Towering walls of water surged west toward the ocean, scouring the bedrock along the way into a larger channel. Gradually Lake Missoula shrank and eventually disappeared...several times. These floods and scouring flows created the dramatic landscape of the Columbia River Gorge east of Portland, and the channeled scablands of the western Columbia Basin.

Over the sweep of time, nature changed the face of the Columbia Basin many times because of large-scale warming and cooling cycles. Whole ecoregions came and went, untold ecosystems and species arrived, expanded, linked, shifted locations, declined, and became extinct—and new ones formed and did the same. And the process continues even now.

Before settlers arrived in the Northwest, the chinook salmon run was the greatest in the world. But when artificial dams appeared in the river, the pace of change accelerated. Salmon populations began declining, with migration runs dropping over ninety percent. Hatchery-raised and stocked fish comprised three- fourths of these migrants instead of native breeders produced naturally in the river.

Today, fourteen population groups of steelhead trout and Chinook, coho, chum, and sockeye salmon in the Pacific Northwest are listed as threatened or endangered under the Endangered Species Act. And it took less than one-hundred-fifty years for these species to reach the brink of extinction. Studies have shown that over two-thirds of the salmon reductions in the Columbia Basin are dam related.

Despite the installation of fish ladders and hatcheries—and even trucking and barging fish around the dams—the huge decline in salmon and steelhead numbers continues. These fish species must migrate between their upstream tributaries and the sea to grow. It is an arduous journey, and when they reach concrete dam faces, the tired young fish must exert extra energy to find the fish ladders. If they do, the structures injure many because concentrations of fish become so dense near the ladders.

Smaller salmon do not bother and just try to slip through the dams' turbines. The death toll is high for these salmon. Many are chewed-up directly by the turbines; others become easy prey because of inadequate or damaged screens.

Nature provided the means for young salmon to make a one to two-week swim to the sea, aided and concealed by the cold, cloudy, fast-moving water from spring snowmelt. The dams have increased migration time of young by one to two months. This is because of long stretches where they no longer have a current to assist them...just miles of still-water lakes to swim against.

Some of those lakes extend for nearly eighty miles. The water sits and warms in the quiet impounded waters and sediments settle to the bottom, so the water becomes clearer. Tired and weakened fish are thus more visible to predators, such as waterbirds and northern pikeminnow, walleye and bass. Due to lower energy reserves, many fish lose navigational abilities and the strength to migrate further.

But the consequences of dams do not stop there. The fish also suffocate to death. When flowing water splashes over natural riffles—shallow sections of cobble—and rapids, oxygen becomes dissolved. Migratory river fish require such oxygen levels to thrive. Warm water cannot retain as much oxygen as cold water. So, increased water temperatures in the lakes behind the dam walls hold less dissolved oxygen to rejuvenate already tired migrating fish.

Further, macroinvertebrate populations that depend on high oxygen concentrations also become depleted. This adversely alters the entire river food web, including steelhead forage. With less food and oxygen available, fewer of those fish who reach their breeding grounds can spawn...and they produce fewer young in the next generation. Then the cycle continues into subsequent years, and the trend of decreasing river fish numbers is accelerating into the future.

But dams cause even more problems for river ecosystems. As the flow of water slows behind a dam, it inhibits a river's major function—to transport its bedload through the landscape. The watershed in rivers like the Columbia produce a great deal of sediment, gravel, and rocks from erosion and weathering upstream. This material enters tributaries and the main channel.

In slow-moving water, this bedload settles to the bottom, where it can lead to siltation upstream of the dam. More than this, it smothers spawning areas, and causes a buildup of toxic elements in the lake substrates. The combined dams on the Columbia have trapped an immense quantity of sediment upstream...enough to nearly fill the Great Pyramid of Giza.

One might suppose all these obstacles would prevent any healthy salmon from migrating and breeding successfully. But there is still more. As a way to increase fish numbers, hatcheries installed along the Columbia raise salmon. Today, nearly two-hundred hatcheries exist in the Columbia floodplain, using the river water to produce more than one-hundred-forty million young fish. Trucks haul these hatchery fish around the dams and then barge and release them into the ocean, where they mature.

Once the fish mature in the seas, they return to the river to breed upstream three to five years later. They soon encounter the dams and again must get past these massive structures. Unlike before dams arrived, now eighty percent of those migrating fish are hatchery reared. This means, of course, that only twenty percent are wild-reared fish.

The artificial conditions of hatcheries are substantially different from those in the Columbia River where currents dominate. In hatcheries, food pellets get dispersed by scattering them on the surface of tanks, where masses of young fish compete. Salmon in rivers, however, have the whole river to spread out and feed well below the surface, where aerial predators such as birds cannot snag them for dinner. Thus, surface-feeding is not normal in wild salmon populations.

Besides trucking and barging, many fry fish get released directly into the river. Evidence shows that once they attempt to return upstream to breed, hatchery fish suffer high mortality. They face hazards for which they are ill-adapted from life in the artificial hatcheries.

Just one-quarter of one percent of barged fish ever make it back upstream to spawn. That is a massive decline from historic levels. Consequently, salmon and steelhead are well on their way to perishing altogether in the Columbia. Recently, scientists found that instead of increasing population numbers to historical levels, hatcheries are actually speeding up the salmon species' extinction.

Why have hatcheries not worked, despite massive public funding? It is due in part to genetic alterations that such man-made facilities induce in the fish populations. Research has found that fish raised in hatcheries that are then released leave far fewer offspring than their wild relatives.

The problem does not end with those offspring but carries over into their wild-born descendants. The implication is that hatchery salmonids that survive and reproduce in the wild are gradually causing genetic problems. Interbreeding has caused the biological fitness of the fewer wild populations to decline.

As with so many other situations—man-induced or natural—the subsequent causes and effects from seemingly benign events keep producing sequences of unintended consequences. Perhaps someday soon, the "wild-caught" salmon you used to order for dinner may no longer exist. You could still get a mass-produced genetically inferior fish that grew up packed tightly in a hatchery tank. Oh, wait, that's mostly the case now anyway, since seventy percent of salmon produced worldwide are "farm-raised."

That may bring warm and fuzzy feelings to household cooks who do not know better, but maybe the label should say something like, "Genetically Inferior Tank-Raised Salmon." But I doubt industry market promoters would ever agree to that.

The more adapted salmon are for thriving in captivity, the less capable they are of succeeding in the wild. The reason is the fish that survive in hatcheries are those with behavioral patterns well-suited to artificial conditions. And they are not those found in wild populations adapted to river conditions. Hatchery conditions shape the genetics of subsequent generations, and within a few years, the hatch-reared genome drifts further away from the wild type.

It is likely hatchery selection pressures are producing an entire suite of changing physiological and behavioral traits. Identifying those and the chain of consequences they produce remains difficult. Doing so might promote management changes in captive conditions to lessen the disparities between wild and hatchery-born fish. But the state of the science is not yet there.

Perhaps all is not lost. Managing the Columbia's hatcheries requires a change in strategy. Conservation of unique genetic material is becoming increasingly important. The key for hatcheries to operate effectively for both native and wild fish is to minimize interactions of released hatchery fish with naturally spawning fish populations.

Part of the strategy could involve letting hatcheries continue producing fish for commercial harvest of migrants in the lower reaches of the Columbia when migrants arrive there. Relaxed rules would also allow expanding harvest limits in the upper parts of the watershed. There, some hatcheries could focus on producing fish that are as similar to wild fish as possible using more advanced hatcheries that mimic river conditions.

For this to work, upper basin hatcheries must sufficiently isolate hatchery fish from wild fish. The intent should target minimizing hatchery fish genetic material in the spawning grounds of wild fish, since the hatchery-raised fish pose a risk to natural fish populations.

But the dams keep producing more adverse impacts. They made it much easier for certain invaders from the sea to plunder far upstream river reaches. They are the equivalent of river "carpetbaggers," taking advantage of the struggling salmon's plight.

Slick, flashy creatures with silver sides swarmed upstream. They were American Shad (*Alosa sapidissima*), an anadromous species that migrate upstream to spawn. On the way, they clash with the salmon heading downstream toward the ocean.

Shad are smaller fish and can bypass dams more easily than salmon and steelhead. Few need to use the tiring fish-ladders—they just swim upstream to the dam walls and slip through the coarse screens on the flow-gates into the pools below.

Historically, no shad runs occurred in the Columbia while Celilo Falls existed. Now over seven-and-a-half million shad surge up the channel to breed. Each female can lay up to one-hundred-fifty-thousand eggs, which hatch and grow in the river and migrate to the Pacific by August. So far, it remains uncertain about the extent the booming shad population may cause salmon and steelhead growth rates and productivity.

Yet, some recent studies have found positive effects in that they provide food for sub-yearling Chinook salmon. Also, shad contribute as much needed phosphorous and nitrogen to the river system as do salmon when they die.

Removing dams and returning rivers like the Columbia to a natural state would provide the best ecological solution. Short of that, a combination of upgrading them, keeping hatchery and wild salmon separate, and matching hatchery fish genetics to respective native species may become the most practical approach.

Dam removals have occurred on other streams and rivers—some even on tributaries of the Columbia. Among these were Marmot Dam on the Sandy River and the Little Sandy Dam on the Little Sandy River, both taken down over a dozen years ago because of the environmental impacts they caused to their rivers' ecology. Removing them became an important step for improving their salmon and steelhead populations.

But dismantling of other dams has also occurred, including over 1,570 structures in the U.S. to restore fish passage and access to habitat. Ecologically, many rivers are better off without dams. Even so, 79,000 other dams remain in place across America.

Fifty years after Celilo Falls disappeared, the U.S. Army Corps of Engineers used sonar technology to survey the riverbed where I watched the windsurfers skim over the calm waters. The results revealed the falls remain intact below the existing lake. Rocky outcrops, carved basins and chutes matched the historic aerial photographs from the 1940s when the falls were in their glory.

For now, though, we have only the echo of falling water that once was but is no more. Now the consequences remain from dams built decades ago without regard for nature. They will persist for a long time, for humans are prisoners of their own hubris. Or, as Alexander Pope knew—mankind suffers from the "Eternal sunshine of the spotless mind." We forget or ignore our failings in the past and repeat them era upon future era. Our species never seems to learn.

Perhaps someday the world may witness the return of the great fisheries of the Columbia Basin—and the roar of water down ancient flumes. At least we can dream about what was and what might be again.

Wouldn't it be wonderful to watch June Hogs again powering their way through crashing rapids? Perhaps Celilo Falls will rise from the depths again. For it is still there...under the silent water.

Soda Butte Creek

A small stream tumbled and splashed over stony riffles into quiet pools and eddies. The water flowed cold and fast, saturated with oxygen and nutrients carried from its mountain headwaters.

With one hand, I swept a long pole under a submerged log next to the bank. Immediately a trout floated to the surface. In my other hand, I held a separate pole attached to a circular net at the end. I submerged the net and gently slipped the fish into it.

The fish lay still in the net, paralyzed. I swung the net sideways and back to the assistant behind me. He towed a flat-bottomed jon boat upstream using a harness. When the net reached him, he grabbed it and tipped the fish into an open cooler that sat in the boat's bow. A steady flow of bubbles swirled in the tub from a hose attached to an air pump.

The associate held the fish horizontally in the water and moved it back and forth a few times to pull oxygen- rich water over the gills. Within a minute, the fish became active again, looking for a way to escape.

Meanwhile, I continued sweeping my pointed pole back and forth across half the fifteen-foot channel. Another crew member with a similar setup did the same on the other half of the stream. His pole swung past me as he brought two fish in his net back to the tub. We continued working upstream against the current in the knee-deep water, sweeping back and forth, causing fish to rise and float, stunned, while we collected them as we went.

We wore chest waders and heavy rubber gloves while we fished—not with rods and reels, but with electricity. It was strictly illegal—except for licensed scientists conducting research like we were. Our work involved electrofishing, a standard field technique for sampling freshwater streams. It remains a practical method even today for assessing population densities and health of fish without killing or harming them.

A gasoline generator in the boat created a weak electrical current that flowed through insulated wires to the anode ends of the metal poles. The current induced a muscular response that caused the fish to swim towards the closest anode pole involuntarily. Quickly they stopped swimming and became paralyzed for a few seconds, then floated to the surface where netting them became easy.

After twenty minutes, we brought the floating lab into a quiet pool and released the harness. We put our nets in the boat and laid a board across the gunwales to provide a makeshift table. On top sat a weighing scale, along with a measuring stick and a clipboard with data sheets.

We began identifying, counting, weighing, and measuring the fish, along with recording observations on health, age, sex, and origin. Slight variations in body markings told us if a specimen had originally come from a hatchery or had naturally spawned in the river. Then we placed each fish back in the stream where they invariably dashed off into the riffles.

The stream typified those that drained sparsely inhabited midwestern slopes covered in hardwood forests—small, fast, and saturated with oxygen. The work we did would provide insights on the stability of fishery resources in the region, and a basis for state fishery managers to better sustain recreational fishing. Most of the fish we caught that day had medium tan bodies and dark spots. These markings identified them as brown trout (*Salmo truttta*), a non-native species introduced into American streams from Europe in 1883.

But we also collected brook trout (*Salvelinus fontinalis*) that day, another species introduced to benefit recreational fishing. Brookies have bright orange bellies with black and white stripes on their abdominal fins—quite striking. We collected data on that chilly November day in the northern Midwest stream, hoping it might tell us if these two species remained in balance and whether they affected natural stream ecology.

Conditions differed, however, in other regions such as Wyoming outside Yellowstone National Park. There, introduced brook trout dominated in surrounding creeks. They remained beyond the park's boundaries until they escaped, eventually marauding downstream native fish breeding grounds, especially those of the cutthroat trout (*Oncorhynchus clarkia*).

Cutthroats, or "cutties," are extremely popular native fish in the Rockies for fly-fishers, with their red coloration on the underside of the lower jaw and gill plates. It looks like they are bleeding from throat injuries. One of those streams brookies had invaded was Soda Butte Creek. Named after an extinct geyser cone that still sits next to it, the channel flows on the east side of Yellowstone in the Beartooth Mountains.

The creek flowed through the *Middle Rockies Ecoregion (17), High Elevation Valleys (17a),* containing bottomlands, terraces, marshlands, and foothills. Ecologists and fishery biologists became alarmed when the invasive brook trout got into Soda Butte Creek. This stream drains into the world's most critical cutthroat rearing grounds—Yellowstone Lake. To fight against the brook trout from ravaging the cutthroat fishery, biologists began electroshocking Soda Butte Creek every year. They removed brook trout whenever encountered. Concerns persisted because brookies could out-breed cutties and keep their own populations high.

History is full of lessons about the devastating effects that often occur when non-native species get introduced into a landscape. The law of unintended consequences usually wreaks havoc on existing ecosystems. In Soda Butte Creek, shock-and-remove did not work. It soon became clear that other measures needed consideration.

The new plan involved killing everything that had gills in Soda Butte—even cutthroats. This was a radical idea to save the cutthroat community—mass murder all the fish in order to protect the community— "ecological cleansing" I called it.

In the fall of 2015, state and federal biologists, as well as Yellowstone's fishery managers, implemented the new plan. Twenty-eight miles of Soda Butte prime stream habitat once again underwent bombardment by electroshock treatments, with brookies and cutthroats alike removed. Harvested brookies ended up dying in piles. A local farmer took all the brookie corpses and buried them in fields as fertilizer. Trucks transported the three-thousand cutthroats collected to temporary holding facilities—fish concentration camps.

Then crews, just following orders, dumped lethal doses of a pesticide called Rotenone into Soda Butte Creek. This killed any remaining brookies and cutthroat, and whatever else lived in the pristine waters that used gills to breathe. A week later, the poison dissipated, and biologists released the previously captured cutthroats back to the stream. There, they have thrived without the brook trout conquering their habitat.

Unfortunately, the recovering cutthroat populations in Yellowstone creeks soon came under siege from a different enemy—more dangerous even than brookies. This time, the barbarians involved lake trout...another invasive species. These fish are native to large bodies of water such as the Great Lakes. Someone—supposedly an angler—spilled a bucketful of lake trout (*Salvelinus namaycush*) into Yellowstone Lake. It wasn't until 1994 that the first lake trout appeared there, discovered where it did not belong.

Yellowstone Lake is the jewel of the Rockies—the largest freshwater mountain lake in North America. All the cutthroat streams in Yellowstone drain to Yellowstone Lake, which is where the juvenile cutties migrate to grow up. Adults spawn in tributaries such as Soda Butte Creek, then the young cutthroats begin their run to the lake in fall. There, they grow to maturity before returning to their spawning streams the following year.

After repelling the brook trout, cutthroats began disappearing from Soda Butte Creek once again. They declined precipitously as the invading lake trout gobbled them up, because few cuttie young survived to return and breed in creeks like Soda Butte. Not only did cutthroats decline, but so did nutrient cycling in the park's terrestrial ecosystems. Without cutties, land predators had fewer fish to eat— then their populations suffered. Causes and effects multiplied until pretty soon, ecological balances tumbled and instability reigned.

To counter the invasion by lake trout, boats deployed long gill nets and fish traps in Yellowstone Lake. These operations removed over 1.4 million lake trout over two years. The lake trout population decline allowed cutthroat numbers to increase in streams like Soda Butte Creek. Long-term balance, however, requires ongoing management and remains uncertain.

One fall afternoon in 1981, I watched a fly fisherman cast for cutthroats in Soda Butte Creek. I was on the trail of a party of interest that had gone missing for weeks, apparently hiding out in the rough mountain country that surrounded the creek twenty miles north. By now I had concerns that the wanted party may have become a gang, biding their time, getting their weapons ready for battle.

A few days before, I had left Butte, Montana, where my company sent me that September to conduct another environmental investigation. With my work completed there, I had several days available to find the perps before flying home. The rental car remained available, so I drove it south to Yellowstone, three-hours away.

I had been there before, for other reasons and purposes. This time I had a different mission—find the elusive missing party before all the fighting broke out. From Tower Ranger Station, I crossed the Yellowstone River and drove east through the Lamar Valley. It lay within the *High Elevation Valleys Ecoregion (17n)*, still part of the *Middle Rockies Ecoregion (17)*, where sagebrush steppe and grasslands dominated the floodplain. Except for riparian areas, much of the sagebrush steppe is devoid of trees offering panoramic vistas as far as the eye can see.

As I drove, strips of Douglas fir and lodgepole pine forest filled lower hillsides and moister drainages of the broadly rounded hills. They protected an understory of blue huckleberry, birchleaf spirea, elk sedge, pinegrass, and heart leaf arnica.

A handful of miles later, the road crossed the Lamar River and followed the right bank. The channel shortly swung south, and a half-dozen miles further, I came upon the river's confluence with its Soda Butte tributary. The road turned north, and I tracked the creek upstream. After pulling over on the shoulder just past the confluence, I reached the spot I described earlier, where the fisherman swirled flies on the water surface for cutthroats.

Beyond the creek, wide open meadows provided an extensive floodplain more than a mile wide. Bright greens, yellows, and browns covered the luscious plain in the early afternoon. I watched herds of bison and elk graze in the crystal-clear distance. There, Absaroka Mountains rose toward a cloudless sky. This was the high, forested, partially glaciated *Absaroka-Gallatin Volcanic Mountains Ecoregion (17i)*. There, rock outcrops, volcanic mudflows, and extensive glacial drift and colluvial deposits bordered the Lamar Valley.

A similar range towered above the road behind me, but the steep wall along the road blocked their view from creek level. These two ranges bordered the U-shaped Soda Butte valley between them where the creek flowed. Glaciers had formed the valley, and they remained too open and flat for the missing party I sought. I knew they would not hide out there on the wide plain.

Soda Butte Creek flowed wide as the road next to it, within low stable banks of grass and shrub willows. The Lamar River continued south while I followed Soda Butte Creek northward. Getting closer now, I thought. Here is where I would pick up the trail to my quarry.

The wide valley at the confluence shrank to half its size as I traveled northward. Steep slopes of the Absaroka mountains rose above both sides of the road, forming high ridgeback ranges. The road pointed north, and far ahead I noticed another range of high, dissected slopes. Snow covered their rugged peaks, which added another few thousand feet in elevation to the already mile-high level of the valley floor. Soon, I would reach that rugged terrain, ready to bushwhack into the high country to find what I had come for—surveillance of some outlaws…another wild bunch.

In this remote part of Yellowstone, I rarely saw another vehicle as I drove. Cooler air from the surrounding mountains drifted down the rugged slopes and side canyons through dark bands of evergreens and across exposed rock faces onto lower slopes. There I could see golden aspen shimmer in the cool breeze. Soda Butte Creek meandered for miles through it all. And the snowy peaks in the distance remained visible through my windshield as I drove onward.

Doubts soon intruded concerning my notion about how the pursuit would end high above the creek in the Absaroka range ahead. I didn't know why, but something nagged at me, involving what I knew about the missing characters' modus operandi. I'm overlooking something, I thought; what was it? Still, I did not wish to abort the mission based on a vague feeling. As a landscape investigator and eco-collector, I felt a call of duty to push on.

I continued tracking Soda Butte Creek northward. After crossing Pebble Creek, the road traveled above the floodplain on a steeper contour. Then, the valley suddenly narrowed as I entered Ice Box Canyon, with walls that rose sixteen hundred feet—so steep and looming that sunshine had trouble getting attention there.

Once out of Ice Box Canyon, the floodplain widened again, and I could see a line of serrated peaks topped the valley walls, and each ran parallel to the channel like a bleached spine with ribs. I could see their deeply fissured side canyons of firs and pines. Rough country with too many places to hide. The thought of searching such a labyrinth reminded me of boyhood snipe hunts—a fool's errand. And yet, my plan involved going off-trail at even higher elevations further ahead—well above the timberline.

Soon, the narrow creek landscape alternated between thick stands of evergreens and occasional low meadows. I studied the landscape while I drove, and the geology confirmed the possibility of finding the party I sought somewhere in all that ruggedness.

Sunlight glinted off the snow dappled peaks through my windshield and sparked a thought about what had bothered me earlier. Then I realized where I might actually find my missing quarry—and it did not include the steep slopes of the Absarokas after all.

Soda Butte Creek swerved east at the Wyoming-Montana border, and I followed it. A few miles later the creek swung south, away from the road, and became lost amid the Douglass firs and lodgepole pines. The road no longer ran near the creek, and within another mile, a dark-brown log structure straddled and blocked both lanes. I had reached the ranger station for the northeastern entrance gate to Yellowstone, at the far edge of the national park.

Snow-capped peaks surrounded the building—the same ones I had followed since leaving the Lamar River. Mineral Mountain rose behind the building on the left, and Republic Mountain dominated the right; both over ten-thousand feet. No other vehicles or people, the only movement a droopy flag on a pole that barely twitched. I eased the car up to the drive-through window and stopped.

A moment later, a friendly ranger in uniform appeared, and I began asking him questions about the group I sought. He and his associates had received no reports of them or their clan lurking about for months. He mentioned other mountainous areas where some of them liked to hangout further west in the park.

Too late in the day for heading there. I asked if anyone had seen them in the past among the rugged slopes nearby. He thought a moment, then mentioned that some had slipped through the area months ago on their way to their hideouts in the high country. When I asked about any trails from there, the ranger shook his head, but pointed behind the car. Less than a half-mile back, he said, I would find a spot on the shoulder wide enough to park, and I could bushwhack from there.

After pulling the car ahead, I made a U-turn and headed the way I just came. Down the road, I passed a tiny break between the thick border of evergreens, swung around and parked on the narrow shoulder next to it. I grabbed some gear and slipped down the road bank through the opening.

The landscape expanded beyond the trees into a strip of short grasses, dry and tawny-colored by this time in the fall. Nothing moved except for the desiccated tops of knee-high grasses swaying in the light breeze.

Across the flat area and far above, fingers of snow filled the steeper ravines on mountain slopes. Just what I had hoped; my hunch might be right. I carried an assortment of gear in my field vest because all sorts of mishaps can occur in rough high country at any time of the year, especially if you go solo in unfamiliar terrain. For that reason, whenever I entered a potentially hazardous landscape, I always took precautions—even for day hikes.

My vest served the same purpose as an old frontiersman's "possibles bag"—except it had tons more pockets. Into them went several camera lenses, a small first aid kit, and basic survival items like water purification tablets, flint firestarter, waterproof matches, a steel multi-tool and hunting knife. I kept a compass, whistle, flares, and energy bars in there also, along with a rain poncho, wool hat, nylon cord, and an aluminum thermal blanket folded thin as a wafer. Enough gear to make it through a few days if bad weather or an emergency came up, but lightweight for traveling.

Binoculars and a camera with telephoto lens hung off my belt in leather holsters, while a fanny pouch held a pair of water bottles. No matter the remote landscape, I always carried similar gear, and wore drab field clothes—no shiny objects or flashy colors that could trigger a nervous animal to flee or a grumpy one to attack.

But I had a hunch I might not need to trek into the rugged highlands. My idea suggested the wild gang might have had reasons to remain at lower elevations. Perhaps they still had a couple of weeks before they needed to move upslope into the highlands. If so, then I might find my missing party closer to creek level where tasty greens still thrived. Maybe there I would locate a group of them—bighorn sheep (*Ovis canadensis*).

During winter months, the sheep stayed above timberline in rugged ravines and alpine meadows, protected from winds, keeping warm with a thick double-layered coat. Specialized hooves enable them to grip the rock humans would need a rope to climb.

In summer months, the sheep descend into the valleys to graze and mate. But the snow that now hugged the peaks stopped hundreds of feet higher than usual. This suggested my elusive quarry might not have migrated yet up into the highest snowy reaches of the mountain ranges. Plenty of time remained for them to climb before the snowpack descended and blocked their access to the high country.

Perhaps I'd find them still in the lower meadows. Based on area size alone, my chances of finding a bighorn in Yellowstone were slim; one sheep per hundred acres equaled only five-hundred in a park larger than Delaware and Rhode Island combined. But I hoped to narrow the chances by factoring in bighorn habits, ecological requirements, and seasonal conditions.

The Rocky Mountain bighorn is the largest wild sheep inhabiting North America. A large ram may weigh as much as a refrigerator and stand half as tall at the shoulder. Mature males spend most of the year in bachelor groups of three to five individuals. They roam the high country protected from predators like wolves and cougars.

Males are not territorial but stay apart from bands of females and young sheep until November. Until then, the rams are the best of buddies, chomping on low vegetation in subalpine meadows and rocky outcrops.

By late fall, the urge to mate turns the rams into warriors that fight against each other. They hang around females, assessing their harem potential. Epic battles soon erupt for breeding rights with ewes, who collect around victors, waiting for breeding duty over the coming weeks.

In battle, rams charge each other at a gallop, their foreheads crashing together with a stupendous crack that can echo off the rugged slopes further than a mile away. These battles may last all day before one ram concedes and backs down. Then the winner with his group of ewes goes off on a mountain honeymoon.

Bighorn spend summers in the valleys, then move into the cirques and cols high in the mountains to pass the winters. But now in September, rams had no urge for battles and the boys would still enjoy hanging with peers, chewing their cuds together.

I headed across the open area toward a stand of evergreens. A few yards later, the grasses ended at a patch of gravel less than a stone's throw across. Devoid of vegetation and filled with loose gravel and cobble, the patch continued on my left and right. It resembled a gravel road with scattered pieces of woody debris on top—dead branches, a few logs, old brush here and there.

But I noticed scour marks along the edges of the gravel, and realized they marked an abandoned channel of Soda Butte Creek, a relict of an earlier time. The flow once followed this route but had changed course, leaving the channel bed and debris behind. I still did not know where the present flowing channel lay, but I had found its tracks.

The lack of any vegetation in the gravel bed told me it probably carried flow earlier that year, during the spring floods. Any earlier, last year's herbaceous seeds would have sprouted and seeded by now. Annuals would show signs of dying and withered perennials would remain anchored in place for another year of growth. I found none of these clues.

Directly across the old channel, thick trees blocked the way, so I turned and followed the dry creek bed to my right. Soda Butte Creek likely shifted back and forth over the flat terrain at least annually, depending on flow volumes. Here, the floodplain had plenty of room to twist and turn as much as nature required.

Stream and river floodplains that wind through U-shaped valleys vary in width. These flat areas are called alluvial valleys, places where meadows live, where shrub willows dig their roots into the banks and nutritious grasses run wild across the landscape.

Glaciers ground down the hard mountain rock to form the broad valleys of Soda Butte and the Lamar River. With the glaciers came meltwater, and it poured through the valleys cutting, shaping, and relocating channels that meandered across the flat valley floor.

Meltwaters and river flows deposited sediment and gravels washed down from the upper slopes. They settled across these valleys, building alluvial soils full of minerals and nutrition to support vegetation and wildlife.

The action of flowing water as it shapes landscapes into geological landforms is one of the most highly dynamic processes in nature...and it never stops. Melting snows provide three-quarters of the annual flow in Rocky Mountain streams like Soda Butte. The dry streambed I walked in was only temporary and therefore considered an active channel, rather than an abandoned one. Flow will come back, I thought, probably next June right after snowpacks thawed.

I followed the old drainageway along the stand of spruce and fir until it ended and the landscape opened into a wide prairie. It resembled a ripened grain field, but no trail wound through it, nor evidence that anyone had ever been there. Unsure which direction to take through the waist-high grasses, I headed toward a large mound in the distance covered in mature pines. I waded my way forward, pushing aside the tall stems on the less crunchy soil compared with the gravel bed. The prairie flats appeared a quarter mile wide and twice as long.

Halfway there, I noticed movement off to my right. Something running. Several things dashed through the tall grasses, nearly hidden. I whipped the field glasses off my hip like an officer under fire with his weapon. They revealed a herd of pronghorn riled by my presence. Almost as uncommon as bighorn in Yellowstone, I watched these ungulates bolt away.

After a moment, the herd of twenty stopped and turned their muzzles toward me. They stared with heads high—sniffing, assessing, working it out. Males displayed their unique black antlers that stuck straight into the air like ancient scimitars. Tan and white coats stood out sharply on legs mostly invisible in the tall grass.

I thought of similar scenes on the plains of Africa, where herds of impala behave much the same, though a completely unrelated species. Convergent evolution had produced similar anatomical forms from different precursor species. Similar environmental conditions and ecological niches in dissimilar landscapes had caused natural selection to produce comparable bodies, behaviors, and physiologies.

Pronghorn (*Antilocapra americana*), though, are unique to North America, since they occur nowhere else. Their heads carry horns instead of antlers, composed of a bony core covered by a sheath made of a stiff hair-like material. Antlers get shed annually, but horns do not. And pronghorn headgear makes them the only animals in the world that have branched horns they shed. The outer sheath falls off every fall and then grows back in the summer. As a member of the family

Giraffoidea, the pronghorn's closest living relatives are the giraffes and okapi of Africa. It seems their precursors evolved there before the continents drifted apart 200 million years ago.

Not only can this animal run long distances, but it is also one of the fastest runners in the Western hemisphere. Pronghorns can sustain a gallop for a half-dozen miles at a constant speed of sixty miles per hour. Cheetahs cannot do that, though they can sprint faster for up to a quarter mile before exhaustion takes over.

Some animals in the herd ahead began grazing, and I moved toward them cautiously while keeping my eyes on the group. They ran when I violated their escape distance again—the gap length between us they would tolerate before fleeing. Most wild mobile species have an inherited escape distance, which benefits one to know while out on the landscape. If you invade it, the animal will usually enter fight-or-flight mode...charge or flee. It is not wise to take the risk if you are not prepared for the consequences.

The herd had stopped again and faced me once they gained enough distance. I continued walking their way and soon the animals began running once more. Just normal pronghorn behavior—run a hundred yards, then stop, turn, and observe potential predators.

As much as I enjoyed trailing the pronghorns this way, I knew they would never let me get any closer. It would not help me locate any bighorn, for the open plain was not their habitat. I turned back toward the pine covered hillock across the plain, and when I reached its base, thick brush along with downed timbers and evergreens promised a tangled climb to the top. No guarantee I would have a view from there anyway.

I glanced at the sun—getting low. To estimate how much time before it set, I extended my palm in front of my eyes, fingers parallel to the horizon. My index finger rested just below the sun, and I counted the number of fingers between the sun and the horizon. Each finger meant fifteen minutes, and four of them showed...just over an hour until the sun would set. Not enough time to waste on the climb and back.

Instead, I hiked around the base through the tall grasses, keeping the trees on my left. I heard my boots scrape more heavily on the ground—a head's-up that the gravel content had increased. The actual flowing channel was surely not far ahead.

The pines thinned out, and soon I heard faint sounds of flowing water, but the creek wasn't visible from the trees until a few moments later. Only then did I have glimpses of it through the leaves, and the noise level had increased. Not far now.

The tree line ended, and the prairie floodplain ran wide again. I stopped the length of several slingshots away from Soda Butte Creek, watching it against the far bank plunge and dash against boulders in a steady rumble. I could not see the water's edge closest to me because at this distance, the drop-off there was too high above the water level.

More gravel, less vegetation lay between me and the near bank, and the ground sloped gently toward the stream. I moved a dozen yards closer, then froze, my heart thumping wildly when I could now fully see below the near bank down to the water's edge.

The bank dropped vertically a dozen feet. But a narrow ledge jutted out over the rushing water halfway down. Five bighorn rams lay resting on that ledge. Four of them stood up and watched me quizzically with their grayish coats and jutting horns—two adults and two juveniles.

The other ram still lay on the ledge but turned its head briefly and gazed at me passively. The breath went out of me when I saw his great twisting horns...more than double the size of the other rams. Both his horns circled the outsides of its scarred face, the tip of one horn gone, sheared off no doubt in ram-to-ram combat a long time ago. Here was a grizzled veteran of uncountable mountain battles, and in another week or so would begin bashing some more heads.

I grabbed the camera from my holster and swung it up, focusing the telephoto lens on the thick neck and head. Digital cameras did not yet exist, but the click of the shutter and whir of the mechanized film-advance seemed loud in the still air. The bighorn turned its head back toward the river—*click-whirr, click-whirr.*

I zoomed in, about to press the shutter release again, when in the viewfinder I saw the massive ram horns swing toward me once again. Oh, yes, great portrait, I thought to myself. While I composed the next shot, the ram swung his horns directly toward me. Even better, thank you, I breathed to myself, feeling the surge of an endorphin thrill.

The shutter button went down and another click and whir sounded. Then the animal rose, climbed smoothly off the ledge and up the steep bank, where he took several steps toward me. Here was the boss, the alpha male facing me down, massive compared with the others. My thrill plummeted to a chill—the ram now stood on my level, just twenty yards away, scrutinizing me.

We faced off like gunslingers at a shootout, so close I could see his brown pupils, an old tear in a horn, and a battle scar near his ear. His gonads hung menacingly, as though he was ready to impregnate an entire valley of fertile females. I felt a gulp in my throat, and my arm and camera slid down to my side and I holstered my camera, ready to bolt and high-tail it off the prairie.

His body rippled with muscle—a living battle tank covered with gray fur trimmed in white around the mouth, rump, and belly. Horns thick as battering rams, which they were, weighing more than all the bones in its body combined. They were hard enough to withstand a rival crashing into them at twenty miles per hour...or a pesky ecologist disturbing its peace.

The ram held its head high with chin elevated, a challenge directed to me the way a disrespected gangster might. His muzzle pointed toward my chest, and he carried hundreds of pounds of solid mass that could launch me further than a horse kick.

This face-off wouldn't last long, I knew. To show I did not pose a threat, I eased my head sideways to avoid looking him in the eye, but continued watching peripherally. A quick glance confirmed the absence of trees to climb or a boulder cluster to run behind.

"Steady, now." I spoke in a casual, even-toned voice loud enough for him to hear me. He watched me impassively, appearing completely unconcerned—no ear twitching, blinking, foot stamping, head-nodding. The other rams still cocked their heads my way, waiting. The big one facing me, though, clearly appeared in charge and master of his domain.

He waited. I sensed he wanted me to move. As deliberately as a retreating dueler, I nodded, then took three slow steps backward. I heard the gravel crunch and wondered if he took it as defiance. But nothing; no signs of snorting, growling or stamping feet that would signify ram aggression.

When I took another step backward, he turned and calmly walked back to the bank. From there, he climbed down to his ledge and laid back down in the spot where I had first seen him. He faced the river and contentedly resumed chewing the regurgitated cud that I interrupted. The ram had assessed me, decided I was nothing but a curious anomaly in his environment, not worth wasting any more time on; he had more important matters to chew over.

Tension evaporated; the river flowed; I stood amid majestic wildlife in their own habitat. A sense of peace surrounded me. I turned around and hiked back with the sunshine on my shoulder. Rocky Mountain high.

The Lure of Eco-Engineering

With a quick twist and tuck, I secured the ribbon-flagging to the elderberry branch using a double half-hitch. I started to move ahead through the marsh, but as my left foot lifted, the boot stayed mired in the muck with my socked foot hanging in mid-air. Instantly it joggled me off-balance. Accompanying the sucking sound, a loud grunt broke the surrounding solitude—my own voice of frustration.

To recover my balance, I put my foot down on the muddy surface— where it immediately sank out of sight in the wet ooze. For a moment, I steadied myself on my other leg and the hip-high steel soil auger in my hand. It had a shaft with a T-bar for a handle at the top and a twelve-inch-long open bit on the other end. I used it like a cane to steady myself while extracting the boot and soggy appendage. Then I hobbled with them to drier ground a few yards ahead to clean things up.

I wore heavy rubber barn-boots with lugged soles, which covered my calves. Without laces binding them to my feet, the suction trapped the boot. Usually this wasn't a problem, but this mud was especially dense with clay and clenched the boot like a rusty bear trap.

If the terrain expected was mostly uplands with dry ground such as fields, woods, and rocky slopes, I usually wore waterproof leather boots with laces well above the ankles. Breathable and rugged with root- gripping soles.

But where I was certain to encounter flooded ground or would cross deeper streams, the rubber barn-boots were best. Just as tough as leathers, but they didn't breathe, sometimes resulting in moist feet. Both, however, protected ankles from sharp rocks, thorns and ground-dwelling creatures like scorpions and snakes.

My teeth clenched as I worked my way to the water's edge where the wetland ended. This soggy mishap would slow my progress, and I still had thirty acres to inspect and flag before the sun set—an ordinary day in the life of this field biologist. The reason I was out there was to investigate all the wetland boundaries on a large vacant property.

A land development company wanted to construct roads and buildings, and needed the delineation performed to get construction permits. Such boundary demarcations required specific scientific procedures, and my project workload as a consulting ecologist over the past ten years had included many of these types of field efforts.

Conducting an official "wetland delineation" involved walking the landscape and flagging areas where uplands changed to wetlands. While cruising, one had to identify functional connections simultaneously among the many indicators possible. A competent delineator needed an ability to decipher the landscape effectively.

The Lure of Eco-Engineering

This required tracking down facts and evidence the way a detective followed crime clues. I had become a sort of eco-detective, a nature sleuth looking for answers in all the wild places. When your senses are fully engaged on the landscape, they can tell you much about what happens around you—on the ground, in the air, within the water and under the soil. Often, changes in the vegetation get noticed first, but evidence of hydrology or soil conditions can tell stories about what is going on in an ecosystem.

Other clues involved the terrain elevation compared with other nearby landforms. Or whether the slope faced a particular direction and received more sunshine or rain annually. And what was the direction of prevailing winds, amount of shade, ambient temperatures, and the kinds of rocks present? Questions needed answering, either before going afield or while on the spot.

Besides direct encounters, tracks, scat, nests, burrows, bones, and sounds provide evidence of animal inhabitants. Deciphering such clues suggests the kinds of wildlife present, and therefore the types and conditions of habitats to expect. In addition, patterns of normal weather, the season at hand, and climate factors needed interpreting, as well as site history, activities of humans, and geographical position by latitude and longitude.

Rugged terrain and dense brush often hindered efforts for delineating boundaries and traversing landscapes, which is why a machete usually hung on my belt. After years of battling sharply spiked thickets in wild areas, some of my field assistants started calling me "Brambles." They said it was because when our machetes dulled, they appreciated my penchant for bashing through extra-thorny brush like a charging moose to open a path. Or maybe it was because I was a stickler for getting the data and could get prickly about it. Either way, the moniker seemed to fit.

Land properties large and small often presented nearly impenetrable conditions with walls of vicious thorns from multiflora rose, greenbrier, blackberry, raspberries, and dewberries. These could shred a field vest like an angry wolverine. Sometimes it took two or three vests to complete a delineation on an undeveloped twenty-mile transmission or highway corridor project, or a three-hundred-acre parcel of densely tangled vegetation.

Field clothes also took brutal assaults from the weather and seasons—heat, humidity, pouring rain, snow, sleet, wind, chewing insects and bird poop. My vest served as a shield, and if I had to make a choice, underwear would get left behind before my field vest. Maybe I'll wear it to my funeral someday.

Often my time on the landscape required making my way alone in a tract far from a road, though on many other projects, I required a field team to cover a site. Navigation depended on old-school skills like orienteering using compass, maps, land features and dead reckoning—since handheld radios, GPS units, and cell phones were unavailable for most of those early excursions.

Many times, I had to drive a field truck to where a lonely road ended. Then I'd shift into four-wheel drive and bounce over the terrain a mile or so to the starting point. From there I trudged on foot to complete the work, even if the weather raged cold and blustery like a three-dog night.

Usually, I spent the day on foot, having to rely on my navigation and field abilities. Much easier having a useful map with topographic contours, but often I didn't have one. Many times, I started early on a sunny morning and by afternoon found myself in a downpour or blizzard far from the truck.

On one particular occasion, I received a call for an urgent field investigation that required I leave immediately and fly six-hundred miles to Sault Ste. Marie, at the northernmost tip of Michigan, in the *Rudyard Clay Plain Ecoregion (50z)* within the *Northern Lakes* and *Forests Ecoregion (50)*. The landscape is nearly completely flat with a few low beach ridges and sandy ground moraines.

Vegetation covered the site's fringes with hardwood-conifer forest, including firs, spruces and hemlocks. Northern hardwood forests contained sugar maple (*Acer saccharum*), American beech (*Fagus grandifolia*), American basswood (*Tilia americana*), and yellow birch (*Betula alleghaniensis*). The main ecotype I needed to investigate involved a complex of poorly drained wooded wetlands and shrub swamps of gray alder (*Alnus incana*) and willows (*Salix spp*).

This large wild property needed investigating a few miles from the historical Soo Locks, which allowed ships to navigate between lakes Superior and Huron.

I arrived to conduct a wetland delineation on a cloudy winter day with freezing rain and bone-chilling temperatures. The nasty weather, project urgency, and the site's remoteness converged to produce a suite of harsh conditions that made a field investigation nearly impossible. Dense sleet fouled my vision and windshield as I drove the rental vehicle from the airport and into the countryside.

I trudged across fields and mixed woods at the site, while snow fell in huge flakes. Eventually, the terrain slope dropped, and I paused where it flattened out; an area where I sensed a wetland might lie under the snow. Visibility had dropped to twenty yards. My first clue that I stood in a wetland appeared when I scraped away a three-inch snow layer and found solid ice rather than frozen soil.

With the steel auger, I chopped through it and bored a hole to sample the underlying soil. Below the inch of ice lay muddy soil, allowing me to twist the bit-end down to a foot and a half. The auger bit, known as a "Dutch auger," looked like a foot-tall soda can with two sides cut out and the bottom came to a sharp point rather than a flat base. The remaining two sides comprised heavy steel with sharpened edges for twisting into the ground. Other times, I used a "bucket auger" with a solid cylinder, but the Dutch version made it easier to extract soil cores except in sand or gravel.

I pulled the auger up with the soggy sample and examined it. After removing my gloves, I rubbed lumps of soil layers between my thumb and fingers to assess their textures. As my fingers numbed from the cold, deciphered the soil color patterns and recorded other data as government protocols required. Land development projects like this one needed wetland delineations conducted in order to get permits before proceeding.

The protocols included evaluating a site's soils, vegetation and hydrology—the amount of water available. I found positive indicators for confirming soil and hydrology criteria, including evidence of a seasonal high water table that covered the surface during the growing season. These indicators included clay texture, iron mottles, gley colors and sulfidic odor. The ice below the snow meant water covered the ground before it froze. Another hydrology clue.

All the clues told me anaerobic conditions prevailed in the soil that developed under long-term saturation by water. This confirmed the hydrology criteria as positive. In addition, water-staining showed on exposed tree roots and trunks in this lower portion of the landscape, which takes years of inundation to develop.

Identifying the species of trees and shrubs during winter did not present a problem, for it was routine no matter the season. In winter, twig forms, bark, habitat, branch shapes, and growth patterns provided clues. However, on that blustery day a few miles from Sault Ste. Marie, lower parts of herbaceous plants lay under the snow cover and required brushing away.

Ecologists consider wetland species hydrophytic, meaning they need wet or moist conditions to live. The species of Juncus, sedges, and rushes I noted met the vegetation requirement for a wetland. And so did the trees, including silver and red maple, green ash, tamarack, and pin oak, along with shrubs such as buttonbush, holly, and red-osier dogwood. Now I had confirmation of all the necessary indicators of soil, vegetation, and hydrology. Delineating a wetland required marking the upland- wetland boundary with ribbon flagging hung on branches or perennial plants about every hundred feet.

After several hours, I completed flagging the wetland boundary while the snow continued to fall heavily. By the time I approached the truck, it had reached my knees.

For several years, wetland delineations became a significant part of my fieldwork, along with other environmental and natural resource projects. I never knew upon stepping into a landscape or ecoregion what I might find. Even if I had recently been there before, something differed the next time I arrived. The challenge then involved finding the cause and assessing an ecosystem's stability and productivity.

Besides field assessments and investigations, I gradually moved beyond them into habitat restorations. Many of those took place on wild landscapes and included ecosystems degraded by human activity. I became interested in improving plant and animal habitats...places where life could thrive on its own.

It wasn't that I had hopes of saving the planet—either from humanity or nature itself. That level of hubris never seemed useful, for I knew Earth could fully take care of itself. If four billion years of planetary self- management isn't sufficient to convince one that nature has things under control, then nothing can. Living nature always adapts...though not necessarily within the time span or manner in which humans prefer.

Many people these days desire a subdued nature, one they can control. They expect nature to respond favorably to human attempts at interfering in its business like tinkering with the Earth's climate cycles. Whether driven by ignorant, short-sighted bureaucrats or a vast herd of emotional environmentalists, neither science nor anyone can predict the impacts on regional ecologies from attempts to manage the world's climate.

Demanding entire societies around the globe to restructure in order to save the planet from humankind is the ultimate in irrational and arrogant thinking. Too few facts have ever been available to support such a wholesale revamping of the planet, because unintended ecological consequences are always likely to occur.

In my experience, major human attempts to control nature usually produce adverse results no one expected. Because we can, we have tried to tame nature with dams, straightened rivers, built in floodplains, drained wetlands, farmed monocultures, introduced invasive species, over-pumped aquifers, erected wind turbines and power lines that kill birds by the millions. I have seen many of these environmental consequences, measured the effects onsite, and implemented practical corrective actions that accommodated nature's requirements. They involved difficult work requiring more objectivity than a mere passion for change.

Just throwing our technologies to control nature is dangerous and fraught with uncertainties. We never seem to know beforehand what to expect when we do it, nor recognize all the past failures from such activities. So why would anyone think humans are advanced enough to implement effective planetary-level projects to control the climate? Hubris. Such arrogance masks the reality in our midst.

But regarding reality, the planet does not have a "fever," nor need our intervention by untrained eco-first responders who are long on passion and short on competence. Such intrusive mega-actions are doomed to failure no matter who promotes them. As Ayn Rand said, "You can avoid reality, but you cannot avoid the consequences of avoiding reality."

Many dominant complex processes determine weather, atmospheric temperatures, and climate patterns. Among these are sunspot activities, moon waxing and waning, tides, El Nino, La Nina, ocean currents, jet streams, cloud movements, water vapor cycling, concentrations of carbon, oxygen, methane, and CO_2, the sun's tilt, Earth's orbit and seasonal patterns, day lengths, solar irradiance. and volcanism.

They all have synergistic effects and consequences. Climatologists and others who insist greenhouse gases like carbon dioxide, methane, nitrous oxide and water vapor from fossil fuels are the primary causal agents in global climate changes overlook basic physics. It is absurd to believe that greenhouse gas elements that form less than 0.04 percent of the atmosphere are the prime factors that control the temperature on the Earth, when there are so many other natural variables contributing to climate, all interacting simultaneously.

No one, including any competent scientist with a computer model or not, understands more than a tiny fraction yet of how any of the assorted climate processes work together or cause long-term temperature and weather patterns—regardless if they come from anthropogenic activities or natural events.

Today's climate change "warmests" focus on anthropogenic effects of greenhouse gas emissions beginning with the industrial revolution in the 1800s. A giant horsefly in the global warming ointment is the proponents' lack of perspective. Their context is limited to an insignificant fraction of time—the 200-year period of the industrial revolution. The proper context is at least the past 600 million years, which they ignore. Scientific analyses of ice cores show that over that extensive span of time, CO_2 and global temperatures have fluctuated up and down. But they do so independently of each other—there is no relationship trend. In other words, no correlation exists between CO_2 and temperatures, and also no causal relationship has ever been documented by scientists worthy of the title.

Frequently over the long-term, temperatures increased when CO_2 went down, and vice versa. In fact, for the past 2.6 million years, temperatures have risen and fallen within a very narrow range between 12.4-14.2°C; insignificant. Currently, the global temperature is near the upper limit of that range at 14.2°C. But for most of the past 600 million years, it has averaged around 24°C, a 70 percent difference. So, today's global temperature is at its lowest, not highest.

Over that same period, the data shows CO_2 declined from 7,000 parts per million to today's level of only 411 ppm—again at the bottom of its range. Despite such high levels of 24°C over Earth's history, life continued to thrive and evolution persisted, adding untold new species and orders inhabiting ecoregions worldwide.

When the entire span of time on Earth is considered, it is clear temperatures have risen far higher than today's for hundreds of millions of years, long before humans inhabited the Earth. The same trend is true for CO_2 levels, which declined from thousands of parts per million to today's measly 411 ppm, a difference of 1,600 percent.

Warmests love to show graphs of how CO_2 and other greenhouse gases have risen along with global temperatures since the 1800s. While true, they ignore the greater span of time that shows both levels have remained at their overall lowest levels in Earth's history for the past 2.6 million years.

Context is everything, and warmests tend to only select time spans that fit their narrative of anthropogenic global warming. By ignoring a proper perspective, climate change warming proponents push mass hysteria that serves socio-political agendas but not the scientific method.

When starting data collection at the lowest level of a range, any increase in trend may seem significant, but actually may not be within the larger context of extended time. With today's CO2 level near a record low, the increase over the past two centuries is trivially small compared to changes in the geological history of life on Earth. With no proven significant relationship between global temperature and CO2, burning fossil fuels cannot legitimately be claimed to cause global warming.

The ignorant are often not aware of how uninformed they are. For the most irrational of the ignorant, the sky is always falling. But nature has more important work than fulfilling our emotional preferences and desires about its climates. As Charlotte Bronte wrote in Jane Eyre, "the mountain will never be brought to Mahomet, so all you can do is to aid Mahomet to go to the mountain." In other words, you and your desires are not the center of the universe, and sometimes, you must accept and accommodate the universe and nature, rather than vice versa.

I wasn't so concerned with imagined dystopian futures as I was with making homes in the present for creatures to flourish in sustainable ecosystems. For me, the restoration work involved landscape maintenance on a regional scale—a more inclusive version of Habitat for Humanity that included an ecoregion's wide diversity of inhabitants—more like "Habitats for Life."

For some time, a notion had occurred to me that if I built a habitat or restored it properly, lifeforms would blossom in diversity and wellbeing. It could also lead to improved human lives because of our innate connectedness with nature. In providing physical enhancements at the regional landscape level, intangible values could follow—such as re-connecting people's instinctive emotional attachments with nature.

We came from nature one way or another and will depend upon its realm while we are here. What remains of us will continue forever as part of the great cycling of matter. By exploring landscapes, we can remain rational stewards of our environments while embracing our personal connections with them. But it takes more than incomplete computer models and a belief system. Factual knowledge from many disciplines, on-the- ground experience, and proven techniques are required.

My collection of ecosystems expanded with my work as a private consultant, along with a professional workload that increasingly focused on restorations. My earliest included shoreline stabilizations on the Chesapeake Bay. For these, I began recommending installations of emergent plants and sea grasses adapted to brackish waters.

Many areas of the nearly twelve-thousand miles of the bay's shoreline had eroded from storm waves, poor land use practices, and decades of ship and powerboat wakes. Crumbling wharves and banks had cut further and further landward, washing millions of tons of upland soils into the bay waters. As a result, native seagrass beds below the banks had become decimated in the Chesapeake Bay within the *Chesapeake-Pamlico Lowlands and Tidal Marshes Ecoregion (63b)*, a subset of the *Middle Atlantic Coastal Plain Ecoregion (63)*.

Eroded soils silted river deltas, created shallow bars, and brought toxins to the bay's living resources. This occurred not only in urban-suburban shoreline areas but also in rural properties next to the Bay.

Customary practices to protect the shoreline's banks had traditionally involved engineered solutions, including steel pilings and concrete revetments, or riprap composed of light gray and white limestone rocks thrown together randomly over a slope. Riprap often washed away and limestone is unnatural to the coastal plain ecoregion. The nearest quarry lay seventy miles away in the Appalachian foothills of the Piedmont. Worse, these fully artificial structural revetments often failed, and I began looking into using more natural and enduring approaches that would protect banks, adjacent lands, and submerged grass beds.

This focus on natural restoration required merging practical ecology with engineering principles. That meant involving certain specialists—hydrologists, geotechnical and materials technicians, civil engineers, as well as drafters, construction professionals and design layout staffs. Problem was, most engineers knew little about science, especially biology and ecology. And I knew only a rudimentary amount of engineering. Essentially, we did not speak the same language, and approached solving landscape problems from very different directions.

I knew it was going to be up to me to educate the engineers about applied ecology once I educated myself about engineering practices and principles. My course was clear—I'd need to become an ecological engineer. Fine, but there weren't any of those back in 1990 when I wanted to combine the disciplines in my consulting practice.

Besides myself, most environmental scientists knew little about practical engineering then, and eco-engineering was not a recognized discipline. Plus, no guidelines existed on integrating ecological principles with those of civil engineering.

It wasn't until three years later that the National Research Council defined ecological engineering as "...the design of sustainable ecosystems that integrate human society with its natural environment for the benefit of both." That fit perfectly with what I had already been doing in my work. Eco-engineering combines research from both theoretical and applied ecology, as well as civil engineering principles.

Civil engineers usually specify sowing grass seeds in the uplands around their structures, then hope they grow without washing away in heavy rains. In addition, once installed, the artificial structures do not grow, reproduce, or repair themselves, though they do erode, rust, breakdown, catch fire and blow up.

The eco-engineer, however, has to deal with living systems that change constantly, and designing their improvements becomes more complicated. Plants grow and die, logs, root wads, and organic materials decompose, weather changes cause biological responses. Food and resources fluctuate with landscape conditions.

For these reasons, the number of variables and the dynamic nature of landscapes requires an ability to evaluate and implement solutions based on a wide variety of science disciplines, in addition to engineering. Even today, eco-engineering is young compared to other engineering disciplines—and it is growing fast into an exciting new field.

When I began treading the eco-engineering path, I knew it wouldn't be easy for me, since it required a steep new learning curve. In addition, I would need to convince engineers they did not always possess the best answers for improving the sustainability of certain landscapes. By far, that was the most difficult hurdle that needed clearing.

Civil engineers I worked with could see and touch the structures they built. It was easy to conduct maintenance tests for structural integrity, wear and tear, performance. But created or restored ecological systems involve natural processes that are often hidden, and therefore of little interest to engineers because they did not have training in sciences like biology and practical ecology. Their focus, I surmised, was always on solving people problems in structural ways, but letting the "bugs and bunnies" fend for themselves.

As long as their structures remained intact and functional, engineers remained contented. The proof of success lay in how well structures met their designed purpose as a bridge, building, highway or dam. That didn't inhibit me from pressing forward with naturalized restorations. I had seen too many over- engineered projects breakdown because they could not sustain themselves against nature. Ongoing maintenance costs frequently exceeded initial design and construction budgets, which hampered funding for new civil works projects that were critical to municipalities, counties, and states.

What I needed from engineering I gained through on-the-job experience, field restoration work, training courses and personal landscape investigations. Where I found opportunities, I convinced our company engineers to include natural materials in their project designs.

As a project manager, I had control of design plan development for the projects I managed. Together with my role as a senior scientist, I gradually developed restoration design plans in collaboration with our engineers. Early on, they were skeptical about the merits of using natural materials for stabilizing streams and riverbanks. Most engineers, though, needed convincing that enough restoration projects were available in the marketplace to justify a shift in company services.

That prompted me to network and gumshoe the marketplace myself to secure funding contracts. Within a few months, I had secured a few, including one with a budget of a million dollars. Soon, I began working on several restoration projects involving natural designs for both shoreline and inland sites. The natural methods proved themselves functional in the field. They worked as designed and were cost-effective because nature maintained them without costly maintenance budgets to worry about. We weren't taming nature; we were restoring ecosystem health.

Soon, I had a team of engineers that could help me turn our construction drawings into reality on the landscapes. For my company's shoreline bank stabilization projects in the Chesapeake Bay, we now installed seagrass beds in the waters below steep eroded banks. The submerged grass beds worked well with naturalized bank protection techniques. These natural beds of plants are crucial for the Bay's ecology and had nearly disappeared because of poor land use practices.

Submerged aquatic vegetation like sago pondweed, eel grass, wild celery, and widgeon grass improves water quality by reducing erosion, trapping loose sediment, and absorbing pollutants. During photosynthesis, underwater grasses release oxygen into the water, which aquatic animals need to survive in the dissolved form. They also serve as cover and habitat for vulnerable young fish and crabs and provide food for migrating waterfowl.

For stabilizing banks, my eco-engineering designs relied upon a combination of structural components and plant materials to grow a dense stand of vegetation to create a living wall to protect streambanks and shorelines.

Sometimes for the structural components, I eliminated traditional concrete revetments in favor of long rolls of compressed coconut hull fibers stacked up the gently graded bank slope. After inserting willows and other fibrous plants into the dense rolls, the banks grew out and remained stable.

On other sites, we buried live branch cuttings of selected brushy species into benches dug on the banks. Projects where only living materials were used without rocks, artificial, or manufactured structures involved "bioengineering," which is a subset of ecoengineering. Foot-high layers of live shrub branches were often set on the benches.

Then, excavators backfilled the benches with soil, leaving the brush facing the channel sticking out. These grew into thick green mats covering the banks. I tried a variety of natural methods, and they worked not only until the vegetation became established, but still thrive after many years.

During the 1990s, my restoration interests expanded to include wetlands, marshes, forest restorations and pond ecosystem constructions. Gradually, the works also included retrofitting dry grass-covered stormwater management basins comprising several acres. Standard practices routinely called for such ponds on sites under construction to capture muddy sediment from runoff.

These stormwater management facilities prevent stormflows from flooding neighborhoods and causing infrastructure damage. In urban-suburban areas, the extensive amounts of impervious surfaces—streets, asphalt lots, roofs—prevent rainfall from infiltrating naturally into the soil and moderating runoff flows.

Engineers had been designing and installing stormwater basins for decades, invariably with structural materials or mowed grass banks and flat bottoms. Often, old basins deteriorated or failed completely over the years—outlets clogged, water level control structures stopped working and banks eroded. Over time, municipalities often ignored managing such basins for various reasons, and the neglect degraded the engineered mechanisms.

Typically, a few inches or feet of water remained from storms but became stagnant and polluted because the outlets no longer worked. Residents began tossing their yard waste, junk, and vehicles over the banks among the invasive weeds. Retrofitting was a way to convert these dysfunctional eyesores to diverse, sustainable, and thriving wetlands. In other cases, I designed a series of sequential wetlands that consecutively cleansed wastewater from leaking treatment plants and piping systems.

In these treatment wetlands, water flowed between cells where each one performed different functions. Some contained various marshes, shrub wetlands, and swamps with trees. A mosaic of special emergent plants promoted natural uptake of various waste toxins. Not only did these designed wetlands provide watery habitats for wildlife and the ecological community, but people in the neighborhood could also appreciate a natural gem in their midst.

Larger ecosystems usually offer greater stability because energy pathways and functional diversity are more numerous and complex. An energy or food web contains many ecological niches, and the more niches, the more stability an ecosystem usually exhibits. For this reason, some of the restoration projects I undertook occupied thirty acres of various wetlands and uplands, and others encompassed a dozen or more.

But not all involved large ecosystems. In 1992, I volunteered to design a two-acre freshwater wetland on the grounds of a county park set in the Piedmont countryside. The three-hundred-acre property was free to the public to enjoy the woods, meadows, hiking trails, and a small lake.

Children needed a place to learn about marshes, the county said. I volunteered to undertake the project for creating a wetland on their land. Because the most important factor in creating a wetland is confirming a reliable source and amount of water for the wetland type involved, I did a field study and found what I needed.

The design plan I offered converted a vacant field near a pond into a wetland with a boardwalk. It included log water level controls and meandering waterways. Construction finished a year later, and soon the vegetation grew robust, and student field trips became routine. The state environmental agency paid a visit and gave the site a high sustainability rating even after thirty years of operating.

Size never mattered to me, for I saw function and value in ecosystems of all sizes. Besides restoring sites involving many acres, I wasn't above taking on even smaller projects than the created county wetland.

In 1999, an opportunity arose to create a freshwater pond on a narrow barrier island off the Florida coast in the *Southern Coastal Plain Ecoregion (75), Southwestern Florida Flatwoods Ecoregion (75c)*. With deep sandy soils, this area once supported forest vegetation consisting of slash pine, longleaf pine, cabbage palm, and live oak species. Saw palmetto, gallberry, and such grasses as bluestems and wiregrass characterized the understory before dense development took over the island.

While natural saltwater ponds and lagoons were once common in such landscapes, freshwater ones were not. They required special conditions to form naturally, and those conditions had never occurred on the island. If any ever existed on this or adjacent islands, they were long gone—paved over or carved up by boat canals eighty years earlier.

Regardless of the history and constraints, the property owner wanted a permanent freshwater pond on his island property located a three-minute walk to Tampa Bay on one side, or the Gulf of Mexico on the other. It wasn't something I had done before, but decided to take on the challenge.

Success depended on keeping salt intrusion out of the pond at all costs. Barrier island ecosystems exist where they do because of ocean conditions, deep sands, and rainfall activity. Storm surges of wind-driven waves and high water levels control maximum elevations on coastal islands. The low, sandy landscape is prone to flooding, which submerges the islands. During hurricanes, for example, shallow inland bodies of water get filled with salty seawater, which would severely impact or destroy any freshwater ecosystem.

When I mentioned to the property owner that no naturalized freshwater pond would survive on his island indefinitely, he still wanted to pursue the project. The challenge then was how to build a pond in a beach environment where its surface lay above the worst storm surge elevation...and expect it to last beyond the next super high tide.

First, I set the pond's water level a foot higher than the highest surge on record up to then. Then we acquired tons of rocks and truckloads of more sand, plus timbers and geofabric. We needed some heavy equipment to create the pond hole, but an excavator would not do because we weren't digging a hole. Instead, we needed a small dozer to push sandy soil into a berm along the pond perimeter.

After compacting and reinforcing, I had stones selectively placed, and native plants installed beyond the pond edge. We were building a naturalized pond from the outside, like making a donut; but formed it into a more aesthetic shape.

A few years after completion, I heard the pond became a curiosity and was featured in a published book. So far, it has survived powerful storms and a major recent hurricane. It remains a tropical oasis surrounded by coconut palms, jungle plants and a small stream with riffles. Several species of fish inhabited it last time I checked. Perhaps it will continue to provide habitat and enjoyment for another twenty- plus years.

That pond was an artificial ecosystem, requiring the owner's regular attention to maintain. Yet, it was a thriving ecosystem, nonetheless. A place of ecological niches and food webs where the processes of nature were available to enjoy and contemplate.

At about the same time as I built that small pond, I began getting more serious about streams and rivers. I had long studied them, fallen into them, sampled their substrates for macroinvertebrates and tagged their fish. Now I was keen to step deeper into their pools and rushing waters in order to restore impaired flowing systems between their banks. Restoring rivers became my next frontier. But first, it required that I gain some expertise in a branch of science that was entirely new to me—*Fluvial Geomorphology*.

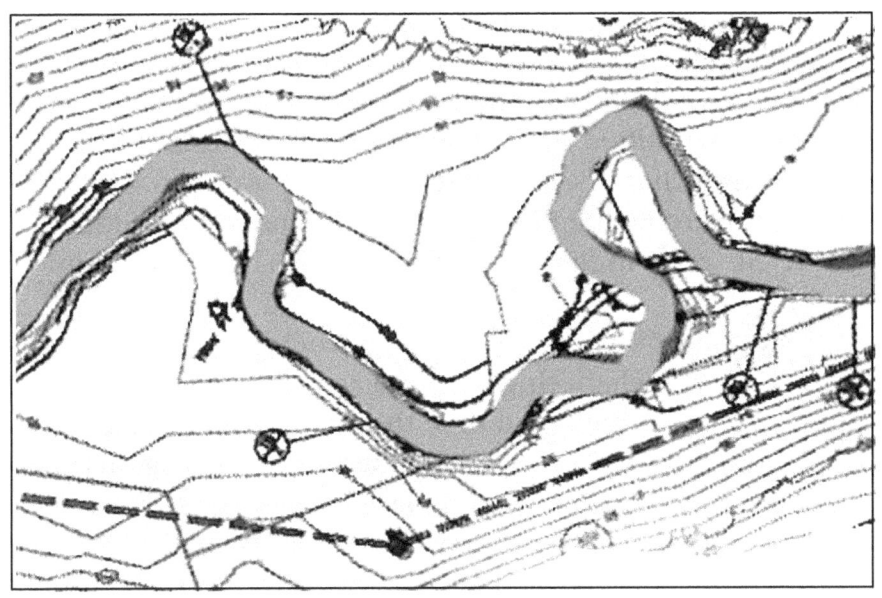

River Morphing

It thrashed its way toward me through the trees, flattening shrubs and small saplings along the way. A single huge eye seemed to loom above its massive yellow body—a cyclops of some sort. Out in front it carried a thick arm high in the air, bent down like a tarantula leg. As it lumbered forward, the arm swayed a few feet off the ground. It ended in a large claw-like appendage with a pincher-thumb.

When the beast came within fifty feet of me, the noise it made drowned out any attempt at shouting. I remained still, watching as it slowly edged closer, clamoring and screeching like some Hollywood transformer. It crunched stones in its path on its way up the dry streambed.

The monster seemed to focus on me and kept coming. I needed to divert it, so I lifted both arms out to the side. While keeping the left one straight, I bent the right forearm up and down with my palm facing the thing. The beast immediately shifted right and went that way until I threw it a different hand signal. With that, it continued on the course toward where I had pointed. The beast had a brain inside it and understood me through our common language.

It stopped next to a pile of large rocks on the stream bank, and the clamoring dropped to a throaty purr. The pincher-arm lowered, and then the claw flexed open from the heavy thumb. The claw clamped onto a refrigerator-sized rock, clenching it tight sideways like some strange T-Rex descendent holding a giant tortoise in its jaws.

But it wasn't that at all, just an ordinary track hoe excavator. I instructed the operator to take the rock a few dozen yards away to a spot marked by a short wooden stake with orange ribbon flagging attached. When the tank treads stopped rotating around the gear hubs, the hulking machine came to a halt with the engine thrumming eight feet from a gash in the stream bank face. The operator throttled down, and the beast went to sleep with the five-thousand-pound rock in its maw. It weighed more than my pickup truck.

The thirty-foot wide channel sat dry because water had never flowed inside. Heavy equipment had dug it the week before in what was uplands. At this point, it appeared like a long raw wound on the landscape.

"We'll set it in the channel against the notch in the bank." I shouted to the brain of the operator behind the cab window. "But hold off a minute while I verify the alignment. I'll need your help down here to do that, so grab a hammer."

River Morphing

Something bothered me about the way the new bank curved, so while the operator hunted his hammer, I grabbed a short wooden stake, a reeled tape measure, and a set of engineering plans I had earlier set near a stump.

I handed the stake and leading edge of the tape to the operator when he hopped to the ground. I told him to cross the empty channel with the items. "Stand in the channel next to the bank across from me while I check something."

The man walked over with the tape, unreeling it from my hand while I picked up the roll of construction drawings. After stripping off the rubber band, I unrolled the bundle and spread the sheets over the stump. Portions of the two by four-foot sheets hung over the edge, but it was flat enough for me to flip the pages to the soil grading plan for this section of the channel.

Before excavating the channel, a crew had previously surveyed the entire length and staked it every fifty feet with station numbers. They then replicated those stations on the design plans I held. I located the station on the map that had me concerned.

With a measuring scale from my vest, I measured the width between the channel bed's lowest topographic lines. The plans showed where the boulder placement should go and the meander curve of the new channel. I had designed these for maximum channel stability based on our previous field investigations. They included geotechnical, hydraulic and hydrology analyses, and geomorphic evaluation.

In my vest, I also kept a small protractor and used it to draw a cord on the arc of the meander printed on the plans, then measured the distance to the arc line. With a hand calculator, I determined the arc of curvature for the meander.

I called over to the machine operator; "Okay, hammer the stake into the bed against the bank, and hold the tape end against it." Then I stretched the tape. Too narrow, just as I had thought. The excavator or the survey crew had made a mistake. Several more measurements confirmed the problem. If left that way, stormflows in the operational flowing channel would undermine the bank protections we intended to install. It would blow-out the channel, causing rampant flooding and mass wasting of the banks. After discussing the problem with the operator, he nodded and got to work digging more soil from the bank. I signaled that I'd check things later.

He also needed to dig the bank back to accommodate the widths of the dozen boulders we would install in a line later. A crew would then place geotextile fabric over the steep vertical bank. It would prevent runoff from eroding around the row of boulders.

While the operator worked, I hiked nearly a half-mile upstream to check on where the new channel started, a dozen feet from the existing one that still carried its normal flow. Those dozen feet acted as a dike to prevent the flow from getting into the unfinished section until the project completed. I wanted to make sure the dike remained intact; if not, water would pour into the unfinished channel, flooding our excavation work.

No problems there. The excavator would remove the dike as one of the last steps in the construction. Then he would fill a few dozen feet of the existing channel so the flow would divert to the new one. The downstream end would connect to the existing channel by removing a similar dike. We would then have a new, more stable channel section that no longer encroached on the adjacent property owner's yards, undermined trees or sloughed bank soils into the stream.

After returning to the track hoe, the operator was ready to set the first boulder. I verified the channel and meander radius dimensions, then gave the go-ahead for the placement.

The operator revved the engine and rolled the excavator forward. It took ten minutes to set the rock in the trench and against the bank fabric, then move it into place so I could check the angle and he could adjust the position. In this way, work proceeded downstream, digging back the bank and trenches, while I selected the rocks by size and shape, and set the angles and spacing for installing them.

Over the next few days, the row of boulders extended forty feet along the outside meander bend. The boulders came from a quarry where they shaped them to about four feet long, three wide, and two high; at least one long side contained a fairly flat surface. It formed the top, sitting next to its neighbors like a row of teeth. The operator set a second, then a third, row of boulders on top, staggering the joints. The wall extended to the bank top, where the steel bucket on the excavator scooped up soil from a stockpile and placed it in the gaps behind and between the boulders.

Using native stones this way involved eco-engineering, and would provide a shield where currents were strongest once water flowed. Soon, mosses and lichens would grow on them and vegetation would hang over the bank and between the joints. The wall would naturally blend with the stream and surroundings and look like nature placed them there. Most other sections, however, would not need a heavy rock wall. There, on inside meanders and straight sections of the channel with less erosive friction, I had designed bioengineering techniques for stabilizing.

A variety of options were used, which allowed nature to maintain them over the long-term. It was 2005, and I had used such techniques on many previous projects. One project involved restoring a stream called "Serenity Run." It flowed— grudgingly— through a corner of a large city on the east coast within the *Middle Atlantic Coastal Plain 63), Middle Atlantic Flatwoods Ecoregion (63e)*.

It flowed through a wooded area of seventy acres. Unfortunately, many years ago, the city used it as a landfill, then abandoned the site and the channel for decades. The Serenity Run project presented many difficulties—controlling flash flooding from city storms and preventing toxins that leached out of the landfill beside it from washing into the nearby Chesapeake Bay.

Flowing ecosystems had threaded their way through my life ever since I began exploring the one down the lane when I was nine years old. My pals and I would enter the woods and follow a path to a small stream near my aunt's house where I was living.

The creek, only a few yards wide, bubbled and gurgled its way over riffles and pools. This was music to me, and in the stream's murmurings I heard stories of the flow's travels from upstream, where it seeped out of the ground as a fresh spring. Since ancient times, it trickled its way downslope and passed the spots where we played.

Small streams are among the best places in a rural landscape where youngsters can find endless nature adventures. There were days when my pals and I entered the woods in the morning to explore the little stream there and didn't come home until suppertime.

Since then, I had crossed paths with countless other river systems. Living on the Susquehanna in Shady Nook was a wonderful way for me and Laura to learn about each other and nature when I was a young student. Much later, I worked with rivers and streams impacted by dams, highways, and natural and human- caused degradation.

Something about water flowing in open channels through the countryside always intrigued me. Why did they come in so many shapes and sizes, and what caused them to change their courses? I learned the answers over years of visiting and restoring streams and rivers, how to recognize the ways channels maintain balance in their environments, and how they adjust to stresses.

Since rivers and streams are such dynamic systems, they change every minute, sometimes in subtle and at other times in sudden and disastrous ways that affect other ecosystems. I gradually felt an urge to do something about the degraded ones—I wanted to fix rivers, but at first was unsure how to go about it. All the solutions I saw in the field at the time involved highly engineered constructions. These included dams, pipes, rip-raped banks, flume-like channels, sheet-piling, concrete weirs, excessive channel widening, narrowing, and deepening, artificial sills, deep plunge- pools, and other modern attempts to control the rivers and streams.

The engineered structural designs invariably concerned one purpose—to convey the waters with their sediments through an area as quickly as possible to avoid flooding or bank erosion. These projects benefited people and their communities and usually worked for a while. But they typically ignored the natural ecological functions of the riverine systems. Rivers and streams could no longer meander naturally across their floodplains. As a result, adverse ecological impacts occurred for fish migrations, natural food webs, and property owners.

Frequently, I encountered excessive sediment depositions where projects had produced over- widened streams, slowing flow velocities, allowing transported soils and gravels to settle out. Bridge abutments deteriorated from high sheer stresses where grading activities narrowed channels too much.

This excessively increased flow velocities and produced scouring of riverbeds. These created "nick-points" where bed elevations abruptly changed, and the scouring marched upstream. cutting deeper into the channel and creating steep gullies with waterfalls that blocked fish passage.

Undercutting of banks from poorly installed protections eroded the banks away by collapsing them and sloughing off soil layers. People's property washed downstream or flooded when designs produced improper channel dimensions and shape. Over ly narrowed channels allowed waters to rise faster and over-top the banks, often causing greater property damage and human heartache than a stable naturalized channel.

In some cases, concrete and steel structures are the only practical solutions. But the dysfunctional streams and rivers I frequently found on the landscape prompted my efforts in restoration ecology and eco-engineering using river morphing principles. The entire process of investigating, designing, and constructing stable channels involved the discipline of fluvial geomorphology, or as it is sometimes known, "hydrogeomorphology"—*HGM*.

The principles and techniques attracted landscape scientis ts' attention in the early 1990s. Mostly theoretical then, only a few pioneers had developed practical techniques to restore degraded streams based on river mechanics, channel forms, geology, physics, hydrology, flow frequencies and patterns.

The more I researched this new field, the more convinced I became it could provide solutions for the flowing streams and rivers that struggled to convey their discharges and sediment through the landscape. Few practical training opportunities for HGM existed in the 1990s, but a small company offered it in Colorado, where I spent a month wading and measuring streams and rivers, and studying practical HGM channel designs.

Not long afterward, I began incorporating HGM into my stream restoration projects. These processes fit perfectly with the bioengineering and eco-engineering approaches I had used previously to restore other types of ecosystems. The HGM added a basic structural foundation for returning the natural morphology, pattern, and mechanics to impaired and unstable flowing channels.

For the Serenity Run restoration, reshaping the channel form and pattern was an important goal of the project, along with stabilizing the banks and bed using natural materials rather than concrete and steel. Equally important objectives pertained to improving hydrological, hydraulic, and geological processes in order to fix problems associated with sediment transport, flow dynamics, and floodplain connectivity.

A stream restoration project, like any other, starts with an assessment of watershed landscape conditions and an initial field reconnaissance of the channel and corridor. I walked the upstream section and found the banks there highly unstable, eroding large quantities of soil into the channel. This overloaded the power of the small stream to flush the excessive amount of sediment downstream and through the system.

Destructive land use practices had overwhelmed the channel and were likely to only get worse as future urbanization produced ever greater amounts of impervious surface. A large amount of water can fall on a watershed during a storm, and the first inch usually infiltrates into the ground. On hardened artificial surfaces, though, most of it immediately runs off into creeks and streams that wash away banks, scour the bed and floods more often than normal.

To reconnoiter the downstream Serenity Run reaches, I set out one morning where the channel emerged into the sunlight from a large box-culvert under a four-lane highway. From the road shoulder, the weedy slope descended steeply toward the channel to the water's edge. Nothing serene about Serenity Run. Severely degraded, it lacked effective functions in more ways than I could float a stick down it—which wasn't even possible due to all the debris.

The width between banks looked as wide as a two- lane road with shoulders, about forty feet. From its source more than a mile upstream of the box-culvert, the discharge flowed through a narrow wooded corridor that cut through the urban area of the city. Apartments and commercial buildings had encroached on the channel for many decades, adding abnormal amounts of runoff from streets, lots, and roofs.

Downstream of the culvert, the stream conditions worsened. As I hacked my way along the choked channel, I noted its many problems and thought of ideas for restoring its natural balance. It had become an ugly, weed-infested, and trash-filled gulley with near vertical collapsing banks. Extensive sand bars had formed, shifting the current against eroding raw banks. Likely no fish had lived in its waters since the turn of the last century, when horseless carriages rode over the box culvert. Now flesh-eating bacteria and syringe needles filled it.

Years of the city dumping trash and garbage up to the water's edge had caused the channel to cut into the solid waste. This erosion had released toxins and old tires, refrigerators, rusting barrels, wrecked bicycles, concrete piping, and other junk that lay strewn in the lower half-mile channel section.

I had observed that the city parked their full-sized garbage collection trucks in a lot near the culvert. There workers hosed them out each day. Twenty or more trucks drove in and out and parked there daily. I watched as all the gooey, stinking mess from the trucks washed across the pavement, then downslope and directly into the stream. Stagnant water in the channel smelled like a landfill in many places and ran milky-gray the way sewers do.

No eager child would ever bushwhack through the briars on the banks to look for adventure or play in that stream. No magic existed there, only neglect and abuse...a place where nature or an ecosystem barely existed anymore. I did not hear music in this stream's flow, only dysfunction and struggle against all the debris in its way.

The stream flowed through the center of the seventy- acre patch of woods that had grown over the earlier landfill. While walking along the channel, stepping around empty oil drums, I reached another ten-foot- high box culvert that the creek flowed through. The odd thing, no road existed on either side; it sat isolated between the banks amid a tangle of brush and trees, the remains of the old access road to the dump site's other side.

That wasn't the only oddity about it, however. I stepped onto the concrete top of the culvert and looked down at the streamflow. A large flat rock lay beneath the rippled water surface, but something about it seemed curious. Through the wrinkled water surface, I saw what looked like writing on the rock. As I studied it from above, I understood it was, in fact...a tombstone.

Based on my watershed investigation, no cemeteries existed upstream for the monument to get washed out from a storm and transported there. Maybe decades ago, vandals had stolen it, brought it in a four-wheel- drive vehicle and dumped it over the isolated box culvert. But only the stream knew for sure, and perhaps it was telling the story in its own musical way as the water burbled over the grave marker's stone surface.

For this abused stream, I knew it would not be easy to restore it. Even if stability returned to its channel, it might not last long because of continued poor conditions in its upstream urban watershed. Uncontrolled storm runoff from so much impervious surface produced frequent high discharges of excessive velocities. A naturalized restoration approach might moderate these "flashy" events, but not if conditions worsened along its urban upper course.

My concerns compelled me to notify the city that long-term success in Serenity Run depended on correcting problems upstream of the highway box culvert. But with the project already approved and budgeted, the city wanted to proceed, regardless. I had my suspicions that nothing upstream would change anytime soon. With that, I was determined to stabilize the stream as effectively as possible, and regular monitoring would show whether it could remain that way.

Although my visual reconnaissance of Serenity Run intuitively told me the stream exhibited highly unstable conditions, I needed much more than my senses and feelings in order to proceed with the restoration project. I needed hard facts supported by field data.

The HGM approach required measuring channel cross sections in the field at selected spots to determine the stream-type based on a hierarchical scale. Usually, we selected a straight section between meanders called an inflection point. First, a crewmember installed a stake on the bank top or somewhere on the face at an elevation I would specify. I selected the spot based on evidence of frequent past flows that left marks and scars at various elevations up the bank's face— morphological indicators.

These were geomorphic clues, difficult to decipher without experience in a variety of stream and river types. Accurately interpreting these bank features is a crucial initial step, because if a restoration design is based on the wrong elevation, the repaired channel will not function properly and failure is usually assured.

Such physical features indicated the elevation of the channel-forming flow, the discharge that had historically shaped the channel to its present form. If the physical features appeared at the bank top, it represented the "bankfull flow." Regardless of where they occurred, these marks were the first critical information collected.

Bankfull flow is important for the HGM approach because river scientists consider it the most effective flow for moving sediment, forming or removing sand bars, forming or changing bends and meanders, and doing work that results in the morphological or shape characteristics of channels. For most channels, this is equivalent to the size storm that occurs about every one-and-a-half years, give or take.

I attached a tape to one stake, then stretched it tight across the channel and fastened it to the other. One crewmember held a measuring rod on the flowing streambed and banks at every foot across the streambed, while I used a surveyor's level to read the height to the tape. In this way, we mapped the channel cross section.

At each foot, we measured the diameters of any rocks above the surface and picked up smaller ones from the channel bed and measured those, too. We also measured meander widths and their arc of curvatures, then used similar procedures to determine the channel slope from upstream to downstream. From this data, I made calculations on sinuosity and pattern of flow.

After that, we dug into the sand bars and collected bucket samples for sifting, weighing, and categorizing soil particle sizes of depositional materials. This told me the types and sizes of sediment and stones that the stream carried. Any restoration project needed to take these into account. Too little stream power meant deposition rather than transport, with mid-channel bars that impeded flow. But excess stream power and erosive forces produced what is known as "hungry water," which scours more material from the banks and streambed. Field indicators of flow problems meant an unstable channel, and Serenity Run had plenty of them.

Information on the vegetation beyond the banks and the terrain went into our field notebooks, including dimensions of the active floodplain. Our field team assessed the stability of the banks along the channel by measuring their relative heights. It showed Serenity Run had highly unstable banks ready to collapse—objective data to support my earlier recon assessment. I processed and analyzed all the field data in order to classify the HGM stream type. The classification of stream reaches provided an indicator of the channel's overall stability, as well as a basis for developing restoration options to stabilize the channel. By knowing the type, I could compare the results with other streams of the same type that served as "reference streams."

The crucial thing about reference channel types is that they are stable, sustainable channels in the same watershed or similar landscapes. Sometimes river morphologists know them well, but in other cases it is necessary to find these within the same ecoregion and conduct the same kinds of field investigations as for the restoration project streams.

We found a suitable stable stream within the larger regional watershed that met the criteria. After collecting similar data as we did on Serenity Run, I determined how the reference stream data compared with this channel. So many critical components departed considerably from the reference channel, which told me not only what needed improving, but where and to how much, in order to restore stability. Objective data must support one's opinion in restoring stream and river channels as it is for most critical situations in life.

In the United States, the U.S. Geological Survey maintained thousands of hydrological gauges placed on streams and rivers that automatically record flow data for flood control purposes. Most have been operating for decades, and I located one installed on a bigger stream in the larger watershed that still functioned. The gauge unit involves a readable scale in feet attached to a simple float that records the water elevations in real time and converts them to discharge values.

After obtaining the digital output files of this data from the USGS, I looked up the discharges for the one-and-a-half-year level storms, as well as each past year's maximum flood levels. From these, I conducted a flood frequency analysis, and the size flow volumes I needed to build into the restoration design.

It was time to get the engineers involved, and I had our water specialists produce digital models of the prevailing channel's hydrological and hydraulic conditions. The results showed where excessive shear stresses—friction—would occur, and where stormflows would overtop banks. I contracted with a geotechnical company to drill holes in particular locations along the channel, extract the soils, and send them to a lab for analysis. Later, I would send the reports to the construction company to plan the excavation and grading activities.

A surveying company staked out the channel stations along the streambank, marking every fifty feet. They also prepared a topographic map with adjacent landscape contours and features they provided to our computer drafting staff.

With all the data collected and analyzed, and the modeling done, I could begin designing the restored stream. This was the fun part, laying out the new channel over the existing one on the topographic plan sheets. Every line I drew, each meander, channel width, depth, cross-sectional view, longitudinal profile, and details on stabilizing structures, had to fit with my calculated values for the stable channel gained from our field investigations.

After many hand-drawn and computer design sheets later, I passed them on to our engineers to re-run new versions of the scour and flood models based on the plans. I made revisions until my engineered features balanced with the model criteria for a stable stream. During various stages of the process, I provide d a new set of preliminary plans to the city's engineers for review.

With final approvals, construction plans were prepared and given to the construction company. The restoration on the landscape began. A few weeks later, I faced down the cyclops track hoe excavator and instructed the operator to pick up the refrigerator-sized rock and place it in the new channel.

On the plans, I had specified various bank and bed features using natural materials that would provide long-term stability once construction finished. These would provide extra protection in vulnerable portions of the channel. In some locations, I used long rolls of flexible logs of heavy burlap stuffed with coconut hull fibers. These would protect the toe or base of the bank where moderate currents slipped passed until native vegetation established.

Where flows were most erosive, I designed a rock wall like the one the contractor built as described earlier. But the restoration called for constructing most of the bank slopes at a less steep angle to reduce erosive forces. On steep banks that was not possible, so I ordered vegetated bench contouring for transitioning uplands naturally with the stream.

The procedure involved grading bank slopes to a gentler angle and cutting benches along the contours at various heights above the water. This produced a step-like face for vegetating with native upland plants.

Before plants were installed, and to give them time to gain a firm foothold, I had crews first lay biodegradable "sock s" filled with moist, nutrient-rich compost and a variety of herbaceous and shrubby seeds. The socks—tubes made from geotextile material, came in rolls up to a hundred or more feet long. When filled with compost, they resembled black firehoses, only thicker in diameter. I had used them on several other stream projects and found them reliable.

The seed and nutrients got mixed with the compost and blown into one end of the dark-colored socks by specialized trucks with industrial blowers—like stuffing a leg of nylons with potting soil and compressing the material. I specified the socks with various thicknesses ranging from four to twelve inches high, with larger sizes used near the future water's edge for normal flows. Crews dragged and laid the long socks onto the benches. They drove heavy wooden stakes through them to hold the rolls firmly in place. Then they stacked sequential layers of socks against the bank slope until even with the bank top. The structure looked like a staircase until workers spread soil between the rows of socks, then blew a final coat of compost over it, so the finished bank face looked naturally smooth. A team installed a grid of open-holed netting over the new bank face to tie all the socks and the entire structure imto a strong, integrated unit.

Periodically along the top portion of the socks, workers cut slits through the netting and geotextile, and inserted individual plants. These included seeds and dormant bare-root specimens of grasses, shrubs, and tree species. The last step involved hosing down the new bank with water from a tanker truck. This washed the surface compost into cracks and crevices and kick- started plant growth.

The contractor watered down the socks each week, and within a couple weeks the seeds sprouted. The saplings grew leaves, producing a natural, stabilized slope full of vigorous, diverse vegetation. Roots gradually pushed through the sides of the socks and formed a natural network that sustained the new bank's stability into the present day.

I used other techniques to protect banks where the channel narrowed too much for grading back and installing sock walls or planting on gentler slopes. Some outer edges of meander bends needed these alternate structures, where our hydraulic modeling predicted currents would flow faster and erode the banks.

These more robust structures included rock or log "vanes." These looked like an arm sloping down from the bankfull elevation to the channel bottom a third of the way across, upstream of the bank tie-in. A dozen or more feet long, the lower end of each arm in the streambed sometimes connected to a shorter length piece called a sill, a few feet wide toward the channel center. The short piece, as well as each arm, rested on footers below the surface, set at a calculated angle with the bank.

Workers shoveled soil and gravel on both sides of the arms, making for a smooth transition with the bank and bed. When completed, only the tops of the boulders were visible, and the narrow structure looked like a natural ramp that sloped from the bank downstream to the channel bottom.

These vane structures did not block the flow because the center piece sat at the bed elevation. They guided higher elevation stormflows away from the bank, reducing erosive forces. They worked because as stormflows neared the structure, the higher water level had to run uphill over the smooth rock arm slope. This caused it to lose energy and take the path of least resistance by swerving away from the bank and spilling off the downstream side of the boulders toward the channel's center at lower velocity. Physics caused these structures to work, making them simple, natural...effective.

The design analyses had predicted scouring of both opposing banks in a few locations. There, I had crews install a pair of rock vanes with sills opposite each other between the two banks, with their sills connected in the channel bed. From above, the entire structure looked like a set of lower false teeth with all molars that sloped down from the banks to the bed.

The restored channel still received the flashy stormflows from its urbanized upstream watershed. But now, its new form and pattern on the landscape functioned without frequent flooding or eroding its banks and carving deeper into its bed.

Rivers and streams play crucial roles in landscapes, maintaining regional water cycles, conveying flows and sediment, and providing habitats, nutrient cycling, and food webs for untold species. Undoubtedly, rivers and streams are the most dynamic ecosystems in the world in terms of constantly changing their shape and flow patterns. They provide travel routes for migrating fish and other animals and bring food to downstream aquatic habitats.

Besides functional roles, riverine systems can mesmerize a person watching from its banks, drawn to the mysteries of its relentless flow. Large rivers impress us with their histories, the power of their waterfalls, their sweeping currents. For some of us, the riffles, ledges, and turbulent water of smaller streams are just as entrancing, prompting deep thoughts and reflection.

And so, for many years, when I would see degraded streams or rivers, it made me want to restore them in their landscapes. Once I found a more natural way to "river-morph," I would return now and then to check on the recovery of my former wild patients. While there, I would listen to the stories they told in the burbling and gurgling of the flow and feel at peace that the songs of river stones had returned to the landscape.

Bootleggers of Cranberry Lake

A soft swish broke the solitude of dusk as my lure sailed over the flat water and landed with a plop thirty feet from the boat. Ripples expanded outward, and the jitterbug danced when the slack in the line disappeared from a twitch of my wrist.

I stood at the stern of the open fishing boat, and Trey sat in the bow and concentrated on threading the barb of a steel hook through a squiggling worm. Late afternoon, and the sun had settled low in the sky. Maybe we still had enough time to catch a few bass for dinner on this mountain lake in the Adirondacks of New York.

The boat sat quietly in the water a few cast-lengths from the miniature island where our campsite lay. Day two of our outdoor family vacation with our children, Trey and Jordon.

We had traveled northward from our home in the Piedmont countryside, filled with expectations that August in 1981.

Such family trips had become our preferred way of interacting with nature, and we undertook many of them over the years, exploring habitats from Maine to Florida and coast to coast.

Sometimes our excursions lasted several weeks to distant wild regions, and once we spent six weeks traveling America in a cargo van I converted to a snuggly camper. We often made local day trips for birdwatching, hiking, canoeing, and other outdoor pursuits.

On this evening, the four of us hoped for solitude, a vacation respite from the worries of daily living. We had found the perfect oasis, alone on a half-acre island in the third largest body of water in the Adirondacks—Cranberry Lake. It lay within the *Northeastern Highlands Ecoregion (58), Lower Berkshire Hills (58d)* with thick, unbroken forest surrounding it, extending for hundreds of miles in every direction. On a map, the lake appeared like a six-legged crab with a central region and long drainageway "legs" stretching outward around the body.

Only one road penetrated this wilderness anywhere near the lake. It passed through a sleepy lakeshore village named after the lake—a collection of small buildings housing only two-hundred people, mostly seasonal residents, and small businesses. Outside of town, a woodsy public campground sat beside the water. We had put up our tent there the previous night, then took it down this morning and stowed it in the boat, along with enough gear to spend a night on the island.

The marina owner where we rented the boat mentioned a clearing there surrounded by evergreens; a pleasant spot to set up our tents. We'd be all by ourselves deep in a wilderness. Perfect, we thought...our kind of place.

Once we left the dock in late-afternoon, the quiet lake surface spread before us. With no other boats on the water, we seemed to have the lake to ourselves. The sun had already started slipping slowly toward the trees in the distance. The low angle caused bright patches of sunlight to glint with golden sparkles all the way to the horizon. It seemed all we needed to do was follow the glistening dapples to our private island.

I estimated we had three hours until the sun settled behind the forest backdrop five miles away. Now, though, we were too far away for even a glimpse of the island. The outboard whined with contentment and the breeze washed over our excitement and passed it along behind us.

A half-hour later I spotted the island and throttled back the engine to trolling speed. Large boulders and smaller rocky outcrops formed a barricade to landing the boat. I put-putted the engine around the island's perimeter, searching for an opening. Nothing looked promising.

The map showed it as Sears Island, which was the largest in a cluster of three tiny islands, with one smaller than a basketball court. I swung the boat around and reversed course for a second patrol. Surely, a landing spot existed somewhere.

On the island's south-western side, a slight break in the rocks. I hadn't seen it earlier because a boulder blocked it from view. Visible now from this direction, I angled toward it, then locked the prop out of the water and drifted into the slot. The bow scraped gravel and stopped on a shoal just wide enough for the boat. When I shut down the engine, a peaceful stillness surrounded us.

Trey grabbed the bow dock line and hopped out. "Tie it to that big root," I said.

He spotted it and leaned down. "Got it." "Are there bears here?" A frown covered Jordon's face.

Trey smiled. Laura patted Jordon's arm. "No, sweetheart." I kept it cheery; "Just us and maybe some squirrels."

After tying off the boat, we all stepped out and followed a short path inland. The clearing appeared, just as the marina owner had mentioned, the size of a doubles tennis court and covered in low grasses and forbs. Mature red spruces and hemlocks towered above us, forming a canopy that filtered light onto the soft blanket of evergreen needles at our feet. They dampened the sound of our footsteps as we wandered about for the next few minutes, exploring nooks and crannies, pointing out various plants and colorful fungi in the tiny landscape.

We returned to the boat and hauled our camping gear to the clearing near an old fire ring made of stones. Someone had placed several large logs nearby to sit, and I turned two other short ones on end and against each other as a makeshift surface for preparing supper. Trey and I set up the gas stove and tent while Laura and Jordon unpacked the food cooler and cooking equipment. While they began prepping for the meal, Trey and I took the boat out into the lake just offshore.

We broke out the fishing rods and began casting for smallmouth bass, hoping to contribute to the menu. Soon, we caught enough fish for dinner and brought our catch back to camp. A sizeable slab of stiff bark lay nearby, and I put it on top of our old metal cooler to serve as a fish-cleaning station. Laura fried the chunks of succulent flesh in butter, and the first bite left no doubts—I had returned to the wilderness.

Afterward, the family sat on logs as the sun set, while I started a fire with dry branches we had gathered. I kept it small—just right for roasting marshmallows for dessert.

The remote lake had attracted my attention while planning our route. Bays and inlets on the maps carried intriguing names. A few seemed associated with families who once lived in the region, including the famous name of Sears. But others had more obscure origins—Cucumber Hole, Witch Bay, and Potato Patch. And what about Hedgehog Bay, Tramp's Retreat and Black Duck Hole? They all seemed to have curious stories to tell, and I wanted to explore some of them.

The name that intrigued me most, though, was Joe Indian Island. It suggested a mysterious past where someone like Tom Sawyer and his mixed blood nemesis, Injun Joe, had adventures there a century ago. To make our exploration more exciting for the kids, maybe I'd work some of those themes into the mix as we hiked about the island.

Before leaving home, I learned that until the mid- 1800s, the only way to get to Cranberry Lake involved hiking Indian trails through fifty miles of wilderness. Mostly just hunters and trappers canoed across the boggy lake then, using their paddles to push aside an ocean of cranberries. When the first road arrived, lumbering companies moved in on the northern border where the village later developed.

With the lumber industry came mills and mercantile facilities in the hamlet, and soon inns and hotels sprouted to accommodate summer visitors looking for a peaceful holiday stay. By the early 1930s, private homes lined the shoreline near the village. Not long after, the State gained control over most of the surrounding wilderness and restricted further building to the already developed shoreline.

When Trey and Jordon began nodding sleepily at the campfire, Laura and I carried them to the tent and into their sleeping bags. The two of us sat together a while longer by the fire, enjoying the solitude and each other's company. The only sounds we heard floated on a gentle breeze from the island's shoreline, where water lapped softly against the rocks and our metal boat. It whispered how lucky we were to have found such peace.

The first thing I noticed when my eyes fluttered open in the early morning was a dewdrop slipping slowly down the tent wall next to my face. We ate a simple breakfast among shafts of sunlight that filtered through the forest canopy and promised another sunny day.

Before heading out to Joe Indian, we had our own island to explore. When we arrived yesterday in late afternoon, we needed to set up camp before nightfall— not much time for scouting about then. But now we had time to head into the little forest around us.

Mossy growth formed an emerald blanket over ground surfaces, sheltered by the conifer canopy. Bright green mosses covered logs, roots, and downed branches. On top of the fuzzy carpet, a miniature forest of mushrooms wore colorful caps and mingled with clubmosses, partridgeberries, ground pines, and arching ferns. No evidence of humans or even Joe Indian's ghost.

We lazed about camp for an hour or so, enjoying our time together with nature. The boat wasn't due back until dusk, and I was keen on exploring other areas around the lake—maybe we'd find a cave on Joe Indian Island like Tom Sawyer did in Missouri, or discover an old, abandoned homestead full of mystery.

My pre-trip research hinted at the region's past of old-time floating camps with illegal whiskey stills. The hootch-makers would move the wooden platforms around the lake, hiding in obscure coves and inlets to keep one step ahead of the revenuers.

Besides whiskey makers, squatter families lived in shacks on platforms permanently anchored to the lake bottom. A spot for settling down, no rent, no mortgage, no neighbors to fight with, no chores, no yard to mow, and fresh fish for dinner from your front door. What's not to like?

Floating decks, though, all but disappeared long ago, abandoned or removed by State natural resource authorities. They pronounced the floating platforms conflicted with the area's wilderness values, causing disruptions to the ambience of the naturally wild setting. I wondered if a few folks still made a living on the lake this way, hidden on a camouflaged platform in some obscure smuggler's cove.

Floating trespassers became part of a squatter tradition that had long existed in the area. Platform dwellers insisted State ownership only applied to the lake's waters. They insisted it did not include the bottom substrates—and since their floating platforms were anchored to the mud; they were legal...as long as they weren't distilling hooch.

The State didn't agree and banned the platforms anyway. As I pondered it, an echo of the Everly Brothers floated on the breeze like it had when I hunted for rad- vectors in Missouri. But now the words in my head sounded different—

Bye, bye homes,
Bye, bye autonomy; hello poverty,
They made us all comply.
Bye, bye my shack, goodbye.

There goes my deck home, there goes my view;
I once was happy, but now I'm blue.
And here's the reason I'm not complete, '
Cause now I'm livin' just on the street.

Back on our island, bellies rumbled. Time for lunch. "C'mon kids," I said. "Let's have a snack; then we'll pack up our stuff—do some exploring on the lake."

After downing baloney sandwiches and a handful of spicy tortilla chips, I stuffed my cheeks with a last graham cracker and reached for a jug to wash it down. I chugged down most of the grape-like liquid. "What kind of juice is this? It's got a funny taste; is this what they're drinking?" I tilted my head toward the kids.

"Not from that jug. We had a few partially filled bottles of fresh juices a couple days ago, and I mixed them together."

"Tastes weird, like soggy socks. Plus, it's very warm; wasn't it in the cooler?"

She shook her head. "No room." "How long in the trunk?" "Since I mixed it up."

"Hmm," I held the container out to Laura. "Sure, you're not trying to poison me so you can leave my bones on this remote island never to be found?" I pretended to gag and grasp my throat, and the kids laughed at Daddy dying.

She looked concerned as she took the jug and sniffed the opening. "Yeah, that's fermenting...we won't drink any more of it."

She poured it out in a clump of weeds. "The plants will love it."

"Ahh, now look what you did—that might've produced an excellent wine in a few more days." I pretended more wistfulness; "We could've added some of those ground-cherries we saw over there, and we'd have some moonshine."

"I thought you said those were toxic to eat; you'd be poisoning yourself."

"They are, everything but the ripe fruit...and those are ripe." "Well, I think it takes more than just a couple of days to make wine, Mr. Expert Vintner."

Jordon whispered to Trey—"What's a vinter?" Trey shrugged. "Must be Amish for winter."

Jordon nodded; they had relatives near Amish communities in Pennsylvania where they often visited; they knew the dialect very well.

"Yeah, but we just add some berries and nature does all the work—wild berry wine from the wilderness," I beamed.

Laura smirked and mouthed the word "moron."

"Well, this moron got you to fantasy island, didn't he?" I sniffed.

"My self-esteem could handle it if you used it as an adjective—'moronic,' since that would only apply to this situation. But 'moron' involves my entire persona at all times, and that is just vicious. So, which did you mean?" Goading her.

"You heard me the first time; now get your butt in gear, Mister." More smirking.

Bested again by the brown-eyed girl. I blew her a kiss in salute. "Okay then, let's pack up the boat and go exploring." Laura stood up and began collecting cups and plates. "Oh, you spilled some juice on your shirt," she motioned.

I looked down at my chest and saw a purple splotch the size of a half-dollar on my tan t-shirt. "Well, that's not coming out. So, guys, the map shows a large and mysterious island over that way...want to check it out?" I pointed westward.

Both snapped alert and their eyes swiveled across the lake somewhere beyond the reach of my arm. I heard a chorus of affirmative yelps and put a finger to my lips. I looked around suspiciously, as though spies lurked about. In my best pirate voice spoken into the back of my hand with a quiet hiss, "They call it Joe Indian Island."

Trey's eyes widened. Jordon looked uncertain until Laura winked at her.

"Still want to go, maties ?" I leaned close and narrowed my eyes like Captain Hook.

"Yeah s!" erupted from our little band of adventurers. We packed away the lunch stuff, then I started the motor and headed into unknown territory. If only we'd had a pirate flag to fly.

Fifteen minutes later, I spotted a smudge of green. "Land ho !" I shouted. Heads shifted and Joe Indian Island grew larger as we approached. A thick mantle of tall evergreens poked skyward like a war bonnet and covered the hundred-acre island. We were still a few minutes out, but the place looked impregnable.

Just then, something glinted on the water far to my left. It did not look like another boat, but some kind of house floating all by itself far out in the lake. "What the..." I slowed the boat. The others looked questioningly at me. "Over there; let's check that out first," I pointed off to the left.

Nearly noon, the sun in full blaze over a breezeless sky. The mysteries of Joe Indian would have to wait. I swung the bow away from the island and throttled up. That quick, we approached a floating platform with a wooden building on top. A rustic, one-story structure of rough boards swayed with the motion of the lake surface. A few floating docks branched outward, and I headed for one of those. No other boats; wonder why?

Twenty feet and closing. Time for throttling the engine down to idle and drifting to the dock. The platform beyond seemed made of solid plywood sheets, empty but for the worn wooden building. The well-aged structure had no adornments, reminding me of something from the 1920s or 30s. I imagined coming upon this place back then on a dark night—the docks thick with boats and string lights, music pouring out of the shack's one window, people dancing the Charleston on the plywood decking—a floating speakeasy.

The place looked deserted, and I was about to push away back to the lake when I spotted an ancient red-soft-drink sign.

Hold on—a speakeasy wouldn't advertise cola beverages, would they? And what hold-out squatter would either, especially with all those bullet holes peppering the classic sign?

Something seemed off here, or it might have been my sudden need for a drink. Maybe it would dilute the fermenting juice that was gurgling in my gut, and the wooziness that had crept into my head.

I nodded to Trey, who hopped from the boat and secured it to a piling. Across the platform next to the entrance door and soft drink sign. I noticed a middle-aged man in shabby clothes sitting on a dilapidated bench against the wall. He wore farmer-style overalls with one chest-flap over his shoulder and the other hung down with the inside facing out. I wondered if that was an intentional warning of casual recklessness, slovenly habit, or just a way to beat the afternoon heat. When he saw me looking at him, he leaned over and rapped his knuckles backwards on the door. It almost seemed like a code-knock. Did he think we came to buy a case of moonshine?

On the piling where I tied the stern line, a handwritten sign warned, "Dock at Your Own Risk." Beside it, a worn board streaked with bird droppings announced "WELCOME" in red letters. An omen?

"C'mon, let's see what this is all about." I helped the others onto the dock. The sun, overhead now, glared off the platform so intensely it made me squint. I took a step forward and nearly stumbled before grabbing the piling to steady myself. Sudden queasiness had caused my balance to falter. I took a deep breath and tried another step—balance fine, but something danced the tango in my belly.

Our little scouting squad followed me across the twenty-foot platform toward the building. I held my gaze on the enforcer spraddled on the bench. He kept his gaze on me; something odd there, unsettling, and then I noticed a large knife in his hidden hand.

I paused my stride and motioned my backup partners to standdown. I watched the man brandish the weapon and make a slicing motion near his lap. It seemed like a warning he might use it on our throats or crotches...until I saw the piece of wood he was carving. Easy now. I stepped forward, motioning the others to advance too. My hand slid toward my hip, and I unsnapped the holster strap on my belt where I carried my old Boy Scout knife...just in case. It might come in handy if I needed to whittle my way out of there.

The guard...or grandpa or whoever he was, went back to his carving. Upon reaching the shack door, I saw the soda sign more clearly—perforated with rusty holes and reddish stains that had dripped down and dried, like blood. I knew I wasn't thinking clearly, and the tango had changed to a jitterbug; I wanted to grab some quick cold drinks and hip-hop back to the boat. Maybe the acidic cola might settle my stomach back to a smooth electric slide.

When I reached for the door handle, I glanced down and saw wood shavings littering the deck. They nearly covered the toes of the man's leather boots—all dry and cracked as though he had owned them since puberty. He slowly looked up at me, and I realized what was odd about his eyes.

Only one eye, actually. I realized it was a white occlusion that fully covered the lens. That made me frown—an old man with cataracts slashing a sharp knife in his lap. That can't end well, I decided. "Okay to go in?" I asked, not interested in waiting around for the looming genital tip-off.

The man shrugged without looking up, and an extr a- large shaving curved off the blade and dropped to the deck, along with a slimy wad of something he spat next to it, which I swear slithered like a slug burrowing into the pile of shavings.

I took that as the local welcome signal since the wad didn't land on my shoe. With that, I pulled the door open, expecting to enter a spacious well-lit room. Instead, what greeted me was a narrow darkened hallway lined with cheap wooden paneling. My pupils, shrunk from the brightness outside, wondered what was down the hall—a trapdoor to the lake bottom, or maybe moonshiners bottling up some white lightning? With my hand still on the door handle behind me, I hesitated to enter the hallway. I looked behind me at Laura. Our eyes locked. I gazed into hers for a moment as though for the last time, then they rested on her tender cheek. I raised my finger and touched the corner of her mouth ever so slightly, a loving gesture. "You've got a bit of mustard there from lunch," I said, and turned back and entered the dark tunnel.

The others followed me to the end, where it connected with a rectangular room; a dim place lined with the same dark paneling. I took several steps forward. The squad took positions behind me and visually surveilled the place.

Straight ahead stood a bar counter made of dark oak. A pair of unmarked taps poked above the smooth surface, but nothing else of note in the room—no stools or anywhere to sit. The only light came from a dirty window behind the bar. Nothing hung on the walls but some spiderwebs, and the counter lacked any menus, coasters, advertising or the usual clutter of a business establishment.

No tables, no drinkers, no pool, no pets; not even cigarettes. It seemed we had walked into someone's personal den. But why keep a soda sign outside, I wondered? I would have turned around and motioned everyone back to the entrance if it were not for what stood behind the counter. A middle-aged couple watched us, expressionless, a younger version of Grant Wood's American Gothic, absent the pitchfork. Still, they did not look welcoming.

I couldn't figure out what caused their blank looks, as though we'd just discovered them in some illegal act...like maybe they made their own hooch in the back. Or perhaps they disapproved of us—I glanced at my family to see if anyone was doing something outrageous like peeing on the floor. Nothing, but my concern persisted for a few seconds along with the silence. Why aren't they saying anything? I thought until I realized I was the one who had barged in there.

I shook my head, trying to clear the fog that had seeped in there since lunch, just before the hokey pokey started in my bowels. The couple looked on the short side, gray-haired and dressed to complement the décor—dowdy. Had we strolled into their living room?

The temperature seemed very warm, no fan or AC; dry sandpaper seemed to coat my throat, and I felt light-headed, as though I'd slugged down a few beers. "Got anything to drink?" I rasped, desperate to quell the squall that brewed below my sternum.

"We got Coke." The woman's voice sounded flat. I shifted my eyes to the man, who seemed to size me up for the number of chops he might be able to get off my ribcage.

I glanced at my chest, wondering the same thing, and saw the purple splotch. "Coke will work. Yeah, I spilled some fermented juice here, and things are fuzzy right now." I hoped that would put us on a fast track to harmony.

But the pair squinted at me with blank stares, as though I might be a revenuer trying to gain their trust.

"Set 'em up barkeep—drinks all-around," I mimicked a bar regular, swinging my arm in the air to include my family. No one even smiled.

I expected to see one of the dour pair fill a nice tall glass with sweet cool cola from a vintage tap. But they hadn't moved a muscle, still staring at me. What are they waiting for? "So, what size do you have?"

"Ain't got but one," the lady deadpanned.

I blinked and tried another ice-breaker. "Well, then...guess it'll have to do, won't it?" I faked a huge belly laugh, my teeth and lips ablaze in phony mirth.

They didn't chuckle. The deal seemed on the verge of going bad. I looked over my shoulder and could see puzzlement on my family's faces, too. I gave them a reassuring half-smile. As my head turned back, I noticed an open doorway near the left end of the bar. I made out several empty wooden tables and chairs within the gloomy interior. A poker deck lay spread over one table. Haze filled the room, smelling of recent cigars.

The furniture seemed slightly cockeyed, and the door frame tilted a bit. I straightened my posture but the room angles continued to shift. I was conscious of the door hinges squeaking at me and thought they were a warning not to enter. But then I remembered the room was floating on top of a moving lake, and my balance almost returned.

My gaze settled again on the poker-faced couple behind the bar. Their blank expressions seemed permanent. I thought they had no intention of serving us anything.

"How much for four?"

Maybe the lady noticed the bead of sweat beginning to run from my left temple. She moved in for the kill. "That will be six dollars."

"Really? That's for a whole case, right—like twenty-four bottles? We just need four."

Neither of them answered. "You mean it's a dollar-fifty apiece?" I sputtered. "They're only a quarter in town."

"You're a long way from town, but it's that way at the other end of the lake." The woman tilted her head north.

The man said, "Maybe they even got some stain remover over 'in-town'—might help that juice spill from your sippy cup." His beady eyes remained on my shirt.

"Hey, we're just here for a drink," I said, wondering how in the world did we end up in a throw-down at a backwater saloon out on this wilderness lake? Then I finally put it together that he was the "Coke Kingpin" in this here wilderness, five miles from civilization. It was clear—if you needed some Coke way out here, you had to deal with this gang.

Except it wasn't all that clear; nothing was clear. But I was thirsty and needed a syrupy fix. "Yeah, okay, we'll take three large." I winced at the thought of handing over four dollars and fifty cents for soft drinks in 1981. But visions of super-sized mugs full of frosty Coke danced in my head—and we were on vacation; time to splurge.

The poker-faced woman reached below the counter and produced three twelve-ounce cans and banged them on the counter. "We only got cans," she intoned. No condensation dripped from the aluminum containers; no hoary frost covered their sides—they looked warmer than my armpits.

I looked down at the red and white cans. My jaw clenched and my voice took on an edge. "Got any ice?"

"Nope, just these here's," the woman sniffed.

I was about to call off the deal when my eye caught the man twitch his arm downward by his side. Perhaps he was just scratching a mosquito bite on his kneecap, but if there was an ax down there, I was prepared to bolt. "Right...here's five dollars. Keep the change."

I snagged the cans and motioned Laura and the children to return down the hallway. Out on the deck again, the enforcer was still at his whittling. But now he had a wicked-sharp end carved on the stick—and his shoe-tops were mostly buried in wood chips. Such chips made great kindling for a wood fire...the kind that could heat up a still or incinerate nosy trespassers in the nearby woods.

The man looked up at me with his sightless eye...like he knew why we had come. He knew we came for the brown stuff, the good brew that could produce a sugar high like nothing else. When he saw us holding the cans, he grunted, though I didn't know if it was from satisfaction, constipation, or a jab to the groin.

I hustled the squad to the boat, relieved to see it wasn't half-sunk or torched. Once I got the motor purring, Trey untied the dock line. We soon skimmed across the open water again. Laura popped the tops on the warm cans and handed me one. I winked at her and she smiled back; the kids were chattering together. A pleasant breeze blew through our hair and the sun remained warm and bright.

While the outboard chugged us along, I sipped my warm cola. Gradually, the funky chickens scratching my insides settled down into a slow waltz and my head cleared. I thought of the man on the bench, the couple, and their hideout. They no doubt escaped paying property taxes by living on their floating platform, anchored to the lake bottom, where the government hadn't yet evicted them. Perhaps they moved locations every few weeks and lived by wilderness rules. Maybe the occupants were just a hardscrabble clan that weren't accustomed to many customers.

But that didn't mean they were up to anything more than a little price-gouging to make ends meet. They probably fished and hunted, living in harmony with the wilderness like those before them. Out there on the water dwelled a kind of freedom unavailable in the modern world, one where human activities made little impact on the larger landscape. At least that is what I thought about as my hand twitched the outboard, and the boat swerved back toward Joe Indian Island. My queasiness had subsided, gentle as a foxtrot now, then faded altogether as we further explored Cranberry Lake.

Loose on the Landscape

Final Call from Wild-Base One

Another August arrived two years later, when we loaded the family car with camping gear again. We wanted to return to Cranberry Lake and the special island we had visited. Our memories from there enticed us to repeat the trip and explore new wild haunts.

This time when we returned to Cranberry Lake, it capped a soggy two-week camping trip in Maine and Canada. We needed a break from hiking slippery mountain trails drenched in rain and fog. The forecast showed sunny weather further south in upper New York State, so we pointed our worn station wagon that way.

We reached the north end of the lake in mid-afternoon and began setting up the tents in the campground, with the dining fly over the picnic table. We intended to rent a boat again for the hour's run to the island, eat supper there, then before dark we would come back to the campground for the night. With half the day already over, we had plenty to do before bringing the boat back before closing at eight o'clock. I told the marina owner where we planned to go, and by quarter to three, we pushed off from the dock.

"We're on our way back to the island," I exclaimed over the engine noise. All heads aboard nodded and smiled.

It's going to be a glorious sunset tonight for a change...before the storm hits, I thought while looking at the sky. Thinly transparent cirrostratus clouds had moved in high overhead, resembling the rippled sands on a wet beach—rain within twenty-four hours.

Winds light, lake surface calm. Familiar spires of hemlocks and spruces appeared on the horizon far ahead—solitude beckoned.

No need to circle the island—it was as familiar to us as our yard at home. I shut off the motor beyond where the shallow rocks broke the surface. I slipped the oars into their locks and rowed toward the gap between the boulders lining the shore. Trey hitched the painter to the same root we used before, and Jordon and Laura exited the boat. I unloaded the cooler and followed them with it along the path.

A few feet from the fire pit, I set it down and looked around. Same rocks and sitting logs; vegetation and soils undisturbed. No one else looked to have visited there for a long time—perhaps since our last trip. Seemed like our island was just waiting for us to come back.

It was a satisfying thought, making the tiny landscape more special. But sometimes when we return to a place, we find very different experiences there. Previous details fade with our memories and new ones attract our attention. We may find features once hidden but now arisen that we never expected. We might have to face events that never happened previously because circumstances were different. But those can change at any moment by coincidence, unrelated except for their timing. Such events appear to arise at random, unpredictable like bingo numbers, birds in a flock, and frost-tracks on windows.

Nothing is truly random, however, for everything in the tangible world has a cause—just not necessarily the same cause for different events. The human mind has a keen ability to recognize patterns in seemingly random occurrences, though correctly interpreting their meanings usually depends on how much rational thought gets applied.

When complex events materialize at the same time and produce significant outcomes, we tend to think a "perfect storm" is the cause. Some think a mystical or meaningful reason has gathered the forces together, though science has its doubts. Usually, such events involve independent variables that occur coincidentally—no causal relationship connects them. That is largely irrelevant for those caught out in the storm, however, for they must struggle to make the best of difficult circumstances.

Since we planned on leaving the island before dark, we decided on no fire tonight. We had plenty of time to relax, so Trey and I went fishing again beyond the boulders—in the same spot we had before. A few bass took our hooks, but we let them go, not needing them for our meal since we had other provisions from our cooler.

We fished for another twenty minutes, then I rowed back to the island where we had our picnic. Water lapped softly against the shoreline rocks and lulled us with its murmurings. Gradually, shadows softened and daylight seemed to yawn, ready for the night-shift. "Okay gang, time to pack up; we've got about an hour to get back to the dock before dark."

"Can't we stay just a little longer?" Trey asked. "We'll miss the sunset."

"Wish we could, but we need time to cross the lake while it's light. We're heading north and so the sun will set on our left—we'll be able to watch it as we cruise."

"Oh, cool."

"Is that where the pot of gold is, where the sun sets?" asked Jordon.

I chuckled. "No, honey, that sits at the end of rainbows. Where the sun hides is where all your best memories are kept, and when you watch a sunset, they come back to you. So, your memories are much more precious than a pot of gold."

"Goody, I can't wait to see this sun go down."

After we loaded the boat, Trey untied the painter, pushed the bow off the gravel, and climbed over the gunwale to sit next to his sister. With the oars in their locks, I started rowing back toward the lake.

Our momentum carried us past the island's rocks, and I shipped the oars. We drifted while I pulled the starter cord on the outboard. It came to life with a hearty whine, and I shifted out of neutral and increased power with the throttle—the whine at once turned into a roar of enthusiasm.

The boat leaped forward like a frisky colt, and everyone's attention focused on the horizon. When I throttled up, the outboard sounded more eager to return to the marina than a stallion racing home to the barn.

But it was just noise and smoke...something wasn't right. The engine still roared, but we weren't going anywhere—the stallion was only running in place.

I released the throttle, and the engine wound to a stop. We sat quietly on the water a few hundred yards from the island.

The propeller must have gotten fouled with something when we landed at the island. After grasping the engine housing, I pulled it toward me so the prop came out of the water and latched in place while I inspected the shaft. The propeller rotated freely when I spun it with my hand.

"That's not good," I muttered. "What's wrong?" Laura asked.

"Shear-pin broke—the bolt that locks the propeller to the shaft."

"How could that happen?"

"Most likely, the spinning prop hit a submerged rock, snapping the bolt off. Half of it is now at the bottom of the lake."

"What are we going to do?"

"Not sur e." I looked around for a spare shear-pin; none. Even a bolt, nail or piece of wire would do in a pinch, but we had nothing I could adapt as a substitute. My eyes rose from the prop and looked at Laura. Stoic, like the children, expecting I'd figure something out.

My gaze then lifted into the sky. All the blue gone now; the white rippling clouds had grown purple. I remembered, "red sky at night, sailors' delight, red sky in morning, sailors take warning." Forget the nice sunset, no orange and red delight out there tonight. A storm approached…and we sat stranded in an open boat at the wild end of a lonely lake with night falling.

The others weren't looking at the dusky sky; their eyes had settled directly on me. I wanted to tell them that Dad would twiddle something on the engine and we'd be skimming across the water in no time again. But with little to twiddle, we weren't going anywhere fast. And even if I had a spare shear pin, no tools lay in the boat to punch out the remaining plug in the shaft and replace it. I'd also need pliers to bend a cotter pin to keep it on, or a wrench to tighten a nut.

Water gently swished against the metal hull, whispering how the lake had us in its grasp now and controlled what would happen next.

A perfect storm was about to give birth on the landscape where the descending night, a broken engine in the wilderness lake, and an ugly squall gathering on the horizon would all intersect.

We couldn't just sit there and wait out the night without protection, risking hypothermia. I ran options through my head, discarding each one as equally risky. Five miles from the marina without a means of calling for help, surrounded by wilderness. No roads, no residences, no other boats.

My eyes shifted from the gathering dusk to Laura. "I could probably row us back to the marina, but they'd be closed by then.
And it would likely take me hours."
"In the dark? What if we get lost?"
"I've got the compass, but it's exposure that worries me—high winds and waves if the storm came up."
"I don't like that idea," Laura said.
"Me neither; best bet is to go back to the island." Trey piped in, "We don't have our tents with us." "Or sleeping bags," Jordon exclaimed.
"We don't need them tonight. We can make a lean-to out of the boat so we'll be dry and out of the wind; plenty of soft hemlock boughs for bedding. With our rain ponchos and space blankets, we'd do just fine. Then row back tomorrow when the storm clears." Practical, logical.

The others didn't look too keen for it; probably thinking about huddling through the night under an upside-down metal container that smelled fishy and banged loudly with raindrops. "We'll drag it to the fire circle where we'll build a nice warm fire and roast marshmallows." Their looks didn't change.

I didn't mention my concerns about if the storm was leading an entire cold front system rather than a single event. Before we embarked from the marina, the forecast stated a sixty percent chance of rain and windy conditions overnight—and for the next few days. It sounded like the lousy Canadian weather we thought we'd escaped had stalked us southward to Cranberry Lake. And without a means of communication, no telling when we might have safer weather to return. The other thing I didn't mention...we only had enough food for another half day.

"What if we row to the lake shoreline over there, past the island?" Laura asked.

"Then what? No assurance there's even a trail anywhere we could easily find. Even if we did, then we'd have to leave the boat with all our gear and hike seven miles around the lake. And we'd have to do it in the dark and rain, stumbling on slippery rocks and roots, risking injuries."

My memory flashed on how we once did that with full packs around Mount Katahdin in Maine. Misery abounded until we finally set up camp near a small pond where a moose and calf walked through to feed on juicy water plants. That encounter lifted our spirits.

Another time, in Michigan's wild upper peninsula, a storm hit our remote camp during the night; hours of lightning and crashing thunder. Our dog got washed away in the adjacent creek, and I had to wade downstream and rescue him from turbulent waters. While driving out the next morning on the isolated dirt road, we encountered a large tree across our route. It had fallen overnight, blocking the only way through the deserted landscape. Fortunately, I had brought along a bow saw for cutting firewood; nothing to do but retrieve it and cut our way past the heavy limbs.

But there on Cranberry Lake, all our options seemed bleak while dusk settled in. "To the island then," I announced.

I dug out our main flashlight and told Trey to turn it on and sit in the bow with it while casting the light over the water ahead. With the oars in place, I began rowing back to Sears Island. Darkness slowly enveloped us, and a gentle breeze picked up.

We were halfway to the island when I spotted something in the darkness far off the right side of the boat. A single pinprick of light glimmered in the dark far away. How far, I could n ot tell. But then it winked out. Blackness again; maybe nothing but a reflection. From what?

"Over there. Did you see that light?" I exclaimed. Heads turned and necks craned. No one had seen it. Then it blinked on again.

There it is, off the starboard bow; could be a boat or someone's flashlight." Laura now saw it too.

"Maybe a hiker or back-country camper."

"Can't be a vehicle or somebody's cabin," I reasoned. "What if it's another floating camp...or the same one we visited near Joe Indian Island last time? Would they even remember us?"

"Let's hope it's a boat," Laura said. "It's bobbing with the water."

"Hard to tell, but we're going to head for it.

Hey Trey, flip the strobe switch on the flashlight; it might alert them that there's someone here in trouble."

The darkness deepened, and with each oar-stroke the island fell behind us, slowly retreating until it disappeared in the night. The only sounds came from the oars dipping into the inky lake and draining water when I pulled them out for the next stroke. Every few minutes, the tiny light disappeared for a moment.

"Boat lights and floating camps don't flicker like that," I said. "Do you see that? It seems to fade and glow every few seconds." "I see it," responded Trey.

"Me too," Jordon whispered.

"Why would it do that?" Laura asked.

"Maybe there's something between us and the light."

"Like what, another boat?"

"A boat hauling aboard something, though what that could be I don't know. Hootch cached underwater? And why would anyone night-fish all the way out here?"

We all stared at the weak glow while I rowed, and our strobe flashed urgently. The distant glow gradually grew larger.

"I don't think that's a boat at all," I finally had to admit. "It looks like it's on land and the flickering is because we're seeing it through all the trees on shore as we move."

I had been rowing for a half hour by then and kept at it for another twenty minutes. The sky flickered for a moment, warning of the coming storm. "Well, it's obvious now that it must be some building," I decided.

After a few minutes, the outlines of a dock emerged out of the darkness, lit by a pole light above it—the source of the glow we had tracked. Amber reflections danced in the water next to the dock. No boats or people about, so I aimed for a nearby piling.

After slipping a line over it, I got out and helped the others do the same. We stood on the planking and looked around. Set back from the dock among the trees, we saw the outlines of a wooden building. Weak incandescent light spilled out from several windows from the single-story structure.

"There's another light over there, and some people moving around," Laura said, pointing further down the shoreline to the right.

I saw movement, and we could hear distant voices in a patch of light through the trees. I heard a thump, but it wasn't possible to see what was going on.

"Let's go up to the house; stay close. Let me do the talking."

We approached the front steps to the open porch. Dull yellow filled the door frame. I led the other castaways onto the low porch and pulled the screen- door open. Inside, we found a large, dimly lit space with simple furnishings and a cleaned-out stone fireplace.

Groups of wooden tables and chairs sat neatly on a plank floor without rugs. It resembled a candle-lit lobby in a worn and rustic mountain retreat.

But I knew it wasn't; it lacked a front desk, service- bell to ring, or helpful staff scurrying about.

We huddled together, alone in an unattended building that shouldn't exist in this wilderness without roads. Goldilocks must have felt the same way when she found the three bears' empty cabin after getting lost in the forest. I was about to go back outside to find someone, but then a young man entered through the screen door.

He stopped short, blinking at the gaggle of intruders before him. "Oh...hi."

I could tell he was trying to place us—flicking through his memory clusters like a counting machine tabulates money stacks. He too must have thought he had entered a strange fairy tale—who are these people and how did they get here?

His eyes settled on mine. "Hello," I nodded. "Sorry to intrude, but our boat broke down on the lake and we saw your lights. Do you think you could help us?" It probably sounded too casual, like I was asking a neighbor to drive us to town because our car wouldn't start.

But as I spoke, understanding spread over the man's face, softening his features like maple syrup poured over morning flapjacks.

He nodded reassuringly. "Let me get someone who can; just wait here." He turned and went back outside.

A few moments later, the door opened again, and an older man entered. He wore what looked like camp clothes, leather boots, dark slacks, and a flannel shirt.

We introduced ourselves, and I explained our dilemma. When I finished, he clucked and shook his head.

"You are incredibly lucky."

Final Call from Wild-Base One

"Yes, we sure are. If it weren't for your dock light still on, we never would have found…"

He waved that away with, "That's true, but your timing is amazing, almost too coincidental; you are lucky to find anyone here at all."

I nodded. "If you guys had gone out, we would have just waited at the dock until you came back."

The man's head tilted back, and he chuckled. I didn't react, wondering why that was funny. Laura and the kids did too. They looked at him, then at me, and I winked back at them for reassurance.

He shook his head as though marveling at something. "You would have had a long wait with all the lights turned off. We should already have left by now, and you never would have found us in the dark. Just good luck that we're still loading the boat. If you arrived here an hour from now, you'd have to wait a very long time." He smiled. "Like nine months."

That jolted me. "Seriously?"

"You've landed at our biological field station. I run it in the summers for SUNY, State University of New York. But tonight is our last for this year—in less than an hour, this place will become abandoned. You got here just in time."

"That's…an amazing coincidence." I stared at him, trying to comprehend the odds that landed us in the only place of rescue with just a few minutes to spare. And other coincidences did not escape me either. Here I am, a biologist, who is depending on another biologist to save us when both our evacuation plans had gotten delayed. I shook my head as though denying the reality at hand. "What's this operation doing so far out here in the wilderness?"

The others began drifting away to investigate the room better, examining animal skulls, twisted tree roots, rocks, and dissecting trays.

"The station is only open for two weeks twice a year, once in June and the other in August. Here we offer field courses for serious undergraduate and graduate-level students. They get to study nature and help us conduct ecological research—not to mention canoeing, hiking, and exploring for fun."

"What a great opportunity; how many students come here?"

"Nearly a hundred at a time. But they've all left except a few of us that are packing up and shutting down right now. Storm's on its way; we need to get moving."

"I think we spotted some of your team through the trees when we docked."

"Probably. They're loading at the other dock." Then he whispered into my shoulder. "There was a black bear hanging around a little while ago where you docked; better keep the family close."

I nodded. "Any room on your boat for us?"

"Afraid not. There's only one still here, and when we get all the equipment and remaining students onboard, we'll be at our legal capacity."

"In that case, we'd appreciate if you could call the boat rental place for us; they're probably still open waiting for their boat."

"We don't have a phone—no wires extend out here. But we have a two-way CB radio we use when necessary. Someone isn't always standing by to take a call, but they are tonight while we pack up."

"Glad for that." Another coincidence that baffled me. "We were going to make the last call a few minutes from now, then we'd pack it up and take the radio with us."

It all seemed so unlikely—breaking down when and where we did, seeing the faint dot of light on the lake, following a hunch, getting there in time. And then only minutes remained before our only means of contact would end. I was at a loss to explain the universe's fickle pathways to fate and fortune. The mysteries of unlikely convergences baffled me; their circuitous pathways to intersection are so improbable to predict in a rational world.

My watch showed eight-thirty when the man and I walked across the room to a small table. He flipped on the CB radio and pressed the mic. "SUNY Central, this is ESF Wild-Base One, come in."

Silence. Then a moment of static. "SUNY Central, this is ESF Wild-Base One; do you copy?"

More static, then someone answered. The biologist quickly explained our problem and requested they contact the marina.

Minutes later, the base called back to confirm. "Lucky again," the director said. "The marina is still open and will get underway with another boat. They should arrive about the time we'll be leaving."

Another unlikely piece of fortune. We shared our gratitude with the biologist, and he left through the screen door to continue loading their boat. We all sat at a classroom table and waited. In the feeble lighting of the quiet room, my limbs relaxed, tension ebbed. We won't be hiding under a boat tonight in the rain, I thought.

The kids soon put their heads on the table and went to sleep. Laura dozed with her elbow on the tabletop, propping her head up. I watched them breathe; glad their minds were somewhere else. Mine was thinking about how it wasn't over yet—we still had a long boat trip back to camp.

Well over an hour passed before the door opened and the head biologist entered with the boat rental owner. We followed them to the dock, where the owner inspected the outboard on our boat.

"Looks like a broken shear pin alright."

"How could that happen out in deep water?"

"Where were you?"

"Just off Sears Island."

"Probably hit an old, submerged stump—one or two of them on that east side; not very deep there."

I gritted my teeth. "You could have mentioned that earlier when I said we were heading there."

The owner didn't respond; he just bent down with a towline and tied our boat's bow to his stern cleats. We stepped aboard and donned life vests. The rescue boat looked similar to the one we rented—just big enough for the four of us to sit upright, but not enough space for us plus the owner, especially for the kids to get comfortable. So, we put them and Laura in our rental boat where they sat on the stern seat facing the lead boat.

I climbed into the tow boat and faced their direction so I could keep them and the motor operator in constant view. If a problem arose, I would grab the throttle from the owner, idle the boat, then yank the towline toward me until I could haul my family aboard as fast as possible. They could float awhile with their safety vests in the water if it came to that.

We pulled away from the dock in tandem, the rental owner maintaining a moderate speed. Minutes later, I watched my family sleep on their stern bench seat while nestled among our belongings. Laura's head leaned back toward the boat's wake, her eyes closed, and arms spread wide, embracing a sleeping child against each side of her—so peaceful, a protective Madonna. Had I needlessly put them in jeopardy?

While the engine droned on, wavelets of whitish water spread away from the moving hull. My thoughts drifted to how we ended up this way. Somehow, we had weathered a perfect storm of events that was ending in our favor. Improbable? Yes, but a more basic question intruded.

Was it right for me to expose my family to the wilderness where danger lurked? Shouldn't they remain in more familiar surroundings where comfort and security are better had—inside pavement perimeters, structured playgrounds, and concrete palisades?

But I had spent much of my youth in such places and knew one could face worse dangers there that could destroy a soul. Never for me again...and not for them, I had vowed. I would show them landscapes and nature, where souls could thrive. Better to encourage them to learn nature's ways instead. Metropolitan living isn't for everyone, yet.

The outboard whined, bow waves roiled past and disappeared into the void. Without a moon or stars for guidance, we moved through a dark ether that bathed us in a warm, gentle breeze. The boats advanced northward, zippering the placid lake open with their silvery wakes. Still, it was after midnight when we reached the campground and pulled the car onto its parking pad. My eyelids drooped and a case of the yawns hit me when I turned off the ignition.

Just a few dozen steps away lay our tent and sleeping bags, where sweet sleep beckoned. I switched off the headlights, then woke Laura. We each lifted a child out of the car. Laura carried Jordon, and Trey followed her toward the tent.

I grabbed some items from the car, then turned and took a few steps to follow Laura, who was halfway along. Something in the darkness moved at the corner of my eye. I stopped and squinted, and the coal-black form of an adult black bear lumbered out of the trees only thirty feet away. The tent lay in its path, and without pausing, the beast walked into our camp.

"Black bear," I said while yawning. I felt too tired to care, but I repeated the warning for everyone to hear. Normal voice, no energy or reason to shout. None of them even looked up. A few seconds and they were already at the tent entrance. I watched them quietly step inside one by one; not sure they saw or heard anything.

My eyes shifted to the bear again, which padded past the tent without halting. I stood exposed, a horseshoe toss from the bear. It turned its head toward me for a moment, then glanced at the picnic table and ambled that way. It sniffed for leftovers, found none, and resumed its walk out of the camp and into the forest again.

I watched it leave, then shuffled to the tent, saw my family cuddled there, then flopped onto my sleeping bag. The storm hit sometime in the night, and in the morning we found our dining fly had collapsed in the wind. And by then, all our footprints and the bear's tracks had washed away. But none of us had heard a thing while asleep in our bags, because our dreams were busy distracting us from the night's worries.

The Batsto Bewitching

Before we married, Laura and I discovered the ruins of an old, abandoned village. We weren't the only ones to have found it, but few had explored it at the time. It once bustled around a cluster of buildings. There, early settlers hacked out a living along the banks of a small, quiet river in the wilderness of the vast *New Jersey Pine Barrens Ecoregion (84b), Atlantic Coastal Plain Ecoregion (84)*.

    The village, called Batsto, had existed in such a lonely place for only one reason—so the inhabitants could rip into the mucky bowels of the riverbanks to harvest bog ore. Pungent odors of charcoal kilns and iron smelters hung in the air over dirt-packed streets. For its inhabitants, it must have seemed like an immense crematorium lay smoldering under the entire village.

But burning the dead was not the building's mission...creating instruments of death, however, certainly was. Residents made weapons, cannonballs, and ammunition from the ore to slay British soldiers and colonial turncoats during the American Revolution.

By the late1800s, most everyone had left Batsto. Then entropy marched right in and began laying waste to everything—rotting this, digesting that, decaying a beam here, a wall there until it all settled into a pile of ruins, weeping nutrients for the benefit of other life forms. Eventually, the State took over the site and restored a few buildings to preserve their history.

Laura and I had read a brief article about the old village. It sounded intriguing—especially since the river offered a way to explore the region. We organized an expedition that spring, deciding to arrive as Batsto's inhabitants once did...by canoeing the last few miles to the village rather than driving to it.

The river flowed southward through the two-hundred square mile Wharton State Forest wilderness, and a suitable launch point lay miles upstream reachable by vehicle on a remote sandy track. Batsto's remains lay a half-day's paddling away, and we intended to combine the canoe trip with exploring the village's leftovers afterward.

The ruins extended over just a few acres. But it lay within the vast uninhabited landscape that comprised twenty percent of New Jersey—over a million acres of the largest natural area on the MidAtlantic seaboard. Scraggly pitch pines and stunted scrub oaks struggled above a dry prairie understory. There they sucked paltry nutrition from the ubiquitous sandy soils. Most plant and animal species could not adapt to the scarcity of resources, even in the pockets of hardwoods that colonized more fertile areas.

This austere ecosystem occupied the region for nearly twenty thousand years. But even long before, the landscape provided a much harsher place—back when today's continents had not yet formed. The land was part of Pangea then, a single vast supercontinent containing all the Earth's future land masses. It was not Earth's first supercontinent during the last four billion years, though it was the most recent.

Before Pangea, only three continents existed 335 million years ago—Gondwana, Euramerica and Siberia. But 200 million years ago, proverbial Mother Earth began undergoing a metamorphosis, induced by cramps deep in her belly. Her molten core rumbled with gas, and partially digested magma regularly spewed out through lava tubes onto her hard tectonic plates.

For eons, Earth vomited her guts out. These plates dried and formed a crusty network that supported the new Pangea supercontinent. All that volcanic and tectonic activity produced internal pressures beneath the plates that pushed against adjacent ones, stressing them beyond tolerance. Pangea began cracking apart like a giant cosmic egg.

Plate tectonics gradually caused North America and Africa to split away from each other. Eventually, they separated into two huge landmasses, Laurasia in the north and Gondwanaland in the south—Mother Nature had slowly ripped her apron in two. As they drifted over millions of years, a new sea formed between them—the Atlantic Ocean. Climates changed many times; sea levels rose and fell over the next 150 million years without any politicians' help or humans fretting about it.

Global cooling produced glaciers in the north that locked rivers and lakes in ice, lowering sea levels. The last retreat of the oceans left deep sands for forty miles inland, forming the Coastal Plain Ecoregion, including the Pine Barrens landscape.

As the Pleistocene Epoch ended 12,000 years ago, another warming cycle began in the region. The last great ice sheet started melting. Melt waters exposed sediment, gravels, mineral soils, and more sand ground from Piedmont rocks by the glaciers further west.

As tundra ecosystems declined with melting glaciers, warm-tolerant colonizers moved in. Pines eventually dominated the overstory, including Jack, Red, and Pitch, along with Blackjack Oak and Scrub Oak. These species tolerated dry conditions and soils with low nutrients, along with blueberries, bearberry, hazelnut, and willow. Prairie grasses and forbs occupied the ground in uplands, and a panoply of sedges moved into low moist areas.

Before Laura and I first made our voyage down the Batsto River on a bright spring morning, we rented a canoe from a local shop. An assistant carried it on the roof of a four-wheel-drive Jeep while we followed in our car to the takeout spot near the village. We left our car there and got into the jeep for the six-mile drive north to our launching point. The route ran along a rough, sandy trail through a pine forest before emerging into an expansive clearing. We unloaded the canoe among the bunchgrasses near the river.

Engine noise faded with the departing jeep, and silence descended. I glanced around, noting the monotony of vast sandy patches thick with grasses and forbs, punctuated by shrubby pines and bushes. The landscape extended as far as I could see—no houses, no human presence of any kind.

We tossed our daypacks in the boat and dragged it toward the riverbank, the metal squeaking and squealing like an eager child. It ended at the water's edge where we hopped inside. Using our paddles, we pushed away from the bank, then the current eased us into the slipstream.

We marveled at the morning sunlight that danced in the riffles ahead of us, along with the gurgling water, the relentless gentle flow, the warmth on the back of our necks.

Once past our clearing, pine forest and hardwoods stretched on either side. Thick trunks and limbs leaned over us, curving off the banks to form living arches that welcomed our passage. Fresh air filled our lungs, a gift from the forest and every green leaf surrounding us. A pileated woodpecker announced our presence with a hearty drumroll that echoed in the forest. Sweet, ethereal notes of wood thrushes hinted at mysteries in the underbrush.

No rocks or boulders blocked our way in this sandy environment, but trees and logs did. Where these had toppled into the channel, they fell short of the opposite side, allowing us easy passage around them. Skylight mixed with the dark water and it seemed we floated on a byway of blueberry puree. It invited us into a mystical landscape of natural wonder, where every shade of springtime dressed the riverbanks, welcoming us to nature's secret pageant.

White and purple violets bloomed on the banks. Yellow spikes of golden-club emerged from the surface of slower moving waters. Blue irises on slender leaves filled grassy openings, and broadleaved pickerel weeds poked above the shallows next to sandy banks.

Colorful warblers darted across the channel, landed on tree limbs on the opposite side, and serenaded us with their ballads. Here and there, green frogs strummed out bass cords to accompany the trills of the songbirds. Their plunking twang sounded like a broken guitar string. Invariably, they would plop into the water with a musical marcato articulation to end the chorus. The river burbled and ferried us along with little help from our paddle blades. We had merged with the slow current and moved with a natural rhythm through a landscape of liquid serenity.

For the next half-hour, the turns in the river presented new delights. Painted turtles sunned themselves on logs before slipping off and disappearing as we approached. Patches of Atlantic White Cedar armored banks with dense branches, a great-blue heron fished from the shallows, wood ducks swam ahead of us and dragonflies landed on our bow.

The trees and bushes eventually dwindled, appearing only in patches beyond the banks. Grassy spaces with heaths, such as huckleberries and swamp azaleas, began to take over. Soon, the channel became nearly lost amid a mosaic of little bush-covered islands that appeared all around us in a vast field of open water. We had entered a broad shrubby marsh with expansive views. Without confinement, the current slowed and we let the canoe drift awhile, barely needing to nudge it around the islands in the open marsh. We paddled through acres of white and pink lilies with heart- shaped pads sparkling in the sunshine. The Batsto had bewitched us.

The channel re-emerged and we picked up the paddle-pace. Banks became lined with dark-green cedars, tall pines and thickets of scrub-shrubs, which blended with the unbroken forest beyond. Now and then we skirted around a log in our way or nuzzled aside a leafy branch. But eventually the turns became gentler again, and we slipped along straight stretches. Finally, we entered the upper end of Batsto Lake.

A light breeze refreshed us as we paddled the last half-hour down the lake. We steered away from water weeds and occasional stumps that poked above the surface. By late afternoon, we beached the canoe at the sandy takeout point at the south end of the lake where we had left our car.

We drove the mile around the end of the lake and wandered around the village's remains. Down a weedy, sandy street there we found a partially rebuilt old mansion, as well as a once-busy blacksmith shop. The weathered shells of worker cabins stood vacant of life on the fringes of the property. Old mining equipment and carriage parts lay about. Timbers and foundations from other buildings baked in the afternoon sun, nearly smothered in last winter's weeds and new spring upstarts.

Hurray for the brave upstarts, I thought, that move-in and restore disturbed places. Colonizers and pioneer plants prepare disturbed landscapes for the new histories that will unfold there. Next time you see a weed holding the soil together in a vacant lot, pat it on its head—"That'll do weed, that'll do."

A few hours later, we returned home to the northern Piedmont, where the rivers are rocky and rolling hills and lush valleys replace the sand barrens.

Ten years later, we wanted to repeat the canoe trip with our two children. By then, Trey was eight years old, and Jordon was five. Still in business, the same canoe rental service Laura and I had us ed before hauled us and the equipment to the clearing by the Batsto River where we launched long ago.

With Trey's eagerness to paddle, we gave him the bow position while I took the stern. Laura and Jordon sat between us. We pushed the boat off the shoal and saw sunbeams in the riffles just as before. But now I pointed them out to our children so they could marvel over nature's pageant too.

On that sunny day in May, pine warblers and yellow throats flitted across the channel. Leopard frogs croaked from the shallows. The river gurgled and water dripped from our paddles as we slid through the downstream meanders. Water lilies again cheered us along through the marshes. Blue spikes of our old pickerel weed friends stood bold against broad, green leaves of arrow-arum and the white stems of golden-club, bright as ever. Stands of cedars and red maples lined the riverbanks still, and the miniature shrubby islands were again sporting fresh spring growth. The Batsto flow had once more shown us nature's splendors and soothed us with her lullabies.

Loose on the Landscape

Although we lived three hours from the Pine Barrens and had explored them several times, we felt drawn to return periodically for more enchantments. The Batsto called us back a few years after we made the trip with Trey and Jordon. We planned to go on a day trip in April, a month earlier than the previous excursions.

A few days before the outing, we learned my sixty-year-old mother, Bea, wanted to visit us for two weeks, which would include the date we had scheduled the canoe trip. The relationship between Bea and I had remained amicable since I was nine, when she dropped me, two younger brothers and a younger sister at an orphanage. I didn't leave there until I graduated from high school.

During that time, I harbored no animosity toward her for abandoning my siblings and me there. Instead, I buried my resentments by focusing my attentions on the natural world. In my younger mind, I viewed her more as a victim of my father Dick, who left her with a passel of kids and few choices.

Still, she didn't fight for her children when it counted...not for ten years, nor did she show an abiding love to them as they remained confined in the orphanage where she had dumped us. Such things might have led to withered futures for me and my siblings, because nurturance never got a chance with Dick and Bea. As a result, cherishing another person was not something I knew much about as a young man, until Laura gradually taught me how—an angel of mercy, so patient and kind.

Bea was mostly a city girl and lived a few hours away in Philadelphia. She said she needed a break from her second husband, Wilson, and their bickering environment. This wasn't the first time, but we didn't want to cancel our family outing because of it. Laura and I invited her along, but also offered her the option of spending the day alone at our home until we returned that night. She did not know how to drive a car and wasn't keen on spending the whole day by herself in the country, so she reluctantly agreed to come on the trip when I held firmly to our plans.

The morning of our trip, she seemed more somber than usual. I presumed the problems with her husband occupied her thoughts. He was a medical pathologist who saw dead people. Fortunately, they all lay on slabs in the city morgue or in slices under a microscope where he determined their cause of death. Yet, he was a gentle and generous man, and we always got along fine. He took Laura and me to one of his autopsies once.

An obese man lay dead on a stainless-steel table, his enormous belly bloated with decomposition gases. The corpse rose in a mound above the side-gutters and drain used to catch his juices when Wilson cut through his organs as though tucking in to a very large potpie.

He soaked up the remaining liquid with a sponge, and it reminded me of sopping up gravy with a piece of bread. Wilson lectured us as he hunted for anatomical clues to the man's demise, but my attention remained on the once-living body of another human that was now carved into a pile of organic waste. He once laughed, yearned, and had a future, which had all ended hours ago with a heart attack.

Whatever the problems Bea was having with Wilson, I hoped a day out with nature would lift her spirits— though she hadn't been in a canoe since she was a teenager. Then, too, her primary connection with the natural world over the past forty years had been walking in parks and tending her city garden.

I began checking the weather forecast a week before our trip; difficult to do in those pre-digital days, but I called local libraries and monitored my weather radio.

It rained over southern New Jersey a few days before our Saturday departure, but the forecast predicted clearing by launch day. To make sure, I called the canoe rental place Friday afternoon. They expected good weather ahead as well.

To confirm, I called again just before leaving home early Saturday morning, and the owner told me the weather was already improving.

That made the trip a go, and we drove several hours for another pleasant day in the sandy Coastal Plain. When we parked at the canoe rental office, the sky remained overcast, but the clouds had thinned. I found the owner working on a crossword puzzle behind the counter. He looked up quizzically, and I asked about renting the longest boat they had for the Batsto.

"That would be the twenty-footer we have in the yard—all aluminum."

"Perfect; how's the river running? Heard you had a lot of rain the last couple of days."

"Plenty, but now the skies should be clear out there." "Any reports of flooding?"

"Nope, the haul trail to the takeout is sand, so it's gotta' be dry by now."

"Great, got my family here, including my mother, hoping for a pleasant time on the river." I mentioned it to flush out any concerns by the agent before committing to the boat.

"Sure, I get it."

"We figure on starting at Quaker Bridge and reaching the village by late afternoon."

"That's a nice trip. You can follow us to the takeout spot where you can leave your car. Then we'll haul you all and the canoe to the bridge where you can launch." "Sounds perfect; that's what we did a few years ago."

I fished out the cash to pay for the rental.

"Just leave the boat on the bank with the paddles at the takeout when you finish, and we'll pick it up later— easy as pudding."

The man called his helper over and explained where to take us. Out on the lot, I watched the two men pull the longest canoe off a rack—longer than a flatbed tow truck. They loaded it onto the jeep's roof rack, then we followed in our old station wagon we called "The Goose." We dropped the car off at the lower end of Batsto Lake, not far from the old village. The river flowed south into the mile-long lake, which was created by a dam at the abandoned town.

We intended to launch six miles upstream, the same spot as we had done in the past. The family squeezed into the jeep, and it headed north along the river in four-wheel drive, bumping and bouncing on the sandy trail through a pine forest. After twenty minutes, the jeep stopped, and we all got out, bending our limbs back into place.

"Looks familiar," I said, glancing about the clearing. "There's an opening in the brush over there on the bank where you can put in." The driver pointed to a dark space between some bushes several canoe-lengths away.

"I remember we launched from here last time, but the weather was better," I mused. My gaze wandered over the scene, the visual impression familiar, yet it felt different this time—the way a hare senses something ominous lurking in a nearby thicket. Maybe it was just the moody weather—gray sky, plants drooping from the drizzle that had fallen earlier that morning, the silence.

Pockets of clumped grasses stood between the jeep and the riverbank like green traffic cones blocking the way in warning. A fleshy patch of prickly pear cactus backed them up with sharp spines. I glanced across the clearing toward the brushy cover along the riverbank where twisted branches and contorted pines grew, some with blackened scars from old battles with brush fires. Limbs arched above, nearly suffocating the dwarf oaks and sweet bay magnolia bushes under them.

Sand sucked at every root, clutched my shoes, and seemed about to pull me under the surface if I stood there too long. Next to me, flattened stalks of wiregrass suggested something had stood there just before we arrived. Its broken stems seemed to pray for deliverance...but the dull sky that loomed over all granted nothing, not even a shadow.

I turned and helped the livery man unload the canoe and carry it to the opening at the channel. We set it on the ground while the family stood together watching with eager faces...except, for the downturned mouth on my mother. They all clutched their small day packs as tight as refugees waiting to board a boat to freedom.

The jeep driver retrieved the paddles while I studied the channel. Only a small stretch was visible before it curved out of sight around dense thickets of trees. On the far side, a wall of leafy branches dragged in the current, obscuring the raw face of the bank. The channel seemed wider than I remembered. A determined stone heaved across might reach the other side, though barely.

On my left through the mist and trees, I could see the low guardrails of Quaker Bridge over the channel. Its single lane connected a deserted country road with the other side—the only crossing upstream of Batsto Village. On the top rail, I noticed a dark patch that suddenly expanded into odd-shaped wings and flew across the channel. Crows don't have wingspans of nearly four feet. A raven, I thought, but realized how rare they were in the Pine Barrens.

I'd heard how a man in 1889 found a nest near his home fifteen miles away with two young ravens in it. He raised them in captivity, naming one "Never" and the other "More." They didn't get along, and eventually "Never" killed "More" and partly devoured him.

I winced while turning back to the group; Nevermore, I sighed.

My gaze shifted to the right, where the water rushed downstream. I remembered the Batsto as a low gradient channel of gentle flow and polite manners. But this stream was in a hurry. The water seemed heavy, full of sandy sediment from the earlier storm. No longer blueberry puree, the flow moved with attitude in mocha-gray. Yet the surface remained smooth as usual, no white-water or standing-waves to unbalance the canoe.

I didn't see any fallen logs in the channel, and rocks wouldn't be a problem in the sandy barrens. Without visible impediments, it was hard to gauge how the boat would handle. The owner had selected it as suitable for us, yet something nagged at the back of my mind. "River seems faster than I remember. Is this usual?"

The livery man glanced up for a second as he laid the paddles in the boat. Despite the lack of sunshine, I saw him squint at the water. "Looks normal, right? You won't have any problems." He twitched his shoulder and pointed above the trees. "And look, the sky is clearing."

Indeed, the clouds were thinning and a few brighter patches poked through. "Hope so. Ever run this river yourself?"

"Nope, just haul the boats, and help in the store." He pointed at the channel. "They say the channel widens out downstream and the current slows," the man responded.

"Good; we can't afford to tip over."

"You'll be fine." The man then chuckled. "Hey, just watch out for the Jersey Devil; it's been known to visit these parts, you know." I gave the man a questioning glance.

He grinned. "You've never heard of i t?" he seemed surprised. "Tall like a man, bat-wings, horse-head, claws, horns, forked tail—scares the vinegar out of folks."

"Vaguely," I shrugged. I'd heard the name but knew nothing else about it. "Sounds ornery."

"Been haunting people out here in the barrens since the beginning; even the Indians saw it."

I played along; "No kidding?"

"Yep, been reports of it killing sheep and livestock too."

"In that case, we'll be sure to keep our bleating to a minimum ," I winked.

"Well, I've got to get going. Enjoy the ride."

While we placed our stuff in the boat, I heard the jeep start, then a straining whine. I looked over to see a rear tire spinning in the sand, then it caught and the jeep shot down the sandy track and disappeared. That guy seemed in a hurry, like the river.

While the stern half-rested on the sandy shoal, the front half of the canoe stuck out into the flow. The lack of an actual bank made my nagging feeling strong er.

We needed to balance the weight with all five of us and keep the boat lining properly in the flow. For this, I had Laura take the bow. Trey stepped in next and got behind her. Bea followed, then Jordon. I slid into the stern seat.

"Ok, everyone needs to put on a vest." I tossed each a standard life preserver—orange and bulging with kapok stuffing. Laura and the kids donned theirs, chatting amiably while I helped them. But Bea refused.

"I don't need one; I'll be fine."

That made me wince. "Mo m, it's necessary; it may save your life

if we tip over."

"I'm not wearing that." She sounded perturbed, as though I asked that she wear a leaded weight-belt.

"We're not pushing off until you do."

"Then just let me get out now and you can all make the trip without me; just go and enjoy yourselves; I'll wait for you."

I'd seen her play this game before. "Look around, Mom, this is a wilderness; the nearest town is nearly ten miles away and there aren't any taxis out here—there's no way out except in this canoe." "You can come and get me when you reach the car.

I'll probably survive."

This wasn't the time for such drama, and I knew the only way to keep my mother from drowning in Lake Woebegone was to keep her in the boat. Logic hadn't worked, but perhaps a little cognitive dissonance might. I nudged her that way at a gentle idle.

"That's hours from now; it'll be getting dark by then."

She stared at the river in silence, stony-faced.

Since that didn't work, I goosed the emotional throttle a bit. "Bears roam about here, and if we get delayed, you could be stuck here with no protection...for a day or two."

More staring. I needed to rev the terror scenario up to full. "You might have to survive on your own for the next five days until a rescue party finds you—no food, no water, no heat...no toilet." No response, not even a squirm; the others sat quietly, watching.

The river gurgled.

Then I fired the emotional afterburners. "Are you going to tell the helicopter crew who winches you up the cable next week that you needed rescuing because you hated the idea of wearing a life preserver?"

That did it; she took the life vest without another word and placed it around her neck and fastened the straps.

"Everyone okay and ready for launch?" It was my cheeriest voice. Laura nodded, and the kids exclaimed, "Yeah, Dad," in unison.

I looked at their grandmother, wondering if bringing her was at all sensible. "Mom, are you ready?"

"Fine." Nothing in her voice sounded fine. If she wanted to act more like cargo than an eager participant, at least the rest of us would enjoy the Batsto's charms once again. Surely, the river's beauty would lift her spirits just around the first bend.

The mass of moving water urged me to join it, and I nudged the boat off the sand with my paddle. As we entered the flow, I dipped the blade gently to guide us downstream.

Immediately, though, I sensed trouble. The current moved much faster than it had looked from the bank. I tried to steer the boat down the channel's center, but the current took control. It swept us toward the far edge, where thickets of trees loomed with branches swept sideways in the current and they extended well-over the channel.

We stroked hard to avoid the trees, straining to pull the bow back toward the middle. It worked, and the canoe swung away from the limbs that bobbed underwater. My memory leaped back to a few minutes ago when I stood on the bank and noticed the same thing...branches dragging in the water. Then I recalled how in previous years they didn't drag, because the banks were much higher then, and their raw sides fully exposed.

Now I made the connection about what had bothered me while standing at the water's edge. I couldn't see it then with such a limited view of the channel. On the open water, however, it was clear—the Batsto River wasn't at all normal...it was in high flood stage.

The tree branches should mark the top of the banks, well above the flow by five or six feet. But now the water level had risen, submerging the bank, and sweeping against the branches' undersides. This meant a massive increase in the volume of flow, twice as fast as we had experienced on the Batsto before...and far more dangerous.

"Morons!" I shouted at the absent boat rental staff, digging the paddle into the flow and yanking hard to pull the boat back toward the middle again. The rushing current curled around our canoe like a thick serpent and shot us downstream, whipping us between the tree lines with each meander.

The others turned their heads toward me with worry etched on their faces. "It'll be ok," I assured them as I again jammed the paddle deep as though into a liquid beast. Water gushed against the boat as we surged ahead in the center where the "thalweg" flowed. Here the river's grasp was strongest, where the current moved fastest, deepest, and most powerful. But it was also the safest route, where ricochets were fewer.

The thalweg line was visible as a narrow rippling of faster-flowing water in the flow that shifted on and off- center depending on moment-to-moment fluvial forces. I held the boat there for the smoothest passage, knowing the best way to ride a beast is to stay on the ridge of its back.

It works until you hit underwater obstructions like sleepers. These submerged logs lurked like crocs just below the surface. When we saw one crosswise in the thalweg, we chose a path around it, pulling out of the faster current if necessary. Running over one of those logs could roll the canoe in a second and put us all under water—where hidden limbs could snag and hold one of us there forever. I had rolled my kayak that way years ago on a remote stream and wasn't about to let it happen here. Stay vigilant, I reminded myself.

As we plunged ahead, sticks and woody debris also fouled the thalweg and caused it to break-up suddenly and disappear— fractured into turbulence and scattering froth in the flow. Then the thalweg would reappear past the obstruction. At bends it shifted and ran near the banks from centrifugal force.

Maintaining the canoe's stability was easier in the straights, but the thalweg constantly whipsawed into tight meander turns to the left and right. There sharp branches threatened, and underwater logs jolted the boat sideways, banging against the metal like a baseball bat pounded against an empty oil drum.

No escape, no calm place to pull over, and no exit. Despite our efforts, the river thrashed its way through the wilderness as though dragging us to its lair somewhere in hell.

At times, the high water overtopped the banks, and no channel was discernible. In those places, the entire landscape flooded, and water rushed over a wide area on both sides, flattening bushes, bulldozing limbs and sending logs toward us like torpedoes.

It wasn't just the river that moved anymore—the whole landscape seemed in motion, angry with the boat of intruders that dared invade its domain. Nature gushed, and we were just some of the flotsam to be jettisoned.

When the channel re-formed, I fought to steer the boat around hazards, but the weight of so many people made the canoe sluggish despite my strokes. Laura did her best, but the river kept heaping more obstacles in our path, requiring moment-to-moment decisions.

Where the channel narrowed, the flow moved even faster until it seemed we would surely capsize. Laura kept at it, bearing my shouted instructions with restraint, overwhelmed by the constantly changing conditions. Frustrated, I bellowed like a captain on a sinking ship—because I was, and we were. Once again, I had put my family in jeopardy by exploring the wilderness with a small boat.

While Laura worked to keep the bow clear of debris, I kept my focus on reading the river and what it was about to throw at us. But then the canoe would slam against the end of a log anyway and cause someone to gasp. Laura and the kids often blurted out hazard locations, but Bea said nothing. Nobody screamed or wailed—but they tightly clutched the sides of the canoe. The Batsto was bewitching us once again, but not in a good way. It had our rapt attention and had captured our emotions. Only this time, it wasn't a pleasant feeling...not even close.

And then the thalweg shoved us on top of another huge sweeper across our path. Suddenly the bow rose high, putting Laura's head a foot above mine back in the stern. The log under Bea's seat acted as the balance point on a teeter-totter, causing the boat to wobble ominously, threatening to toss us overboard if anyone moved a muscle.

The current banged against the stern, nudging it sideways. If the canoe swung parallel against the log, I knew tons of water would push with a mighty force against the side of the hull. In seconds, it would tip it toward the flow and fill the boat, swamping us.

None of us dared take a breath or the current would pull us under the swirling water, where the submerged log lurked in darkness.

Loose on the Landscape

Riding the Dragon

Laura hovered above the sleeper log with the canoe's bow in the air like a breaching whale. She used her paddle to push us backward off the top. My paddle was too far from the log, so I backstroked rapidly, then side-stroked to keep the current from forcing the stern further sideways.

Our efforts finally moved the canoe upstream until we were off the log, free of its clutches. Then we both stroked hard to maneuver toward the end of the log, slip around it and zoom ahead. The great flow surged ahead, clenching us in its hydraulic grasp. I watched mounds of water flexing and rolling like the massive shoulder muscles of a giant cat from the Pleistocene, come for a visit through a cosmic wormhole.

In the sounds of rushing water, the river seemed to rebuke and snarl at us. I snarled back, letting the adrenaline gallop free while I focused on the next hazard in our path. Laura and our kids remained stoic. I wondered if their calmness prevailed because they trusted me for safe deliverance, or it was due to shock from our peril. I couldn't see their faces to tell.

I had brought my family into many wild places before to teach them about the real world —the good, the bad and the indifferent. Whether it involves other humans or risky environments, you can't take on a devil if you don't know firsthand how it operates.

Bea, however, was not so restrained. She had been vocal about our dismal chances since the moment we launched. At first, every few minutes she demanded I pull the boat over like a taxicab to the curb and let her out. "We can't Mom, there's no place to land; current's too fast and the banks are too thick with brush."

She was silent for a few minutes, but then she blurted, "I want to go home right now!"

"As soon as we find a spot, we'll try to stop for a breather."

"Joel, drop me off right now, or else."

"It'll be okay." I was emphatic, but a limb scraped the metal boat with a loud screech—it sounded like the river was laughing hysterically.

I hollered at Laura to swerve as a sharp branch loomed toward my mother. The family had enough to worry about, so I kept the thought to myself that if the boat capsized in the middle, no one could simply walk over to the bank and climb out. The current was far too strong for that. It would rush them downstream the way it would any log.

The Batsto had been carrying water and debris through the Pine Barrens for a very long time. I later learned both the river and the withered landscape were places where myths could always find fertile ground. Myths had long thrived there, and their roots went deep. Beyond the handful of all communities, few people found hospitable homes among the odd shaped pines and stunted shrubs of the Pine Barrens. And those that did, who swore by the legends, felt there was something malevolent and unnatural there. This usually involved supernatural entities they believed lurked among the scrub oaks and pines. Most often it was the Jersey Devil they had in mind. When we launched the canoe that morning, I didn't see such a creature sitting on Quaker Bridge. But I saw a raven, I think. And we all know what Poe told us about them.

Most accounts ascribe the origins of the Jersey Devil to 1735, when a Quaker woman from England lived in "The Barrens." After producing twelve children, she made a pact with the Devil to surrender her next one to the demon if he would make it her last birth. It seemed to me a particularly desperate approach to birth control.

As the story goes, she delivered a bouncing infant demon sporting a horsey-goat head with horns, bird legs with hooves for feet, claw hands, forked tail and bat-like wings. It was apparently so bouncy that it immediately sprung right out an open window and escaped.

The little devil supposedly thrived among the swamps and contorted vegetation of the barrens. It grew up into a right proper demon, harassing and haunting innocent folk that dared trespass on its turf. People reported many confrontations periodically during the next two centuries. Stories of the Jersey Devil describe red glowing eyes, scales, and fire coming out of its mouth.

Whatever it was, it seemed this malevolent presence had been haunting the region long before settlers arrived. The native American Lenape tribe had another name for the Pine Barrens…"Place of the Dragon."

They weren't the only ones who used that term. Early Dutch explorers bushwhacked their way through the bleak landscape, noting features and rivers. They called the area "Drake Kill." In the Dutch language, "Drake" means dragon, and "Kill" is their word for stream and river. Hence, they called the Batsto "Dragon River."

How curious that English settlers, native Americans, and Dutch explorers during different time periods invoked the name of the same mythical monster—something dragon-like, very similar to...the "Jersey Devil."

Over the years, people reported the demon getting into chicken coops and farms, destroying crops, and killing animals. Sightings came from at least fifty different towns in the region, where it terrorized residents. Sheriff posses periodically formed to apprehend the creature, and for a time, a $100,000 bounty was offered for its capture, dead or alive.

Chaos reigned for a week in mid-January 1909, when a veritable plague of Devil sightings occurred throughout southern New Jersey. According to reports, it wreaked havoc upon town folk—attacking trolley cars and people at social gatherings. Newspapers reported police firing upon it, along with announcements of many school closings, and businesses that shut, their owners too afraid to open their shops.

Mass hysteria and mindless fears were as common back then as they are even today. Irrational beliefs undermine problem-solving and determining root- causes of events. History shows us that once mass hysteria rages, it can quickly damage a promising society— Salem witches, Jonestown in Guyana, "War of the Worlds" radio broadcast, climate change obsession, Covid-19 panic.

At times, however, events may sweep a person helplessly to a conclusion they might never have desired or understood. It is then one might feel victimized by uncontrollable forces. But that never gets one to safety; better to count on skills, wits and perseverance.

We rode the Batsto dragon to an uncertain future, straining to keep the canoe upright. Countless times, I jammed my paddle into the swirling flow and wrenched the shaft toward me, pushing the bow away from a protruding branch that threatened the family. But this allowed the current to snatch the stern instead and swoosh my end sideways.

There were places, though, where the dragon rested, and it was those I sought when my own muscles ached more than I could bear. These were the eddies, where the current swirled back upon itself, producing quiet water. I looked for them on the downstream sides of logs and the inside bends of meanders. I'd angle our way into them for a few moments before shooting out into the rushing current again.

The river was having its way, threatening each moment to sweep one of us out into the current with a protruding branch, or gouge the hull and flip the boat.

We pushed on, constantly shifting strokes and our course in the hyper-flow; it was all we could do. My watch said we had spent two hours dodging obstacles and fighting to stay in the thalweg, but it felt twice as long. Nothing happened in slow-motion the way they show in movies. Time seemed to move increasingly faster, accelerating with the surging current. Changing scenes flicked past my vision as though we were on a wild rollercoaster to oblivion. Too much was happening in the same moment for my mind to keep up with new corrective actions. At any moment our situation could change dramatically if I faltered or made the wrong move.

The dreary sky cleared, and I began overheating in the hot sun, so I took my tee shirt off. We came around another tight turn where the current pushed the canoe immediately toward the outside bank.

White cedar trees formed a dense phalanx with sharp bayonets of broken, jagged branch stubs thrust toward us. The current, stronger than my strokes, swung the stern against the cedar branches. Immediately I felt a biting pain in my left side and knew one of the ragged spikes just gouged me. I yelped and saw blood gush from the wound; no time to examine the puncture. I furiously draw-stroked to pull the boat away so the others would avoid a similar stabbing.

Laura and I inched the canoe back toward center-channel into the thalweg, where we cannon-balled through a straight section before hurtling into another turn. Ahead, a large log had toppled from the bank and lay across most of the channel, blocking our passage. It wasn't submerged like a sweeper but lay horizontally with a foot of space between the log and the water surface, its trunk thick as a barrel.

"Log!" I yelled to Laura. We started our back-paddling routine, but the current fought us and won. The canoe hit the log sideways with a metallic thump, trapping us lengthwise against it by the thalweg flow. Tons of water pushed against the submerged part of the boat, causing the topside edge to tip dangerously upstream. The enormous force of flowing water tried to pull us under the log in a white froth. In seconds the canoe would swamp like the edge of an empty pot dipped under the surface.

The relentless side pressure on the hull prevented Laura and me from pushing the boat away from the log with our paddle blades. The top rail of the canoe dipped further toward the flow. I leaned over the upstream side, thrust my blade deep into the current and jammed the end into the sandy channel bottom with the shaft braced tight against the hull.

It held, and the canoe stopped tipping...but only for a handful of seconds. I had just enough time to relax my arm muscles briefly and relieve the burn for a moment. My head filled with the sound of rushing water. It gushed around the paddle shaft, canoe edges, and the mass of limbs and leaves that bobbed in the flow at the end of the log.

Then the force of the current undercut my blade tip and ripped it out of the streambed. Without my tight grip on the shaft, the current would have swept the paddle away and under the boat. Instantly I re-braced the paddle against the gunwale and thrust it deeper into the sandy bottom. It provided leverage to counter the hydraulic pressure, but it succeeded only as long as my strength lasted. I could not overpower the current and hold thousands of gallons of angry water back for long with a wooden stick.

My only option was to relax every few seconds, then jam and pry again, fighting the river and losing each time the current scoured out my blade tip. I glanced sideways at the others. They leaned hard against the side of the boat that chaffed the log and stared with ashen faces at the rushing water creep closer to the canoe's top edge.

I held on and stared at the rising flow relentlessly pounding against the hull. Water churned white with oxygen as though the river was salivating, anticipating its chance to devour us finally. The river no longer gurgled; it roared in our faces.

Fatigue sapped my strength; thoughts became jumbled, insisting I relax my arms for good while my muscles screamed for mercy.

A calmness descended. It tantalized and wooed me to give in— to let go and allow the river to take us where it wanted. I felt a voice— let go...let go now.

The voice was irresistible, but my arms continued to hold the paddle against the gunwale. Now I was fighting not only against the river but also myself. The wound in my side oozed red streaks down my ribs and needed plugging. I felt the paddle loosen in the sandy bottom again...desperate chaos was only a few breaths away.

I peered at my family again. Fear had spread over their faces while they watched rivulets of water leaking into the boat. The top edge of the log lay just above their heads and ranks of branches protruded into the air. Branches, thick with leaves and tangled twigs—almost a wall; but perhaps not an impenetrable wall.

"Laura, Trey, grab hold of those branches sticking from the log above your head and try to hold the boat really tight against the lo g." They did, and I resumed prying against the flow. The combined effort was just enough—the top portion of the canoe stayed above the water a little longer. The load on my arm muscles lightened a smidge The rivulets of water coming over the top slowed to a trickle.

"Now try to pull yourselves and the canoe along the log to the left, toward the bank."

Seconds passed; I felt the boat slip along the log toward the bank nearly a foot, then it stopped, and I heard both of them grunt.

Trey gasped. "It won't move—can't budge it any further."

I winced and pried harder...no use. What was preventing the canoe from slipping through the water along the log face? I leaned back to look at the tapered stern and saw the end wedged in a crook of a branch stub on the log at the waterline. It seemed the dragon had snagged us with a claw, preventing our escape.

Sweat made my hands slip on the paddle shaft. More water quickly slopped into the boat and soaked my lap. I heard bodies behind me shuffle to avoid getting wet, causing the canoe to wobble, and allowing another bucketful to splash inside.

I held the roiling water at bay for a few more moments. "Trey, see if you can climb up on the log." He was behind Laura near the front of the canoe and hoisted himself up onto the log.

"Now Laura, throw him the bow line so he can tie off the boat on a limb. Trey, leave some slack in the line and work your way along the top of the log toward me."

While atop the log, he fastened the line, then gingerly stepped between a network of sharp branches for nearly twenty feet until he reached the point above me at the stern. "Dad, you're bleeding from your side."

"I'll be okay; I need you to take Mom's paddle and see if you can help me pry the tip of the stern back out of the crook. Maybe then we can move along the log toward the bank. Laura, hand Trey your paddle."

Trey took it; a moment later he nudged the boat a few inches—not enough to get past the crook in the limb. The current shoved the canoe back against the log. He tried again, "It's not working Dad." He was right.

My grip on the slick paddle weakened further, sweat burned my eyes, and the boat started tipping ominously again. More water sloshed inside until a thin curtain of it washed over the rail. In thirty seconds, the added weight of water in the boat would pull us lower, putting the gunwale under water. My mental clock began ticking down, counting the seconds.

"You can do it Son, give it another mighty try, but this time pull the stern back toward where the bow sits." He did, and I yanked the paddle from the bottom and used the last of my reserves to power stroke the bow forward. With the bracing removed, more water splashed over the side, and I quickly pulled out of the paddle stroke and thrust the blade down again to stop it. The flow was too powerful; I couldn't hold on for long, just a few seconds more and it would be over—*ten...nine...eight...*

My strength gave out, sucked away by the river. Out of options, I needed to let go, switch attention now to a rescue plan before my family got swept downstream out of sight. An image flashed in my head of my children floating face-down against the log, while another of us couldn't reach the surface. It felt as though my whole life had coalesced into its final moment of being.

My mind went numb, filled with the incessant river roaring in my ear, surging relentlessly as though bursting from a dam breach. I heard a voice again—"It's done; let go...let go of the paddle.

A great sadness enveloped me that I had failed to save my family. My hands relaxed, but my cramped fingers would not open. Rescuing the others would be impossible if my fingers wouldn't work, and I only had seconds to assess who was in worse jeopardy. I was about to triage my family on the fly while we were still in peril...would we all make it?

"Let G o," the voice called again. Then more urgently..."Let Go, Dad—we're out of the crotch ," and it was my son speaking to me.

I blinked and glanced at the stern, saw it was true, and immediately backpaddled. It was a feeble attempt, but the boat inched backward along the log toward the bank, ever so slowly. "Laura, stand up and untie the bow line from the branch above your head where Trey attached it."

She did, and I handed Trey the stern line. "Take this and work your way to the bank while pulling the boat." He crouched and slowly stepped along the log between the branches while I backstroked to move the stern away from the log and toward the bank. My arms responded, feeling like stretched taffy, nearly useless and disconnected from my body. Out of the crotch and thalweg, the stern slid toward the bank as less force pushed against the hull.

When the stern touched the bank, the fast current evaporated, and we sat in a quiet eddy. Trey got back in with the rest of us and everyone took a breath.

We sat quietly in the shade, inches from the brushy growth lining the channel edge. It was so tangled and thick, however, we could not exit the canoe or even see the actual bank. It didn't matter, because now only slack water lapped against the hull, and we could rest.

I breathed deeply, feeling the tension dissipate. "Is everyone okay?" All but Bea turned and nodded. I saw relief blossom on their faces, but Bea seemed lost in her thousand-yard stare. We drank from our canteens and sat in silence. I closed my eyes and let the burn in my arms slowly ebb away.

But then I became conscious of the pain in my side. I looked at where the dead tree stub had speared me and saw a ragged gash the diameter of a quarter. Blood oozed from it and formed a red trail that ran down and stained my shorts. How deep the wound went, I couldn't tell, nor if a rib had cracked or broken.

Laura looked back at me. "Let me see it."

I twisted my side toward her, and it caused me to wince now that the adrenaline rush no longer masked the pain.

She could see it from the bow. "Ooh, you need to stop the bleeding."

I unzipped my pack and took out a clean red and white bandana—the kind farmers kept in their coveralls. I poured canteen water on it and dabbed the wound. I pressed the wadded cloth tight against the wound for a few minutes. Then I tied my shirt around the bandanna and my chest. We grabbed our paddles and backstroked several canoe lengths upstream and away from the bank. We now had enough room to stroke our way around the log's leaf mass at its far end. Instantly, we entered the thalweg current once again.

The channel remained hemmed-in by dense forest on both sides right up to the water's edge. We sluiced our way downstream as though riding a water slide, then rounded another bend where the river had narrowed and the flow ran faster. Laura and I struggled to keep the correct alignment as the flow swept us toward the outside of the bend, only to find a most unexpected sight.

Standing waist-deep in the channel on the inside bend across from us were two nearly naked people. A young man and woman of college age were shivering—bare-skinned except for their skimpy swimsuits. The man stood with his arms crossed, hands clasping opposite shoulders, hugging himself. The woman's black scraggly hair hung straight, as though she had just stepped out of a shower. Both looked more forlorn than lost kittens in a rainstorm. No boat, no life preservers, no equipment, and obviously no idea what to do. Thick brush and trees formed a barrier ten feet behind them and cast shade where they stood in the cold water.

"Oh my gosh," Laura exclaimed.

"What are they doing here ?" Trey asked.

"Looks like they're in trouble," I said. The current whisked us faster than a bobsled into the meander.

"Can you help u s?" the man pleaded. "We flipped and lost our canoe and all our gear."

"Please, please," the woman mewed.

The fast current only afforded a few seconds of view from the moment we saw the couple until we came abreast of them across the channel. I had taken my eyes off the river when I saw them, and now it was all we could do to keep from foundering in the flow. I shouted over to them. "Really sorry; wish we could help—but we have no room and there's no place we can pull over. We'll notify someone when we make it out ourselves.

The man nodded. "Okay, thanks."

"But you gotta' get out of that cold water quickly—hypothermia comes fast."

The woman made a bleating sound and seemed about to cry. And that quickly, they were out of sight as the boat swerved into the next turn. I hoped the Jersey Devil hadn't heard her bleat.

"Poor people," Laura sighed, shaking her head. "Geez, that's really awful," Trey agreed.

Jordon jerked her head and looked at me with eyes wide and brows raised.

I forced a grin, "Everything will be fine, sweetheart." Bea did not speak but stared off the starboard side with the resigned look of a condemned prisoner about to be executed.

I knew the couple had few options there in the depths of an untamed place, miles from help. They had lost their only transportation. With no warmth, gear, clothing, food, or water, things would worsen for them. Making the most of it, I knew, was in their own hands.

I couldn't figure out why the pair stood in the water and shade as though waiting for a bus. With April's chilly water temperatures, they would become hypothermic within less than an hour, unless they exited the water and warmed themselves in the sun. They needed to get out quickly by beating back enough brush to find the bank, then pick their way downstream for miles to Batsto Village.

We continued dealing with our own dilemma. Twenty minutes later, I spotted something else unusual around a broad curve in the river. A sandbar appeared, the only one we'd seen that day. It had formed along the inside edge of the curve where sand had settled out in the slower current next to a high bank. It formed a small beach, plenty wide enough for us and the boat. Even better, the sand extended up and over the bank, providing a view of the distant landscape.

"Head for that bar," I quickly called to Laura. "Use draw strokes as fast as you can, so we don't get carried past it."

We swung the canoe toward the sand, and the current brought us closer in a smooth glide. Seconds later, I heard the pleasing crunch of soft sand under the bow.

We all stepped out, stretching our legs. Exclamations of relief came from Laura and the kids. My mother said nothing and seemed a bit dazed as she scooped out a spot halfway up the sandy bank and plopped herself down.

I noticed her sallow face. "You okay, Mom?" But she didn't answer, other than a slight nod. I wanted to reassure her again and opened my mouth. But it seemed she wanted to be left alone, so I stepped away.

One by one, the rest of us sat on the sandy bar with our legs stretched out, faces to the sun. Jordon picked up handfuls of sand and let the grains fall through her fingers, as though thrilled it was dry. After a few minutes, Trey soon got up and started exploring, and Jordon followed.

By now it was mid-afternoon, and I felt hungry. "Let's eat our lunch. It's probably the only place we'll find."

Laura nodded. "Dig out the first-aid kit so we can dress that wound."

I grunted, now conscious of the pain again, but stood and went over to the boat where I retrieved the daypack and canteens. Laura taped the gouge with gauze and a sterile pad. We all sat in the sand near the water's edge and had a picnic.

After lunch, I climbed the bank for a look around. It rose a dozen feet in a gentle slope. In every direction, the dense woods had given way to small open stands of pinewoods that dotted the landscape amid head-high scrubby bushes. No trace of human presence—we were alone in a lonely place where the river flowed incessantly below me.

I returned to the beach and sat down, letting my mind drift. The sounds of flowing water began speaking to me as I studied the current. And in its murmurings, I understood why the flow was so fast and full of fury this day.

The weather reports I'd heard before we left home covered the whole Pine Barrens and southern New Jersey regions. But more rain than predicted must have fallen over the Batsto watershed portion. During the night, the river level kept rising from the excess rain in its upstream watershed and feeder creeks. The main channel must have overflowed its banks in the darkness long before we arrived.

The canoe rental owner should have known what was happening in his own watershed. He was in the business of outfitting people where safety is always a concern...running rivers. Only fools take rivers for granted, for they are dynamic, high-energy systems full of huge hydraulic forces—even when not in flood condition.

What mattered now was navigating my family to safety, regardless of what the river threw at us. "Ok, everybody, time to go. Grab your stuff and let's get back in the boat."

We pushed off and merged with the current once again. Soon the channel widened and fewer logs and brush-traps blocked our way. With renewed strength, my senses seemed keener to the channel sounds—I could hear nuances now in its gurglings, and patterns to its babblings. They betrayed the river's hazards like a poker player's "tells" give away another gambler's hand.

I knew what to expect now from this river and it hadn't yet beaten us. Let the dragon's fury whip at us and the Jersey Devil wreak havoc around our feeble boat—we would handle it.

Laura seemed more relaxed, and our paddling became better synchronized. After a while we entered Batsto Lake, where the current dropped to drifting speed. The tops of the stumps we'd seen on earlier trips had disappeared, submerged in the high water. We had found none of the couple's gear or their boat. After another half hour of paddling, we reached the boat landing. A handful of people milled about the little beach and picnic area.

With the crunch of sand under the canoe, I heard sighs and exclamations of relief from my family. They made me smile for the first time that day. After they piled out of the boat, they stood in a cluster with their stuff while I pulled the boat up the sandy slope. I retrieved my backpack, flipped the boat over, and walked toward the group.

A young red-haired man about my age came over to us. "I saw you come in; you all didn't just canoe down the river, did you?" He sounded doubtful.

I nodded. "Yes, that was a nasty trip; river's at flood stage, and dangerous."

His eyebrows raised. "Any problems?"

"We passed a couple far upstream who lost their boat and gear. I told them I'd notify someone who could help them."

"No kidding; how far upriver were they?"

"I'd say at least an hour and a half as the crow flies; they were in pretty poor shape, standing in the water with just their swimsuits. Didn't see another soul on the river, though."

The man shook his head. "You sure were lucky. They closed the river and the lake this afternoon, because the water level is way too high."

"Wish they'd done it before we launched."

"Guess you aren't aware that someone drowned up there today because of the dangerous conditions.

My head jerked up then. "That's terrible, could have been u s." I felt a need to kick something, like the boat rental owner who failed to know the conditions.

The red-headed man said he didn't know details of the drowning, but he mentioned additional incidents he'd heard about that afternoon. Several canoe parties out on the lake had capsized, swamped their boats, and lost their gear. After he heard about the drowning on the local news, he drove over to check things out himself.

The sun slipped low on the horizon, dark soon. "Well, we've got a long drive ahead of us, so we need to get going. But we'd really appreciate it if you know who we might contact around here about the couple we found on the river."

"Don't worry about it. I live around here, and I'll contact our local police. They'll handle it."

"You sure?"

"Yeah, no problem. I'm going home now, and I'll call the precinct from there."

I thanked him, and he turned and began wandering off. The family followed the path to our car. Before following them, I looked toward the upper reach of the lake. My gaze then shifted into the distance far beyond, where the river still flowed…and perhaps a young couple still shivered in cold water, terrified with darkness on the way.

I knew the river would run fast up there for days yet. Then things would return to normal…except for those whom the river damaged, and those left behind. We were all exhausted, and I needed to get my family home to a familiar and peaceful place. And that remained far away.

I was about to turn and head to the car when I noticed large wings flapping over the water in the distance. It was a raven again, this time flying across the lake, heading upstream. Perhaps it was going to Quaker Bridge. I heard the raven call. Its raucous, throaty hail seemed not so much an admonition this time, but a salute of sorts.

The river, I knew, didn't care about folks or their fears; its power came from impassive natural forces acting upon the landscape. No need for human inventions like demons and dragons to explain its business. Myths and monsters are nature's way of helping humans cope with dangerous and unsettling places when the mind has no rational answers. For some, however, they are the only explanations that seem to make sense when the inexplicable prevails.

When I was young, my father Dick seemed like a monster at times, instilling fear and punishment, then abandonment as though my siblings, mother, and I were trash to be discarded. Dick's tormenting eventually made me stronger, and so did my experiences with nature.

I had seen the best and worst of the Batsto and became bewitched each time for different reasons. I dug the car keys out of my pocket, turned and walked toward the Goose. It was right where we left it, sitting peacefully among some pines, unruffled. The whole family leaned against the doors, their faces drawn, sweat-stained, hair limp, eyes drooping. They looked like weary disaster survivors waiting for extraction from some desperate place. I unlocked the doors, and they all crawled in as though a big featherbed lay inside.

My arms ached on the steering wheel, my back throbbed, and it felt like something was chewing on the wound in my side. I still had hours to drive and bring my family home.

Guardians of the Enchanted Isle

A sharp bark and the whoosh of flapping wings erupted from a lone dead cypress. The wood stork's raucous call echoed in the primeval landscape of still black water, quaking peat, and moss-dangled trees. In the gloom of another time, the great wingspan and heavy bill of the startled bird might have been mistaken for a Pterodactyl.

The bird lifted off the snag and lumbered away, croaking in protest at a pair of canoes that slipped quietly under its barren perch. In the lead boat, I watched the stork flap its wings, the dark undersides alternating with its white body. It seemed to flash a warning against penetrating too far into this mysterious landscape.

Quiet descended again, broken only by the plunk of our paddles. The mid-morning had unfolded breezeless and humid under a sun that had risen over the vast wetland for tens of millennia. For the past half-hour, we penetrated alone through the heart of the Okefenokee Swamp. With each push of the paddle, we moved another canoe length into a landscape uninhabited by humans. My brother Kane, seven-year- old Jordon, and ten-year-old Trey, followed in a canoe behind the one Laura and I occupied.

We carried a rough map that marked the destination we sought— an isolated wooden platform somewhere in the vast wilderness around us. We intended to set up our tents and spend the night there, elevated a few inches above the dark water. But first we needed to avoid the Cretaceous killers that waited along our route.

We pretended that the thin veneer covering our boats would protect us if we just concentrated on the rhythm of our paddle strokes. We focused on steering through marshlands and mats of floating organic matter called "peat blowups." They formed when methane from decomposition loosened compressed peat on the bottom and bubbled chunks of it up to the surface. Our shoulders ached when pushing through these dense flats, like trying to escape quicksand.

The blowups did not hinder the monsters though, for soon they were all around us. Some had even bobbed up next to our canoe, staring at us from the water weeds, snapping their jaws with deep-throated growls as we breached their chosen territories. These snaggle-toothed creatures, armor-plated leftovers from the Cretaceous Period and contemporaries of dinosaurs, had changed little in sixty-five million years.

We paddled among killer alligators (*Alligator mississippiensis*); swamp-dwellers ruled by instinct—the largest reptiles on the planet today next to crocodiles. None of us knew what lurked in their primitive brains at any moment, or if our presence would unleash an explosion of violence.

We had dodged several meaty adults and many smaller versions of the predators along the way, the tops of their armor-plated heads and unblinking eyes, barely visible above the water surface. There they lurked, watching us, some waiting for a chance to snatch one of us, pull them under and rip their flesh into turkey-sized chunks to swallow, with all the trimmings.

Yet they were not the only killers in the swamp. Before the canoes passed under branches along wooded sections, we glanced upward in case water moccasins or other snakes hung there, ready to drop into our laps. Biting insects pestered us and carried potential diseases. Even some plants were killers—Venus flytraps, pitcher plants, sundews—capturing and digesting unwary insects in their prison-like bowels.

The information on the platform we sought stated it should have just enough space for our two dome tents plus gear. It was the only solid surface for miles around where we could spend the night. The many small, wooded islands and clusters of cypress trees we navigated around were off-limits for camping, left entirely to nature. I had reserved the platform weeks ago, and now carried enough supplies for a couple of days, and little else beyond our wits.

But if we did not arrive within the next four hours, it meant we had gotten lost, or worse. Meanwhile, I absorbed the sun on my back and the wild scenery of the largest and most primitive swamp in North America.

After setting out, we paddled through an open marsh covered in water a few inches to several feet deep. As we moved deeper into the heart of the wilderness, we passed tree-covered islands that confused the way forward. Known as hummocks, they contained the only dry land within the six-hundred square mile soupy landscape.

These mounds formed around fallen trunks or branches where peat settled long ago, or blowups piled up, allowing shrubs and trees to grow. Organic soils eventually developed from the decay of their leaves and woody parts. The mounds grew as more trees found suitable substrate there and supported hanging mosses and rootless air plants above the swamp floor. Only the larger hammocks appeared on our map, but I followed my compass and my senses. In the decade before cell phones, we had no means of contacting outside help.

The *Okefenokee Swamp Ecoregion (75g), Southern Coastal Plain Ecoregion (75)* contained marshes, swamps, cypress stands, and deciduous islands. It extended thirty-eight miles long within southeastern Georgia and northern Florida. Today it lies forty miles from the Atlantic Ocean. But during the Pleistocene, wave actions built sand dunes that became a terraced bar along the ancient coast.

It trapped the low woodlands behind, inhibiting drainage across the entire floor of the Okefenokee. As the terrace grew, the woods became saturated and the upland trees gave way to wet-tolerant species. In time, the entire region flooded permanently and became a marsh-swamp ecosystem. Sphagnum moss dominated the open areas for thousands of years, where it decomposed into peat. Today, the peat has accumulated more than a dozen feet thick.

When our progress through the swamp stalled from the densest peat blowups, I climbed out of the canoe and pushed it by the stern through the dense material. In other areas, we steered around living sphagnum mats so thick we could stand on them. When we did, the entire floating mat shook the way a waterbed does when someone steps on it. Such wobbly ground is why native Americans called this region the "land of the trembling earth."

Tannins constantly leached from the submerged peat and kept the swamp's water the color of dark tea. It looked unclean and dangerous to drink, but the mild acidity from the tannins purified it from harmful microorganisms. It was potable, though to me it had an earthy taste.

Besides open water and marsh "prairies," the Okefenokee contains bog forests and scrub-shrub pockets interspersed with wooded hummocks. Those drier strips of land we passed contained thick stands of cypress and upland forests. Masses of Spanish moss draped from branches in long tendrils, shading tree leaves from sunlight. It usually caused no harm to the trees other than slowing their growth rate. Still, buttress-rooted cypress festooned with hanging moss evoked a sense of mystery along our route.

Since its beginning, the forces of fire and water have controlled this landscape's features and very existence. During droughts, fires from lightning strikes ignite exposed peat and burn off the vegetation. Historically, many of these fires have been so severe in some locations that they killed all the woody plants there. More than that, they burned away the root mat and upper part of the peat beds. These deeper fires formed large depressions that flooded when the rains returned, creating ponds and open marshes. The last fire to rage across this land with sufficient intensity to create a marsh prairie occurred in 1844.

During our trip through the prairies, we found other, smaller pools in the marshes unrelated to the weather. Alligators excavated these in the peat to hide in cooler depths. Sometimes I noticed muddy soils with flattened herbaceous growth leading from the water to hummock interiors—alligator trails. These predators will go on land to feed on injured animals and carcasses, and to nest.

As reptilians, they have a keen sense of smell and can detect carcasses from several miles away. We didn't need to worry about it, but alligators can also smell menstrual blood. Evidence shows they can perceive a single drop of blood in ten gallons of water. We kept our hands above the surface as we paddled, and lunch scraps remained in the boat within sealed bags.

We remained watchful, never knowing when we might encounter one of the scaly creatures, which we did frequently. Sometimes they lurked under the placid surface with just their eyes and nostrils above the water, waiting. Many times, we failed to spot them when they hid among the lily pads until our canoe came within a few feet. Then they quietly submerged as we passed, or thrashed with their tail, giving our nerves a jolt.

Gators have lived in these environs since the swamp developed. They and other flora and fauna there today also lived during the Cretaceous period one-hundred-forty million years ago. That was a time after the Mesozoic era ended. Dinosaurs thrived in the Cretaceous, together with other reptiles, amphibians, birds, and shrew-like mammals. And then one day sixty-five million years ago, Chicxulub visited the Yucatan Peninsula in Mexico. It came in hot and hard, a massive rock six miles across.

The blast generated a core of super-heated plasma of 10,000 degrees. The thermal pulse lasted a handful of minutes, but it produced a massive shock wave and air blast. This radiated across the seas, over coastlines, and deep into the continental interior. Winds exceeding six- hundred miles per hour sent a pressure pulse that scoured soils and flattened trees. The Okefenokee region did not escape, nor did animals and vegetation that lived in its ecosystems, including dinosaurs.

The Cretaceous ended the instant Chicxulub arrived. As the ensuing blast hit, it threw up a dust cloud that obscured sunlight for years. That blocked photosynthesis in plants—and destroyed countless ecosystem food webs. The climate had changed dramatically in a moment. And it launched one of the planet's greatest mass extinctions where eighty percent of existing species gradually vanished forever.

New habitats and ecological opportunities arose, and competition from dinosaurs dwindled. With their extinction, mammal evolution exploded, and in only sixty million years, hominids appeared. Modern people arrived only three-hundred-thousand years ago. We eventually spread into every continent, valley, plain, desert, shore, and hillside.

Our species of hominids settled in the Okefenokee over 4,500 years ago. Before then, the area was too dry to support

Guardians of the Enchanted Isle

thriving human communities. Gradually, small bands of Native American cultures occupied hummocks and drier pinelands throughout the swamp from 2,500 B.C. through the 1830s.

Their story is a familiar one. When the Spanish missions appeared in the 1600s, they brought diseases for which the native inhabitants had no immunity. By 1700, government military forces and warrior raids by Creek tribes had decimated the numbers of early native inhabitants.

Later, Seminoles moved into the void, along with remnants of other regional tribes. They sought refuge from European settlers and military harassment in their traditional lands.

This cycle went on for years. Colonists pushed natives from their lands, Seminoles raided settlements, and settlers and the military chased Indians back to the swamp. Eventually, all-out war erupted between the

U.S. Army and the Seminole Nation. In 1818, a small band of Seminoles followed their chief Billy Bowlegs into the Okefenokee to escape capture. The band increased in size over the next twenty years and the swamp became known as a refuge for Seminoles and escaped slaves.

Billy and his band repeatedly attacked homesteads near the swamp. An armed militia finally drove him and the last of the Seminoles out of the Okefenokee and into greater Florida by the mid-eighteen-hundreds.

Once the military permanently chased the natives out, settlers naturally moved in. However, no great wave of new inhabitants rushed in on the heels of Billy Bowlegs. Settlement of the swamp occurred slowly. Few thought the land had any value. Difficult access through the interior, periodic outlaw attacks, and hazards abounded.

But most of the original settlers had large families and were skilled swamp-dwellers, which allowed them to persist in the wilderness. The activities of early settlers differed little from Indians in terms of their effects on the environment of the

Okefenokee. Sometimes they intentionally set fires to clear out vegetation. Otherwise, these inhabitants exerted little control over the conditions in the swamp.

Yet, fires were normal and necessary in this landscape, and lightning fires produced much of its habitat diversity and productivity. By setting fires, the few early settlers only helped nature to sustain the great swamp environment. The thick bark on the trees allowed them to withstand the natural and early settler fires; they were designed for this habitat.

The situation changed by the late1800s when the turpentine hunters descended upon the landscape. A high demand for gum resins encouraged the tapping of pine trees. Years of scarring trunks for the substance left pine trees vulnerable to more frequent and destructive fires.

Intact longleaf pine bark protects the trees against fires, and their cones require the high heat produced to open and scatter their seed. But when slashed pine trunks burned while dripping flammable gum and resin, the trees lost their protection. Many 300-year-old pine stands turned to ashes from fires they normally would have easily survived. Turpentiners were exploiters rather than stewards of the swamp and protecting their source trees rarely occurred to them.

Some old-growth longleaf pine stands remain, their trunks still scarred, alive today because no fires have yet come their way. But most uplands have lost their canopy of pines. Now they grow young, thick stands of broadleaved hardwoods with tangled understories.

Schemes for exploiting the Okefenokee's resources moved from turpentine collecting to more invasive operations. One involved development of a ship waterway, called the Suwannee Canal. The Suwannee Canal Company constructed it in the 1890s to drain most of the swamp for logging and farming of rice, sugar cane, and cotton. After three years of digging, the canal had penetrated nearly a dozen miles into the swamp. But the company went bankrupt before completing the project, saving the Okefenokee from devastation. Today, the Suwannee Canal remains one of the primary means of access to the interior of the swamp.

We had launched our canoe trip where the canal began on the Okefenokee's east side. The banks had naturalized with trees and shrubs bordering each side.

Other than the channel's straight course, no evidence of its artificial origins remained.

After the canal venture failed, another company built a railroad into the swamp's western edge and used it for logging operations.

Logging camps housing hundreds of workers occupied Billy's Island. When timber operations finally ended in 1927, so did most of the cypress and mature pine trees throughout the swamp. Vast tracts of wetland cypress ranging between 400 and 900 years old had disappeared forever.

Once-secluded Billys Island became a bustling "boom town" of 600 people. Lumbermen, railroaders, turpentiners and entrepreneurs penetrated the deepest reaches of the Okefenokee. The town of Billys Island contained a sawmill, general store, schools, churches, a machine shop, hotels, and cafes. The face of the Okefenokee had drastically changed. Billy Bowlegs would not have recognized the place.

After logging ceased, very few seed trees remained to enable cypress to regenerate the expanse of its historical stands. Lumbering had changed the landscape so much that cypress could not recover their former acreage through natural seeding. Most areas where cypress once grew in the Okefenokee may never return to their pre-logging condition. Exploitation of the swamp ended when the federal government purchased it as a national wildlife refuge.

Unlike the exploiters, native peoples left little evidence of their activities from 4,500 years of occupation. Today's explorers might stumble upon a created mound, a few shards of pottery, or a dusty military campaign report in a local library.

As we slipped through its waterways, we felt a connection with the swamps' human history in the places marked on our map. Mysterious places popped up everywhere—Cravens Hammock, Strange Island, Blackjack Prairie, Bugaboo Island, Minnie's Lake, Mixon's Hammock. But you will not see the likes of Billy Bowlegs or his associates. Any traces became buried long ago under the peat, burned by a purging fire, or corroded and washed away by the tannin-laden waters. But we had set our course to glean the essence of the present Okefenokee with its restored natural functions—its rhythms and ecological structures and driving forces. And there was something more that I sought. I hoped to find a lead from William Bartram's trail from 1770. He recorded an old Indian legend he heard from some Creeks during his travels in the great swamp.

The legend told of a small party of Indians that were hunting game in the swamp long before settlers arrived. From a far distance, they had seen what appeared to be a village paradise on an enchanted island surrounded by a beautiful lake. As they tried to reach it, they only became lost in the confusing tangle of the swamp.

Many times they glimpsed this enthralling settlement through the mist. But each time they pushed toward it, they thrashed about in perpetual labyrinths. They would reemerge briefly and see it again before it disappeared and then reappeared through the foliage.

Their strength dwindled to exhaustion, and they nearly reached the point of perishing. Then a group of beautiful Indian maidens mysteriously appeared, shared food with them, and took them to their enticing village. The hunters called the maidens "Daughters of the Sun," who later helped them find their way out of the swamp and home. The story spread, and groups of Indians who heard about the enchanted isle tried to find it but never could.

No one ever discovered a road or pathway to the hidden paradise, although some claimed to have found evidence of its existence in certain signs. They swore they heard the sounds of canoes being built, footsteps on hummock trails, and perhaps the giggle of maidens in the distance. The legend intrigued me enough to keep a sharp eye out for a glimpse of that enchanted isle hidden somewhere within the Okefenokee.

Our own adventure began after loading enough gear and supplies for an overnight stay. That seemed long enough to get a taste of this unique wilderness, but barely sufficient to explore more than a fraction. We pushed away from the dock through cola-tinged water. Thickets of trees and shrubs lined the banks of the Suwanee Canal, and yellow-eyed grass, pickerelweed, and bladderwort swept by the sides of our boats. Our paddling moved us slowly down the canal, helped along by a barely perceptible current.

We kept away from the thick buttresses of cypress trees and a profusion of knobby "knees." These hard root protrusions jutted a foot or more above the water like miniature traffic bollards. Their function remains unclear, but some evidence suggests they transport oxygen to the roots where it is lacking. Others suggest they stabilize the tree in the shallow soils. In another cypress swamp I once sawed off a knee and inspected it. Indeed, the interior was highly porous and light in weight—quite suitable it seemed for aerating the roots.

After an hour of paddling the shady canal, we found a break in the trees and entered a marsh prairie. The landscape blossomed into an expanse of sunlight and open water filled with wetland plants. Water lilies with white flowers carpeted the surface, along with floating heart, golden club, wampee, and arrow arum. Small islands of shrubs, cypress, and black gum trees presented a mosaic panorama.

We floated on a root-beer colored pathway beside scaly denizens from another time. American alligators had changed little since emerging from the primordial ooze during the Cretaceous. They didn't need to; their design made them perfectly adapted to the freshwater wetlands of warm southern climates.

The marsh prairie we entered seemed endless, and empty of other people. As we moved deeper within the swamp's bowels, I could smell its dank primitiveness in the decomposing peat. I heard it breathing in the grunt of an alligator and saw its rust-colored lifeblood swirl in my paddle strokes.

We had merged with the swamp, becoming part of it as much as anything else there, captives of its rhythms and mechanisms. Imperceptibly, we had slipped into its waterways to move through its realm. In turn, the swamp produced the oxygen we breathed, the water we drank, and a complex ecosystem to admire.

Our canoes swept under strange trees with their limbs resembling candelabras. The moss draped over them and shared space with white ibises that preened and glared at us. Their scarlet faces and legs made a striking contrast with their snow-white bodies. One looked down at us in silence, then lifted a foot. It paused in mid-air with it, then reached up and scratched its face like a puppy strumming its itchy ear with a hind leg.

Other birds also appeared and disappeared one at a time as we rounded a copse of sweet bay here or button bush there. We passed great egrets and snowy egrets, along with great blue herons and their tricolored cousins. They stood knee-deep and statue-still in the russet water, waiting for a meal to present itself.

A green heron warned us with a hearty "SCAUP!" from a willow tree. A small flock of wood ducks winged overhead, resembling a military fly-over salute. It seemed as though we'd soon find Stephen Foster sitting on a stump, smiling as we slipped past his cabin.

We entered a channel barely wide enough for a single canoe. Shortly, dark clouds rapidly moved in, obliterated the sun, and drenched our exposed bodies with a downpour. It occurred so suddenly we did not have time to grab rain ponchos from our packs. An avalanche of heavy rain crashed onto the landscape, roiling the surrounding water.

We quietly sat in our boats and endured the soaking, welcoming the cooling it provided for our burning muscles. So much rain fell that a translucent veil seemed to have descended upon the landscape, like viewing the marsh from behind a waterfall. I rested my paddle across the thwarts and let the heavy raindrops pound against my bare back.

Through the veil of falling water, I studied a lone egret, watching us unperturbed from the shallows next to a hummock. Water cascaded off its long plume feathers. As I watched it watch us, I thought about how we were all trivial players on the great Okefenokee stage. We all took our mutual cues from the director— raw nature.

After ten minutes, the rain slowed, then stopped. Lily pads reclaimed the surface, the egret speared a toad, and the sun dried us off while we continued our adventure.

Our paddles dipped in and out of the placid water at a slow but steady pace. The restored sunlight glinted off neverwet leaves that disappeared under the surface as our strokes pushed them aside. We glided past a group of tall broadleaved trees near the edge of a hummock, and something large became visible among the branches.

When we approached closer, I saw the tufted ears of an adult Great Horned Owl sleeping quietly. One of the largest I had ever seen. It stood nearly two feet tall, gray- brown, a feathered tuft over each eye. No doubt it was patiently waiting for dusk. Then it would awake, stretch, and take silent flight, swooping after some unsuspecting ground creature for its evening meal.

Red-bellied turtles, cooters, and pond sliders scattered off logs as we approached, diving for the mud or a tussock of grass. I wondered how often one of them ran out of luck and it got snatched off a log while snoozing, clamped in the jaws of an alligator.

I'd heard stories about swamp folks of old sitting on their isolated porches in the evenings. They listened to loud cracks coming from the swamp waters around them. They knew then that a gator had chomped through the hard shell of another hapless cooter. Sometimes when they rose from their rockers and shuffled off to sleep, they had to first pull a canebrake rattler or two from under the bed.

We finally found the wooden platform surrounded by water near a hidden hammock. We deployed our pop-up tents, and before the sun set, prepared a simple dinner. Kane and Trey fished a while over the deck edge and waited for dark. Kane had brought along a tiny charcoal pan with short, foldable legs and set it on the deck. He reached into his pack and pulled out a compressed wood fire log. After setting it alight in the grill pan, we enjoyed a pleasant fire after sunset. It provided the illusion of a wood-fired campfire, making for a delightful ambience.

Darkness fully descended the way theater houselights dim into black nothingness before the show begins. And in a few moments the night chorus began with philharmonic melodies from all directions. The symphony included a variety of vocals involving frogs, toads, crickets, katydids. Splashes in the darkness added emphatic notes along with the sounds of night birds. An alligator bellowed in the distance, adding deep bass notes. A Long-eared owl sang to us, asking the eternal question—Who cooks for you, who cooks for you-all?

Unseen creatures hid among the foliage, the water lilies, the bottom ooze, and in the swamp waters above and below the surface all around our tiny platform. Habitats everywhere thrived with a diversity of niches that supported the swamp's enormous biomass. It was all fueled by wind and water, storms, and wildfires that constantly moved through the landscape.

Unique places still existed in the Okefenokee— nooks and holes where the endangered Red-cockaded Woodpecker still lived. Other rare species included the Bachman's sparrow, Carolina chickadee, brown- headed nuthatch, and pine warbler.

Because of the large-scale human projects of the past, the timelessness of the Okefenokee once seemed near an end. The turpentine industry had taken a severe toll by repeatedly tapping the uplands around the swamp. The longleaf pines on virtually every island were dying prematurely. Tree snags and downed deadwood accumulated. It acted like tinder, producing more frequent and hotter than normal wildfires. They ravaged the islands, hummocks, and forest periphery, burning root mats and peat lands too deep for timely recovery.

By 1937, the creeping death of the swamp seemed inevitable. Then, the federal government gained ownership and established the Okefenokee National Wildlife Refuge. Eager to restore the swamp, managers could not help meddling with nature some more. Efforts involved controlling water-level fluctuations and suppressing fires. It seemed obvious that reductions in the swamp's water levels from droughts caused adverse effects on ecological functions. Without water, wetland plants could not survive.

The government's solution involved building a low, five-mile-long dam across the Suwannee River. This waterway is the main drainage that flows through the swamp. The dam's purpose—to hold normal water levels in the swamp during periods of drought to prevent fires from burning through the marsh prairies. Lightning fires in drought conditions historically removed surface plants from the prairies. This exposed the peat that underlay the bogs and swamp waters.

The accumulation of peat, dead marsh vegetation, and woody debris smothers seedlings and ground cover plants. Natural fires in the swamp burn fast. Ground layer vegetation and excess organic litter become reduced to ashes. The released nutrients such as phosphorous and potassium are then available to develop new marsh growth.

Fast fires rarely damage the trees, deep roots or buried seeds. When the rains come again, fresh growth begins once more, emerging from the ash, invigorated by the released nutrients. In this way, nature keeps the swamp communities vigorous and productive over the long term.

The Okefenokee had developed these sustainable nutrient and water cycling mechanisms over thousands of years. Despite periodic fire and water fluctuations, the swamp ecosystem remained stable.

Sustainability would have persisted had humans not disturbed them. Turpentining, lumbering, dredging canals, building railroads and dams, had put the swamp on a path of degradation. Their cumulative effects were killing the Okefenokee.

Mother Nature had long ago provided the means for dealing with issues of water fluctuations. Several natural small dams called sills were already present within the swamp. But most people seemed to have ignored their importance. These natural impoundments effectively maintained water levels in a series of steps.

The government's managers decided to improve nature by constructing the low earthen dam across the Suwanee River. It did not control water levels as the managers and public had envisioned. It has altered the hydroperiod in the Okefenokee—the frequency and duration of inundation, including water elevation levels. More "improvements" followed by a program of intentionally setting fires during the dormant season. Its intention was to reduce the levels of combustible materials on upland areas of the swamp.

The sill and prescribed burning cures proved worse than the disease...the swamp continued to die. Fires set in the dormant dry season are more destructive to the forests on islands and uplands. In that period, brush and trees contain more dry woody structures. They cause hotter fires that move slowly because managers select windless days for setting them. Unlike natural fires, these conditions often kill mature trees and can get out of hand, destroying larger areas of the swamp.

Nature needs to control the Okefenokee's natural business if it is to remain a wilderness. Continuing reasonable protections for backcountry visitors allows nature to reclaim the great swamp. In this way, the ecosystem should endure until its regional climate changes, as it did when the Pleistocene arrived. That climate change allowed the swamp to develop.

American Indians moved in and out of the swamp to hunt and fish. They found deep meaning in its diverse habitats, and it prevailed upon their imaginations. Such was the power of its landscapes that its mysteries became woven into their legends. The enchanted paradise story the Creeks told William Bartram became one of them. It illustrates the deep feelings of those who wandered in from beyond its borders.

To them and those who lived there, the swamp was not only a source of food but a great mosaic within which it was easy to become hopelessly lost. Its myriad marshes, wetland forests, sloughs, and creeks offered nurturance and sanctuary, but also danger and death. Killers from the Cretaceous still roam there, seeking flesh from the weak and unwary. The swamp changes its shape and beneficence with the seasons. While Indians were familiar with its geography, they did not understand the landscape well enough to be fully comfortable within it. Such is the case with many of us who wander off to discover this wetland world for ourselves.

As we paddled our canoes back to where we started the previous day, I had plenty of time to reflect on the glimpse I had of this great swamp. I understood what an enigmatic place it was for the Indians and others in the way they felt both fearful and attracted to it. The enchanted maiden legend reflected their understanding of this duality of the Okefenokee environment. More than that, the legend reminded them about the natural world at large—where both providence and misfortune can arise wherever one dwells.

Many of us cannot help being drawn to strange and wild places despite our ambivalence. We go to examine and understand their features, to immerse ourselves in them and seek out what they portend for enriching our imaginations and our lives. We may never find an enchanting paradise, but our search may tell us much about the places where we look for them, as well as many truths about ourselves.

Dark Passage in Middle Earth

Somewhere ahead of me in the darkness lay the source of muted roaring. Distant water, I thought, and lots of it. The rumbling reminded me of cataracts. The kind that drown other sounds out with hydraulic thunder from crashing white water. But I knew waterfalls didn't exist there.

The path narrowed, barely discernible in the nighttime gloom. A few steps later, I paused and cocked my ear toward the sound, trying to judge it better. More clearly now, it was surely water—but not from a river; more like distant ocean waves pounding a shore. But it came, I knew, from miles below the surface.

I could feel it drawing me deeper into a realm that had changed little in hundreds of thousands of years. I stood in the lair of what was once the planet's greatest beast, one that came and left over two million years ago, but still waits for the right conditions to rise— and destroy much of the world again.

While it slumbered, I walked forward through the deep nocturnal hues of wilderness places where darkness hid details in the gloom. Not of the melancholy type of gloom, but the atmospheric quality of nighttime. The murkiness hampered my vision, along with a heavy mist that engulfed everything.

More than a mist, I realized, as I walked further on. The cloud hugged the ground in a bluish tinge, swirling slowly in front of me. I could feel it drift past my cheeks and around my legs. The fog thickened as I continued to move ahead, and my skin became noticeably warmer despite an otherwise chilly night. It wasn't the weather, but my unseen quarry that made me hunch my shoulders and keep my knees slightly bent. I was prepared to move fast, as though stalking something furtive and dangerous, which I was. At any moment I could break through the crust and fall into the monsters' maw.

Indistinct shapes came and went as I passed them in the darkness—no edges anywhere. My eyes darted between vague bushy forms and clumps of grass, looking for movement of night creatures on patrol. My footsteps landed softly on the hard ground, leaving no impressions where I carefully placed them to avoid stumbling into whatever was waiting for me just ahead. A short way on, I stopped again, listening for any nuance in the growing roar of water. I was close now, near enough to discern subtle variations in the rushing sound. Hazards would soon emerge; be sharp, I breathed.

I moved through an ancient landscape, a remnant of primordial Earth that persisted long after the beast went back to slumbering. But that did not mean danger had vacated the area, for it waited on the unwary to take a misstep.

Even so, the flashlight on my hip remained off. I hiked in the darkness of a moonless night to experience nature as ancestral humans had—letting their raw senses guide them. Then too, artificial light would prove useless in the fog, scattered by the droplets, destroying my already limited night vision. Without it, I became one with the landscape rather than a mere observer.

Earlier, when I began, the stars provided just enough light to navigate the crusty terrain. Once I descended to lower ground, they disappeared, hidden by the mist. Odd how, in the absence of a breeze, the mist drifted toward me in the gloom with each step, beckoning me forward. Its fine water droplets reflected just enough starlight to see a dozen feet ahead. At times, I poked the ground with a stick I carried to test the thin surface.

Soon, a mild bitterness seeped into my nostrils and tripped my tastebuds. The odor resembled rotten eggs, and I knew at once hydrogen sulfide now permeated the mist. Enough of it lingered to act as a warning, but too little for toxic concentrations that would lead to instant death. I remained alert for any signs of dizziness, headache, burning eyes or breathing problems.

An old expression bubbled to the surface about when you encounter a strong sulfur smell, you know the Devil is about. I doubted he was lurking there that night, but perhaps I was trekking through someone's version of hell, or perhaps it was only the devil's kitchen. I recalled how John Colter, a scout for the Lewis and Clark Expedition, had wandered through a similar place a few miles away. His stories about it spooked those he told so much it became known as "Colter's Hell."

And now I scouted an even more extensive and restless landscape within the vastness of Yellowstone, the crown jewel of wild America. I had entered an area of the *Yellowstone Plateau Ecoregion (17j)* of the *Middle Rockies Ecoregion (17)*, and knew why that smell was in the air. It came from underground, deep below the thin surface, working its way silently up through cracks and fissures. It was the monster's breath, a foul reminder it remained restless.

Others had encountered its dangers not far away in a small, steep ravine near a remote hot spring. In 1897, something strange occurred there. Explorers found the undamaged carcasses of many bears, elk, rodents, and insects. Another time, they found eight fresh bear carcasses there with no signs of trauma. Later tests showed poisonous levels of carbon dioxide and hydrogen sulfide gases had accumulated in the windless ravine. The monster's breath had killed them. Now the place is known as "Death Gulch."

The gases still kill when conditions are right. Twenty years ago, five dead bison appeared in one of the park's geyser basins—just a few miles from the one I traversed. Two adults, two calves and a yearling, lay on their sides with all their legs perpendicular to their bodies as though someone pushed them over while they grazed. Their unusual position showed the bison had died together rapidly, though they showed no signs of predation.

The evidence again pointed to high levels of hydrogen sulfide and carbon dioxide that had become concentrated from poor air circulation. I wasn't particularly worried about that because I was moving over open terrain, and air currents were keeping the mist moving.

To check the sulfur smell's direction, I jolted my head up and sniffed deeply, then side-to-side the way a panther picks up the scent of prey. Stronger just off to my left, the sulfur smell confirmed the cause of the rumbling sound I had been hearing—a geyser erupting somewhere in the darkness. The vaporized water it sent skyward produced the dense mist around me and sent it drifting. It felt cool on my skin, telling me the geyser still lay further ahead. Any warmer and I would feel its wetness on my cheeks.

After several minutes, the gushing noise diminished into the background, telling me I must have moved further away from it. Now, other noises emerged from the darkness. I heard gurgling off to my left and sloshing somewhere on my right. Something ahead in the fog seemed to boil, bubbling like a witch's' cauldron—the devil's kitchen never closed.

Though barely visible in the dark and mist, the landscape surrounding me had no equal anywhere else on planet Earth. Only four other places in the world have sizeable concentrations of hydrothermal features—Kamchatka Peninsula, Russia, El Tatio in the Atacama Desert, Chile, New Zealand's north island, and Haukadalur Valley, Iceland. Yet, none of those come near to matching the size, diversity, and activity of features in Yellowstone's geyser basins.

The thin, crusty surface around me was all that lay between me and an underground labyrinth of sinuous channels that led to the center of the Earth. I could never journey there the way Jules Verne's protagonists did, but hints about what stirred below seethed around me.

My dark passage over ruptured ground covered the most active part of Yellowstone's geyser landscape, and I had to remind myself I was still treading through Middle-earth; not Tolkien's vision, but the actual geological realm between the atmosphere and lithosphere we call the biosphere. Life, however, was nowhere in sight.

While I doubted any hobbit ever wandered among Yellowstone's geysers, such landscapes might easily inspire tales of myth and mystery. Some stories from our youth never leave us and can tantalize our imaginations for a lifetime. They can heighten the impact of experiencing an actual place decades later, where fantasy and reality intersect. Upon arriving there, it is sometimes difficult to tell them apart. Then, the shadows become monsters and breezes bring foreboding.

For a moment in the geyser basin, my mind recalled images I had formed as a youngster while reading about bleak Mordor in the "Lord of the Rings." Much later, I would learn how the film version captured that landscape from scenes in New Zealand's Taupo Volcanic Zone. There, Mount Ngauruhoe served as the main stand-in backdrop for Mount Doom. Many scenes of Mordor came from adjacent Mt. Ruapehu, which has produced several of the world's most powerful eruptions.

Yellowstone has a volcano too, larger than any in the Taupo Volcanic Zone. My nighttime walkabout took place on the floor inside its caldera...the monster's mouth. I had come there alone, in the dark of night, like John Colter did in his own wing of the devil's kitchen, but he had weapons with him, and I did not.

My presence fulfilled a dream of my youth—to tread in the footsteps of wilderness explorers and the frontiersmen I loved to read about. Most likely, none of them who wandered through there ever realized the significance of where they were. Each step I took brought me deeper into the maw of an enormous geological beast...the seething caldera of a supervolcano, one of the planet's greatest of all time.

The geyser sounds and sulfur odor proved it still stirred far underground. I had descended to one of the crater's lowest elevations, where the Earth's crust was thinnest. Pressurized groundwater heated in underground reservoirs by the Earth's magma core reached the boiling point, forcing hot water to rise and spill over the terrain where I walked.

So far, though, the hydrothermal features hid in the surrounding murkiness, rumbling and bubbling not far away. On either side of the vague path I walked, the Earth's skin had cracked, and hot liquid seeped onto the surface like running sores on a syphilitic boar. Here nature's scabs had been ripped off, letting the open wounds ooze and spurt.

This was a place where Earth's pulsing rhythms occurred every moment, where one could contemplate the enormity of what lay beneath their boots...processes capable of destroying much of the planet's life once again. The beast had risen three times in history, the most recent over three-hundred-thousand years ago. And still it simmered, fed by the network of reservoirs, tunnels, and tubes that led miles below me, where the vast magma chamber had been melting rocks since the planet formed.

A dark narrow pool appeared next to the path, less than a few dozen feet long and half as wide. Faint hydrogen sulfide fumes wafted toward me. The water surface bubbled as though something alive was trying to emerge from the depths.

Once past it, the roaring geyser sound faded, and the air became cooler. Drifting further away now, I pulled my wool cap tighter around my ears in the September chill. My breath formed its own small cloud of mist before I realized the fog had thinned.

When I lifted my eyes from the path, a barren land emerged, darkly reminiscent of a predawn battlefield of smoking ruins. In the half-light, it seemed as though I had just missed an epic battle, something from ancient tribal warfare where first peoples fought over a productive land ten thousand years ago. Both sides must have lost, leaving a dismal landscape. Was I a poet, I might have mourned that the land never healed and still wept for all the lost souls. But none of that ever actually happened, except in my imagination.

Another minute of walking brought me to a fork in the path. The right one, more distinct, led uphill to higher ground. I chose the more obscure one that descended deeper into the caldera. Soon, I passed two larger boiling pools, and found the air temperature had risen again. The heat from the thermal features made the surroundings comfortable. Frosty breath no longer tracked my passage.

Others who came this way during daylight had met misfortune here. A man had gone missing in 2022 and someone found his foot still within his shoe, floating in a nearby hot spring. In 2016, another man and his sister went to find a steaming spring to "hot pot"—soaking like a hot tub. He accidentally fell in while his sister recorded it on her cell phone.

Rescuers found his body inside the pool, where the acidic water had quickly dissolved nearly all of him. The parks' geysers and springs are acidic because they are fed by thermal water deep underground that is full of sulfuric acid. The acid is produced by microorganisms that break down hydrogen sulfide in the subsurface rocks and soil.

As I moved on, the hot springs disappeared in the darkness along with the mist. Soon, in the clearer air, I noticed several scattered plumes a few hundred feet away. Geysers spewed steam over the broken ground with tall columns of spray that arced in the air, then floated across the raw landscape.

For a moment, some of the droplets drifted toward me and settled on my face. They slid down my cheeks, then paused at my chin where I licked them—pure water, no sulfur. The beads of warm water physically linked me with the ancient water from the Earth's depths. I took comfort from this tangible connection—that my existence, and all creatures, came from lineages that depended on such eruptions. The ejected water accumulated in the Earth's early atmosphere, condensed, and fell over eons to fill the oceans, allowing life to emerge.

The surrounding caldera changed moment to moment as thermal features started and ended their cycles, and minerals in the steaming water deposited and drained across one of the most primitive landscapes on the planet. Here, powerful geologic forces clashed with the raw materials of Earth in an eternal war of relentless energy transformations. The same primordial processes on display had created landforms and continents for the past four and a half billion years.

The relentless geological activity allowed only a scattering of bunch-grasses to establish themselves in an otherwise desolate place, a moonscape with geysers and spewing grottoes. A few steps ahead, my boots scraped rougher ground, where a circular hot spring a dozen feet wide emerged from the mist. Several concentric rings surrounded the steaming perimeter, with the outermost composed of warty-looking mineral deposits. The chalky crust had settled onto the path, causing my boots to crunch.

Small wavy channels of hot water drained away from the rings, leaving deposits in muted orange, yellow and brown. Each color was produced by a different species of bacteria that fed on the minerals and thrived in the warm water temperatures. Some types, including cyanobacteria and chloroflexi, got their energy through photosynthesis.

In addition, heat-loving fungi lived in the roots of panic grasses that grew sporadically where pockets of soil collected. I could see several clumps of them nearby. The symbiotic relationship between the plants and fungi helped both species survive higher temperatures than each could by themselves.

Though mostly hidden in the darkness that night, the ecology in the geyser basin depended on warm water algae that inhabited the wet ground next to the colorful rings. There, ephydrid flies lived among the algae mats and rivulets, and ate the algae. The flies lay their eggs in peach-colored mounds, often on the surfaces of the mats. They become prey for spiders, beetles, and birds, and are a key part of the local food chain, which includes geese, elk, and bison. These carry energy and genetic material far beyond the hot spring environments and into surrounding landscapes.

While standing at the circular spring, I noticed a gulping sound nearby that began from inside an empty cavity of a small whitish dome. It stood only a few feet high, and soon the cavity filled with water and overflowed. After another minute, the water began splashing upward, and then spouted six feet into the air. Smaller spurts followed, and shortly the eruption died down. The hole drained with a sucking sound, the way a bathtub gurgles down a last slug of water.

Whitish calcium carbonate deposits called sinter blanketed the ground, and the only way through led past a waist-high mound. An inactive geyser. It stood off by itself—a quiet sentinel on a vacant plain. I stepped ahead amid soft sloshing noises off to the side. Suddenly something whumped loudly in the darkness like an industrial washing machine.

Something up ahead caught my eye through the light mist. I angled my way toward it and could see another mound in a broad circular field of carbonate. This one, larger than the last, had a more irregular shape coated in deep gray geyserite, a hydrated form of silica. Like the lonely sentinel geyser cone I just passed, this one too sat dormant, waiting until its time came again to gush.

The way forward led through a broken field of bleach-white siliceous sinter, and the ground in that direction appeared unstable off the trail. I leaned over the left side of the path and jammed the walking stick into the ground. The surface held, so I scraped it with my boot.

Just below, a thin layer of darker material emerged. After removing and flicking my flashlight on, the color shined green like a deep shade of pond scum. Clearly, a photosynthetic microbial community chugged along just underfoot, every bit as productive as those in the algae mats of hot spring outflow channels. The sinter cover protected the community from harmful ultraviolet rays and acted as a mulch to retain moisture and prevent storms from washing the lifeforms away.

I took a tentative step forward, then moved ahead a few yards, testing with the stick. Soon, my feet felt warmer, and I sensed the ground had become too thin to walk on. To continue could lead to death—boiled alive in the scalding water lying inches below the surface—cooked like a chicken in a stew pot. Others had gotten severely scalded in such places on this landscape. Every year, rangers rescue visitors who punch their feet through the thin earthen crust into boiling water—the monster's revenge for trespassing, it seemed.

I backed up and searched for a way around the fragile ground. A faint route led over a harder surface, and just as I moved forward again, a high-pitched scream pierced the gloom behind me. It only lasted five seconds, but I knew immediately what it was. The shrill note began with a one second prelude, a guttural bellow that rose trumpet-like, then dropped into several hollow grunts.

A rush of delight surged through me, for it was the other prime reason I had come that night. This was the literal call of the wild, a sound of rough timberlands, remote mountain valleys with rushing streams. It was the sound of a bull elk bugling in the foggy darkness of the ancient geyser basin.

It was the same call that Pleistocene hunters heard in this very place when they came there ten thousand years ago to hunt. I imagined such a hunter, clothed in animal fur and carrying a spear and bow for hunting elk meat for his clan. I pictured him wandering into this strange place of gushing hot waters and strange noises. Here he might have spent the night, letting the water-spirits he trusted keep him warm on a chilled night, like they were doing for me.

If the hunter had been there before, he likely had no fear of the place, for the cultures that came there respected and revered it. They knew it was not an evil place because the great beasts came there as well. Ancient people who passed through recognized the geyser basin and the other thermal features as sacred, full of mystery and power.

The elk call echoed again, but further away this time. And slightly different. This bugle sounded deeper, clearer. It was a sound of self-assurance, of dominance. It was another male, an alpha with a nearby harem of cows, or a challenger who warned the first rutting bull away by calling him out.

I stared into the dark mist, waiting; I expected another call. Soon, the silhouette of a large elk appeared. It had a great rack of antlers and slowly walked toward me. We were dozens of yards apart, and he showed no sign of noticing me as he came down a short slope of ground. He turned sideways and raised his head. A second later, it came...*A-a-a-a-a-a-a-a-eeeeeeeeeeeeee-oh! Ee-uh. Ee-uh. Ee-uh.*

This, the challenger, had responded to the alpha with his shaggy mane and thick cape of dark hair around his neck. Even in the gloomy fog, he was magnificent as he uttered another threat with his head lifted. He paused, looking toward the higher ground from where he had emerged.

The dominant bull, unseen, answered him again, no less forcefully. The challenger raised his head, then took several steps and disappeared into the fog. Such challenges and confrontations would go on until mid- October—their way of sorting out the breeders from the "wanna-breeders."

With the duel over for the moment, I walked on. The way led through a mix of conifers on elevated ground where the mist thinned. The trees ended, and the landscape opened again, but empty of geyser mounds and springs. Instead, I had finally reached the Firehole River.

Before me, a most unexpected sight materialized. Under the starlit sky, a natural channel of dark water flowed while waves of steam rose off the heated surface. Hard, whitish carbonate coated both banks. Ribbons of black liquid from the adjacent geyser field drained down their slopes. Starlight glistened in the flows, and the steaming river brought to mind an alien landscape—the kind I imagined from science fiction books I devoured as a kid.

This place of primordial nature; it's all about energy transformations, I breathed—and I am just part of the grand process, bits, and pieces engaged in quantum mischief. How fortunate that amidst such raw power and danger, a human can sense beauty. It is possible because nature provides this emotional buffer to shield our sentient minds against the indifference and harshness of the universe. It is nature's way of getting humans to continue living and transforming the planet's energy.

Reluctantly, I turned and left the riverbank, contemplating the thought that beauty and meaning can appear from seeming pointlessness. Nature drives us, and all lifeforms, to process its elements and various forms of energy. We have no choice in the matter if we intend to continue living.

Yet no creature is perfectly efficient at it, and so nature provides opportunities in the form of ecological niches and pathways for other lifeforms to process the rest. Dr. Seuss was right about "Oh, the places you will go," but it applies to more than wonderment for children. Yes, even our molecules will all go somewhere else someday, and we cannot know the new forms and spaces they will manifest. What was once us will never die, for we are merely a temporary consolidation of those elements, though with sentience.

While some may make rational, existential sense of all the random events that produced us, others have no doubt that intelligent design is responsible for it all. Either way, every moment of every life on Earth is an experiment that tests a design. What matters is that each of us chooses the reasons we get out of bed every morning and proceed with the business of living. Thank our lucky stars and the powers that made them, for the gift of enduring and our senses of beauty, gratitude, and love.

Whether we enjoy our presence while alive is largely a matter of the meaning we derive from the experiences we find as participants.

And sometimes, participation is enough. There is much merit to the Taoist expression—The journey is the reward." Exploring landscapes had become my journey, and I had found many rewards in doing so. Standing that night beside the Firehole River had given my midnight ramble special meaning.

After moving away from the riverbank, I entered another area of desolate terrain. The silent outlines of dormant cones covered in geyserite seemed everywhere. Together with steaming pools surrounded by sinter, these features provided a continuation of the dystopian landscape I had navigated for the past hour.

The fog soon became too thick to see beyond several yards again, and hot water sounds fizzed and splashed around me. I moved cautiously forward. In a few moments, another large shape loomed ahead. In the mist, it appeared as another geyser cone, though darker. That and its mass caused me to slow my steps, for I had a hunch about it.

A few steps later and I paused a dozen yards from the shape, letting my mind interpret why the mound remained darker than the other cones I had come across. In the shifting mist, an outline emerged and triggered an association with something I had seen before in another time and place...a bison with its body resting on the ground sideways to me.

It lay beside a small hot spring, a bubbling cauldron of liquid with steam. It swirled and mixed with the fog already there. The animal's great blocky head and recurved horns proved it was a male.

My pulse quickened, for I stood well within its attack distance. But the bison had not noticed me—eyes closed, flanks heaving contentedly with each breath, head slightly lowered, facing ahead, sleeping. Frozen in place, I glanced to my right and left. No other dark forms nearby; just a lone bull soothed by the warm steam wafting off the hot spring next to it.

I watched it another minute before he sensed me, for his eye flicked open. It was the only part that moved, and the beast remained otherwise motionless. As it lay in profile, I could only see his right eye. But it was large and stared at me without blinking. A pale ring circled the rim, making it seem especially large. Most likely an infection, I decided.

We were two very different creatures momentarily sharing the same warm space. He looked peaceful, soaking in the heated vapors, letting them condense on his shaggy coat and run down his side to pool around his haunches.

But I remained attentive to any twitch or change of posture, snorting, or raising of its tail—signs of aggression. I had seen other bison bolt to their feet and charge an intruding person before they had time to flee. It only took three seconds for its horns to catch and swat the stupid teenager as he bolted, barely escaping with his life.

In the dark on this barren landscape under a mantle of fog, few protective options existed for me. With hot water hazards everywhere and without a tree, rocky point, or geyser dome to climb—escaping became elusive. But nothing about the situation seemed threatening; the beast remained still, having assessed and dismissed me as a low risk.

Before taking to the trail that night, I had anticipated a chance encounter with such an animal. When the weather turns cool, bison and other wildlife roam through Yellowstone's geyser basins for the warmer conditions. They rarely become perturbed easily and tend to tolerate humans until their space becomes violated, which I had not done.

Still, my hand slipped slowly to my hip and rested on the flashlight, my finger on the switch. I waited, primed to whip it out and turn it on its bad eye, before waving it to confuse the two-thousand-pound bull if it charged. Then I'd toss it at it and run in the other direction. With its poor eyesight, especially in the dark fog, I might get away with it.

While keeping my attention on the bison, I took a few slow steps backwards to put distance between myself and the beast. Soon, the respiring mass dissolved in the fog. We had parted in peace at the bottom of a seething caldera, as quietly as we had met—two strangers in the night without a common language and ignorant of each other's intentions. We had agreed to tolerate each other. It was an ancient ritual, one that had played out between different lifeforms over eons in that raw and inhospitable place. A few minutes afterward, I cut across more broken ground, and soon a new deep rumbling reached my ears. It grew louder with each step, and in another minute, the rumbling had become a modest roar. I could not see the source through the gloom, but it seemed very close.

Then, an irregular whitish mound appeared in the mist. At first, its size was difficult to gauge, but after another few steps I could tell this was the largest geyser dome I had seen that night. Rising nearly twelve feet tall, it sat on a base of geyserite twenty-feet wide. An irregular opening three feet in diameter gaped at the top, and a dense column of hot water roared continuously out of it. The plume rushed upward nearly a hundred feet before I lost it in the steam and fog.

I had hoped to find this geyser, and now it stood there before me, gushing in a spectacular eruption. Among the largest of all geysers in the world, Castle Geyser remained aloof to me, though I felt captivated by it. Cascades of warm water fell like platinum braids, down and down until they splattered on the sintered ground.

Starlight, filtered by the mist, refracted the water droplets into a dozen shades of purple, pink, and violet. The low-light settings in my camera captured the otherworldly scene. I heard the roar, felt the fine spray on my face, and smelled its freshness. This was nature's show—an opera of unrestrained hydraulic power that was bursting from the cone, whooshing geothermal energy under enormous pressure from deep inside the Earth.

There I stood, in a corner of ground-zero, among the places where the planet's water cycle begins from underground. The ejected precious liquid burst into the night sky, beginning the process that would sustain life there and elsewhere. Its vapor rose, drifted in the atmosphere, then later would condense as rain, mixing with water from fresh springs, lakes, rivers, and oceans. Castle Geyser had been active for over a thousand years, based on carbon-14 tests of its cone. I was fortunate to encounter the eruption, which normally only goes off twice in twenty-four hours, and lasts twenty minutes.

After that, the plume turns to pure steam for a half-hour, then shuts down and goes to sleep for nine to twelve hours.

The activity that sustained the hydrothermal features within the geyser basin started sixty-six million years ago when a new cycle of volcanic activity uplifted the region's topography. Then, over two million years ago, the Yellowstone supervolcano erupted for the first time, forming the great caldera where I roamed.

This eruption was a monster, among the largest volcanic eruptions known, and covered nearly six thousand square miles with ash, as far away as Missouri. The eruption ejected thousands of times the volume of material that blasted out from the 1980 eruption of Mt. St. Helens, in Washington.

I wasn't thinking much about another super- eruption in the geyser basin that night. Scientific evidence then and now has not convinced many scientists that it will ever happen again. Geological records have shown that such planet-shaking blasts are extremely rare, usually only once in a region.

With the remaining steam and rushing air spewing out of Castle's cone, I turned from the spectacle and worked my way back through the desolate landscape. I soon found a more defined trail that led me to my starting point on higher ground.

In the distance, the sounds of geysers continued in the devil's kitchen, where timeless recipes, cooked in warm broths, were served to the landscape in bubbling pools and sloshy grottoes. The mists had long vanished by then, dissipated in the crisp night air. Above me, a vast field of stars filled the deep purple sky from horizon to horizon, their edges now clear and sharp. The great Milky Way seemed to smile at me as though the heavens were pleased that I had made the effort to experience one of its special places in a state of primordial rawness.

Earth had formed in the Milky Way long before it became my home, and I had just gained a glimpse of its childhood landscape among the geysers and hot springs. There, its growing pains remained on display. During that moonless night with few visual cues, my other senses had allowed me to navigate through the danger zone unscathed.

Despite the chill in the air, a warm glow filled my heart with gratitude that I not only came from this Earth, but it would remain my home for life. Never would I need to question whether I belonged here, for clearly, I did. My roots went deep here, all the way to the center of the Earth.

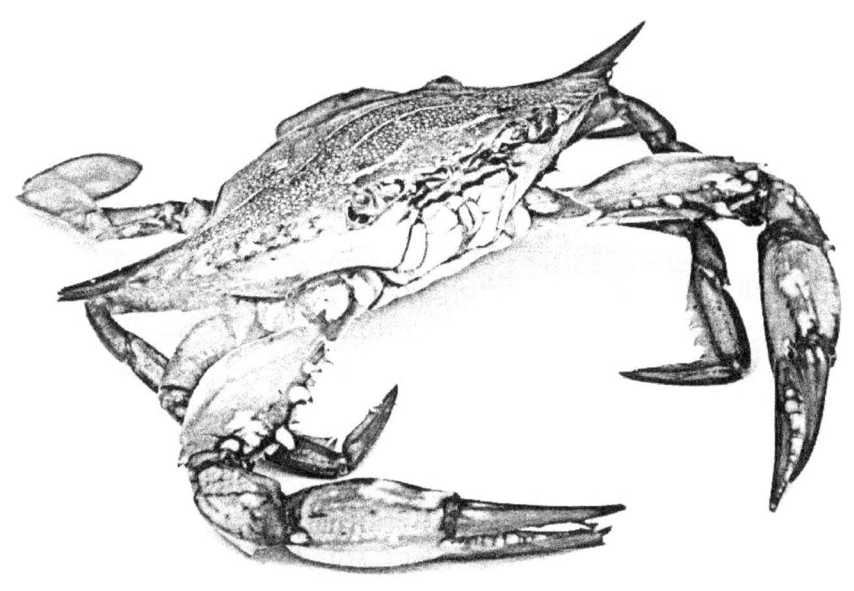

Chara's Wake

A fast little lady came into my life long after Laura and I married. I used to go out with her sometimes, and Laura knew about it. She had a place down on the Chesapeake. We often went on trips together when I was a young man, cavorting about with the wind and waves. We explored all over the Chesapeake Bay region, where we raced along on the wild side, leaving stragglers in our wake. She was a good friend and partner to me, literally. More than that, she offered me joy, and her name, Chara, meant just that in

Greek—a feeling of inner gladness and delight. That is what I heard anyway, from the man who sold her to me.

She was petite—only a twenty-two-footer. It must have been an exciting moment when she first slid into the water in 1967 as a Columbia sloop. Heads surely turned to see her decks gleaming and shackles sparkling. In her younger days, she was a competitor, and no doubt won her share of races.

But when I met her in 1986, she had matured and left the racing circuit to the newer and faster boats of her class. She remained cute though, and alluring with her white fiberglass hull, and was far more experienced at sailing than I was in those days. In fact, when we first met, I knew nothing about handling sailboats. Had never even been on one before.

Chara's lineage began in Europe during the seventeenth century. A new ship design had emerged that the Dutch referred to as a sloop. These cargo sailboats contained a single mast, with one headsail in front and one mainsail attached to the mast. Their maneuverability made them ideal for the Bermuda trade with North America in the 1600s.

Chara was a miniature version, a racy day-runner with similar assets. Her spinnaker sail on the bow fastened to the front mast cable and could billow out- front with the best of them. Among other charms, her cabin could sleep four, with a small galley and stowage capacity for a week's trip on the bay.

She also had a tight little stern that housed a purring outboard motor for navigating around docks and slips. Her simple cockpit had bench seating along the sides and a wooden tiller for steering. It looked like an ax handle that protruded into the cockpit from the stern and attached to the underwater rudder. Her deep and heavy keel prevented knockdowns and capsizing in stormy weather.

In short, she had the right stuff for fair and foul conditions alike, and for dodging here and there on windy bays. She was not a fancy gal with lots of accessories—not even a working compass when I met her.

Yet, sailing her was a purely organic experience, completely tactile using just the wind against a bit of cloth and my own confidence. Unlike a bigger, heavier boat, she was as nimble and sleek as an otter, attuned to the most subtle shift in a breeze or swell, or twitch of her tiller. She responded the way a vintage sports roadster did on curves—low, smooth, pulling delightful Gs as she charged ahead. I could feel the roll of every wave and the force of every gust through her hull the way a road's roughness vibrated through a sports cars' chassis.

In more modern sailboats, automation operates everything—sail hoisting, winch-winding, steering, course plotting. Chara, though, required constant hands-on attention the way one keeps ahold of the stick shifter and wheel of a roadster. She had a basic design, but lived a high-maintenance lifestyle, sometimes a bit too needy. It took a lot of touchy-feely involvement to bring the best out of her. She always needed something from me.

When I wasn't tugging her lines and keeping her on course, she kept me busy dressing and undressing her sails, and grinding her winches. When we got together, she rarely complained when I sailed her hard, then tucked her dripping hull into the dock berth. She was born for such workouts and easily performed them. Since she was special, I set her up in her own place and paid the rent. It was a cozy slip in a marina near the mouth of the Middle River, a dozen miles from Baltimore.

Our relationship started when Mark, a colleague of mine, introduced us one breezy day. He invited me to join him and Chara and another male friend for a day trip. Mark had been going out with her for several years, and now and then had mentioned her attributes at the office where we worked.

We spent a fun-filled day together on the bay, drenched in salt spray, my senses pounding with exhilaration. We skimmed the waves heeled-over with the beam-rail an inch from the bow wave. Nothing stopped us for miles ahead. We whooshed for hours through wind and rollers under a cobalt and cotton sky soaked in sunshine. Jimmy Buffett, iced beer, and raunchy jokes flowed with the slipstream.

Before the afternoon ended, I sensed a budding attraction to the little sloop's sassy gait and beguiling ways. She belonged to another, though, and I was content during the next year with the memories of my time spent with her that special day. Thoughts of her would float to the surface occasionally when I reminisced about my favorite fun days of all time.

But when Mark's roving eye landed on a different sailing beauty, it provided Chara and me the opportunity for an exclusive relationship. He offered her to me, suspecting I had a roving eye for her.

The tantalizing possibilities wooed me for a few moments. I soon came to my senses and realized it was a preposterous idea. It seemed almost loony for a complete non-sailor like me to own a sailboat larger than the one I used to play with in the bathtub.

But after a few days of self-rationalization, I felt a compulsion to possess the captivating Chara against all odds. Especially since Mark had sweetened the deal with a promise to teach me how to handle her; he would show me the secrets of sailors and sailing.

That was all I needed, plus the four-grand in cash he wanted. I didn't have that kind of spare savings, so I arranged a loan from my bank. I knew it was a risky thing to do for such a non-essential purchase. But Chara had charmed me beyond reason...and I just had to possess her at any cost. She had beckoned me with promises of adventure, and I could not resist.

When I made my case to Laura, she naturally seemed concerned that I wanted to spend serious time with another female. A manufactured pile of fiberglass, no less, that could sink our relationship. She thought my mind had become waterlogged and had short-circuited my reasoning faculties.

I assured her my motives were noble, and my relationship with Chara would never interfere with what Laura and I had developed. I shared my visions of how Chara would benefit our whole family. She would bring us memorable sun-filled days on the bay. We would have breezes in our faces, spray soothing our warmed bodies while dashing toward an open horizon, giggling all the way. We would join the boating community, which would welcome us with billowing canvass and wishes of good fortune and "Godspeed." Our whole family would become skilled sailors, I enthused, free to roam with the breezes to exciting ports of call.

Laura balked at first, shutting the portal of opportunity against my windy idea. I sulked for days, imagining desperate scenes with Chara slipping her moorings, drifting out of my grasp. My visions of us dimmed; no longer sliding peacefully in sun-dappled waters, downing endless umbrella drinks to bouncy reggae tunes. Something infatuated me about her sleek decks, her swaying boom, and leggy mast, the swish of the breeze on her sails, the way she glided when winched up tight.

Laura eventually gave in. Perhaps because I promised that someday soon, I would transport her and my new love across the bay on quiet zephyrs for a sunset meal of blue crabs on a romantic dock. With another lady now in my life, wild adventures to come began filling my dreams. I saw Chara and me outracing storm fronts, heeling hard on the wind with the mast and mainsail almost skimming the waves.

Mark met me at Chara's slip, where she quietly swayed in greeting at the dock. Her bow faced me, nodding gently, seeming to say, "I've been waiting for you."

I contemplated the alluring creature. Her two front cabin windows reflected my bewitched gaze. In the subtle breeze, she sashayed her beam-fenders at me, beckoning me to come and play. Without hesitating, I handed Mark the check. Chara did not seem to mind at all that someone else owned her now.

I did not know Chara's boom-vang from her jib clew then. But we became acquainted right after I took her out by myself. We clicked from then on—tackling the open water where life comes at you fast and sometimes furiously. The entire Chesapeake Bay became our playground. This vast landscape encompassed sixty- four-thousand square miles.

Mark joined us the first few times we left the dock. It was then he taught me all the parts of the boat, nautical terms, and commands. He showed me how to hank and set the sails, winch, steer into and off the wind, gybe and read the tell-tails to gauge the wind strength and direction. These foot-long pieces of colored yarn remained tied to the side rigging cables that stabilized the mast at the beam. Sailors had been using tell-tales for centuries, like rudimentary windsocks.

After Mark's basic hands-on training, the sloop and I worked things out for ourselves. I soon learned that when left to herself, she was a passive sort, a drifter who accepted whatever the winds would bring her way. She usually let them push her around willy-nilly without complaint. It was merely her nature, I decided.

But when we went out together, things became different. Much better when I took charge, though sometimes she groaned and resisted. I became the dominant one, always issuing orders, pulling on her sheets, and cranking winches to get her motivated in a particular direction. Usually we moved along smoothly, but occasionally we had some difficulties until we adjusted to each other's needs. Sometimes I got my way and other times she did. Yet, whenever I gave her some slack, she always turned back into the wind. It was her preferred go-to place.

Chara could be contrary in other ways, like when we sailed on a beam reach. Then her sails always pulled downwind, forcing me to tug incessantly on the tiller in the opposite direction. We'd fight about it briefly, then one of us would assert themselves and things would return to normal...until the next wave or wind-change. Sometimes it was aggravating the way she responded, turning away from my overtures in favor of every gusty breeze that happened along. But when I looked deep into her hull, I realized it was best for the two of us to work together. I was confident we could get past her flirtations with fickle winds.

I was aware Chara had a difficult past, a tragic divorce from her ex, an owner before Mark came along. When I handed him the check, Mark told me what he knew of the previous breakup before he met her. It seems that the man that took up with her some years ago came to a mysterious ending. No one knows exactly what happened between them, but it must have gotten rather ugly on the open water one sunny day. They made a date with the wind—the two of them alone, probably looking for some fun. Neither of them returned to port.

Even back in those days, Chara had a reputation as a delightful companion, but helmsmen found it unwise to push her beyond her limits. She could be an indifferent sloop at times—toss you overboard, then turn her perky transom and let you fend for yourself in the water.

That is apparently what happened on that peculiar occasion. Details remain vague, but a few days after leaving port, someone filed a missing person's report for her companion. Eventually, he washed up on a rocky shore half eaten by the crabs. Enough flesh remained to identify the fellow, though the cause of death remained suspicious.

Some days later, others found Chara miles away, battered and listing on a shoal with water filling her hold. Once towed back to the safety of her berth, she got her insides pumped out and blow-dried. After some cosmetic work, she returned to her old self. Authorities investigated the gash on her captain's head, but no evidence ever linked her to the mishap.

She never divulged what happened and refused to talk about it with me. But others speculated the fellow wasn't as attentive to her as he should have been. Perhaps he had too much to drink, or gybed when he should have tacked, and she slapped him with her boom. That could have easily knocked him into the bay. While he struggled to stay afloat, the indifferent lady probably sailed away without him.

But her past didn't bother me; my infatuation refused to believe she would ever harm me. After all, she was not some sailboat serial killer of ship captains. And I had no desire to change her. Oh, sure, I always felt a dab of paint here and some polish there couldn't hurt, but her simple appearance was fine with me. She always wore a gelcoat in gleaming white, accented with a powder-blue stripe along her topsides. It was just enough to bring some color to her profile.

She didn't need an autopilot system or fancy gadgets and gauges to stay a course—she had me, and I soon learned to navigate mostly by sight, sound and feel. Like a sports car, she needed my hands on the wheel to guide her—the tiller in her case. If I just wanted to relax for a spell, I'd rig up some bungee cords to hold the tiller where I wanted my hands-free.

Having her wardrobe changed was something we did often, though only canvas outfits would ever do for her. Fortunately, she always let me choose her sails and hoist them on. Yet those times when she wore nothing at all were also special for us. Then she'd slip around naked with her mast and forestay sails dropped to the deck.

This always happened when we glided into or out of the marina, with just her pert spreaders sticking out. They would fly proudly, her banner jiggling in the soft breeze for all the world to see. She didn't care. Then I'd tie her lines to the pilings and tuck her in the slip with a little pat on her stern.

When we went out on the bay together, she usually dressed in her mainsail, accessorized with a jib on her bow. When conditions called for it, she would go fully loaded in her largest foresail—the Genoa. And once in a while she went topless with only the tiny storm jib snapped to her forestay like a bikini. She had a saucy spinnaker in the sail closet, too. When filled, it's billowy mass allowed us to make downwind runs in a blaze of color.

But sometimes, with the tiny storm jib in a fresh blow, I could barely keep up with her as she frolicked with the wind. Then it was all I could do to keep her under control. And sometimes conditions became ominous, and I needed to yank her around and heave- to for our own good. Then I could catch my breath and consider our options, for she seemed to have no sense of caution.

But she also had a forgiving nature—if I blundered, she never foundered, even in the worst weather. When we close-hauled in a howling wind, she could show how nimble she was. If I was slow in loosening tension on the sail to spill off some pressure, she instinctively headed right into the teeth of it by herself—just the way she was made to do.

This action always slowed us down so I could bring things under control. Like a weathervane pointing directly into the wind, resistance became futile when she heaved-to. This involved setting the sails so her jib would sail us one way while the main pulled us in the other. Instantly we would slow down and cease heeling- over.

The wind forces would cancel each other out, causing the sloop to stay still. Then I could take a breath and make adjustments for getting underway again with a better set to the sails.

Now and then, her rigging groaned when asked to comply with a task, or I might bark at her when she did not respond as quickly as requested. But mostly, we jaunted along quietly, and I could enjoy the scenery and reflective thoughts. In time,

I came to understand her better, to know how she might perform in certain situations. I learned to appreciate the nuances of physical forces that motivated her to move in the way she did.

Sometimes we spent the entire night together anchored out in some corner of the bay. Now and then we would go off by ourselves—drift away on the tide with a rising moon to a secluded spot in some gentle cove. Here we would sit, gently rocking under an indigo sky amid lapping waves and the distant flicker of signal buoys. I loved to listen to her rigging tapping against her mast as she swayed to the wind-swells at anchor. Those metallic tinklings murmured like a heartbeat and lulled me to sleep snug in her berth.

But when the wind was up, so were our sails. I would arrive at her slip unannounced and off we would go. Such times we had heeled to the gunwale on a freshening breeze, when the wind gusts and rolling waves were ours alone. Then we enjoyed piling up the knots, jib and main taut as a drum balanced by tons of water against her keel, pushing us forward in a slippery dash. Rigging hummed in perfect pitch with the rush of water against the bow. Tell-tales so tight in the slipstream they barely fluttered.

But then who noticed, when it was the wind on my cheek that told me we were flying sure as an arrow. If the breeze crept toward my earlobe, I would draw the tiller as a violinist his bow to head up a fraction and tweak our passage to the limit. When my upper lip felt the breeze, I would bear off a tad so we would regain the perfect track.

Wind, sail, and hand. Nothing was more basic or more important in those special moments. Yes, the earth moved for us then, her rotations driving the winds that sustained the bond between us. We captured her breath in our sails and flitted across her fluid surface with nothing before us but a clear horizon.

Through Chara, I encountered new and exciting things that once lay beyond my own imaginings. She taught me much about her world, a watery realm of wind and weather that could be frightening, yet navigable. She helped me face and overcome countless challenges.

Take the trip to Rock Hall, for example. Laura and I had planned to take the kids sailing one Saturday. We intended to meet Mark and his family for dinner at a bay-side restaurant on the eastern side of the Chesapeake—a seventeen-mile trip over the water. We would gorge on fresh crabs, then spend the night with Chara anchored at a marina in a secluded inlet. On an afternoon created especially for sailing, we tacked our way out of the Middle River. The shoreline guided us with its olive-tinged forests, bright sheds, and gray docks.

When we reached the open bay, I checked the navigation charts and set the sails for a broad reach. I manually checked the compass every few minutes to maintain the azimuth I had selected for the dockside restaurant. I logged our progress and locations by the marked buoys we passed and calculated our speed by gaging the length and height of the bow wave at the waterline.

Chara had a maximum hull speed of about six knots or seven miles per hour. That might seem turtle-like, but on open water with a stiff breeze, it feels like ninety mph in a convertible roadster. That will blow your cap off and make your hair flow straight back. This is caused by the "apparent wind."

The apparent wind at any moment consists of the combined speed and direction of the "true wind" and the wind produced by the boat moving through the air. Everyone who has run a sled or pair of skis down a hill understands this; the thrill is not just because of the wind blowing, but also the wind you make by moving.

A true wind—the actual breeze velocity—coming across the bow increases the apparent wind induced by the speed of the boat. Apparent wind is important to sailors for setting effective sail angles. It also allows them to anticipate how much power the wind will generate from a particular point of sail.

At four miles out from the dock, Hart Miller's Island appeared on our starboard beam. I used it as a marker to reset the sails and shift course to a more southeasterly direction around the island. The day was gorgeous, and the trip uneventful. After nearly four hours, I spotted the dock for the bayside restaurant. We dropped the sails a hundred yards away and drifted up to the dock mere feet from the outdoor tables filled with diners.

After securing the boat, we joined Mark and his family, who had arrived earlier in their new sloop. We ordered enough blue crabs for everyone, sprinkled with the region's famous spicy seasoning, and steamed live in large pots. When the shells turned reddish-orange, servers dumped heaping mounds of them on long picnic tables covered in brown wrapping paper.

We cracked the hard shells open with wooden mallets. To get to the succulent white meat in the claws and joints, we used small seafood forks and picking tools like those used in any dental office. It was a messy affair, which is half the fun. When combined with abundant pitchers of beer, the social ambience is difficult to beat. And so was the scene overlooking dozens of yachts bobbing at their slips and moorings.

The wind disappeared and calm prevailed as the sun fell lower on the horizon. It is easy to dillydally in a place like that, get caught up in the moment and lose track of time. No big deal, unless it is. Like when you still have a distance to go in the dark, on a sailboat, in unfamiliar waters.

We only stayed twenty minutes too long, just enough time to down the last of the beers and pry a final morsel out of a remaining fat crab claw. But that was more than enough time to change the course of destiny we had planned for ourselves that day. After taking leave of our friends, the family and I hopped off the dining platform and onto Chara's deck.

We cast off the lines, and I motored offshore before running up the sails and heading north. Our anchorage for the night lay less than a mile and a half up the coast, a forty-five-minute trip, by my reckoning. Since I had never sailed in those waters before, I had planned to get there well before dark to avoid any problems.

But I had misjudged how fast the sun sets in those parts. With our twenty-minute delay, dusk had settled around us soon after we turned northward. I steered by the tiller, my eyes scanning the water continuously off the port bow, where I expected to encounter a flashing green navigation buoy. I had noted it on the chart before we started our bay crossing. It was a warning to keep the marker on the port side in order to stay in deeper water.

With darkness falling fast, I asked Trey to retrieve our best pair of flashlights from the cabin. I sent Laura and the kids topside with one and stationed them near the bow as lookouts. The evening gloom descended quickly, and the buoy did not appear even with the aid of the flashlights. Perhaps we are too far east of it, I thought. The shoreline also remained invisible, lost in the gathering murkiness. I nudged Chara a few degrees westward and slowed her to a glide.

But the buoy still did not appear. Shortly the wind began picking up enough to make the tell-tails stream. Chara surged ahead. "Come'on buoy, where the hell are you?" I soon realized we had missed it. A creepy feeling clutched at me like a pair of crab claws pinching my finger. Hard-shell karma seemed at work. It whispered that we had become lost on the open water at night...revenge for feasting on so many of their kind.

I reviewed my actions since leaving the restaurant. We must have drifted off course when I first swung north in the dwindling light, going further west than I'd intended. Then later I made it worse by altering course a few more degrees. That all meant the buoy was actually east of our position.

This is what you get, I berated myself, from dawdling over crabs and returning to the boat later than we should have. As if to show her agreement, Chara suddenly began bucking like a strapped mustang. The bow rose, then immediately slammed down onto something hard and unyielding the way a moving car jolts off a speed bump. She shuddered, and the mast clanged loudly as the halyards and cable stays banged against it. We had just hit something so firm it caused the mainsail and jib to spill all their wind and flap loudly, useless as a fouled parachute.

The sudden force caused Laura and the kids to bounce and stumble on the deck. This put them at risk of getting tangled in the sails or thrown overboard, since no handrails bordered Chara's deck. A grab bar extended along each side of the cabin, but nothing protected one from going over the sides other than a sturdy set of sea legs. Sailing aboard her required a good sense of balance gained from experience.

"Get to the mast and wrap your arms tightly around it but stay clear of the boom." I realized we had strayed from the deeper water and were now in a shallow area with Chara's heavy keel crashing on the compacted bottom. Her fixed keel was not retractable, like some other sail boats. It extended five feet below the hull and its torpedo-shaped base held a thousand pounds of lead. Chara's heavy bottom was a blessing in rough weather by acting as a counterweight to strong winds and capsizing. But her keel would not tolerate bouncing off the bay floor for long. It threatened to crack apart the bottom of her hull.

The boat continued to rise and slam, rise, and slam every few seconds. Worse, the wind freshened, producing white-caps and wind-driven rollers around us. The restless water came with the elevated wind speed, but also because the waves now rolled across shallower water.

It is the same reason tsunamis have such tremendous power— water driven a long-distance builds energy in the depths. But when the bottom grows shallow near a beach, the wave structure condenses like a spring and grows vertically. Then the increased energy is released as the wave surges inland. The booming sounds transmitted through the hull by the pounding keel were never supposed to happen on a sailboat. I wondered how long it would take for Chara to shatter apart and cast us into the dark water.

The rudder lifted out of the flow with each bounce, and so I had no means to steer the boat any longer. It was only functional when the wind and waves moved the boat forward and water pushed against the rudder's sides. Normally, I controlled the rudder's angle to the current by moving the tiller from side to side. Changing the angle altered the boat's direction.

In calm conditions without steerage, Chara would have sat still in the water. But with each bounce, the wind-driven waves pushed us ahead in a leapfrog motion—bang, rise, hop, then crash and repeat. Ironic that all day I had commanded the wind, weather, and water to do my bidding and take us where, when, and how I wanted. But now nature had retaken control— and my family and boat were entirely at the mercy of the bay and its shoal.

Not only was I no longer in charge, but few options existed to get us off the shallows and back to deeper water. I fired up the outboard and engaged the prop, expecting to out-power the waves. Each time the hull hit bottom, the prop would submerge for a second and I would rev the outboard to gain some forward momentum. But it had no effect because immediately the next swell lifted the prop out of the water.

Soon the wind shifted and came from behind us, whipping the water into frothy waves that threatened to spill over the transom and swamp the boat. Worse, the wind and waves moved us further into the shallows. Seconds later, my eyes detected a line of white frothy water fifty yards beyond the bow. The froth-line became clearer with each keel-hop, forming a near- horizon that extended into the gloom on both sides of the boat.

"Breaking waves," I shouted. The boat was heading straight toward a band of boulders that churned breaking waves into the frothy band. Soon we would crash onto those rocks. The navigation chart flashed in my mind—we must be off the Swan Point Peninsula, heading for the boulders placed there to protect the wild shoreline. We had strayed northwest much too far. The outboard became useless as a replacement for the rudder, so I shut it off.

Chara's sails whipped uselessly, blocks and pulleys clanged, rigging groaned; I needed to go forward and drop the main and jib sails before they ripped apart. But the sloop's relentless bouncing shoved me off balance every few seconds. My eyes swerved toward the cabin roof and the handholds mounted along its length. I wasn't sure I could let the tiller drop and dash there without the boat tossing me overboard. I judged the distance to the rail at eight feet—only a couple of seconds away…long enough, without support, to stumble off the deck or get smacked by the swinging boom.

A snap shackle hung from the backstay cable that steadied the stern end of the boom. The short cable attached to the shackle, known as a pigtail, remained detached while sailing the boat, where it jiggled and swayed. Since I preferred not ending up as crab-scat like the previous owner, I reached up with my free hand, grabbed the pigtail and snapped it onto the tip on the end of the boom. It kept the heavy boom from swinging, though the loose mainsail attached to it still flapped wildly. It had to come down.

On the next rise, I released the tiller and the rudder slammed sideways out of control. Immediately, the deck tilted steeply, but my sea legs held and my rubber-soled deck shoes prevented my body sliding. I coiled and leaped through the final few feet of the cockpit with my hands reaching for the cabin roof grips.

One of them caught the roof railing like a talon grabs a branch, and I pulled the rest of my body toward it. With both hands clasped on the rail, I looked up to see my family splayed out on the cabin roof, hugging the mast and the other set of handrails. They looked terrified.

I waited for the hull to crash down, then broke away from the rail and snagged the mast, encircling it in my arms. I hauled down the mainsail and fastened it to the boom with its straps.

Half the boat length remained between the mast and Chara's prow, where the jib remained fastened to the deck and forward cable-stay. The smaller sail flapped threateningly like some wild poltergeist. My hold on the mast loosened, and I pulled myself along the last section of cabin roof rail. From where it ended, six feet of dark, shifting deck loomed. I needed to cross it to reach the flapping jib. The wind howled while the deck bucked and lurched. Spray soaked my skin as I dove for the jib shackle. I released the sail and wrestled it like an anaconda, twisting it around the cable-stay to secure it for the moment.

After snatching the anchor and its chain off the stanchion on the bow, I stumbled with them along the deck toward the cockpit, dragging the attached line. I reached the cockpit and stumbled inside, then dropped the anchor at the stern.

After looping the line's free end around a stern cleat, I threw the anchor out as far as I could. But it did not catch or dig into the hard bottom, and Chara bounced ahead. I pulled the anchor in and recast again and again, in different directions and distances. But the waves were too strong, and we continued our bumpy march toward the rocks.

Time was growing short, and darkness surrounded us. Black sky merged with black water so thick I couldn't tell them apart except for the line of white water ahead. I worried about the white caps driving against the straining hull, pushing us toward the nearby rocks without an anchor to hold us.

As I tossed it out again, I shouted to Trey to get the spare anchor from the cabin's bow locker and bring it to me. When he did, I cleated the line and threw it off the port stern. With the main anchor off the starboard stern, the pair could hold a grip in the mud. It slowed our advance, but the relentless wind and waves pulled the anchors loose every few minutes, and I had to recast and reset the hooks now and then.

But at least we were no longer hurtling to the rocks. The pounding, though, continued with Chara pitching, rolling, and crashing on the bottom. She was taking a severe beating with each jolt, listing to port, then starboard, then back again.

I heard a cracking sound and realized her fiberglass hull must be fracturing. I beamed the flashlight into the cabin and saw several inches of water sloshing. Floating equipment and dislodged gear swirled between the storage bin sides that lined the bottom perimeter of the single aisle. I had painted the bins solid white, but now a continuous dark band had appeared six inches above the cabin floor. The section of the bins below this band flopped back and forth as the keel slammed down on the floor of the bay. The hammering must have finally caused a rupture in the hull where it attached to the keel.

I grabbed a life vest, slipped it on, then snatched three more and handed them through the cabin hatch to the others at the mast. If the boat was coming apart, we were moments from catastrophe. I turned on the strobe flashers to mark our location. The anchors were holding us in place as the wind howled and halyards snapped and clanged in my ear. Waves pounded against the transom and spray shot into the cockpit of the reeling sailboat. I heard another cracking sound above the wind. Only one thing left to do.

I reached inside the cabin hatch and flipped on the VHF radio. Thoughts about what was coming loomed darkly...defeat, helplessness. I hesitated with the mike in my hand, watching the water in the cabin slosh back and forth. With a sigh, I flipped to Channel sixteen and pressed the send switch.

"MAYDAY, MAYDAY, MAYDAY, this is the sloop, Chara. Repeat— this is the sloop Chara; call sign *Charlie—Whiskey— Tango— Uniform—8364*. We are requesting immediate help off the south end of Swan Point, near Rock Hall. Steering disabled in high winds— endanger of breaking apart on the leeward shore. Need immediate assistance."

I kept calling until I received a response ten minutes later. Eventually the Coast Guard made contact, and I explained our situation, specific location, and need for a tow. The dispatcher acknowledged, but every few minutes he came back on the radio asking me again for all the same information without offering confirmation of assistance.

Swan Point is a major landmark on the Chesapeake Bay and is the only such designation anywhere near Rock Hall. Navigation charts clearly show it, and why the Coast Guard seemed clueless was beyond me. Without GPS technology yet, the only way I could provide latitude/longitude coordinates was from a chart inside the cabin. But under the present conditions, that was not practicable. So, I repeatedly provided the information requested by the dispatcher until I wanted to switch off the radio and take our chances with the elements. Instead, I fired off two flares a few minutes apart into the blackness overhead and saved the last one for later.

Chara was too small to carry a life raft or tender, but we would all float in our life jackets if we abandoned ship. It was the rocks that worried me, since we could get smashed upon them, or get injured by the disintegrating boat.

We remained in peril for nearly two hours while the anchors held. Eventually, a pair of tiny glowing red and green dots grew larger off our stern. Finally, the dots came close enough that I could see they belonged to a private powerboat that had responded to our Mayday call and located us. The two men aboard, private citizens, tossed us a line, and I hitched it to our stern cleat after I hauled in the anchors.

I restarted the outboard. By then, the rocks loomed large and the crashing of waves had drowned out the wind and hull banging. Less than thirty feet separated us from shore. After repeated attempts, the men pulled us off the shallows—just as the Coast Guard came back on the radio with another information request. I cursed and switched off the radio.

Once we reached deeper water, we conveyed thanks to our rescuers and untied. I then examined the cabin more closely. With all the cabin lights on now, I could see Chara's hull had not actually ruptured. The cracks I heard had come from heavy gear inside the cabin bins crashing against the doors. A mess, but no serious damage.

What appeared in the weak flashlight beam as fracturing of her fiberglass structure was only a crack in her surface gelcoat layer. A superficial problem, like small stress cracks in a plaster wall, easily repaired. All the water in the cabin had come from waves splashing into the cockpit and from water spilling out of the bilge because of all the pitching and rolling.

Now, as we slowly motored on our new course to the marina, we let our tensions ebb; no more crashing waves, thrashing boat, or snarling rigging. Shore lights flickered, and the waves returned to gentle swells.

The sudden change in conditions made it seem we had slipped through a portal into another dimensions' maelstrom, only to have come back out unscathed. As the adrenaline rush dwindled, an overwhelming desire to sleep hit each of us. Laura and the kids dozed up on deck. In the cockpit, I forced myself to concentrate on the boat, our course, and the reassuring purr of the engine. In fifteen minutes, I skirted the breakwater for the marina I had targeted before leaving Chara's slip.

We entered the harborage. After four hours at the bay's mercy, we had found a haven near midnight. I drifted into a designated berth and secured the boat. How comforting it felt finally to have reached Gratitude Marina, a more relevant name I could not imagine. We surely were not the first wayward travelers relieved to find shelter there. After bailing the water out, we crawled into our berths while soft winds rustled the rigging like a lullaby. Chara rocked gently, soothing away our cares. I listened as long as I could, grateful for her caress—until the blackness of peaceful, dreamless sleep overwhelmed me, and I surrendered to it.

Lost in Translation

The loud whapping of the helicopter blades frightened a troop of howler monkeys in the canopy. They bolted in all directions as the noise shattered the peacefulness of their morning. Some dove for lower branches while others leaped onto adjacent trees in the rainforest.

None of the other seven people onboard seemed to have noticed the howlers. They were engaged in reading maps or writing notes— the noise inside the aircraft was much too loud for talking. For the past half hour, my focus concentrated on the trees in the unbroken forest below.

I studied the canopy and the distribution patterns of the many varieties of trees in the vast emerald landscape. The large crowns of dominants poked like cabbage heads above the main canopy cover. They had pushed the crowns of lesser competitors aside to claim a greater share of the sunlight. Such savage indifference also allowed the dominants to suck more of the sparse nutrients from the soil around their roots, and then pump them upward where most of the leaves waited.

Lesser species struggled for their share of resources in the dominants' shade. Flying above it all, I saw the forest as a vicious battlefield, though it appeared peaceful and benign. Constant robbing of nutrients, space, and water produced the distinct variations in the vegetation patterns I observed. Some trees preferred the sub-canopy, others the understory, and many more stayed in the ground layer.

Vegetative warfare. It never stops, even after death, when microbes, fungi, insects, and scavengers compete for decomposing resources. These natural battles involving plants and animals for territory and resources occur wherever life exists—on the ground, in the waters, under the surface, and in the air.

And at the moment we were skimming treetops over a vast area of Colombian rainforest. Earlier, we had taken off from Medellin, the country's second largest city. The helicopter provided the only practical way to reach remote jungle destinations where roads did not extend.

We had panicked the howlers while still in the foothills of the western Andes, heading toward the headwaters of the Rio Sinú river. To get there, we would need to cross rugged peaks of the Paramillo Massif. This is a mountain range of the West Andes, at the northern end of the Cordillera Occidental (West Andes) range in Colombia. The steep highlands there comprised an area known as the *Alto Sinú*.

Nearly thirteen-thousand feet above sea level, the forested slopes captured rainwater that served as the source of water for the Rio Sinú. This is the largest river in Colombia's Caribbean Region, after the Magdalena and Cauca rivers. It flows from south to north for hundreds of miles before merging with the Caribbean Sea on Colombia's northern coast.

The Sinú landscapes lie within the *Magdalena-Urabá Moist Forests Ecoregion*, designated by the country's code *NT0137*. The Sinú watershed is vast—more than the area of America's Glacier and Yellowstone National Parks combined—3.5 million acres. Precipitation in the Alto Sinú drained down jagged mountain slopes within the upper third of the river's watershed. The Rio Sinú flowed through the Andes before entering its foothills and continuing into the flatlands of the lower plains on its way to the Caribbean Sea.

As the helicopter passed over giant kapok and cecropia trees, I watched their branches sway in the propwash. Bromeliads perched upon lower limbs and thick twisting vines wound up trunks that reached two- hundred feet above the ground. Rubber and banana trees slipped under the aircraft's landing skids as we rotored ahead.

Forty minutes later, the helicopter approached a sheer face of vertical rock. Still some distance away, I could see flat-topped summits of the mountain range flank both sides. They jutted upward out of the rainforest, while steep verdant folds of wooded slopes covered their lower sides.

The pilot headed straight for one of the mountain walls about halfway up its face. Why, I wondered as the aircraft shuddered in the turbulence of an updraft. As the pilot approached closer, a rocky outcrop appeared on the vertical wall. The helicopter swooped in and hovered a few seconds above a level area, and then it landed. The whapping noise and engine whine diminished and then ceased. We had arrived at our temporary base-camp.

After stepping to the ground, I moved out of the way and set my gear-bag down. Sun on my face; it felt good, but I pulled my cap brim lower against the glare. The expansive view around me immediately popped into sharp focus and reminded me of a postcard from Machu Picchu.

On the cliff shelf, both the helicopter and base camp offered the only flat surface on the otherwise sheer wall. From there, tropical forest blanketed the surrounding mountain slopes. Vegetated ridges and drainageways plunged downward, then down further until lost in the mists. Diaphanous cloud-fingers of water vapor drifted upward the way lazy steam rises. Dappled sun filtered through the trees near me, and the call of rainforest birds echoed in the forests below. The high humidity made my pores start weeping sweat.

I turned away with my bag and followed the others from the helipad across a boarded walkway that bridged boulder-strewn ground. On the far side, a man stood watching as I approached him. He had dark hair and medium olive skin—a Colombian for sure, barely out of his teens. Waiting for us, I thought. He smiled— he had a gun.

It was a military assault rifle, and he held it strapped over his shoulder, pointed at the ground with his forefinger placed straight along the trigger plate...the ready position. He wore a uniform of dark camouflage—heavy black boots, military brimmed cap, and a neck bandanna for absorbing perspiration from the humid conditions.

As I passed him, he nodded as though expecting me. I smiled back uncertainly, and a few yards further ahead, the area swarmed with uniformed soldiers, most of them carrying weapons. Others unloaded jeeps and trucks of crates and supplies. This looked like an active firebase, but for what reason, I could not tell.

A soldier led our group to a large open canvas tent where we sat on cargo and ammunition boxes. We chatted a few minutes among ourselves, then two men came in and introduced themselves. They wore casual clothes with fashionable synthetic vests that looked fresh off the shelves from an upscale safari boutique.

Mine, on the other hand, consisted of thick duck- canvass, made for bushwhacking, peppered with thorn nicks and dirt stains. We all shook hands and grinned broadly, for these were our clients from downtown Bogota.

They represented a company that had hired the consulting firm I worked for out of Washington, D.C. We provided technical services for environmental and engineering projects worldwide. The clients worked for a large private utility company called Urra, which constructed and managed large water resource projects. They hired our firm in the early fall of 1981 to conduct environmental studies in the Sinú River watershed for one of their projects.

The company's headquarters in Bogota wanted to construct a dam for the upper reaches of the river—in the Alto Sinú's rainforest. To gain the approvals and permits, the Colombian government required a scientific assessment of potential impacts to the region's rainforest ecology. Our clients needed my company's expertise to proceed with the project known as the "Urra Dam."

As a result, my firm sent a reconnaissance team of scientists and engineers to this remote wilderness location. This included me as lead ecologist, plus a geologist, hydrologist, forester, several engineers, and our principal in charge of the project, Frank Kellar.

We had arrived in Bogota from the States the day before to conduct initial field operations. The immediate intent was to gain an overview of conditions in the Sinú watershed and prioritize environmental issues to further investigate at a later time.

In the weeks before leaving, I had assembled what little information existed in the scientific community and government sources. Not much on ecological conditions, but I reviewed topographic maps, aerial photos, geological reports, and historical accounts on human occupation. These provided context on geographical and social issues of the region.

While conducting my pre-field research, I traced the Rio Sinú's course on maps through the northern end of the Western Cordillera of the Andes. The region lay mostly within the southern portion of Colombia's Department of Córdoba. Only the lower half of the river that drains those mountains was navigable and served the towns and cities that existed there.

But in the vast rainforest region of the upper third where we had landed, only occasional muddy tracks and trails wound through the wilderness, mostly hidden under the canopy of tropical jungle. Based on my background in forest ecology, I knew the rugged terrain and remoteness of the upper region made it suitable for a high diversity of tropical plants and wildlife.

It also made it an attractive habitat for something much more dangerous than all the jaguars in the country. This menace walked on two legs...armed and hostile communist guerrillas. When we encountered the gun-toting Colombian soldiers on the cliff side landing zone, I realized firsthand the seriousness of the sociopolitical landscape we had entered. The military was not there primarily for our protection against predatory wildlife, but to hunt and kill the guerrillas regardless of our presence.

Long before our arrival in Colombia, various paramilitary bands, drug cartels, and anarchist groups took refuge in and controlled extensive areas of the region's countryside. Each pursued their own agendas, including insurrection against the prevailing government.

Communist guerilla groups had been fighting the Colombian military in the rainforests of the Sinú for decades. But in the late 1970s, the illegal cocaine trade mushroomed and became a major source of profit pursued with widespread violence. Local citizens living in isolated rural towns often found themselves caught in the middle, where many of them had been slaughtered, kidnapped for ransom, forced into involuntary labor, and had their homes and possessions seized and destroyed.

It wasn't until we landed on the cliff shelf with the helicopter that I understood we would roam terrain held by some of these terrorist groups. With all the military scurrying about the base we had choppered into that humid day, the situation seemed secure for the moment.

We spent an hour under the canvas tent discussing our field plan, going over safety protocols, reviewing maps and laying out our itinerary. We wrapped it up just after noon, and without announcement a group of middle-aged women in plain clothes brought in a few pots and trays of food. They silently set them on a side table cafeteria-style. One woman ushered with her hands toward the food.

We rose one by one and filled paper plates with the offerings, which included odd chunks of bony meat I assumed was chicken bathed in a bland gravy, unseasoned beans, and fried plantains. It was a simple meal reflecting the remote wilderness location surrounding us.

After finishing the meal, we collected our packs and left the tent. Outside, a man waited with several armed soldiers. When we collected around him, Miguel, one of our client representatives, introduced the man as our local guide. Our group fell in line and the soldiers deployed, with one following behind the guide, another in the rear and the last took a position mid-column. The guide led us along a steep path through thick tree cover and down the mountain. The trail eventually broke out of the jungle at the Sinú River. There, three dugout canoes bobbed in the water against a low bank. Nearly thirty feet long, each boat came from a single tree hewn by hand in the rainforest. Passengers had to sit one behind the other by climbing over the thwarts as in any canoe.

In the stern of each, a local man sat next to an outboard motor. Although any of the boats could accommodate six people, only three of us got into each one, allowing our daypacks to have sufficient space. The soldiers turned and disappeared back into the jungle. As the foliage closed behind the last soldier, I wondered who would provide us with protection.

While waiting for the boats to load, my eyes swept the surroundings. A few shafts of early afternoon sun penetrated through the trees in a hazy mist along the far bank. Sunbeams splashed the lower plant growth in random patterns of bronze and gold. The broader scene reminded me of cathedral forests I had explored, ere whispering seemed expected. And except for our voices, the surrounding jungle kept its silence. My scan revealed no visible creatures in the trees or on the ground, not even a bird.

I gauged the river's width at about seven of our canoe lengths. Dense vegetation bordered both sides of the channel and blocked any view beyond. The foot-high banks grew thick with vegetation, which told me this part of the river remained exceptionally stable. Certainly, the channel had not changed its course for a very long time—hundreds, perhaps thousands of years.

Based on the size and shape of the channel, I realized we were in the far upper section of the river, close to the headwaters. There, among the highest peaks, a network of springs and small streams would have merged into the main channel. Downstream from the canoes the waters flowed for nearly two-hundred-fifty miles and the channel would double in width along its course.

The guide spoke to his steersman for a moment, then stepped into the bow of the lead canoe. The boat handlers soon fired the engines, shattering the jungle quiet. All three boats angled into the current, one behind the other. I had selected a rustic wood seat in the center section of the first boat, where my observations would remain mostly unobstructed.

Impenetrable forest arched over the banks and formed a shady canopy as we moved quickly downstream. The current flowed swift and unrestrained in the river without rocks, logs, or debris to slow it down. Boat engines whined loudly and powered us at even higher speed down the channel where the water ran deepest and fastest.

After twenty minutes, the engine whine changed to guttural growling as the boats slowed. A few moments later they drifted toward shallow water against a bank, where the handlers shut down the motors.

We maneuvered the canoes alongside each other and tethered them together. Everyone stayed in the boats because the jungle was too thick to exit. We had a project discussion on the water, where the guide informed us we sat at the upper limit of the proposed reservoir behind the concrete dam. It meant that based on the engineers' prior analyses, the impounded water would extend to where we sat. For nearly twenty miles downstream, the river and rainforest would then lie under the permanent lake.

The channel section we just ran would remain normal. But then it would widen from here as it merged with the lake. No longer a couple hundred feet wide between banks, the lake would extend nearly three miles wide and fill the valley. While to some, visions of a massive pristine lake emerging in the rainforest might seem desirable. I knew, however, lakes were not natural in this region, especially at such a high altitude in the Andes.

Natural inland bodies of water in Colombia are not true lakes, because they have no surface outlets. While they look like lakes, they are called lagunas in Spanish and are very shallow bodies of water compared to most actual lakes. Lagunas and lakes both have inlets that supply them with rainwater. Groundwater, streams, and rivers also flow into them. But lagunas are closed basins that regulate water levels by evaporation and groundwater seepage or underground rivers. Consequently, lakes and lagunas are quite different ecosystems.

During our impromptu canoe meeting on the Rio Sinú, I scanned the riverbanks. But nothing special suggested the upstream shore of the lake would occur precisely where the boats were located. It was just a remote spot in the wilderness that matched a calculated point on a topographic map. Physics would define the exact spot once the dam became operational.

A few minutes elapsed, then the boats were off again, heading further downstream. A quarter of an hour later, the jungle along the left bank vanished, and an acre of open ground occupied the space. It was a section of level floodplain filled with a variety of dense herbaceous growth, but nothing else occupied it I could see. Jungle succession, I thought, plant pioneers establishing a foothold in a clearing. Sunlight bathed the area in lime-green hues—a vivid contrast to the deep emerald shades of the continuous jungle surrounding it.

Moments later, we passed another opening in the trees. It seemed twice the size of the previous one. Downed trees and stumps smoldered; smoke swirled upward and hung just below the treetops in the background. A few flames licked up the trunks of others, but I saw no people.

Slash and burn, I said to myself. Others had been here before us. The fires seemed deliberately set to create small fields. They would later grow cultivated crops on them—local agriculture in the rainforest. Who could live so deep in this tropical wilderness, I wondered, to make a go at this kind of primitive farming?

A short distance downstream, yet another opening appeared, but this one had a hut standing just back from the river. A simple square dwelling with a thatched roof, it stood in the clearing by itself. The one-story wooden structure sat on log stilts elevated eight feet off the ground. Essentially a roofed platform, the hut had no walls—just a railing around the sides attached to the stilt logs. Without walls, the dwelling's sides were fully open to the weather and air currents, which helped prevent mildew and insect problems.

Another log with a series of notches cut into it leaned against the frame and served as a ladder to enter or exit the elevated house. A child stood on the ground outside next to a woman in a faded pink dress, and she was holding another small child in her arms. They watched us pass but did not wave or smile; nor did we. Only a few hundred feet separated us, but we remained worlds apart; merely strangers ogling strangers.

These, I was certain, were Emberá Katio people, whose ancestors had lived along the Sinú River for thousands of years, though they seemed the only ones there now. Perhaps, I thought, the man of the house was the one who was out burning the field we saw.

I watched the family until the jungle closed in again, restricting views to a few feet beyond the riverbanks. I thought how often throughout their history had indigenous Emberá people seen foreigners coming and going along their river. The small family in that clearing were pioneers trying to hew out a simple living in the wilderness.

They were not asking much from society, just the opportunity to survive mostly on their own. Noble certainly, but savages surely not; Rousseau, the philosopher, had it mostly right. The indigenous family I saw would fulfill his romantic "uncorrupted savage" idea. But how might they change if a lake soon replaced their river and homestead?

The Emberá Katio lived in a simple society, close to the land. Our project team, however, came from a complex society—and some members of our group had consequential plans for pioneers such as these. Might those involve a kind of savagery, I wondered? And would "progress" in the form of a vast lake in their midst force them to abandon their traditional lifestyle for cramped urban living far beyond the rainforest?

Now, though, we were just passing through their neighborhood, and had entered the landscape where the river would no longer flow if the dam project proceeded. These inhabitants and others like them would have no home nor prospects, for they would lie under the dark depths of an artificial lake. Were they even aware of what others were planning for them? I asked myself.

More openings appeared with similar houses. Occasionally we saw other small indigenous families and single houses, or a few men working the fields between stretches of rainforest.

Yet, dense tree cover still dominated the land, and the limited slash and burn activities in this part of the Sinú valley produced benefits to the rainforest. The practice created occasional small openings in the canopy where sunlight could penetrate. This produces higher plant diversity, and the borders form ecotones where new niches support important habitat for a variety of animal species adapted to edge environments.

In the clearings, shade-intolerant pioneering plants find open ground to establish a foothold. These provide alternative food sources for local wildlife populations. Habitat variation and species diversity make the rainforest biome highly productive.

Sound slash and burn agriculture is sustainable because it does not depend upon outside inputs based on fossil energy for fertilizers, pesticides, and irrigation. The ash from burning provides a rich source of nutrients that last for a year or two, then the farmers abandon them. Nature quickly restores them to rainforest again.

As historically undertaken by indigenous peoples, subsistence slash and burn farming remains an ecologically harmonious method of cultivation. In places such as along the

Sinú River where the human population density is low, the process increases nutrient cycling in the forest.

This is the main reason Amazonian rainforest soils are largely infertile—most of the nutrients remain locked up in vegetative biomass, including the estimated sixteen-thousand varieties of trees. It may take a hundred years or more for a large tree to die naturally. All that time, it withholds nutrients from the larger ecosystem that are stored in its tissues.

Even when trees fall, they provide many ecological benefits. Decomposition of dead branches and roots into basic elements occurs slowly while they remain standing. Once fallen, though, the humid environment speeds up the process. Decomposers and detritivores rapidly break down plants into forms that new seedlings can gobble up in no time. While it leaves the soils impoverished of nutrients, it maximizes ecosystem productivity by maximizing biomass growth and carbon sequestration.

For the relatively few local subsistence farmers, cutting down a patch of trees, however, is very labor intensive. Instead, they slash the bark of tree trunks and bushes with machetes and axes. By girdling the trunks, the trees die because they can no longer pump nutrient-carrying sap up to limbs and branches. Once they are dead and dry, the farmers burn them down from their base to ashes, which releases nutrients back into the soil.

Sustainable slash and burn techniques have passed down through the generations of indigenous peoples like the Emberá Katio. Their farmers knew how to scrape out a firebreak around the perimeter of the fields before they burned, to avoid destroying the forest beyond. They also knew about wind and moisture conditions, and crop rotation patterns to optimize their efforts.

Humankind and nature had coexisted in ecological balance along the upper reaches of the Sinú River for centuries, including when our canoes plied its waters. Local inhabitants somewhere nearby most likely also carved the canoes we rode in out of downed logs.

We motored further downstream, and I watched the land become more rugged beyond the channel. Sloping hills began appearing in the background above the trees beyond the riverbanks. For the next thirty minutes, I saw no further evidence of human activities.

Suddenly the channel narrowed to half its previous width, and the handlers throttled back their outboards again. The boats floated toward the right bank, and we tied them to some trees.

All the team members began stepping from the dugouts onto the low bank, while the boat handlers stayed with their boats. The rest of us milled about on the bank, a flat shelf that extended only a dozen feet from the water's edge before ending at a vertical rock face. My legs tingled from so much time cramped in the canoe, and I stretched them while the others gathered in a group. I walked a dozen yards along the bank and looked up to examine the wall of rock, but within a few feet it became lost in the foliage.

It told me that this river section must have encountered an especially resistant rock face, and even after eons of rushing water, the channel had reached its lateral limit at this hard rock. I pulled aside some vines and could see the dull, hard surface of the rock underneath.

I glanced across the river, and it appeared similar— lianas, snaking vines and understory trees climbed a vertical wall, partly visible from where I stood. These walls, I noted, were likely the reason the channel was so narrow there compared with upstream.

The other team members had started a discussion, and I walked over next to Kellar as he listened. "So why stop here?" I spoke softly, not wanting to interrupt the others' conversation.

He leaned his head toward me while the discussion continued. "This seems to be where the clients want to place the Urra dam breast. The mountains form a pinch-point here on both sides of the river—shorter width means lower construction and material costs. And they can secure the concrete end walls to the hard rock."

Nodding, I let the engineers debate the pros and cons of that while I moved away and began taking notes on the plants. A line of leafcutter ants wound through the underbrush and across my path. I stopped to observe the parade.

Each ant hauled an irregular piece of green leaf far larger than itself. They cut the leaf parts with their chainsaw-like mandibles and carried loads many times their body weight. The flat leaf-blades waved back and forth with the insect's efforts—part of a miniature conga-line with swaying emerald fans. The ants were taking the leaf parts to their underground nest where they would cultivate them as fertilizer for fungi. Later, the adults would feed the fungi to their young, while continually sending out other expeditions for more bounty. Another instance of jungle farming.

I watched the line of ants disappear under the foliage. My attention moved to the surrounding vegetation. No signs of birds, mammals, or any other creatures. I returned to scribbling in my field notebook. Out of the corner of my eye, I saw a man in a maroon plaid shirt paddling upstream toward us in a canoe. It was small, only a quarter the size of ours, and he pulled alongside our boats. The man got out with something in his hands, but I could not tell what it was.

Continuing my inspection of the area, I all but forgot the man whom I took for a local. A minute later, I noticed he was showing something to several team members. They shrugged and shook their heads, and the man approached another of our crew closer to me. It was then I could tell the man held an animal pelt of some kind. My interest immediately perked up, and I stepped over to him to take a better look.

As I did, the man's eyebrows popped upward, and a half-grin played on his lips, sneaky like a Cheshire Cat. I sensed he wanted something. He twitched the skin at me and said something in Spanish. I made signs and stuttered that I did not understand.

He must somehow be part of the Colombian team that was supposed to meet us here, I thought. Maybe the group told him I'm the wildlife guy, and he wants the animal identified.

Miguel saw us and stepped over from the discussion group. He nodded at me. "He wants to sell it to you."

"How much does he want?"

The two of them exchanged words in Spanish. Then Miguel looked at me again. "He won't say, but if you want it, then just give him a few dollars."

"How many?" I asked. Miguel shrugged.

The man held the skin while I examined it. It was about two and a half feet long, covered mostly with black fur with a few brown streaks; white patches marked the throat and belly. It looked like a species of small fox, so I told Miguel to ask him where he found it. "He says he killed it in the forest nearby."

"Does he have a local name for the animal?"

He spoke a few more words to the man, and he responded, shaking his head. "He says 'no'—he's never seen one before."

The animal had a variety of canine features...long slender muzzle, bushy tail, short legs, thick, bristly hair. I noticed it had small, rounded ears, which seemed odd for most foxes. I had never seen anything like this animal and was keen on identifying it later.

My hand reached for my wallet. I opened it and started putting single American dollar bills into the man's palm. After two, I looked up and the man's eyes stared at my hand. Two more went in his palm—the eyes never blinked. One more. I checked his face, a slight frown. I hesitated, but then slipped two more dollars to him. His head remained bent, and the palm never twitched. That was seven, and I was about to wave him off.

But I examined the pelt again, turning it over and checking the quality; skillfully processed. I laid down a few dollars more and flipped my hand away in a questioning gesture. That was ten; worth it to satisfy my curiosity. The man lifted his head, smiled, and handed me the fur. I nodded, but he had already turned aside and began walking toward his boat.

I rolled the skin up and watched the man paddle away. Once he disappeared, Miguel said, "I recognized him; he was released from prison about a month ago."

"No kidding?" But I was barely paying attention— absently trying to figure out where to put the skin. "Was he poaching wildlife or something?"

"No. He murdered another consultant who was investigating the dam site here like you guys." That cool tone of Miguel's again.

I looked at him sideways and patted the rolled skin. "Right, and this here is the last of an endangered species."

Miguel grinned. He raised his eyebrows and nodded. "It's true; he thought the consultant was going to take his land away and replace it with the dam, so he shot him dead with a revolver." Miguel shrugged again, then said, "It was kind of a misunderstanding...sort of a problem with translation."

I stared at Miguel, trying to decide if this was his little joke on the naive gringo with the ragged field vest. "Lost in translation, huh? Glad I didn't haggle with him."

Miguel smirked. "The consultant was describing how the dam would flood the valley and the man's land would disappear, so he would have to move far away. He meant it would occur eventually, since it would take at least a decade to get the dam built."

"The guy that just left thought it was something that would happen like in a week or two. So, he dealt with it like it was imminent—blew his head off."

My eyes darted to the pelt, then settled on the tangle of jungle next to me, contemplating his words. After a few seconds, it occurred to me I was staring at a strangler fig that had crept up a small tree. Its thick tendrils wrapped around it the way a python squeezes the life out of a capybara.

"He went to prison for a year," Miguel said. "They just let him out. Interesting...here he showed up again—probably wanted to see what these new consultants had to say."

"Come on." I threw him a dismissive wave. "Why didn't you mention this to the others?"

Miguel shrugged, with his own Cheshire Cat smile. "He wasn't holding a gun, and he didn't seem upset."

I felt my eyes narrow and my hand tightened on the pelt. "Neither do pythons before they squeeze the life out of you," I muttered.

"Huh?" he said. "Never mind."

"I'm not kidding, Joel; you just dodged a bull—; I mean, you got a nice skin there. Glad it went okay."

My tongue pressed hard against my cheek lining, but I said nothing further, just stepped past my client to rejoin the others. Keep an eye on this one, I thought on my way over there. The surroundings might seem benign, but danger and death lurked everywhere—creeping through the underbrush, hanging from trees, arriving in dugouts with carcasses to trade.

Although the rainforest appeared peaceful and the lives of the indigenous Emberá-Katio people seemed pastoral, the Sinú valley had seen considerable violence over the past four-hundred years. Jungles are like that, but beyond natural predation, there is a heart of darkness about them when humans invade. Joseph Conrad understood this while writing his novel that inspired Coppola's film "Apocalypse Now." Suddenly, I felt it too on the banks of the Sinú River.

The invasion began two thousand years ago when the ancient Zenú people began inhabiting the flatter elevations of the lower Sinú valley. They were the first to establish a civilization far downstream of the Alto Sinú in the wide alluvial plain. There, six-thousand feet lower in elevation, they called their capital city Fincenú. It lay near the river where they had cleared away the jungle, about thirty-six miles downriver from where I purchased the mammal skin.

In addition to the city, the Zenú maintained extensive irrigation, drainage, and agricultural works. These people also mined gold and crafted fine jewelry used in trading. The surrounding mountains contained veins of gold pushed up from the Earth's depths millions of years ago. Over centuries of erosion, flakes, and nuggets washed down into creeks that fed the Rio Sinú.

The Zenú buried their dead in earth mounds and placed gold objects in the graves with the bodies. Their main burial center was based around a ciénega, a large marsh near the Sinú River called Betanci. Mounds once lay thick along both banks that stretched for fifteen miles. Some were twenty feet high and nearly ten times as long. The Zenú reserved the largest for chiefs, filling them with gold and other riches. Archeological evidence points to a highly developed culture supported by a substantial population during pre- Columbian times.

But the Zenú were not just a pastoral civilization; not in Rousseau's "noble savage" sense. But then, what cultures ever were, considering that humans have always been an aggressive species. Warfare for the Zenú was essential to their way of life. Cannibalism and public displays of human trophies became important for gaining prestige. Flayed skins and even arms and legs stuffed with ashes were common household furnishings. Female warriors, celebrated for their fierceness, often led the armies. As is usually the case, not long after humans enter a landscape and gain a foothold, they exploit it. The Zenú were no exception.

But in the early 1500s, the winds of change blew a fleet of conquistadors to Colombian shores. Under the command of one Francisco Becerra, they dropped anchor in the Gulf of Urabá in the west where today the Panama and Colombia borders meet. The Andes rose above them like a massive wall protecting a golden city. Undeterred, Becerra took one-hundred-fifty soldiers inland through the jungle. They never returned.

Eighteen years later, Pedro de Heredia, another conquistador, landed in what is today the city of Cartagena on the northern Caribbean coast of Colombia. He sent an expedition of two-hundred-fifty men to explore the Sinú valley.

They proceeded up the river in native dugout canoes, similar to those used on our expedition nearly four-hundred-fifty years later. When Heredia's men learned about a large city in the region, they marched toward it in their armored chest plates, helmets, and swords. As they approached Fincenú, they noticed the large concentration of mounds and buildings. Once at the city center, though, they found it sparsely populated. Bright sunlight flashed off the soldier's armor onto empty buildings and dusty streets.

The ruling chief was a woman named Tota, and she informed the men that the land had once been populous. But most of the people had died from a strange disease after a group of bearded men like Heredia's appeared years earlier. They showed Heredia stacks of Spanish arms and equipment. It looked like Becerra's ill-fated mission had ended at Fincenú, along with the lives of thousands of the indigenous Zenú soon after.

Befitting a proper conquistador, Heredia had his men loot the gold from the graves of the Zenú. Over eighteen months, they stole more than two billion dollars' worth of gold. These Spaniards devastated the indigenous Zenú to where they disappeared from the landscape. The jungle grew back, smothering the extensive grasslands the Zenú had created more than a thousand years earlier. The culture vanished along with their mounds, buildings, and language.

Nothing of interest for the Spanish lay upstream of Fincenú, for no gold existed there. Riches abounded in the river and rainforest, but these were living resources that the Emberá-Katio people depended upon for survival. They had formed a different culture than the Zenú, living in simple villages and on subsistence farms in more rugged terrain. There they grew vegetables in their small slash and burn plots, hunted animals for food in the forest, and fished in the river. They were safe from the invading forces...at least for a while.

The Emberá-Katio are members of the larger Emberá population that mostly reside in Panama and the Sinú region. Some refer to themselves as the Katio Indians, but most seem to use the hyphenated name.

Daily life went on for the Emberá—until rumors of the Urra dam posed a threat to their lifestyle and culture. If these were not enough to worry about, then the arrival of another kind of exploiter provided even more of an existential threat. It was a source of terror and murder...and involved roaming bands of those armed guerrillas— which were far more numerous than conquistador Heredia's gang.

They began appearing in the jungles of the Sinú after 1964, when The Revolutionary Armed Forces of Colombia (FARC) and the National Liberation Army (ELN) formed as the military wing of the Colombian Communist Party. Since then, these and other Marxist groups had been engaged in a civil war with Colombia's regular army.

Gradually, conflicts with government forces began pushing these rebels into less accessible areas, including the jungles and rugged mountains of the Alto Sinú where the Emberá lived. These were terrorist organizations funded through kidnapping, ransom, extortion, and illegal drugs. When they needed supplies or recruits, they sometimes attacked people that lived along the river, forcing youngsters into their ranks, decimating families like the ones we passed on the river. The Emberá had no gold, but the few resources they did have were often plundered by these terrorists.

Our project team soon left the proposed dam site on the river and headed further downstream a few miles. We did not encounter any guerilla forces then, nor on the way back to the mountain base where our helicopter sat. We left there just before dark and turned to Medellin.

From the airport, we drove in shiny taxis through neon streets that took us to our hotel—a twenty-story steel and glass structure offering a large lobby decorated with indigenous art. After tossing my field gear on a chair in the bedroom, I turned the air conditioner higher to deal with the humidity.

Then I took a shower, changed into a suit and tie, and made my way to the upscale restaurant on the top floor. There, I ate an elegant dinner with my other team members and shared a few bottles of fine wine. We made toasts to the project's success, a productive day...progress. I too held my glass up, though a hollowness had seeped into my heart and I couldn't wait to return to my room, confused about the implications of my work relative to the sweeping social and political conditions in the region, and the proposed dams' impacts on its ecologies.

Twilight

Log canoes and the helicopter provided our primary means of travel over the next two weeks. They allowed us to access remote locations in the Sinú region and more populated sites downstream. The river's vast watershed drained through two-hundred- sixty miles of rugged mountain rainforests, steep hills, and flat plains. We flew over remote locations each day, studying the landscape and river below like a condor on the hunt.

At various times, one of us would spot something that needed closer scrutiny, and the pilot would find a clearing and set down or hover a foot or two off the ground. Then our team members would grab gear and jump out to inspect the area of interest.

An overview of the Sinú's natural resources and ecological state of functioning needed critical evaluation in order to assess potential effects from the proposed Urra hydroelectric dam. That did not mean, however, that the Colombian government had much enthusiasm for our work. The bureaucrats and vested interest groups preferred to just proceed with getting the project under construction. Environmental, social, and economic issues seemed mostly a nuisance relative to the financial benefits they perceived.

The impetus to conduct our environmental investigation derived more from concerned national and international organizations. No substantive environmental laws existed in Colombia then. They would come years later, reluctantly, through various ministries of government.

While Colombia's National Code of Renewable Natural Resources and Protection of the Environment was adopted in 1974, it had no teeth, little specificity. Critics argued that most of the articles of the Code only regulated the public's right of access to natural resources. But it did not effectively protect rights related to health or environmental impacts related to land development projects. Nowhere did it define specific environmental regulations, except to transfer the duty to conserve natural resources from the government to the private sector. Environmental investigations fell to companies like Urra's hydroelectric utilities, though no standards or procedures existed to undertake them.

Our team of scientists and engineers had no capacity or role in making policy decisions regarding the Urra dam project. But we had experience and standards to follow from our respective professional disciplines. Besides scientific principles, we also had NEPA. The U.S. National Environmental Policy Act provided our guidance on documenting and reporting our investigatory findings.

The company hired us to provide objective investigations regardless of anyone's opinions or agendas. That required careful observations, an ability to connect disparate bits of knowledge, and draw reasoned conclusions that matched the evidence.

In this way, field ecologists are like crime detectives—they let the evidence speak for itself. Both detectives and ecologists understand how patterns of cause and effect can lead to predicted outcomes and solutions. The first step in crime solving and science is to examine the scene, which was what I was doing along the Rio Sinú.

A primary question remained ever-present on my mind...what does the evidence tell me about how the Urra Dam project would affect the natural resources of the river and its watershed? I scrutinized conditions from the air, the river, and on the ground.

But getting to the Sinú region required flying commercially from Medellin. Before the initial one- hour flight from Bogota, flight staff warned us to expect a difficult landing at the Olaya Herrera Airport. Its runway, hemmed in by dense city infrastructure, left no room for pilot error. International jumbo jets need lots of airspace to make turns. Things seemed normal until the jet made its final approach from the east. As we passed over a steep band of green mountain ridges, my upper body jerked sideways in my seat without warning. The plane shuddered violently, and I felt my stomach drop.

It felt like when I used to ride roller coasters and they shot downward too fast. Turbulence from updrafts lasted for minutes...I was sure the plane was falling from the sky.

The jet then banked steeply as though it would flip over; g-forces shoved my upper body against the window while the seat belt dug into my hip. The plane held the angle far too long, it seemed, while also still dropping in altitude.

I strained to look out the window and saw a mountain range ahead. We were heading straight for it. The cityscape below was crammed against the slopes that towered above it. Streets packed with buildings lay in a narrow bowl ringed by the mountains.

Shortly, the extreme attitude of the aircraft became worse, as its wingtips canted even more vertically. The turn radius tightened, and the turbulence increased, but the aircraft slowly moved parallel to the slopes instead of head-on.

I felt the plane make an agonizingly slow swing to the left; the runway came into view when the wings leveled out. Then the nose of the jet swooped down like an eagle diving for a fish. The pavement came at us fast. The wings wobbled as the tires squealed for mercy on the tarmac and the engines reversed thrust to decelerate. My head almost hit the seatback in front with the hard braking maneuver—necessary because the runway ended over a thousand feet shorter than Bogota's.

We seemed to have landed at the bottom of a metropolitan fishbowl. My hands shook while unlatching my seat belt, and I wanted to find a wall to slam my chest against to push my heart back into its ribcage.

But such landings at Medellin were routine for the pilots. During the following week and a half, we flew into and out of that city frequently. As I waited for takeoff each time, I thought of pie. As in American Pie, and whether this'll be the day that I die.

Most of our helicopter flights into the Sinú originated from Medellin; smoother than the jet flights, but noisier than a kitchen garbage disposal running on worn bearings. Once the rotorcraft cleared the mountain wall surrounding Medellin, we flew west over the Andes. At first, heavily dissected slopes appeared, covered in rainforest and open patches devoted to cattle ranching and farming.

Within minutes, though, most of the fields disappeared, as did the roads. Unbroken rainforest ruled the landscape all the way to the horizon.

The green mantle of trees-controlled conditions in the ecological community below the canopy. The largest trunks and crowns ruled lesser forms by taking the most space and sunlight. Yet, a rich understory prevailed below the treetops, offering innumerable habitat niches for other plants and wildlife.

As we flew over the Alto Sinú, I was impatient to set down and explore remote areas that were yet untouched by humankind, even the Emberá. I discussed my plan with the pilot, with a request to have someone local who could accompany me—someone with deep knowledge of such secret places.

Jenkins, a forester on our team, wanted to join the mission. He mostly had an interest in commercial timber issues, while mine focused on the state of overall ecological processes and activities. The guide would help us navigate through the uncharted forest and make sure we could return on time to the pickup point later in the day.

If we did not show up at the specified time, became injured, or got turned around and lost in the dense growth, there could be a lengthy wait for a ride out.

The pilot made a radio call, then flew a few minutes downriver to a small village in the open plains at a much lower elevation than the proposed dam site. He landed there and a man with a machete got in. He propped it unsheathed between his knees and we flew back toward the high rainforest.

Eventually, the guide directed the pilot to an opening in the canopy created by several large trees that had fallen. Remains of their root mats lay upended, exposed, indicating they likely came down naturally in a storm. The debris made it impossible to land the aircraft among the rotting logs, so the pilot hovered and the three of us leaped from the cargo door.

My feet landed in the waist-high grass while the downwash from the blades blew it into pulsing waves around me. We immediately moved through the herbaceous growth toward the edge of the forest, and I heard the deafening noise of the rotors fade. The helicopter had left to take the engineering team members to different locations in the valley where construction would occur.

Just outside the tree line, I motioned for the other two to stop a moment so we could confer. By turning the elapsed time bezel on my watch, I set it for two hours—our allotted time, then showed my wrist to the guide. Pointing to my watch, I made a small circle over it to indicate two revolutions, then pointed to the forest ahead. I asked the guide if he could take us as far as possible into the forest and return us to the clearing within the dial setting on my watch.

It was immediately clear our guide did not speak any English, and we did not speak Spanish. How could such an important factor get overlooked in choosing a guide? I asked myself. If the guide didn't know what we were looking for, then how could he lead us there?

After some faltering words accompanied by fumbling hand gestures, the guide nodded. What he was agreeing to, I was unsure. This wasn't a good start, but our metal whirlybird had just flown away.

After a moment, I gave a thumbs-up, and the guide turned his back. Jenkins and I followed him, and we stepped into the forest.

The first thing I sensed was the silence—no twigs crackling, leaves fluttering, or even the sound of our own footfalls. There was no doubt we were in the subdued light of an old-growth community—perpetual twilight. Trees of immense size hoarded the light in the canopy one-hundred-fifty feet above us, allowing only small points of sunlight to glitter through to the forest floor. I stood in a virgin climax rainforest.

Devoid of thick plant cover, the floor offered a spacious understory where walking remained easy. In some places, only a few inches of composting leaves and detritus lay on the surface. But a thin mineral soil layer the color of beige putty occupied most of the ground.

I picked up a handful and kneaded it between my thumb and forefingers, pushing it into a short ribbon. Beads of moisture oozed out, and I felt the sticky texture of clay with hardly any organic matter. It confirmed my suspicions; the myriad of plant structures around us had locked up most of the ecosystem's nutrients. Whatever died quickly decomposed and got sucked right back up through the massive roots of the canopy trees. Smaller plants scrambled for what remained as litter before the dominants could grab them.

The moist clay made navigation slippery underfoot, because its exceptionally tiny pores inhibited rainwater from infiltrating rapidly in the shallow substrate, so it stayed near the surface. Despite the low nutrient content of the soil, trees grew to immense sizes.

They got that way by developing extensive disklike root mats, often several hundred feet in diameter. These huge fibrous mattresses were efficient in collecting nutrients and water and providing support for their immense trunks and branches. In addition, huge buttress roots grew from the ground to against the trunk, as high as fifteen feet above the soil. Jenkins and I measured the girth of some giants at eighty feet around, with trunk widths of forty feet—nearly as long as a semi-truck trailer.

The canopy tree trunks did not encroach on one another, spaced according to their root mat perimeters—where one edge ended, another began. In this way, and by hoarding the sunlight in the canopy, the dominant trees controlled the entire rainforest ecosystem. All other plants below the treetops fought for scraps of space, light, and nutrients. I walked in a war zone similar to the one I had observed from the helicopter on our first flight from Medellin, where the howlers bolted through the canopy.

Between the great trunks grew a boundless variety of smaller trees, shrubs, and herbaceous plants. Some bore leaves the size of umbrellas, shading out adjacent competitors, while thick woody vines strangled smaller trunks. A profusion of epiphytes, mosses and air plants had overtaken territory on the surfaces of the vines and tree branches, smothering leaves of their hosts. Fungi sent forth masses of branching threadlike hyphae that pierced living and dead plant tissues like bayonets. The damage they caused allowed diseases to invade, producing discolored leaves and stems on some vegetative growth I passed. All part of the systems' energy cycling.

Nature takes a long time to develop climax ecological communities—hundreds and sometimes thousands of years. It is why they are so rare in the modern world filled with humans. For most tropical landscapes, the end-stage in natural ecological succession is the classic climax forest. The one we moved through would persist until nature produced a different climate regime...or humans sufficiently degraded the environment. Presently, however, it functioned as an efficient, stable ecosystem, without evidence of disturbance by man—no trails, trash or even slash and burn plots. Mankind had never been in this part of the rainforest before.

The forest's structure differed from the tangled, impenetrable growth that colonizes early successional stages and logged-over tropical forests. Navigating through such second-growth forests is often impossible, requiring constant machete work or heavy machines. Most Hollywood jungle scenes get filmed in second-growth rainforests where every step requires whacking vegetation. We, however, did not need to use the machete even once.

We slipped deeper into the forest, where the air stayed dense with humidity and my field shirt seeped perspiration. Much of it came from the abundance of plants that released water through their leaf pores as a byproduct of photosynthesis called transpiration.

The leaves also produced great quantities of oxygen. I sensed a freshness to the air, and the smell of decomposing organic matter similar to the inside of a thriving greenhouse. It was unmistakably the smell of life, and of death, and endless renewal.

A constant low hum pervaded the forest, barely above perception, as though a giant heat pump or air exchanger was running in the distance. But it was not anything mechanical at all, just the combined buzzing from millions of hidden insects and other creatures going about their daily lives. It felt like I was inside an immense living entity, which I was—one of nature's grand factories humming along at top speed.

Yet, in the heat of the day, we heard few animal sounds in the forest, and the stillness became palpable. Though when darkness arrived later, unseen rustlings, peculiar noises, thrashings, and death cries could erupt anywhere from the creatures of the night shift.

In the daytime gloom, though, lianas and strangler figs clamped around tree trunks and heavy branches because they provided scaffolds for themselves in a relentless climb to steal the sunlight. The bromeliads and other epiphytes fastened themselves with tendrils and gathered moisture and nutrients from the air, rain, and dust. Their leaves became microhabitats for a rich and diverse variety of other organisms—insects, amphibians, fungi, bacteria, and slime molds. Other insects and bacterial varieties lived on and inside the fungi and molds.

Such tiny microhabitats also existed on the forest floor, forming the lowest layer in the surface rainforest structure. This tropical ecosystem depended on a high diversity of structures and species to maintain and process all the potential energy pathways. All life there lived in habitats for which they were adapted, occupying different ecological niches, meaning they filled specific functional roles within the ecosystem—their specific jobs. Plants and animals performed these roles within every layer of the forest.

In the semi-darkness of the rainforest, multitudes of niches nested upon still more niches that wove a massive food web. I could see the results with every step along our route. Plant and animal tissues provided substrates for bacteria, whose niche included decomposition functions. The bacteria are fed upon by occupants in first-order consumer niches that involved protozoans within rainwater habitats, including amoebas and microscopic crustaceans within bromeliad cups.

Carnivorous insects of the second-order niches consume the protozoans, passing the remaining unprocessed energy to larger invertebrates that stalk their prey from countless surfaces. Vertebrates in every layer hunted invertebrates and weaker vertebrates. The actions of each species defined its ecological niche. Every species must perform its part efficiently, or another one would soon fill that niche. The laws of thermodynamics must be served.

It was a complex layered world of green, where life oozed from every surface. It was why I could smell it in the air around me and hear it in the steady hum. Countless living things endlessly processed, transformed, and recycled nutrients and energy.

When I inhaled, I imagined myself within the lungs of a massive living organism that pulsated to the rhythm of its own respiration. Its rhythm became my rhythm as I breathed in the rainforest's fresh oxygen the plants were pumping out. With each breath I exhaled, the great forest absorbed the carbon dioxide back and reprocessed it to oxygen again, and again.

In so doing, the forest and I and all the other respiring animals there depended upon each other— plant to animal– animal to plant, organic to inorganic and back again. We respired together, breathing for each other in a symbiotic dance that only the living can appreciate.

After several hours, I checked my watch...twenty minutes to go before we needed to meet the helicopter. Jenkins nodded when I mentioned it, and we halted the guide and tried to let him know. But things got sort of lost in translation and he did not seem to understand. I watched the machete in his hand, hoping he didn't think we were talking about bringing in loggers to cut the rainforest down. Images of the man who sold me the mammal skin flashed through my mind.

We pointed to our watches, swirled our fingers in the air like whirlybirds, and made walking gestures back the way we had come. We only knew our route lay somewhere behind us, for we had become absorbed in our work. Without the guide, we would find ourselves lost, unable to even navigate by sun or stars under the closed canopy.

I gave the guide another thumbs up gesture, smiling with my eyebrows raised—understand? The guide nodded several times and immediately turned and headed off the way we were already going...deeper into the rainforest.

Jenkins and I swiveled our heads toward each other and blinked, trying to figure our next step.

"He's the guide, and we were pretty clear on the instructions," I said. "Best to let it play out; he's got to go home too."

Jenkins shrugged, and we followed the guide. As we did, my thoughts turned to what I remembered about constructing a raised platform for spending the night in a jungle. I began looking at the vegetation with a different eye, including which of the umbrella-like leaves would be best for keeping the nightly downpour off us.

When I glanced at my watch again, the bezel said we only had five minutes to go. But I could not see the forest edge anywhere around. I had noticed different plants since we last stopped and knew we had not been that way before.

Jenkins caught up with me and grabbed my arm. "What the hell? I don't think we should keep going this way."

"Look, we don't know which way we're actually going. He could just be circling back in a wide arc, and we don't know it.

Why don't we keep going? We'll know in a few minutes whether that's the case or not."

"And if it's not, then what? It's after four and the little light we have now will be gone soon."

"Then we'll use his machete to make a shelter and tie it together with vines; We'll start a small fire for protection—everything will be fine."

Jenkins winced but loped ahead to catch up with the guide. I followed, glancing at thick patches of moss that might make the platform more comfortable to sleep on. Soon, my expectations became confirmed—we broke out into the clearing to find the helicopter sitting quietly. Someone spotted us and the rotor blades began their windup as we waded through the rolling waves of grass.

Once airborne, I could observe the Sinú River far below, and the way the steep mountain slopes confined it to a narrow slot between them. The Andes were young, only thirty million years old. They rose when the continent's tectonic plate collided with the adjacent oceanic plate.

My thoughts recalled the geologic history of the Andes below us. Ten million years ago, the off-shore plate began subducting— pushing under the continental plate, thrusting the land skyward tens of thousands of feet all along the western side of South America. Rivers and streams formed new drainage patterns, cutting through the uplifted rock. Gradually, over four million years, peaks and ridges remained standing as erosion sluiced away nearby rocks and sediments into the streams.

The vertical down-cutting through the newly uplifted land continued until it could go no further— where the base-level elevation exists today. As the alluvial plain that formed in the lower Sinú valley became flatter and wider from erosion, the river's velocity slowed. That allowed the channel to meander across the alluvial plain long before I flew down the valley and documented it.

The helicopter followed the Sinú channel northward, downstream toward the Caribbean Sea. As we left the high rainforests of the Alto Sinú, I studied the gentler landscape below. The steep slopes had turned into verdant green hills far from the proposed dam. The land remained covered in forest for several miles, but large clearings soon began appearing near the river in this central valley region. Then larger deforested tracks became clear, which grew in size the further downstream we flew. By the time we reached Tierralta fifteen air miles away, forests had become rare on the landscape. The Sinú channel had carved a floodplain there over five miles wide.

The rural municipality of Tierralta held sixty- thousand people then, but we dared not land there because a war was underway. The Popular Liberation Army (EPL) was fighting paramilitary groups for control of the surrounding cocoa plantations that supported all the narcotics trafficking. Without doubt, it was a violent place to live.

As we passed over, the level of poverty became evident— narrow, dirt streets lined by low, shabby houses with rusting corrugated roofs. A dingy grayness seemed to pervade the crowded spaces, mostly absent of motor vehicles.

We continued all the way to Monteria a hundred miles further downstream, still within the central region of the valley. There the Rio Sinú floodplain had expanded to twenty-five miles wide, and the channel flowed through this city of two-hundred-thousand people at the time. The inhabitants called themselves costeños and their city "The Pearl of the River Sinú."

Once covered in rainforest, this region was where the Zenú settled, clearing the land before the Spaniards arrived. They converted the landscape into savannah and crop fields, which were still visible as we conducted our surveys. But modern inheritors of the valley had long ago converted most of the cleared areas around Monteria to cattle pastures and coffee plantations.

Further downstream along the Rio Sinú, we entered the lowest reaches of the valley. This part of the alluvial plain extended north to the ocean. The tropical forests were long gone, replaced by extensive pastures and large agricultural fields. Towns and cities erupted from the plains along the river and networks of roads connected them.

The wet season still lay upon this part of Colombia in early October when I came there. High amounts of rain typically fell daily and washed into feeder creeks and drainageways before adding to the Rio Sinú's flow. Along its course through the lower reaches, the fresh water replenished the large system of wetlands—lagunas, ponds, marsh, and swamp complexes of critical importance for wildlife, both native and migratory.

In these wetlands, ciénegas, and remaining lower jungles, other biologists in other times had found substantial populations of diverse species of ducks, raptors, flycatchers, and other songbirds that spent the northern winter months there. The wetlands also provided nurseries for many important fish species, both fresh and salt-water.

It was fortunate Jenkins and I had conducted our field operation in the Alto Sinú rainforest when we did. Soon after, a major weather front moved into northern Colombia and dumped a massive amount of rain. Far too much for the level plains of the Sinú to absorb through the soil surface. And so, the streams filled and flushed the water into the Sinú River. The volume of flow overwhelmed the system and the river's banks overflowed, flooding the lower plains in the Sinú landscape.

Our helicopter pilot was about to take off from a site in the Alto Sinú where we worked that day. The rotors *whapped* after I climbed in, and I waited for liftoff. But the craft stayed on the ground. I heard the radio crackling, and the pilot engaged in a conversation with his dispatch.

When it ended, he turned and informed us that the flooding had become catastrophic, and the aircraft needed to divert to undertake rescue operations in the lower floodplain. Our work in the rainforest ended for the day, at least.

The aircraft then headed downstream, following the river for miles, passing over patchworks of fields and small woodlots. The landscape looked the way I had seen it over the previous week. Soon, however, signs of the flooding appeared in the fields near the river. With each mile, the floodwaters consumed more of the land, spreading further away from the channel, which had all but disappeared.

I lost track of where we were, but eventually flooded land appeared below as far as the eye could see. We flew over a densely populated area, a city whose streets and small buildings lay under water. The only evidence of a river channel were the miles of old houseboats that lay in adjacent rows crammed next to each other, marking the sides of the river corridor.

The floating shanty town contained dilapidated houseboats of all sizes, shapes, and colors. Some sat half underwater and showed damage. People stood on their roofs gesticulating as we powered onward. Radio calls came fast and furious and the pilot turned to us and announced he had to drop us at the nearest safe place before commencing rescues.

That turned out to be Monteria. We had flown over it days before. First settled by the Zenú, the city now looked its age under the low gray ceiling of storm clouds and pouring rain. At least it had an airport, constructed a few miles north of the city, and that is where we landed.

It had one runway; not a busy airport compared to major cities of the world. We found a small bus that delivered the team to a hotel that had seen better days and plenty of worse nights. We found enough empty rooms for each of us to have our own.

The hotel had the look of something built in the 1950s, still hoping to display a no vacancy sign on the door someday. My room was large—too large for me to kick my boots off without fear of ever hitting the opposite wall. I know, I tried it. Yet it was all but empty, except for a double bed, a torn leather chair and a distant set of drawers. It felt as cozy as an empty stockroom.

We ate dinner in the hotel restaurant at a long table. It, too, was larger than necessary, but the tables had white tablecloths and padded chairs. It reminded me of a Bogart movie from the 40s, black and white and shabby all over. One of our clients told the group not to order any salad because of dysentery concerns. I immediately removed the lemon wedge from my water glass.

For some reason I felt slightly uneasy there until I noticed a dark lump on the floor across the room. While wondering what it was, it scooted under the next table...a monster cockroach, the kind that could bully a small dog.

I didn't say anything but was glad to get back to my room. I went into the bathroom that had no toilet where a commercial-sized bidet ruled the space. I glanced into the tub and saw a silverfish the size of my shoe running laps around the porcelain edge trying to get out. How about that, I thought to myself? Here I am in the middle of Colombia staying in the Hotel California.

Check-out was early, and we piled into a bus heading for the airport. Still overcast and cooler than we had experienced on previous days. The cold front had remained over the lower sections of the valley.

Downtown traffic seemed typical for a city that size, and it took fifteen minutes to reach the outskirts. There, the urban setting dwindled to Latin American suburbia, and then to rural poverty and open fields. The unpaved one-lane road to the airport ran straight— hardly wide enough for two vehicles.

That didn't matter though, because people on foot far outnumbered cars or trucks coming or going.

A solid line of locals filed along the roadside, spilling onto the dirt track and causing our bus to start and stop frequently. Everyone headed in the same direction, shuffling along to the airport four miles away. People wore plain clothes—men, women, and children alike. I watched the procession through the open windows of the bus and thought how the absence of noise seemed peculiar. The travelers moved along within inches of my window as the bus crept along the road, but the sound level of their activities remained subdued.

No one seemed to be in a particular hurry. Few smiles lit their faces, as though they dreaded their destination and having to board a plane. Most carried considerable loads on their backs in sacks, baskets, and crates. They contained all manner of things—market goods, household supplies, clothing, chickens, children.

Wooden carts of all sizes hauled heavier loads, pushed or pulled by hand, or by burros, piled high with goods. Animals bleated, squawked, squealed, and barked from inside or on top of large burlap bags. These mostly contained coffee beans or vegetables.

We handed over our luggage at the airport, and returned to Medellin without incident, except for another harrowing landing. But that wasn't the case with retrieving our luggage. We exited the plane from the aircraft stairs on the tarmac and security staff directed us to proceed to a staging area not far away, next to a line of long outside tables. We stood in the heat and humidity and waited an unusually long time. Then baggage carts pulled up. Handlers dumped luggage on the tables, and the passengers scrambled to locate their own bags. After signing some kind of form, we could take our belongings.

I had only brought one small leather suitcase, and when I found it, the top had been unzipped and my clothing stuck out on all sides like lettuce spilling out of a sandwich. Someone had riffled through the bag and left the top flopping.

I lifted the lid and checked to see what was missing. Several things were gone, including an extra camera, lenses, and my bush knife. My main one still lay in my carry-on. I groused to Miguel next to me, and he shrugged without a word. No officials hung about, and I thought of stomping off to find someone. But then remembered where I was—and it wasn't Kansas anymore. Instead, I yanked the zipper closed and stormed off toward another waiting bus that took us to the hotel.

At least, I thought, the culprits had left the animal skin in there...probably considering it totally worthless. Later, I studied the skin the man in the maroon shirt had sold me on the Sinú River. I determined it came from a very secretive and little-understood animal—a short-eared fox (*Atelocynus microtis*). While not actually related to foxes, it has similar morphological features, and fills a comparable ecological niche— hunting small animals and living in dens on the ground. The mammal is unique and endemic to rainforests in the region like the Alto Sinú. This meant the species originated in the Amazon rainforests and occurs nowhere else.

Many other mammals inhabited the jungles and wetlands of the Sinú valley. Among them, two Colombian tapirs, manatee, capybara, jaguar, spider monkey, several tamarins, spectacled bear, cougar, ocelot, jaguarundi and the giant anteater—the most endangered of them all.

Endangered birds also made the Sinú rainforests home, including the harpy—its largest eagle, as well as the blue-billed curassow, and the great green macaw. Many more species of birds, reptiles, amphibians, and arthropods occurred there, but biologically, this was one of the least known ecoregions of Colombia.

When we finished our work in the Sinú valley, we made our final flight from Monteria to Medellin. While still in the air, I began merging my notes and observations on my findings over the previous two weeks in the region. Just a start, for much more work lay ahead in the coming months. Still needed were analyses, cause-and-effect confirmations, functional dots connected, ecological and environmental impacts assessed, conclusions reached, recommendations derived, and we would prepare an objective, comprehensive report written and delivered.

All of that would take place back in the states, in our corporate offices. I would ride the elevator up to the seventh floor of the gleaming building where I worked in my pinstriped shirt and tie, far from the lush rainforest. There my team and I would work in windowed, temperature-controlled offices trying to figure out what kind of ecological future lay ahead for the Rio Sinú, its valley, and the people who dwelled there.

During our last flight out of Medellin, I watched the sun set on the landscape. As twilight settled over the Alto Sinú rainforest, I felt a sadness come over me. Not because I was leaving and soon heading home, nor because the day had ended. My sorrow was for the of the Rio Sinú and the Emberá who would lose their way of life when the lake arrived and smothered their landscape and all the forest beings under its still waters. Changes were coming to the rainforest, and unintended consequences lay on the horizon. Those were yet undefined as the Alto Sinú approached twilight. Like always, beyond the twilight, darkness holds more uncertainty, for the way ahead is obscured. On my last night in Colombia, I slipped between fresh sheets in the king-sized bed and reached to turn off the lamp. As I did so, my eye fell on the rolled-up skin sitting on the dresser across the room. All those human lives taken by terrorism, for...what? My hand paused a moment on the switch. Then I pressed it, and the room went dark as a night in a jungle.

I stared into the gloom at where the rolled pelt lay. A variety of disjointed images began crowding my mind...the Zenú, golden treasure, conquistadors, jungle leaves dripping rainwater, whapping helicopter blades, howler monkeys, rising mists, smoldering trees, log canoes, rushing river, pink dress, a raised hut, man in a maroon shirt, Cheshire cats, murder on the riverbank, guerrillas, automatic weapons, the dam project, toasts to progress, impending ecological impacts, the mysterious animal whose remains lay neatly rolled up a dozen feet away.

Each image pulled my mind in a different direction, all competing for attention. Weary, I begged myself for sleep, yet the thoughts kept coming. But then, they coalesced into a unified whole. I realized then that at the center of it all was the Rio Sinú.

For millions of years, it remained a river that brought life to its steep slopes and valley. Its reliable flow and channel provided a means of travel that also brought hardship and death for many people who settled there and still persisted.

Yet, the river continued to flow and provide sustenance for the remaining Emberá Katio people who knew how to endure in the rainforest. But now plans were afoot that would put the river itself in danger. The greatest of all landscape threats was gathering on the horizon...one the river, its people, and its resources could not survive, should it come to pass. Rivers die when their waters stop flowing. For the Rio Sinú, all that was, is, or might be, would cease to exist when the coming deep lake waters flooded the valley.

Into the Kootznoowoo

The small plane droned on through the wide Gastineau Channel. On both sides, steep green mountain slopes tumbled down to the water. Ahead, Juneau, Alaska, sparkled in the late afternoon sunlight three thousand feet below. It lay nestled like a fairytale city at the base of Mount Juneau in the delta of the rugged Gold Creek valley.

Spruce and fir forests surrounded the isolated capital, their dark verdant tones contrasting with the pearl-white buildings, cerulean blue water, and azure sky. For as far as I could see beyond the green slopes, endless snow-covered mountain ranges filled with glaciers marched to the horizon. In the clear air, the beauty of it all popped the view into three-dimensional relief like a holographic image. How wondrous it looked as awe flooded my senses and nearly took my breath away.

The single-engine Cessna began its descent, returning to the airport north of Juneau after a day on Admiralty Island, a half-hour away to the south. The fifteen-hundred square mile land mass the size of Rhode Island lay deep in the Alaskan wilderness, nearly unpopulated by humans.

A rugged coastline, old growth temperate rainforests, towering mountains, and alpine tundra with permanent icefields dominated the vast island. Dense hemlock, western cedar, and Sitka spruce blanketed much of the landscape. The forests dwindled high on the mountains into alpine meadows dotted with miniature pines and waist-high spruces. Carpets of ground-hugging flowers, lush grasses, and low herbaceous plants occupied the surfaces, along with dwarf dogwood, bunchberry, heart leaves, and others.

Extensive lowlands covered the central interior and supported an endless number of lakes and streams. Grizzly bears (*Ursus arctos horribilis*), also known as brown bears, were prolific on the island. Population estimates showed over 1,500 bears roamed the wilderness—about one per square mile...exceeding the number of people living on the island. Grizzly bear numbers comprised ten percent of Alaska's entire population of the species. In addition, more brown bears dwell there than in all the other states combined. While more bears wandered the island than people, bald eagles outnumbered bears—about 2,500 lived on Admiralty Island...more than all the bald eagles known to exist then in the remaining United States.

Admiralty Island's only permanent community, Angoon, lies on the western border of the island on the inside passage. Its people are mostly Tlingit Indians, descendants of the tribes that controlled the straits for centuries. The Tlingit call Admiralty Island "Kootznoowoo," or "Fortress of the Bears," for good reason.

The island is home to more than just brown bears, eagles, and five-hundred Tlingit. Black-tail deer thrive in the rich sedge meadows and in the old-growth forests. Mink, marten, and otter are common along the islands' shores, together with countless varieties of birds.

Earlier that morning in mid-August, Laura and I made our way to the small plane passenger pickup gate at the far end of the Juneau terminal. We met Dutch there, the owner of the plane. He arrived right on time in field clothes, with a fifty-caliber revolver strapped to his hip. He looked in his early fifties, with graying hair and a pleasant face.

After a cordial greeting, we stepped outside onto the airport tarmac. There we hopped into Dutch's van and he drove us a mile and a half to the lagoon where his Cessna floatplane rested in the water tied to a dock. Other small planes flanked each side of the watery airstrip, and now and then one would taxi down the channel to take off. In between, prop planes landed at the far end and taxied on their pontoons to the docks.

Dutch stowed our day packs, and we climbed into his plane. Soon, we lifted off the water and headed south toward Admiralty Island. The small plane flew over expanses of glittering water, snowcapped mountain ranges, lofty peaks shrouded in fog, and green valleys with winding streams.

The remoteness of our destination made it unreachable except by floatplane or a sizeable boat. The island also seemed endless— nearly a hundred miles long and twenty wide—the seventh largest island in the United States. No roads penetrated through the vast interior, though lakes provided places for landing a small plane.

Thirty minutes after taking off, Dutch descended toward the water on the island's east coast, twenty miles from Angoon on the opposite coast. He landed in the five-mile-wide Seymour Canal and taxied until the plane floated a stone's throw from the shoreline at the edge of a tidal flat. He shut down the engine, stepped onto the pontoon and hopped into the water in his rubber boots.

Morning mist lingered in pockets along the shore. After retrieving a rope from the cargo area, Dutch waded with it to shore in the foot-deep water. He secured the line to a stump, then returned and helped us collect our gear. My daypack and field vest carried my usual field gear, but also an assortment of cameras, lenses and two pairs of binoculars. Both Laura and I wore knee-high rubber boots and followed Dutch to the gravel beach.

While Dutch double-checked that the plane remained secure to the stump, I glanced about the area. A dense forest lay beyond the shoreline and steep slopes rose two-thousand feet in front of us, forming a surrounding arc. Dutch led us inland through the forest. We passed giant hemlocks, spruces and firs festooned with yellow-green moss and gray beard lichen. Some trees had aged hundreds of years, with branches that swept to the ground.

Moss draped over logs, stumps, and rocks, leaving the ground humpy with a soft green carpet. We walked through a temperate rainforest where copious precipitation and year-round mists soaked the land. Over two hundred inches of rain fell each year. Most of it came in winter, but trees extracted summer moisture from foggy days and produced the blanket of dripping moss that kept the forest moist.

Such temperate rainforests are rare ecoregions on planet Earth. Most of them occupy narrow coastal strips of land between an ocean and a nearby mountain range. Warm ocean currents need to lie close in order to moderate the climate, and the nearby mountains block the rain so it washes into the lower coastal forests by streams. A tiny fraction of the world's land was ever temperate rainforest, and Admiralty Island forms part of the largest area of these forests on the planet.

We walked a mile on a rough trail, then Dutch swung right and we followed him beyond the forest through waist-high grasses. The way led downslope and into a large open meadow. Near its center a great log sat bleaching in the sun, the remains of a forest giant now toppled. Dutch stopped there and set his daypack down. We had arrived at our destination.

Fifty yards in front of us, a small stream with banks only a few inches high flowed through the meadow. Known as Pack Creek, it rushed from the forest several hundred yards off to our left and swept across our view toward where the distant tidal flats lay on our right. The flow in the twenty-foot-wide stream began six miles away, high among the peaks of an unnamed mountain. Migrating pink and chum salmon used the stream to make their seasonal runs upstream to spawn in Pack Creek's headwaters. We had reached the *Coastal Western Hemlock-Sitka Spruce Forests Ecoregion (120)*, and breathed in some of the purest air of our lives.

We stood by the waist-high log, exposed to the sun as it burned away the last of the mist. In the meadow, lime-green sedges, olive-colored rushes, and other herbaceous growth thrived in the open lowlands. The darker tones of conifers composed the dense forest behind us and across the creek for a few hundred yards to another tree line.

In the island's pristine interior landscape, streams wound through the cathedral-like forests in valley bottoms, and Pack Creek was one of countless examples. We rested at the great log, sitting on its smooth, bark-free surface. Dutch and I chatted about the terrain and the salmon for a few minutes. It was not long, though, before a bald eagle (*Haliaeetus leucocephalus*) appeared and flew up the stream channel before landing on a spruce branch at the forest border just behind us. Its pure white head left no doubt it was an adult, and it watched the stream from its high perch.

Soon it launched from the branch with its six-foot wingspan and swooped low toward the channel. It landed with a splash at the water's edge. My binoculars had followed the flight, and I could clearly see it had caught a fish in its talons. The eagle hopped onto the gravel bar where it began tearing at the flesh. The salmon flopped its tail, but the bird's sharp claws held it fast. Red streaks oozed from its wounds as the eagle stripped off meat with its beak before swallowing it.

The bird soon finished its meal and flew over the treetops and out of sight. While Laura and I spoke in low tones, I scanned the meadow and the forest edge every few minutes with binoculars. Two of my cameras sat on tripods next to me, one with a powerful telephoto lens attached.

I glanced over my shoulder and noticed something move at the tree line. It had a dark, almost black form— an animal of some sort. I nudged Laura and cocked my head toward it. The creature crept out of the forest into the meadow, seemingly on high alert—ears erect and forward. A young coastal brown bear tentatively made its way downslope through the meadow grasses. The same species as the grizzly of interior Alaska and the Rocky Mountain region.

But Admiralty Island's bears are much larger than those varieties. Males average 1,400 pounds compared with 700 for inland grizzlies. Coastal grizzlies are larger because of the greater abundance of salmon, their main food. And I was certain this bear wanted some.

The bear filled my camera's viewfinder as it waded half hidden in the growth. *Click-Whirr* went the motor drive. Every few yards, the young bear's head popped above the sedges and sniffed the air. It focused on the tree line on the far side of the stream in front of it. Satisfied, it worked its way toward the water. When it reached a hundred feet away, where the grass and sedges became shorter, it sprinted to the stream edge.

This adolescent looked three to four years old and wore a dark chocolate coat. Its small size and hesitant behavior suggested it had left its mother earlier that spring but was still too young to breed. Subadult males avoid adults of either sex because of the latter's high aggressiveness.

Grizzlies are solitary animals, except for mothers and their cubs. Confrontations between bears in the wild often get nasty. One of them is usually more aggressive and chases the other off...unless a male wants to eat a cub, which sometimes happens. Occasionally, where salmon run thick and fishing is easy, foraging bears will tolerate each other as they gorge on fresh fish.

But avoidance was surely the reason the young bear took its time to make certain no adults were about. Before entering the meadow, it likely had watched us for a while from the brush, and decided we provided no threat compared to potential grownups of its own kind. At the creek, the youngster leaped off the foot-high bank into the water; *Click-Whirr* went my camera again. It splashed about a few moments and came up with a salmon in its mouth. Like the eagle, it carried it onto the open space of a gravel bar and began eating its catch.

The bear quickly consumed what it wanted and abandoned the remains to run toward the stream for more. It was agile enough to bring back two more fish and eat them before it sensed it had overstayed its luncheon welcome. The juvenile suddenly scampered back to where it had emerged from the forest behind me and disappeared.

A moment later, across the stream another bear appeared at the wood line. Much larger, this bear had the cinnamon-colored fur and size of a fully grown, healthy female. When she began moving, I estimated her height to the shoulder at three feet. That made her nearly 600 pounds...nothing anyone would want to tussle with.

She had the look of a predator that might have torn one or all of us to pieces if she had a mind to—assuming Dutch didn't stop her with his revolver first. A fifty-caliber bullet in her cardiac cage could make her pause and review her options about attacking. That kind of ammunition could halt the charge of a galloping grizzly before it gets a few paces from your nose.

Fortunately, the bear lumbered toward the stream through the far meadow and stopped at its edge. She surveyed the flowing water as though it served as her own private salmon banquet. The bear paused once it reached center-channel, then moved its head back and forth and up and down, as though trying to decide which of all those juicy salmon she wanted to make into filets. She then galloped through the shallow water, chasing fish.

The salmon tried to avoid the slashing claws by leaping away and dashing ahead. I could only see the backfins of the fish as they dodged claws in the shallow water, but the stream was full of them. Random splashes by fish and bear occurred all over the channel. The bear darted up the channel, then turned and ran back downstream, kicking up gallons of spray. Its full attention focused on slippery salmon.

She jammed both paws under the water, came up empty, then leaped ahead several times. I imagined her frustration…mind-muttering to herself how she wanted that salmon—no, the one between her legs was better; wait, it got away; go after this one—where did it go? Over there, forget that one— there's more over here.

She bounded up the channel again, accompanied by a cluster of screaming gulls flapping wildly above her, rooting her on so they could get the leftovers. A male raven sat on the bank calling encouragement with a repetitive wonk-wonk. The feathered bunch all knew that if the bear got lucky, they did too. Their bird brains signaled to let the big hairy creature do all the slippery lifting and bring the scraps to the gravel bar banquet table for these crafty scavengers.

Finally, the bear stopped again, breathing hard. All her effort had gained her no fish. She stood still for a moment, water draining off her shaggy coat. Her neck stretched forward, and she shook her head, throwing arcs of water droplets across the stream. Most of the gulls settled on the gravel bar, chattering with disappointment. The raven walked up and downstream along the bank, shouting as it went—*croooaaak, cur- ruk*. He reminded me of my old varsity soccer coach shouting encouragement from the sidelines.

The bear ignored the crowd of onlookers and ambled a dozen yards further in the knee-high water, her stubby tail still dripping. A moment later she resumed her fishing strategy of loping all over the channel, unable to focus on a specific fish. More dashing, more spray, more bad luck.

The gulls cheered her all the way, dodging each other from above while letting their rivals know who should get the choicest leftovers. The raven strutted, clearly perturbed, watching the commotion—*wonk-wonk, cur-ruk.* Sounded like cursing to me.

The bear kept at it, and ten minutes later she drove her head and shoulders under the surface. A moment later, she produced a fat salmon in her jaws. She bit down, and with the crunch that followed, the fish ceased thrashing. The crowd of onlookers screamed at fever pitch. I half-expected the raven to shout "Sc- OOOOO-rrr!" like some European play-by-play announcer at a soccer finals event.

With both her forepaws planted on the carcass, the bear used her sharp teeth to pull the skin off, then ate it. Next, she tore out large chunks of flesh, chewed a few times, then swallowed and bent down for another bite. A few gulps later, she was back to fishing again.

She caught the next one in less time and seemed to have a feel for how the salmon reacted to her efforts. When the bear sampled her third fish, she spit out the meat. This one may have contained a less tasty oily flavor than the others. Or, she might have snagged a less tasty chum salmon that usually migrate later in early fall.

The bear left the remains on the gravel bank and bounded back to the stream for another. After eating four fish, the female had enough of chasing salmon. She walked out of the stream and laid down in the cool grass to rest.

I had an inkling all that effort had made her tired, and she needed some time to belch up some of that fish oil in her belly. Ten minutes later, she rose and wandered far downstream toward the tidal flats. I lost her when she moved out of sight.

Salmon are not the only food that sustains Pack Creek's bears. Lyngbye's sedge is one of the earliest plants to green-up in the spring and provides one of the first opportunities for bears to replenish energy reserves after hibernation and before salmon migrate. They graze heavily upon it along Pack Creek, as well as skunk cabbage and silverweed roots in the nearby woods.

During summer, various woodland berries such as salmonberry, blueberry, elderberry, currants, and devil's club berries provide a significant portion of the bears' diet. In the fall, bears return to the rich herbaceous meadows where they chase salmon. By then the sedges have gone to seed and the bears spend their time digging and feeding on the roots of rice root, lupine, angelica, and cow parsnip. Hunting food is a full-time occupation for bears.

We ate our own lunches on the log and felt the comforting warmth of sunshine on our cheeks. The wild ambience and the natural rhythm of the present moment soaked into my thoughts. I contemplated our good fortune of watching bears hunting in their natural habitat far from any other humans—a place that most people did not even know existed. Yet, I knew that in another season when salmon did not fill Pack Creek, the bears would not be so tolerant of our presence; likely get snippy and want a taste of our livers.

But during our day on Admiralty Island, pink salmon were running, and little else mattered to the grizzlies. The number of salmon in the stream varied, particularly by weather. Rain helps wash the chemical "scent" of the upper watershed downstream, making it easier for returning adult salmon to navigate back to the stream reaches where they hatched.

Storms and flooding inhibit salmon numbers in the small streams. We could not predict such things in advance, nor how hungry the bears of Pack Creek might feel on any particular day. But on this day, the bears so far were leaving us alone, desperately seeking salmon.

While Laura and I watched, a channel full of salmon pushed themselves upstream to breed in the waters of their birth. The upper reaches near the headwaters contained considerable quantities of large woody debris, such as logs, fallen trees, branches, and roots. They also have gravel bottoms, and there the females scrape out shallow depressions three by six feet, called redds. They do this by sweeping the gravel with their tails, letting the small stones wash downstream.

A female pink salmon carries up to 2,000 eggs and deposits some in the "redd." They stay there because the current flows above the lower redd bottom. Males take turns hovering over the eggs, depositing sperm. The female then brushes gravel over the nest before making another redd nearby. She may deposit eggs in several more before her egg supply is exhausted.

Spawning streams are typically dense with salmon, and redds can cover the entire channel bottom at breeding sites near the headwaters far upstream. But in less than a week, all the adults will die. Their health rapidly deteriorates over several days as their reason for living becomes fulfilled. The vitality is no longer needed that sustained them to overcome great obstacles to reach their place of destiny. To live any longer would consume precious resources that their young require. So, they die. All of them. Even the ones that did not get the chance to breed. They will decompose, releasing nutrients back to the stream ecosystem to help grow the emerging new generation.

As I sat on the log in the meadow chewing a sandwich for lunch, I noticed a dark spot in the tree line far off to my left, where the stream emerged from the forest. It did not move and looked like a stump. I had not noticed it before, so my eyes squinted to bring it into sharper relief.

But then it moved, and I knew it was another bear. It walked with a saunter that announced this animal was used to taking complete charge of its affairs. I put down my sandwich and raised the binoculars.

The hump on its back looked massive and its shoulders shuddered as powerful muscles propelled the animal in seeming slow motion out of the forest toward us. A very large male, certainly well over 1,000 pounds—half a ton. He held his head level, signifying authority, and ambled along the stream.

The bear entered the water directly across from us by stepping leisurely into it like the boss-bear he was. He paused, looked down for a few seconds, then swiped with a front paw. A fat salmon leaped to the surface and flew onto the gravel bar, flopping and bleeding.

The bear walked over and planted one forepaw on the fish's tail. Lowering his head, he opened his jaws, clamped onto the fish and snapped upward, holding a large wad of skin and flesh. He chewed, swallowed, and then rapidly finished the appetizer. He waded back into the stream to find more fish.

Squawking gulls descended on the carcass, diving, squabbling, pushing each other aside for the remains. The patient raven watched the melee, then stalked over and shouldered its way through the gulls with its guttural croaking—*wonk-wonk*. All the gulls backed off, and the raven pecked at the carcass as though he had ordered the bear to serve it up just for him.

The bear fished and ate salmon for a half hour before wandering off. No doubt later he deposited a hefty pile of scat somewhere deep in the forest, which flies, fungi, and microbes would immediately swarm over. The remains would decompose into a rich source of nitrogen and other nutrients to be carried by rainwater into the surrounding terrain. They would seep into the soil and nurture plants such as a berry bush, or even a spruce seedling near a stream.

Someday perhaps, the spruce tree would mature, die, and topple into the stream. There its twigs, leaves and bark would rot, providing food for a wide variety of organisms like stoneflies and mayflies that lived under the cobbles in the cold-water riffles. Recently spawned fish would eat these benthic macroinvertebrates and grow into larger fish. The waste they produced would flow downstream to the Pack Creek tidal flats. There they would support the estuary ecosystem and marine life in the Pacific Ocean.

Thus, decaying salmon bodies nourish many land and sea animals during the fishes' migrations, after they die following spawning, or once ingested by bears and eagles. Those nutrients become distributed throughout Admiralty Island's larger terrestrial ecosystem in wildlife scat, and after those animals in turn decompose upon death. Some of those dead salmon nutrients find their way downstream to the tidal flats where clams and Dungeness crabs ingest them. Other tissue parts wash into the Seymour Canal and eventually into the sea. And so, the salmon die and what was fish becomes sustenance for something else, for a while.

But without woody debris, the salmon populations of Pack Creek and other salmon streams would perish. Decaying leaves and dead wood supply food for more than aquatic insects. Periphyton attach to their submerged surfaces in the streams and consists of algae, but sometimes a mixture of algae with cyanobacteria, microbes, and detritus. Periphyton serves as an important food source for the aquatic invertebrates and zooplankton. Many species of young salmon also eat the zooplankton.

When salmon hatch, they remain hidden in the gravel and live off their nutrient-rich yolk sac until they can eat insects.

They find protective cover among the woody debris and gather strength for their journey downstream to coastal waters.

Pink and chum salmon hatch in mid-winter and swim up out of the gravel in early spring to migrate downstream to the sea. Pink salmon will remain there maturing for two years then migrate back up streams like Pack Creek in early July to mid-October. Nature's system has worked well for countless millennia. Birth, growth, migration, spawning, and decomposition play critical roles in supporting new salmon offspring, allowing the salmon-bear cycle to continue.

Admiralty Island—Kootznoowoo—is a place where bears are supported by fish and spread the nitrogen rich bodies of salmon throughout the forest as they wander about. The annual salmon run both depends upon and contributes to the Earth's natural geochemical cycling of nutrient materials, including oxygen, carbon, nitrogen, phosphorous, and sulfur derived from rotting fish. Through underlying complex processes, nutrients are used and recycled through these integrated and linked systems.

The salmon-bear and geochemical cycles combined are all about the transformation of energy from one form to another and back again. Along the way, living things tap into the energy and material cycles to survive and perpetuate their kind.

The availability of nutrients and energy for sustaining life changes constantly, and every species must adapt and utilize those resources for their own benefit. Salmon do it, bears do it, gulls, ravens, and every plant species at Pack Creek does it. Even humans do it, for we too are part of earth's great web of cycles. In nature, there are checks and balances that usually keep one species from exhausting resources that would ultimately be catastrophic for its populations. That can happen when links in the cycles get damaged or broken. When that happens, the ecosystems that depend upon them suffer. But the day we visited Pack Creek, nature operated at full capacity. All the links remained intact while we glimpsed the great cycles in action.

Mature salmon would gather at the mouths of streams such as Pack Creek the following summer. Their bodies would undergo physiological changes in the estuaries before they make the run upstream. While there, their bodies become transformed to tolerate freshwater again. The changes would be irreversible, as they faced an entirely new life ahead.

As with leaves that change color in the fall and bears that emerge from hibernation, nature signals the salmon it is time for their molecules to begin a new journey; time to recycle. The salmon would begin returning to Pack Creek because habitat conditions there remain suitable.

It doesn't stop there, however. As the salmon struggle up the channel toward the gravel beds of their birth, the brown bears of Kootznoowoo take some of them for food, leaving plenty for the birds and others. Then the bears would leave Pack Creek and return to the forest edge. From there, they would disappear, merging with the thick foliage. Not long afterward, they would feel an urge for digestive relief to deposit some of the ingested salmon molecules in their waste. More than an urge, it would be another call of the wild. One that, for the bears and for ecoregions everywhere, should never be taken for granted. Without recycling on a grand scale, life could not endure.

A Piedmont Legacy

Four-hundred years ago on a site nearly fifty miles west of the Chesapeake Bay, any wandering hawk could look below while soaring high in the slipstream on a bright summer morning. It could see an immense grayish-green blanket stretch to the horizon. The broad-leaves of giants a hundred feet high rippled on a rolling plain so dense only occasional sunbeams broke through to spotlight a floor dark with humus.

Although most of the large trees have vanished by now, the vast plain known as the *Northern Piedmont Ecoregion (64), Piedmont Uplands (64c)* still extends from New York City to Alabama. It derives its name from the Italian term *Piemonte*—"foot of the mountain." People by the tens of millions inhabit this land from rural areas to urban centers such as Trenton, Washington, D.C., Richmond, Raleigh, Columbia, and Montgomery.

In Maryland and Virginia, the Piedmont begins upstream of the bay's tidal creeks—where flatlands of the Coastal Plain shift to an undulating landscape.

There dark, sandy loam soils of slow meandering tidal creeks and rivers, give way to faster, less sinuous streams with riffles and pools underlain by clayey soils in oranges and browns. These brighter grains of soil are all that remain of mountains that once towered here—and the seas that covered their eroded bases long ago. Today's placid land-swells give no hint of the cirques, cols and boulder outcrops from the past. Pick a stone from any Piedmont flower garden. It likely once perched thousands of feet higher on some ancient, ragged precipice.

For years, Laura and I tended one of these flower gardens. It sat on a nearly three-acre remnant of a hundred-acre farm in the northern Maryland Piedmont where we made our home for nearly forty years. From our porch, the sweeping view always included a pond buffered by trees and shrubs. And beyond that, fields and forest that bounded for more than a mile. It was a comfortable scene, and one we never tired of watching.

Were we to soar with the hawks today, our property would appear as a humble polygon, one of millions on a living patchwork quilt. The rural countryside blossomed with blocks of tawny grain, cornfield strips, rustling woodlots, and hedgerows framing scattered houses. But four hundred years ago, only winged creatures had the privilege of such an aerial view. Then, rather than a kaleidoscope of shapes and colors, it was the unbroken blanket of grayish-green forest that rose and fell in waves to the far horizon.

In even earlier times—far more than a billion years ago— no landscape existed here. Just an ancient restless sea of water shifted over a lifeless earth. Eventually, plates that formed the earth's crust collided deep below the waters, crumpled their leading edges, then thrust jagged peaks skyward. In time, cliffs and crags broke through the watery realm and poked the clouds.

Thus, the Grenville Range was born, as massive and sharp as any that exists in the present world. But those raw slopes and all the grit that composed them completely washed away into a new sea within the blink of a geological eye—a mere 150 million years.

The sea endured for another hundred million years before a further period of mountain building, wearing down and disappearance beneath yet another ocean occurred. Then 400 million years ago, the Appalachians twisted and folded the sea bottom into rock spires surpassing the Himalayas of today. At lower elevations, dinosaurs tramped through the swampy ground, munching marsh plants and each other. Over time, wind and rain eroded the most resistant rocks of the Appalachians to their present modest profile. Weather sluiced away all the less durable mountains to the east, leaving the Piedmont with its knolls, hillocks, and wide valleys.

About twelve thousand years ago, glaciers further north began retreating, and humans moved onto the Piedmont. The climate, still on the cold side, grew spruces, firs and hemlocks that swayed in the frosty air. Before we lived on our little plot, Pleistocene flora and fauna sought their living in a boreal forest amid pockets of open tundra. Saber-toothed cats, giant ground sloths, mastodons, and woolly mammoths roamed about with those early humans. By 6,000 years ago, the climate had moderated and conifers with needles relinquished the land to their flat-leaved cousins of today.

From our porch I often marveled about these titanic changes that over the eons have occurred just under our feet, reshaping the land repeatedly between mountains, seas, flatlands and rolling hills. At various times, the surface where our house sat had shifted thousands of feet higher or lower—sometimes in the clouds and other times under miles of ocean, compared to its present elevation.

Such thoughts provided a sobering perspective on our significance regarding the earth and its great rhythms. But for now, tectonic activity has quieted, and no one knows what will occupy the space under our rocking chairs thousands of years from now.

After the glaciers retreated, broad-leaved deciduous trees gradually dominated the Piedmont landscape. They formed the unbroken climax forest that the wandering hawks soared over. The canopy of leafy parasols intercepted and tamed the erosive power of billions of raindrops. This was a time when trees with deeply furrowed trunks and sixty-inch girths held the planet in place with enormous roots.

Anxious warbler masses descended each spring—battle-songs honed and warrior-plumage flashing—in a desperate seasonal landgrab for miniature homesteads. Pileated woodpeckers hammered away here on snags and the echoes announced their constant search for succulent grubs. Great-Horned Owls watched silently from heavy limbs for a breakfast entrée on the forest floor. It often appeared in the form of a white-footed mouse that shuffled into view.

Larger mammals—raccoon, fox, deer, wolf, and mountain lion— considered this swatch of the Piedmont home at one time or another. This was a land where the chestnut tree reigned supreme in a gallery forest, along with maples and hickories. Black cherry, sassafras and flowering dogwood shared the sub- canopy with the likes of serviceberries. But the low light and enormous trees kept the understory sparse, and as spacious and quiet as a cathedral.

Gray squirrels chattered in our treetops then, as they do now—the most ubiquitous creatures of those old- growth Piedmont forests. It remains unclear whether squirrels expanded oak and hickory forests, or the trees caused the increase in the squirrel population. Consider that acorn and hickory seeds are too heavy to become effectively dispersed by wind. Thus, it was the industrious activity of squirrels in burying and forgetting to retrieve nuts and acorns that was a primary factor in the expansion of oak-hickory forests throughout the Piedmont.

Because of their occasional faulty memories, squirrels inadvertently helped spread the forests—and used them as superhighways. The thick network of branches afforded these furry aerialists a means of traveling miles across the Piedmont without ever touching the ground.

Hunter-gatherers roamed throughout the northern Piedmont since the Pleistocene. But 500 years ago, few of them wandered large portions of the region in our area, because tribal warfare had left a vacant land.

Warring Iroquois descended from lands in the north, later called Pennsylvania, and drove the resident Algonquians southward out of the area. After the invaders returned home, hundreds of square miles remained a "no-man's-land" until settlers arrived. The land in this northern portion of the Piedmont remained largely unoccupied, except for temporary hunting camps. Consequently, most contacts with settlers at the time occurred along established trails that served as travel and trading routes for tribes such as the Iroquois, Conoy Piscataway, as well as the Susquehannocks, Shawnee, Tuscaroras, and Delawares.

Along one of those well-worn Native American trails near our present home, a small creek drained a tiny valley. Any Susquehannock scout could easily leap across it without breaking stride. If the scout followed the creek upstream, he would have found a spring of freshwater seeping from the earth, the origin of the stream's sweet flowing waters. Most likely, after a refreshing drink, he would have left that cool shady spot and continued his journey without another thought of the spring or the tiny stream it fed.

Many years later, European settlers started arriving in the northern Piedmont frontier. Those from England arrived first, then Germans moved into the region later. By the late 1600s, small pioneering outposts pushed eighty miles west from Philadelphia. Others worked their way north out of Baltimore, but even by 1720 settlers found the land mostly unoccupied and did not need to fight indigenous people for the land.

Indian scouts continued to roam the extensive uninhabited tract that included where the small creek flowed and its spring bubbled out of the ground. But now the land formed part of the new colony of Maryland, and King Charles I of England claimed ownership of all the land. To generate rental income from prospective settlers, he allowed land grants in the early 1600s.

Initially, the king's agent, Lord Calvert, declared over two thousand land grants in that northern Piedmont region. Each request required a name for the parcel, and ledgers dutifully recorded them as given by the applicants. Many seemed straightforward—*George's Lot* or *Susen's Fancy*. Others expressed optimism, such as *Neighborly Kindness, Fellowship, Eve's Garden, and Canaan*. Some settler candidates, though, must have had a foreboding when they entered names like *Valley of Strife, Discontentment, Scheaming Defeated* and *Keep Your Wife At Home*. Then there were many whose meaning must have been a mystery to all but the grantee—*Cold Saturday, Can't You Be Easy and Let Me Alone, Bellyache Ticket, Tumbling Down The Hill* and the very curious—*Bite Hime Softly*.

The earliest land grant along the Indian trail where the fresh spring fed the tiny valley's creek occurred in the mid-1700s. With high hopes of making the 1,755- acre tract a productive homestead, the settler who acquired the grant gave it the name *Bountiful Chance* [nom de plume].

The settler and his family cut and cleared the forest by hand where they wanted to grow crops and graze livestock. They burned the brush and stumps after digging them out with picks and shovels—acres of them. Locust trees provided posts for fences and corrals.

At various times over the centuries, the large parcel was sold in pieces, and tenant farmers rented the property's log house, or it stood empty for years until 1835. When the Bountiful Chance property went up for sale again, it retained the name but only encompassed a hundred acres. A hopeful couple noticed the land's potential for homesteading and purchased it.

They, like any worthy settlers, knew what to look for when it came to living off the land. A reliable water source was always identified first, preferably a freshwater spring associated with a small stream in a protective valley. A homesteader would then assess the land's suitability for farming by examining the tilth of the soil, its moisture content, and stoniness. The new prospective farmers then studied the topography to determine if they could build a house and barn with natural protection against the wind and weather.

The new owners of Bountiful Chance found all the necessary features they needed tucked within a protected little valley—potable water, rich soil, hillocks against the wind. They owned and farmed the site for a decade before it went to auction twice more. The first mention of a substantial house on the hundred-acre parcel occurred in the advertisement for the sale in 1871. It noted that the "valuable little farm" was improved with "...a 2 story log dwelling, also an excellent log Switzer Barn, a Hog House, Wagon Shed, Carriage House, Blacksmith Shop and Dairy. Most of the improvements are of recent construction and in good repair. There is also an Orchard of 150 Apple Trees and a variety of other fruits of the choicest kinds."

Bidders also learned about the reliable spring, and how the parcel contained workable fields with ten acres in timber. The farm had changed little over the past ten years—except for the new barn and some minor improvements to the house.

Among its attractive features the advertisement for the sale touted "A good dairy over a never failing spring."

A successful farmer acquired it and built a new house in 1886. It included a full-length roofed porch one story above the ground. It made sense to put the kitchen in the cellar, only steps from the springhouse. A fireplace stood in the basement for preparing meals, smoking meats and heating the upstairs living areas. The house stood as a typical working farmhouse of the period—modest and functional.

Over the next decades, the farm sold multiple times, with various pieces carved off until the previous portion with the house and barn became whittled down to its most recent size of just under three acres. Most of the rest bordered the previous parcel and continued to grow crops and graze dairy cows within thirty feet of the house. A long, tree-lined lane led from the main road and through the fields to the house, a quarter-mile away.

When Laura and I took ownership of the small plot in 1975, we delighted in the pastoral scene of fields, hedgerows, and woods in front of us from the raised porch. It overlooked a two-acre pond, marsh, and the "never-failing spring" that lay within a few hundred feet of our house. The flowing spring always matched its reputation, never once ceasing even during the severest droughts.

The spring fed the pond, and its outlet formed the headwaters of the little creek. It flowed toward the distant main road through a wet meadow between valley slopes only a thousand feet wide.

Though our porch looked over the pond and creek, we could barely see the distant main road. Traffic there remained a faint mumble on the unusual occasions we heard it at all, as when hot, humid days made the air less dense. We added to the house's modern conveniences, yet kept the original structural and architectural features. The lower part of the barn and the wagon shed remained.

A Piedmont Legacy

Beginning with our first summer there, we began adding trees, shrubs, and gardens, but kept the view from the porch. We nurtured flowers because we knew they offer grace to the perceptive and a reminder of renewal to the anguished. We raised Trey and Jordon, plus a host of barnyard and other animal companions on the property with us. Although Laura and I worked elsewhere, our family often pursued activities in keeping with the previous homesteaders, such as raising and storing food from our gardens. We came to feel a kinship with others who once dwelled there and scrabbled a living. A county historian once came by and inspected the little farm remnant, then added it to the state's list of sites with local historic interest.

While sitting on the elevated porch, we liked to watch the birds and wildlife that wandered past and those that came to the pond. We shared the land with deer, fox woodchucks, opossums, raccoons, skunks and many other mammals. Wild geese, herons, egrets, and waterfowl visited the pond and sometimes nested. And every spring our lower field still beckoned meadowlarks to send their sweet melodies drifting over the land. A pair of wild geese came every spring to nest near the pond and lead their young through the lush grasses in the meadow.

We grew more than enough vegetables to feed those that shared our home and stored many in a root cellar, including a year's supply of potatoes that always lasted until the following spring. The apple trees from former times had long disappeared, so we planted a small orchard with apples, peaches, plums, and cherries, and harvested buckets of grapes, blueberries, and wine berries from planted borders.

I constructed a water garden full of colorful Koi and goldfish. Though not native species, they were descendants of wild carp, but full of color and beauty. Pathways wove through the property and connected quiet resting-places with rustic benches. Buttercups filled the open areas in springtime, their little yellow flowers a bright mass of natural exuberance. Patches of grape hyacinths sprouted in the meadow, and their round blue flowers hung like tiny pearls.

The converted wagon shed offered shelter for our many pets— sheep, goats, ducks, and geese. We fenced in a pasture for them and composted their manure for our gardens the way nature and past settlers did. We would collect our grass clippings and use them for mulching to prevent weeds and avoid using toxic sprays.

Our free-ranging chickens always supplied a steady supply of fresh eggs. Now and then we coaxed a reluctant hen to see the merits of going broody and raising a family of chicks. And we came to realize that these deceptively simple birds have much more to offer people than drumsticks and omelets.

We had a neighbor a mile away, a dairy farmer, who leased the land around us for many years to grow crops. He cared for the land by using traditional methods—spreading manure from his dairy cows as fertilizer, rotating crops, planting cover crops of grain to prevent erosion after harvesting his main crops of corn, soybeans, wheat. We bought our hay from him for our own livestock. He never farmed the meadow between our house and the pond, leaving it as a natural buffer to absorb erosive runoff from storms. This kept the pond free of sediment and algae that would drain off the sloping fields.

One summer day in 2000, I learned that the owner of the adjacent thirty-acres of farm fields sold the land. A subdivision developer purchased it, who planned scores of new homes packed tightly upon the landscape. The new buildings would encroach within a few feet of our house—and would completely block the view we enjoyed for nearly three decades from our adjacent porch. By then we were middle-aged and alone on the shrunken farm since our children had long ago moved away.

Land developers undertake projects in order to reap financial profits, and we understood this, as well as the local county's desire to reap more property tax revenues. But it's all about how many building lots can get squeezed out of the landscape. Each one is a discreet profit and tax generator, so more lots mean greater revenues. The power players soon began speeding up the approval process without our knowledge.

We did not hold illusions that ordinary residents like us could prevent the coming suburban invasion. It seemed the best we could do was approach the developer with ideas for protecting as much of the landscape as possible. We offered ideas for keeping as many surrounding natural values as possible within his subdivision design plans.

These included changing the initial design configuration to fewer but larger lots, which could generate the same profits and tax revenues because larger lots would sell for more, increasing their property tax value. We also urged the preservation of the two- acre pond, and avoiding destruction of the marsh. We suggested the developer consider adding blocks of native trees and brushy edges for small wildlife travel corridors between cul de sacs.

To discuss these matters further, we invited the developer onto our front porch one morning. The development company owner stood at the railing with a smirk as he pointed his finger straight out toward the pond and described his pet vision.

"The street will come off the main road through the wetlands. Then it will cut across your lane and curve right so it runs parallel to this porch a few dozen feet from this railing. The houses will have their backdoors about forty feet from here."

This wasn't news to us. A few weeks earlier, I had gone to the local municipality and seen the draft plan that accompanied the building permit application. It showed the main subdivision road lined with basic starter-homes running between our porch and the large pond.

As the developer looked over the porch railing, lost in his dreamscape, I said, "Your design is unworkable; there isn't enough room between us and the pond for the road and houses with front and back yards. I compared ground measurements to your design plan."

The man's head swiveled toward me with a quizzical look on his face.

I added, "You would have to drain or encroach at least thirty feet into the pond to accommodate all that. Why can't you eliminate these three lots here and regain them up on the hill where the lots are twice as large? That way, you have the same number of lots and can retain the pond and buffer with an intact natural corridor. And we could retain this open area between us and the pond."

He shrugged. "I need to stick with the plan we have—fewer complications."

"Then your road width wouldn't meet the State's requirements, and it will eliminate our quarter-mile lane. Do you expect us to pay for connecting to the new street you construct so we can access our property from the main road?"

He looked to the right. "You could realign your driveway over there."

I glanced that way and said, "That would mean our water garden, all the shrubs and mature trees there would need to come out." "Afraid so."

"Who gave you permission to take out our lane and require us to relocate this part of our driveway? We certainly never gave it to anyone."

"Don't need any. You only have a simple easement for your lane, so by law we only must give you a reasonable means to access the main highway, not the route of your choice. The new public street fits that requirement."

"That might be true if our lane was only a simple right-of-way, but you haven't done your homework; our deed says otherwise. Legally, you need our permission to make any modification to it."

His eyes shifted from the shrubbery on the property boundary back to me. I noticed his jaw had clenched. "Our information says you don't have a metes and bounds survey but only an access easement."

"Your sources are incorrect—it's metes and bounds; surveyed, plotted, and written into our deed. You need our permission."

The man's gaze faltered, and he turned toward the pond again. Then his voice perked up the way someone tries to distract from a blunder. "It sure is peaceful here now, but in six months there will be a whole new neighborhood. Kids bickering in the back yards right there, car doors slamming, lots of lawn mowers, people arguing during the night. You might consider moving soon, before construction even starts."

After he left, Laura said, "It seems obvious he's not interested in our ideas for making adjustments to their plans."

"No question about that, and it sounded like his doom and gloom estimate within six months was meant to scare us, so we'll move away without interfering."

And later we learned that the complications the developer hoped to avoid had gained verbal acceptance from the local municipality because of an ordinance loophole from 1979. Also, back then, no substantive environmental regulations existed for subdivision projects. No need to avoid or mitigate wetland or marsh impacts, keep patches of trees, manage stormflows against erosion, or conduct environmental investigations for rare and endangered species like bog turtles that were rumored to inhabit the marsh.

We retained an attorney and challenged the development based on its design flaws and disregard of environmental and historical issues. We repeatedly met with the developer and municipality to negotiate protections for the landscape and our access lane.

Our efforts forestalled the project but did not halt or restrain it. The developer proceeded with plans to design imitation-colonial homes around us. It looked like Bountiful Chance would soon become Suburban Destiny.

After over 200 years, a rural lifestyle on the farm remnant was finally coming to an end. When we sat in our rockers on the porch, we often thought about the crop fields and meadows that for centuries had so reliably converted rain and sunlight into food for people and wildlife. We continued to enjoy the familiar scene in front of us, but now we also waited for the changes we could not prevent. We envisioned the fields and woodlots sprouting asphalt, aluminum siding, and plastic. And we waited for the traffic and houses that would block our pastoral view.

Tucked as we were in a natural corner of the landscape, few neighbors lived nearby. No citizenry marched on the nearby town hall to keep the area's rural character. The site's long lineage of homesteading and farming seemed not to matter as the planning and approval process moved forward.

Capitalism and profit motives helped make America great, but it also destroyed many cultural, historic, and ecological landscapes. Historically, as population growth increased in the Piedmont, so did the demand for new housing, which spurred an onslaught of subdivisions on already occupied land. Sometimes, perhaps often, the money trail of untold numbers of grand development projects over the past half-century often revealed a pattern of collusion between governments, venture capitalists, developers, and shortsighted citizens.

When the subdivision project around us emerged, our municipality seemed eager for the additional tax revenues. Spanking new homes were coming for a demanding population emigrating from Baltimore, which would no doubt "stimulate the economy." Rumors emerged of a different developer taking over and constructing a higher density complex of apartments and townhouses.

A new developer with deeper pockets and a phalanx of legal experts was needed to deal with our pesky driveway issue. Soon the new developer took over the project, one with more political connections and a track record of bullying his way onto natural landscapes and stripping them away for condos and clone-houses. To avoid having to comply with recent reforestation laws, his crews cut all the trees where his houses would go. This included the mature borders along our lane that provided habitat and travel protections for wildlife. By doing this before the subdivision gained approval, the forest laws would not apply.

The larger Piedmont landscape then did not resemble what the early settlers saw, its surface now scraped, flattened, gouged, and covered with cities and towns. The living patchwork quilt had gotten tattered and was replaced with artificial structures, throngs of people and snaking highways.

And now change was again upon the Piedmont—in our backyard this time. But as we sat together and talked on the porch, we realized that the history of this landform had always involved change. Mountain building had occurred through uplift and volcanism, then wearing down of rocky peaks to flat peneplains.

Later, the entire landscape subsided under nameless seas, followed by advance and retreat of flora and fauna. Most of the Piedmont had seen displacement of native peoples by warring tribes and sometimes by settlers. And the little farm had seen many exchanges of ownership and partitioning until the farm became restricted to our little knoll and three tiny acres.

It was a story as old as civilization itself; nothing to see here. Move along now and make way for modern progress because we all supposedly live in enlightened times with smarter people. Traditional values and sentiments change, and nowadays far too many consider protecting rural vistas and viewsheds irrelevant. Their history and benefits are less important than acres of parking lots, wind turbines, electric vehicle charging stations, cell towers, and the glare of ubiquitous sodium lights.

Our landscapes remain at the mercy of its inheritors. As the author Philip Roth once said, "In America everything goes and nothing matters..." But citizens have the power to require good stewardship in managing the land, if they understand why it is important.

And yet, regardless of whether the adjacent subdivision materialized, changes were coming. Even nature had not yet finished shaping the landscape here—or anywhere else in the Piedmont. Although earth tremors and mountain building had ceased to be worrisome for millions of years, the process of breaking down and wearing away landforms had never stopped. Through weathering and erosion, the landform's soil skin was imperceptibly but relentlessly still undergoing a facelift.

We did not doubt the inevitable. We understood that the journey of the Piedmont is one with an inescapable destination—eventual extinction. And more buildings and asphalt would not deter the process. The subdivision would only be a brief side-trip on this geological odyssey.

Grain by grain, the remnants of the region's mountain remnants that now composed the soil nurturing the grasses under our feet, would someday wash to the streams. They would find their way into the Chesapeake Bay thirty miles to the east. In a distant future—eons after our own departure—even the underlying bedrock would decompose, and our rolling Piedmont would again become something else, perhaps flattened into a featureless plain.

And then the next sea may cover it. Just as it had many times before. To be sure, vegetation and careful land stewardship could slow the rate of soil loss. But such efforts could never forestall the planet's natural process for nutrient cycling. For when it comes to natural laws, there are no loopholes—gravity and entropy always win.

My wife and I had sought to maintain a connection with the little Piedmont farm's past by the way we lived on a tiny fragment of it. But its natural features, beauty, and traditional values remained threatened. Previous changes had mostly been slow, taking place over centuries or millennia. In contrast, the impending changes now facing the little farm would come swiftly—requiring only months to complete.

As the future pressed upon us, we imagined how it would unfold. Images of what would come swirled in our minds. We imagined new "starter-home" clones constructed in the little meadow between us and the pond, then on the field slopes of the valley, and finally where the pond once nestled before it became filled in. Our glimpse into the future focused on the first-time homeowners who moved out of distant urban apartments, eager to purchase and begin a new life "in the country."

I had seen these scenarios dozens of times in my career—the death of rural areas in favor of creeping urbanization, where nature takes a back seat to creatures with cell phones that stalk the landscape looking for new nail salons and pizza shops. In our minds, few would likely have the same appreciation as we did for this landscape. They would expect the level of community conveniences and services they were used to; places for teenagers to hang out, stoplights, sirens, fueling stations, soccer fields. The demand for more infrastructure would increase; new strip malls and fast-food drive-throughs would require more roads and paved areas. Traffic congestion and suburban chatter would replace the songs of meadowlarks that once greeted us in the mornings.

When we visualized the future, we saw the "never- failing spring" now paved over, and the creek piped all the way to the main road. The wetland it once flowed through had dried up, infested with aggressive weeds. They too were opportunists with the means of exploiting a fragile landscape. But these vegetative colonizers did so without diesel-belching earth-moving monsters, the whine of circular saws and the pounding of a thousand hammers echoing across the land. Those were far more ominous than the rat-a-tat-tat of a few hungry woodpeckers in the deep woods that thrived here 400 years ago.

For the first twenty-five years we lived on the Bountiful Chance remnant, we had watched a slow march toward replacing natural features with people features. But the effects did not change the rural character of our corner of the Piedmont because they were modest and gradual.

But by the time we got wind of the subdivision plans, development had started to accelerate in our region. The new project would increase impervious pavement, roofing, and mowed lawns all around us. Instead of infiltrating, rainwater would get diverted to sewers and ultimately flow into the Chesapeake Bay. Consequently, very little rain would recharge the groundwater anymore. For centuries, the spring and creek provided its sweet liquid sustenance to support natural communities. In our vision of the future, they would nurture life no longer—the development would bleed the old farm to death.

While we despaired of the coming changes, we understood those who wanted to pursue the American dream of owning a plot in the countryside. We were one of them. And who were we to hold back progress in an era when homesteading and living in harmony with the land was unnecessary, according to urban planners?

Modern anxieties and lack of practical skills seem to terrify many in recent generations from putting out meaningful efforts toward stewardship of rural landscapes. They seem overly concerned about manicuring their lawns, trying to decide how to fit a third car into their garages, poisoning every insect, and deciding where to attach the satellite dish and internet cable.

We wondered if anyone who would then live in the new subdivision would know anything about or have any interest in the little plot's history. Would it matter to them that once, grand mountains challenged the clouds here? Would they dream about the ancient seas that once occupied this land, or the people who had later camped here, and those who tended the fields and struggled to make a living on this insignificant patch of rolling Piedmont? What would remain to inspire them with such thoughts?

During the next two decades following our initial challenge to the subdivision, my family raised enough environmental issues to stall the approval process temporarily. But as those issues resolve, the project looms ever closer and our options dwindle. Our world will not fade away, but others will soon rip it out from under us with their subdivision project.

The landscape as we knew it remains intact for now, and we intend to enjoy it as long as we are able. Laura and I still sit on our porch watching the scenery and wildlife. Now, the arthritis in my joints limits me from rambling landscapes the way I used to do. But nature remains just over the porch railing and I never tire of it. We had long hoped to find a peaceful retirement on our morsel of the old Bountiful Chance homestead. But now that we have reached that phase of our lives, we have some doubts about how much peace will prevail for us here. Even so, we will continue to press for protections for the landscapes around us, and elsewhere. More meetings on the subdivision surely lie ahead, and we intend to continue working to protect our driveway rights and the landscape's ecology.

At the most recent meeting with the municipality's planning and zoning board, the developer asked me with a scowl as it ended following my presentation, "Who do you think you are expecting to stop progress?" I responded we had a legal right to protect our lane access rights and a duty to conserve the environmental features around us.

It wasn't the time or place to remind him that as our populations grow out of control, gobbling up more natural landscapes, we risk losing the ability to sustain ourselves and vital ecosystems and habitats. It is a pattern that has occurred throughout the history of human civilizations. The dominoes begin to fall first in local natural areas containing streams, lakes, valleys and hillsides. Soon, adjacent ecosystems are affected, then the surrounding ecoregion productivity declines, along with those next to it, as ecological linkages become impaired and disconnected. Incremental and cumulative impacts reach the level of nutrient, water and energy cycling.

Once enough naturally productive land becomes too scarce or abused, a tipping point will occur where resources and habitats become unsustainable for those who inhabit the landscapes. What do we do then, eat bugs and manufactured "meat" and live in pods like bees hoping our digital connections fulfill us? It takes more energy to do these things than it does to live sustainably from the landscapes to which we are adapted and have thrived for thousands of years. Live in your cages if you like, but I'd prefer raising my free- ranging chickens and sitting on my porch, where I gain inspiration to get out of bed the next morning.

Laura and I are little different from those before us who dwelled on Bountiful Chance. They too sought to enhance their lives in a changing world by working in concert with the land. Like them, we seek a suitable balance, and will adapt where we must. Surely previous inhabitants of this landscape were similar—grateful for the privilege of resting here awhile on its gentle Piedmont slopes. Such a privilege it was to feel the caresses of its summer breezes, nourished by its rich soils and serene horizons. How fortunate we were to have enjoyed such pleasures for so long.

Someday always comes. The best we can do is appreciate the opportunities nature offers us as participants in the grand scheme of life. It allows us to strive for higher levels of well-being, to change ourselves and adapt. Regardless of what comes, life on this planet will endure, as surely as landscapes will inevitably change forms. It will go on as long as nature itself exists—until the universe winds down or something else replaces it.

No need to fret about such things. Better to stroll down a lane and explore the wonders in meadows and teeming puddles left over from last week's rain. When I last walked through the meadow overgrown with knee- high grasses and forbs, a patch of milkweed plants caught my eye. Their stiff stems rose above the surrounding weedy growth, their large, dried pods opened to reveal masses of cottony tufts of silky seeds. I remembered how Monarch butterflies used to flock to this patch and feed on the leaves in summer. But they had all migrated south by then. Someday they would return and find their favorite milkweeds had vanished, their former food patch under someone's gleaming deck.

A slight breeze tickled my arms. It was enough to launch seeds from the pod into the air, where their tiny white parachutes carried them far across the field. I watched some of them drift into the distance and out of sight. Nature was dispersing the seeds further into the landscape where they would land and sprout next spring's new crop of milkweed plants. These would bring nutrients to other places and nourish the lifeforms there.

Nature will continue managing the landscapes regardless of what humans do. Their projects and cities may last for a while, but we cannot escape the rhythms that move the Earth through its grand cycles. What was once Piedmont will likely become something else in time.

But perhaps in some distant future eons from now, a sentient being will happen to notice the likes of buttercups brightening a pleasant day on a patch of ground. Wouldn't it be nice if it inspired them to learn all they could about that and other landscapes on Earth, and all they offer to the life that dwells in them?

Appendix

LEVEL III ECOREGIONS OF THE CONTINENTAL UNITED STATES

Ecoregions are identified by similar geology, physiography, vegetation, climate, soils, land use, wildlife distributions, and hydrology. Four levels exist, but only representative Level III ecoregions are on the list, in no particular order. Level I divides North America into 15 broad ecoregions. Of these, 12 lie mainly in the United States. Fifty Level II regions give a more detailed delineation of Level I areas. Level III divides the continent into 182 smaller ecoregions. Of these, 104 lie mainly in the United States. Level IV is a subdivision of the Level III ecoregions. See EPA's website for more information: *https://www.epa.gov/eco-research/ecoregions*

Marine West Coast Forest
1 Coast Range
2 Puget Lowland
3 Willamette Valley
111 Ahklun Mountains and Kilbuck Mountains
113 Alaska Peninsula Mountains
115 Cook Inlet
119 Pacific Coastal Mountains
120 Coastal Western Hemlock-Sitka Spruce Forests

Western Forested Mountains
4 Cascades
5 Sierra Nevada
9 Eastern Cascades Slopes and Foothills
11 Blue Mountains
15 Northern Rockies
16 Idaho Batholith

Appendix

17 Middle Rockies
19 Wasatch and Uinta Mountains
21 Southern Rockies
41 Canadian Rockies
77 North Cascades
78 Klamath Mountains
105 Interior Highlands
116 Alaska Rang
117 Copper Plateau
118 Wrangell Mountains

Mediterranean California
6 Southern/Central California Chaparral/Oak Woodlands
7 Central California Valley
8 Southern California Mountains

North American Deserts
10 Columbia Plateau
12 Snake River Plain
13 Central Basin and Range
14 Mojave Basin and Range
18 Wyoming Basin
20 Colorado Plateaus
22 Arizona/New Mexico Plateau
24 Chihuahuan Deserts
80 Northern Basin and Range
81 Sonoran Basin and Range

Temperate Sierras
23 Arizona/New Mexico Mountains

Great Plains
25 Western High Plains
26 Southwestern Tablelands
27 Central Great Plains
28 Flint Hills
29 Central Oklahoma/Texas Plains

Appendix

30 Edwards Plateau
31 Southern Texas Plains
40 Central Irregular Plains
42 Northwestern Glaciated Plains
43 Northwestern Great Plains
44 Nebraska Sand Hills
46 Northern Glaciated Plains
47 Western Corn Belt Plains
48 Lake Agassiz Plain Eastern Temperate Forest
32 Texas Blackland Prairies
33 East Central Texas Plains
34 Western Gulf Coastal Plain
36 Ouachita Mountains
37 Arkansas Valley
38 Boston Mountains
39 Ozark Highlands
51 North Central Hardwood Forests
52 Driftless Area
53 Southeastern Wisconsin Till Plains
54 Central Corn Belt Plains
55 Eastern Corn Belt Plains
56 Southern Michigan/Northern Indiana Drift Plains
57 Huron/Erie Lake Plains
58 Northeastern Highlands
59 Northeastern Coastal Zone
60 Northern Appalachian Plateau and Uplands
61 Erie Drift Plain
64 Northern Piedmont
66 Blue Ridge
67 Ridge and Valley
68 Southwestern Appalachians
69 Central Appalachians

Appendix

70 Western Allegheny Plateau

71 Interior Low Plateaus

72 Interior River Valleys and Hills

74 Mississippi Valley Loess Plains

82 Laurentian Plains and Hills

83 Eastern Great Lakes and Hudson Lowlands

84 Atlantic Coastal Pine Barrens

Northern Forests

49 Northern Minnesota Wetlands

50 Northern Lakes and Forests

58 Northeastern Highlands

62 North Central Appalachians

Tropical Wet Forests

76 Southern Florida Coastal Plain Southern Semi-Arid Highlands

79 Madrean Archipelago

Taiga (3)

101 Arctic Coastal Plain 102 Arctic Foothills

103 Brooks Range

104 Interior Forested Lowlands and Uplands

106 Interior Bottomlands

107 Yukon Flats

108 Ogilvie Mountains Temperate coniferous forest

35 South Central Plains

45 Piedmont

63 Middle Atlantic Coastal Plain

65 Southeastern Plains

73 Mississippi Alluvial Plain

74 Mississippi Valley Loess Plains

75 Southern Coastal Plain Tundra (2)

109 Subarctic Coastal Plains

110 Seward Peninsula

112 Bristol Bay-Nushagak Lowlands

114 Aleutian Islands

About the Author

Joel Everett Harding is the pen name of a professional field ecologist who has spent decades exploring the wild places nature offers us. The author has professional credentials in a variety of scientific fields, including ecosystem ecology, wildlife biology, animal behavior, habitat restorations, and bio-engineering,. He has been a scientist to private industry, federal, state and local governments and nonprofit organizations. His personal adventures and scientific investigations have taken him to landscapes throughout North America and elsewhere. He has enjoyed "collecting" ecosystems and wildscape experiences of all sizes, from puddles to rainforests and everything in-between. He lives in the rural mid-Atlantic Piedmont region, and when not visiting the wild places, he prefers painting scenes that have inspired him.

www.ingramcontent.com/pod-product-compliance
Lightning Source LLC
Chambersburg PA
CBHW071310150426
43191CB00007B/566